The Tangled Complexity of the EU Constitutional Process

Offering a fresh view on the EU constitutionalisation process, the new edition of *The Tangled Complexity of the EU Constitutional Process* presents three main points: the idea of constitutional complexity, the tension between constitutional evolutionism and constitutional constructivism in the process of European integration, and the functional nature of conflicts in the evolution of the EU. Because of its prodigiousness, European law produces consternation among constitutionalists accustomed to traditional patterns of power.

This book argues that while constitutional conflicts have frequently been depicted as elements of disturbance along the path towards legal coherence, they are physiological and might even be functional to the development of the European legal order, which should not be understood in a deterministic manner.

The new edition will be of particular interest to academics and students in the disciplines of law, international relations, and political science.

Giuseppe Martinico is Full Professor of Comparative Constitutional Law at the Scuola Superiore Sant'Anna, Pisa.

Routledge Research in EU Law

Available titles in this series include:

Gender and the Court of Justice of the EU
Jessica Guth and Sanna Elfving

The EU and the Proliferation of Integration Principles under the Lisbon Treaty
Francesca Ippolito, Maria Eugenia Bartoloni, Massimo Condinanzi

Migration Law and the Externalization of Border Controls
European State Responsibility
Anna Liguori

Member States Interests and European Union Law
Revisiting the Foundations of Member State Obligations
Marton Varju

EU Law Enforcement
The Evolution of Sanctioning Powers
Stefano Montaldo, Francesco Costamagna, and Alberto Miglio

Constitutional Law and the EU Balanced Budget Principle
Elena-Simina Tănăsescu and Eric Oliva

Delegation of Powers in the EU Legal System
Annalisa Volpato

The Tangled Complexity of the EU Constitutional Process
The Frustrating Knot of Europe
Giuseppe Martinico

www.routledge.com/Routledge-Research-in-EU-Law/book-series/ROUTEULAW

The Tangled Complexity of the EU Constitutional Process

The Frustrating Knot of Europe

Second Edition

Giuseppe Martinico

Routledge
Taylor & Francis Group
LONDON AND NEW YORK

Second edition published 2023
by Routledge
4 Park Square, Milton Park, Abingdon, Oxon OX14 4RN

and by Routledge
605 Third Avenue, New York, NY 10158

Routledge is an imprint of the Taylor & Francis Group, an informa business

First edition published by Routledge 2013

British Library Cataloguing-in-Publication Data
A catalogue record for this book is available from the British Library

Library of Congress Cataloging-in-Publication Data
A catalog record for this book has been requested

ISBN: 978-0-367-46703-6 (hbk)
ISBN: 978-1-032-31620-8 (pbk)
ISBN: 978-1-003-05652-2 (ebk)

DOI: 10.4324/9781003056522

Typeset in Times New Roman
by Apex CoVantage, LLC

Contents

Preface to the second edition: Why a new edition? vii
Preface and acknowledgements to the first edition xvi

1 Only a drop in the ocean? An attempt to classify the debate about the notion and the nature of the European Constitution 1

1.1 Introductory remarks 1
1.2 When concepts matter: what do we mean by 'constitutionalisation', 'constitution' and 'constitutionalism' at EU level? 3
1.3 Dealing with the literature: what about the 'efficient secret' of the European Constitution? Some attempts at classification 10
1.4 The persistent terminological ambiguity with reference to European constitutional law 17
1.5 Concluding on fundamental rights in EU law 34
1.6 Final remarks 38

2 Dealing with constitutional theories of European integration 39

2.1 Plan of the chapter 39
2.2 Multilevel constitutionalism 39
2.3 Constitutional pluralism 43
2.4 Complexity as 'the efficient secret' of the European Constitution 56
2.5 From complexity to constitutional synallagma: some examples 63
2.6 The idea of a complex 'order' 65

3 Constructivism, evolutionism and (mega) constitutional politics in the EU from 1992 to 2010 76

3.1 Plan of the chapter 76
3.2 Constitutional constructivism versus constitutional evolutionism 77
3.3 The discontents of European constitutionalism and their relations with constitutional constructivism 90

3.4 The (attempted) hijack of the acquis communautaire *92*
3.5 The Maastricht Treaty as a turning point in the relationship between the ECJ and national governments 94
3.6 Pupino*: a frustrated attempt to limit the interpreter? 98*
3.7 The season of the conventions and its products 100
3.8 Article 4.2 TEU as the apex of a constitutional crescendo 105
3.9 The Charter of Fundamental Rights of the EU 112
3.10 Final remarks 118

4 The multiple crises of the European Union (2011–2021) 120

4.1 An existential crisis 120
4.2 The impact over the EU constitutional system and the reaction to the pandemic 128
4.3 Why the European Union is not (only) an ordoliberal entity 141

5 Complexity in action: from the structure to the actors 148

5.1 Plan of the chapter 148
5.2 Multiple loyalties and complexity in action: how hard it is being a judge in a complex legal order 150
5.3 The idea of constitutional conflicts as a direct consequence of the constitutional complexity of the EU 153
5.4 Back to case law: a possible typology of constitutional conflicts 159
5.5 Conflicts by convergence as one of the unexpected consequences of the constitutionalisation of the EU 180
5.6 The importance of a consistent interpretation as a technique for recognising fully fledged 'conflicts' 190

6 On the future of constitutional conflicts 195

6.1 On European monstrosity 195
6.2 Pushing the incoming tide back? Some notes on Brexit 197
6.3 Past and future of constitutional conflicts 204

Index 215

Preface to the second edition: *Why a new edition?*

Very much has changed from the date of publication of the first edition of this book, in 2012. At that time, constitutional pluralism[1] was the dominant constitutional theory and judicial dialogue was a trendy concept. Nowadays, instead, constitutional pluralism is under siege. Moreover, populist governments in Hungary and Poland have abused 'constitutional-pluralistic' concepts like that of national identity, and this has again placed doubt on the dominant narratives of that period. Scholars have also criticised Constitutional Courts for the abuse of the national (according to another terminology, constitutional)[2] identity argument. In this sense, Halmai[3] has also blamed the German *Bundesverfassungsgericht* (BVG) for offering other Constitutional Courts a problematic series of techniques by provoking, in this way, a dangerous escalation of constitutional conflicts. Against this background, constitutional pluralists[4] have been accused of offering arguments to autocrats and populists to justify violations of the values set out in Article 2.[5]

This debate is emblematic of the crisis of the constitutional paradigm in European studies.

1 For an account of the different strands of constitutional pluralism, see K. Jaklic, *Constitutional Pluralism in the EU*, Oxford: Oxford University Press, 2014.

2 For instance, E. Cloots, *National Identity in EU Law*, Oxford: Hart, 2015, pp. 163 et seq. and G. Di Federico, *L'identità nazionale degli stati membri nel diritto dell'Unione europea. Natura e portata dell'art. 4, par. 2, TUE*, Naples: Editoriale Scientifica, 2017, p. 15.

3 G. Halmai, 'Abuse of Constitutional Identity. The Hungarian Constitutional Court on Interpretation of Article E (2) of the Fundamental Law', *Review of Central and East European Law*, 2018, pp. 23 et seq.

4 On constitutional pluralism, see: N. MacCormick, 'Beyond the Sovereign State', *Modern Law Review*, 1993, pp. 1 et seq.; N. Walker, 'The Idea of Constitutional Pluralism', *Modern Law Review*, 2002, pp. 317 et seq.; M. Poiares Maduro, 'Contrapunctual Law: Europe's Constitutional Pluralism in Action', in N. Walker (ed.), *Sovereignty in Transition*, Oxford: Oxford University Press, 2003, pp. 501 et seq. More recently: M. Avbelj and J. Komárek (eds.), *Constitutional Pluralism in the European Union and Beyond*, Oxford: Oxford University Press, 2012. K. Jaklic, *Constitutional Pluralism in the EU*, Oxford: Oxford University Press, 2014.

5 R.D. Kelemen and L. Pech, 'Why Autocrats Love Constitutional Identity and Constitutional Pluralism. Lessons from Hungary and Poland', *Reconnect Working Paper*, No. 2, 2018, https://reconnect-europe.eu/wp-content/uploads/2018/10/RECONNECT-WorkingPaper2-Kelemen-Pech-LP-KO.pdf

Despite all these developments, the basic argument made in the book remains the same: my idea is to present constitutional complexity as something capable of coping with these developments. In this sense, my book developed an alternative theoretical proposal on the role of conflicts in European constitutional law. The starting point was represented by the ambiguous role of conflicts in the account proposed by constitutional pluralists. As Avbelj pointed out, constitutional pluralists, especially Kumm,[6] treat

> integration as one legal practice whose overall coherence depends on the search for the best fit balance of shared normative commitments that, in a vein very similar to socio-teleological constitutionalism, is nothing but destined, which is also at least implicitly desired, to lead the integration to an ever more **integrated, unified and hence non-conflicting entity**.[7]
>
> (emphasis added)

By taking a different approach, in my book I argued that while constitutional conflicts have frequently been depicted as elements of disturbance along the path towards legal coherence, they are actually physiological and might even be functional to the development of the European legal order, which should not be understood in a deterministic manner. Against this background, in the last chapter of the first edition I looked at some factors that could trigger new constitutional conflicts.

The first edition of this book was blessed by many positive reviews[8] but also received some (fair) criticism. Also, a special symposium of a Brazilian journal was devoted to this book.[9]

Indeed, while reading their generous reflections on my book, I was tempted to substantially modify huge parts of my volume. This is perhaps inevitable since many years have already passed from its publication (and this is another reason to thank my colleagues for the attention paid to it).

6 M. Kumm, 'The Jurisprudence of Constitutional Conflict: Constitutional Supremacy in Europe before and after the Constitutional Treaty', *European Law Journal*, 2005, pp. 262 et seq.

7 M. Avbelj, 'Questioning EU Constitutionalisms', *German Law Journal*, 2008, pp. 1 et seq., p. 14.

8 K. Granat, 'The Tangled Complexity of the EU Constitutional Process: The Frustrating Knot of Europe', *European Law Journal*, 2014, pp. 284 et seq.; L.I. Gordillo Pérez, 'The Tangled Complexity of the EU Constitutional Process: The Frustrating Knot of Europe', *European Law Review*, 2014, pp. 884 et seq.; G. Delledonne, 'The Tangled Complexity of the EU Constitutional Process: The Frustrating Knot of Europe', *European Journal of Risk Regulation*, 2013, pp. 422 et seq. S. Iglesias Sánchez, 'The Tangled Complexity of the EU Constitutional Process. The Frustrating Knot of Europe', *Revista de Derecho Comunitario Europeo*, 2013, pp. 1270 et seq.; P. Castillo Ortiz, 'The Tangled Complexity of the EU Constitutional Process. The Frustrating Knot of Europe', *Revista de estudios políticos*, 2013, pp. 325 et seq. C. Cantore, *Book Review: G. Martinico, The Tangled Complexity of the EU Constitutional Process*, Routledge, 2013, www.diritticomparati.it/book-review-g-martinico-the-tangled-compexity-of-the-eu-constitutional-process-routledge-2012-xiv-19/

9 G. Delledonne and J. Pinheiro Faro Homem de Siqueira (eds.), *The Tangled Complexity of the EU Constitutional Process. A Symposium. Panóptica,* 2015, https://papers.ssrn.com/sol3/papers.cfm?abstract_id=2655988

The first critical element shared by all the contributions is undoubtedly the attention that I paid to courts and judges in the origin and evolution of the complex constitution of the EU. In this respect I must say that this choice reflects the very 'court-centric' nature of the debate in this area, an element stressed, among others, by Komárek.[10] This is true, but in spite of what recent scholarship argued about the 'diminishing importance of courts' in the current phase of the European integration process,[11] courts still play a major role. It is sufficient here to think of the important decisions given by both Constitutional Courts and the Court of Justice with regard to the financial crisis.

Moreover, the present author has been one of the first to apply concepts borrowed from Chantal Mouffe to the world of courts.[12] Recently, other studies have tried to do the same, and in a way, this seems to confirm the promising potential of this intuition.[13]

However, the importance given to judges in the volume does not exclude the possibility of extending the considerations made therein to institutional actors other than courts.

Parliaments offer an example of this: what I wrote in the first edition of this book about judges can be recovered with regard to parliaments as well. Parliaments have similar incentives to interact in a complex system; this has been explained by Manzella and Lupo, who employed the formula 'euro-national parliamentary system' to refer to the progressive construction of a compound parliamentary arena ('that is to say, being it constituted both by the EU Treaties and by the Constitutions of the Member States'[14]). The EU Treaties, especially after the coming into force of the Lisbon Treaty, are rich in provisions referring to the role of national parliaments, and this offers further proof of the complex scenario in which parliaments have to act nowadays. In spite of such a richness, this has not avoided a certain marginalisation of national parliaments during the economic crisis.[15]

However, as I tried to show elsewhere,[16] what I wrote with regard to judicial actors in Chapter V of this book can apply to political actors as well. Indeed, it is

10 J. Komárek, 'Institutional Dimension of Constitutional Pluralism', *Eric Stein Working Paper*, No. 3/2010, 2010, https://papers.ssrn.com/sol3/papers.cfm?abstract_id=1575522

11 N. Scicluna, *European Union Constitutionalism in Crisis*, Abingdon: Routledge, 2015, p. 135.

12 C. Mouffe, *The Return of the Political*, London: Verso, 1993; C. Mouffe, *The Democratic Paradox*, London: Verso, 2000; C. Mouffe, *On the Political*, Abingdon: Routledge, 2005.

13 D. Michelsen, 'Agonistic Democracy and Constitutionalism in the Age of Populism', *European Journal of Political Theory*, 2019, pp. 1 et seq.; R. Mieńkowska-Norkiene, 'The Political Impact of the Case Law of the Court of Justice of the European Union', *European Constitutional Law Review*, 2021, pp. 1 et seq.

14 A. Manzella and N. Lupo (eds.), *Il Sistema parlamentare euro-nazionale. Lezioni*, Turin: Giappichelli, 2014, pp. 270–271.

15 D. Fromage and A. Herranz-Surrallés, 'Introduction. Executive-Legislative (Im)balance in the European Union', in D. Fromage and A. Herranz-Surrallés (eds.), *Executive-Legislative (Im)balance in the European Union*, Oxford: Hart, 2021, pp. 1 et seq. p. 6.

16 G. Martinico, 'Interjudicial Dialogue and Interparliamentary Dialogue in the Constitution of the Union', in N. Lupo and C. Fasone (eds.), *Interparliamentary Cooperation in the Composite European Constitution*, Oxford: Hart, 2016, pp. 39 et seq.

not the first time that the idea of dialogue has been applied to parliaments. Among others, this idea has been developed by Barak-Erez, who explores the dialogue among legislatures as a vehicle for legal transplants.[17] The EU institutions are familiar with the formula of 'political dialogue' introduced by the Barroso Commission, a phenomenon that goes beyond the mere inter-parliamentary dialogue since it involves the Commission as well.[18]

Looking at cooperative interactions, scholars have noticed the importance of Protocol 1,[19] especially Articles 9 and 10.[20] More in general, today inter-parliamentary cooperation in the EU develops through different channels (Conference of Community and European Affairs committees of parliaments of the European Union – COSAC; Joint Parliamentary Meetings, Joint Committee Meetings, Meetings of Sectoral Committees etc.).

More recently, new arenas of 'second generation'[21] have been created: the Inter-Parliamentary Conference for the Common Foreign and Security Policy and the Common Security and Defence Policy (CFSP/CSDP),[22] which gathers delegations of the national parliaments of the EU Member States and the European Parliament[23] and the Inter-Parliamentary Conference on Economic Governance of the

17 D. Barak-Erez, 'An International Community of Legislatures?' in R.W. Bauman and T. Kahana, *The Least Examined Branch – The Role of Legislatures in the Constitutional State*, Cambridge: Cambridge University Press, 2006, pp. 532 et seq. See also: D Barak-Erez, 'Legislation as Transplantation', in N Lupo and L Scaffardi (eds.), *Comparative Law in Legislative Drafting. The Increasing Importance of Dialogue Amongst Parliaments*, Hague: Eleven International Publishing, 2014, pp. 17 et seq. and M. R Ferrarese, 'Il dialogo tra Parlamenti e il dialogo tra corti: nuove tendenze del costituzionalismo', in C. Decaro and N. Lupo (eds.), *Il 'dialogo' tra Parlamenti: obiettivi e risultati*, Rome: Luiss University Press, 2009, pp. 317 et seq.

18 http://europa.eu/rapid/press-release_IP-09-1368_en.htm

19 Protocol on the Role of National Parliaments in the European Union.

20 Article 9: 'The European Parliament and national Parliaments shall together determine the organisation and promotion of effective and regular interparliamentary cooperation within the Union'.

Article 10: 'A conference of Parliamentary Committees for the Affairs of the Union may submit any contribution it deems appropriate for the attention of the European Parliament, the Council and the Commission. That conference shall in addition promote the exchange of information and best practice between national Parliaments and the European Parliament, including their special committees. It may also organize interparliamentary conferences on specific topics, in particular to debate matters of common foreign and security policy, including common security and defence policy. Contributions from the conference shall not bind national Parliaments and shall not prejudge their positions'.

21 D. Fromage, 'Parlamento Europeo y Parlamentos nacionales después del Tratado de Lisboa y en un contexto de crisis: ¿Un acercamiento de grado diverso segúnelámbito?' in P. Andrés and J.I. Ugartemendia (eds.), *El Parlamento europeo ¿esta vez es diferente?* Guipuzcoa: IVAP, 2015, pp. 223 et seq.

22 Decisions of the Conference of Speakers of the European Union (EU) Parliaments at its meetings in Brussels, on 4–5 April 2011 and in Warsaw, on 20–21 April 2012, establishing an Inter Parliamentary Conference for the Common Foreign and Security Policy (CFSP) and the Common Security and Defence Policy (CSDP), www.europarl.europa.eu/webnp/cms/pid/1932

23 J. Wouters and K. Raube, 'Europe's Common Security and Defence Policy: The Case for Inter-Parliamentary Scrutiny', *Leuven Centre for Global Governance Studies Working Paper*, 2012, www.readcube.com/articles/10.2139%2Fssrn.2274804

European Union, established by Article 13 of the Treaty on Stability, Coordination and Governance (TSCG).[24] This mushrooming of phenomena has suggested the existence of a 'Multilevel Parliamentary Field',[25] an arena that seems to represent dynamics similar to those recalled with regard to judicial actors. Without going into detail, it is sufficient to refer to recent works here.[26]

Does inter-parliamentary cooperation look like inter-judicial dialogue? The answer depends (of course) on the definition of dialogue adopted.

For instance, many of the activities that scholars label 'parliamentary diplomacy'[27] recall the activity performed through so-called judicial networks but on this scholars are split. According to Claes and de Visser, for example, these meetings are relevant and sometimes work as important channels to favour a proper dialogue between judges and judiciaries,[28] since 'extrajudicial exchanges, both in writing and via personal contacts, score much higher as they allow for a free exchange of ideas and arguments on a more equal footing and even give room for deliberation on common issues'.[29]

On the contrary, these formal or informal meetings of judges have not been included in his notion of dialogue by Tzanakopoulos. Indeed, while, on the one hand these meetings 'may be important for the formation of the judges' understanding and opinions on the interpretation of rules of (international) law',[30] on the other hand

> it is neither accessible to the legal researcher nor can its impact be easily demonstrated on publicly available evidence. It is thus easier to ascertain the presence and effects of inter-judicial dialogue when these are evident through referencing, discussion and cross-citation of foreign court decisions in domestic court judgments.[31]

24 Article 13 TSCG: 'As provided for in Title II of Protocol (No 1) on the role of national Parliaments in the European Union annexed to the European Union Treaties, the European Parliament and the national Parliaments of the Contracting Parties will together determine the organisation and promotion of a conference of representatives of the relevant committees of the European Parliament and representatives of the relevant committees of national Parliaments in order to discuss budgetary policies and other issues covered by this Treaty'.

25 B. Crum and J.E. Fossum, 'The Multilevel Parliamentary Field: A Framework for Theorizing Representative Democracy in the EU', *European Political Science Review,* 2009, 1, pp. 249.

26 C. Fasone, 'Interparliamentary Cooperation and Democratic Representation in the European Union', in S. Kroger and D. Friedrich (eds.), *The Challenge of Democratic Representation in the European Union,* London: Palgrave Macmillan, 2011, pp. 41 et seq.

27 C. Decaro, 'Esiste la diplomazia parlamentare?' in C. Decaro and N. Lupo (eds.), *Il 'dialogo' tra Parlamenti: obiettivi e risultati,* Rome: Luiss University Press, 2009, pp. 315 et seq.

28 M. Claes and M. de Visser, 'Are You Networked Yet? On Dialogues in European Judicial Networks', *Utrecht Law Review*, 2012, pp. 100 et seq.

29 Claes and de Visser, 'Are You', p. 106.

30 A Tzanakopoulos, 'Judicial Dialogue as a Means of Interpretation', *Oxford Legal Studies Research Paper*, No. 71/2014, 2014, https://papers.ssrn.com/sol3/papers.cfm?abstract_id=2497519

31 Tzanakopoulos, 'Judicial Dialogue'.

Going beyond EU law, well-known studies have shown important differences between inter-parliamentary and inter-judicial dialogue, differences that are connected to the features of the actors involved in these interactions:

> First, as noted, individual legislators are motivated to look for inspiration in foreign legislation mainly when the legislation touches on value issues, such as the recognition of same-sex marriages. In matters requiring expertise, the parties to the international dialogue are the professionals who draft the laws. Second, the so-called dialogue often assumes the form of a monologue, namely, countries adopting foreign models of legislation usually do not serve as legislation models for other countries. Eastern Europe adopted Western models of legislation but has never been viewed as a relevant source of legal inspiration by American lawyers or legislators. The judicial community, by contrast, is more egalitarian. Because this is a professional community, worthy precedents from small countries can be a source of inspiration also to judges active in countries that are politically and economically more powerful. Third, even when legislatures use the information regarding laws in other countries, they do not limit the scope of their learning to the legislative arena. A legal principle originally introduced in the exporting country by way of judicial interpretation will sometimes be adopted in the importing country by way of legislation. In other words, legislators refer to any relevant source of inspiration, without granting priority to the principles created by their legislative counterparts.[32]

In light of these considerations, which emphasise the absence of a common background for the international community of legislatures[33] and the lack of a sufficient degree of 'variety' in the exchanges between parliaments Barak-Erez argues that 'the dynamics of legislation influencing foreign legislative initiatives should rather be described as based on inspiration without a community'.[34]

32 Barak-Erez, 'An International Community', p. 546.

33 'Judges and rights activists share a common background – either professional (in the case of judges) or ideological (in the case of human rights activists) – as well as similar value systems. By contrast, members of legislatures in different countries do not share a common background. At most, and only to a limited extent, members of parties with similar ideologies have a shared background (conservatives, socialists, "green" parties, and so forth). Moreover, members of legislative bodies feel accountable mostly to their constituents. This is their most significant link and the only one that can guarantee their professional future. Members of legislative bodies are also less exposed to their colleagues in other countries. Leading party members may take part in delegations visiting other legislatures, but most legislators stay at home. International institutions encouraging cooperation between legislatures for the purpose of mutual learning and experience sharing do not seem to be relevant to the daily work of ordinary legislators', Barak-Erez, 'An International Community', p. 545.

34 Barak-Erez, 'An International Community', p. 544.

Another important difference is given by the nature of the actors: while parliaments are often conceived as provided with legislative discretion, on the contrary

> courts are in general reactive institutions: they are called upon to adjudicate on the initiative of the parties that come before them. They thus react on the initiative of the parties, rather than on their own initiative, to the positions taken by other courts . . . . They may not be allowed to consider *proprio motu* points not raised by the parties.[35]

Finally, there is another possible difference connected to the 'reactive' nature of courts: inter-judicial dialogue is supposed to start from concrete cases, while inter-parliamentary dialogue often deals with a broader object, sometimes even with entire policies. Inter-judicial dialogue (at least for those who believe that courts should decide 'one case at a time'[36]) is thus supposed to be evolutionary and incremental, without a constructivist design behind it,[37] while parliaments are frequently depicted as the bearers of a general and abstract will. Very often this distinction does not correspond to reality, but it offers a good basis for a deeper analysis.

However, these differences should not be overstated: inter-parliamentary and inter-judicial dialogue may work in tandem to improve the protection of transnational constitutional goods or to face those challenges that present a cross-border nature (among others, new technologies and counter-terrorism).

Another point frequently mentioned in the generous book reviews concerns the relationship between evolutionism and conflicts.[38] In my view, it is possible to acknowledge the importance played by conflicts without falling into constructivism, and this can be explained by relying on Hayek, who distinguished between 'action' and human 'design'. Regaining this distinction, one could argue that only the latter is deeply present in the very idea of constructivism, as I tried to explain in Chapter III.

Last but not least, Pablo José Castillo Ortiz stressed that 'some sceptic approaches to the EU "constitution" should be taken seriously by anyone who wants the EU to become a fully-fledged constitutional system' and that the "no-Constitution" thesis is actually, then, a tool for the achievement of a fully

35 Tzanakopoulos, 'Judicial Dialogue'.

36 To borrow the title of a famous book: C. Sunstein, *One Case at a Time: Judicial Minimalism on the Supreme Court*, Cambridge, MA: Harvard University Press, 2001.

37 'A conception which assumes that all social institutions are, and ought to be, the product of deliberate design', F.A. Hayek, *Law, Legislation and Liberty, vol. 1, Rules and Order*, Abingdon: Routledge, 1973, pp. 5 et seq. The dualistic structure of Hayek's thought links the idea of constructivism to that of order, which can be conceived in two different ways: order as κοσμος (spontaneous order) and order as ταξις (constructed order).

38 For instance: M. Goldoni, 'Staging Conflicts in the Context of Constitutional Complexity', in G. Delledonne and J. Pinheiro Faro Homem de Siqueira (eds.), *The Tangled Complexity of the EU Constitutional Process. A Symposium. Panóptica,* 2015, https://papers.ssrn.com/sol3/papers.cfm?abstract_id=2655988

democratic and constitutional European Union'.[39] I took his point; it is true that even theories denying the existence of a real Constitution at EU level can serve as a *stimulus* to give new blood to the necessary public debate on how to make the EU more democratic. However, to confirm the reasons why I do not embrace sceptic approaches in my book, I would like to recall two counter-arguments.

First of all, sceptics often accept labelling a given community as 'constitutional' only under certain circumstances that – and this is my main point – at a closer look are sometimes not even present at national level.

Here comparative law helps a lot. Many other legal orders that share some similar difficulties to those that have been seen by the EU can be labelled unequivocally as constitutional, for instance Canada, which has been experiencing 'constitutional odysseys',[40] or Switzerland, which has been suffering from a semi-permanent constitutional revision.

In this respect, Fossum[41] compared what Russell called 'mega constitutional politics' with the semi-permanent Treaty revision process described by de Witte[42] by showing their common features: lack of legitimacy, constitution-making processes driven from the top, and exclusion of some actors from the constitutional dynamics.

These constitutional processes thus display similarities: the necessity of involving citizens and national parliaments in order to overcome the democratic deficit of the Union, the difficulty of finding 'a satisfactory and comprehensive constitutional settlement',[43] the important role played by courts in reshaping the relation between centre and periphery, intergovernmentalism and asymmetry, which have been increased after the entry into force of the anti-austerity measures.

My second point is that studying the constitutional function performed by national and supranational judges does not imply accepting the status quo or denying the democratic concerns related to the lack of involvement of the national and supranational political actors, being here the explanatory and normative levels distinguishable.

In this respect, complexity offers an alternative theoretical proposal able to understand the origin and the current version of supranational constitutionalism.

39 P. Castillo Ortiz, 'The contested 'Constitution' of the EU and the Quest for Everdemocratic Constitutionalism', in G. Delledonne and J. Pinheiro Faro Homem de Siqueira (eds.), *The Tangled Complexity of the EU Constitutional Process. A Symposium. Panóptica,* 2015, https://papers.ssrn.com/sol3/papers.cfm?abstract_id=2655988

40 P. Russell, *Constitutional Odyssey: Can Canadians Become a Sovereign People?* Toronto: University of Toronto Press, 1992.

41 J.E. Fossum, 'The Transformation of the Nation-state: Why Compare the EU and Canada', 2004, www.mzes.uni-mannheim.de/projekte/typo3/site/fileadmin/mid-term/fossum/CanEU38.pdf

42 B. de Witte, 'The Closest Thing to a Constitutional Conversation in Europe: The Semi-Permanent Treaty Revision Process', in P. Beaumont, C. Lyons, and N. Walker (eds.), *Convergence and Divergence in European Public Law*, Oxford: Hart, pp. 39 et seq.

43 R.S. Kay, 'Book Review Essay: Canada's Constitutional Cul De Sac', *American Review of Canadian Studies*, 2005, pp. 705 et seq.

In other words, complexity can explain how European constitutional law works without identifying a model to be followed or the final destination of the European journey (confirming its non-apriorism).

Instead of reshaping this book completely, I decided to come back to some specific questions by either updating or clarifying some points included therein. I also added a brand-new chapter looking at the most recent developments in the field. I must humbly admit that ten years ago my English was much poorer, and I have tried to remedy that in this second edition.

Many of the friends who had helped me with the first edition also gave me useful comments for this second version. I would like to thank in particular Paolo Addis, Edoardo Bressanelli, Giacomo Delledonne, Umberto Lattanzi, Leandro Mancano, Silvia Nuzzo, Fabio Pacini, Leonardo Pierdominici, Orlando Scarcello. Thanks to my fiancée, Lelia, and our *bad boys*, Mav and Nino, for their love and support.

Unless otherwise stated, this book reflects the events that took place up to 5 November 2021.

This second edition is dedicated to the memory of Paolo Carrozza and Alessandro Pizzorusso, who taught me a lot and whom I miss so much.

Pisa–Firenze
17 December 2021

Preface and acknowledgements to the first edition

Anche se quel musical sul pasticciere . . . e beh, sarebbe un po' tutta un'altra cosa . . .

(Nanni Moretti, *Aprile*)

It is definitely not the best time to write a book on European constitutional law: after the 'knocks' taken in the French and Dutch referenda and the disappointment produced by the Reform Treaty, the recent developments concerning the financial crisis seem to cast new shadows on the EU by questioning some of the pillars of the traditional narrative:

> It is common in this literature, as well as in the broader political discourse on Europe, to think of the European Union (EU) as a one-way street towards ever-greater integration. Such a viewpoint is well captured in the colloquial 'bicycle theory' of European integration, which holds that – just as a cyclist – the EU's survival depends on a constantly forward trajectory, with stasis leading to collapse. The recent, and continuing, sovereign debt crises of several EU states has cast doubt on this accepted wisdom.[44]

Despite this, I shall take the risk of writing a book on the constitutional dynamics of the EU, trying to present what is, in my view, the core of the EU's constitutional structure. In the following pages, I shall anticipate the structure of the volume, which is divided into five chapters.

The aim of the first chapter is to offer a brief overview of the international literature regarding the concept of European Constitution and European constitutional law. I insist on the polysemy of some key terms in this debate: constitution, constitutionalisation and constitutionalism, limiting, of course, my attention to the particular meaning that they can acquire in this field of research. As we will see in Chapter 1, by the formula 'constitutionalisation' of the EU legal order, authors

44 M. Turk, 'Implications of European Disintegration for International Law', *Columbia Journal of European Law*, 2011, pp. 395 et seq., 396.

normally mean the progressive shift of Community law from the perspective of an international organisation to that of a federal state. Another meaning of constitutionalisation of the EU legal order can be found with regard to the progressive 'humanisation' of the law of the common market.

It is just one of many examples that come to mind when trying to apply categories of national constitutional law to the EU level. In this respect, the proclamation of the Charter of Fundamental Rights of the EU (EUCFR) gave – at least – new blood to the debate about the writing of a European Constitution and the possibility of a Bill of Rights at the supranational level, since it asserted the possibility of giving the rights a written dimension at the supranational level, overcoming the European Court of Justice[45] (ECJ) logic of *ius praetorium* in this field.

In the second chapter I analyse the latest trends of the European integration process in light of the notion of complexity (*à la* Morin),[46] conceived as a bilaterally active relationship between diversities.

This notion of complexity comes from a comparison between the different meanings of this word as used in several disciplines (law, physics, mathematics, psychology, philosophy) and recovers the etymological sense of this concept (complexity from Latin *complexus* = interlaced).

I argue that the EU legal order is a 'complex' entity that shares some features with complex systems in natural sciences: non-reducibility, unpredictability, non-reversibility and non-determinability.

The aim of this chapter is to contribute to the theoretical debate on EU integration by completing some points that may have been neglected by the main constitutional theories of EU integration (multilevel constitutionalism, constitutional pluralism).

In the interlaced nature of the EU, a very important role is played by the whole of the legal and permanent flows that connect the constitutional levels (national, international, supranational, subnational), determining the outcome of the interaction between the constitutional levels/poles.

As we will see, the peculiar structure of the EU favours interactions between the interpreters of the constitutional levels/poles and the continuous exchange of legal materials among them.

Scholars have been focusing their attention on judicial dialogue and judicial cooperation, while I have tried to pay attention to some borderline phenomena that are not univocally classified in the literature.

In the third chapter, I focus on some attempts at dominating and reducing EU constitutional complexity, reading the last 20 years (from 1992 to 2012) of constitutional politics at the EU level in light of the idea of constitutional constructivism.

45 After the coming into force of the Reform Treaty, the official name is Court of Justice of the European Union. However, for the purpose of this work I will use the acronym 'ECJ'.

46 This means that I am not going to employ Niklas Luhmann's understanding of complexity, for instance.

As we will see, rarely have these attempts worked, and the debate on the constitutional failure is the product of frustration induced by the impossibility of dominating (completely, at least) the constitutional complexity of the EU.

In the fourth chapter, I move to the consequence of complexity on the actors operating in the complex legal system. The reasoning behind that is as follows: a complex (i.e. interlaced) legal system forces actors operating at different levels to interact with each other. These 'interactions' may assume different dynamics: they can be cooperative, merely competitive or even conflicting.

Sometimes conflicts among levels are only apparent (virtual conflicts), and sometimes they are fully fledged conflicts that expose judges to a sort of 'constitutional dilemma',[47] with the interpreters forced to renounce one of the two constitutional norms at stake. This confers a key role on those actors that operate at all levels (national, supranational, international), in particular the national judges. They pay the price of complexity every day, trying to solve those antinomies that complexity may produce.

In this part of the volume, I try to show how the nature of the antinomies in such a context presents its own peculiarity by providing concrete examples taken from national or supranational case law. However, sometimes there are antinomies that present a particular – constitutional – tone involving the necessity of establishing a priority of one of the constitutional levels over the other, in other words, involving a clash between the constitutional supremacy and the primacy of EU law (to borrow the language employed by the Spanish Constitutional Court).[48] In this chapter I try to identify some types of constitutional conflicts and to show how they may sometimes have a systemic impact on the life of the EU by causing a change in its fundamental principles.

The final chapter tries to offer a reflection upon the destiny of constitutional conflicts in the future of the EU by listing a series of factors that, in my view, will feed a new season of constitutional conflicts, confirming the 'polemical' spirit of European law.

This book gathers the product of two years of seminars and courses devoted to the great themes of supranational constitutionalism and held at the Scuola Superiore Sant'Anna, Pisa, the European University Institute (EUI) and the Centro de Estudios Políticos y Constitucionales (CEPC) in Madrid.

47 On the concept of 'constitutional dilemma' see: L. Zucca, *Constitutional Dilemmas- Conflicts of Fundamental Legal Rights in Europe and the USA*, Oxford: Oxford University Press, 2007.

48 *Tribunal Constitucional*, declaración 1/2004, www.tribunalconstitucional.es. 'Supremacy and primacy are categories which are developed in differentiated orders. The former, in that of the application of valid regulations; the latter, in that of regulatory procedures. Supremacy is sustained in the higher hierarchical character of a regulation and, therefore, is a source of validity of the lower regulations, leading to the consequent invalidity of the latter if they contravene the provisions set forth imperatively in the former. Primacy, however, is not necessarily sustained on hierarchy, but rather on the distinction between the scopes of application of different regulations, principally valid, of which, however, one or more of them have the capacity for displacing others by virtue of their preferential or prevalent application due to various reasons'.

Individual chapters and an early version of this volume were presented at seminars held at various Italian and foreign universities; I would like to thank colleagues and friends who agreed, on those occasions, to provide their comments: Alberto Alemanno, Antonella Angelini, Matej Avbelj, Enrico Bonadio, Giuseppe Bianco, Francesca Biondi Dal Monte, Carlo Maria Cantore, Paolo Carrozza, Roberto Castaldi, Marco Dani, Giacomo Delledonne, Cristina Fasone, Delia Ferri, Filippo Fontanelli, Marco Goldoni, Andrea Guazzarotti, Luca Gori, Giulio Itzcovich, Andrea Lollini, Miguel Poiares Maduro, François-Xavier Millet, Fabio Pacini, Maribel González Pascual, Ernst-Ulrich Petersmann, Leonardo Pierdominici, Alessandro Pizzorusso, Daniel Sarmiento, Marta Simoncini, Antonello Tancredi, Aida Torres Pérez, Vassilis Tzevelekos, Guilherme Vasconcelos Vilaça and Lorenzo Zucca.

I could never have made this work without the library staff of the Scuola Superiore Sant'Anna, EUI, CEPC and of the Centre for Studies on Federalism in Moncalieri.

This work, as always, is dedicated to my wonderful family: *ve lo dedico con tutto il cuore, grazie.*

Madrid
2 May 2012
Giuseppe Martinico

1 Only a drop in the ocean?

An attempt to classify the debate about the notion and the nature of the European Constitution

1.1 Introductory remarks

What is the 'efficient secret'[1] of the European Constitution? In 1867 Walter Bagehot, an essayist and journalist, wrote one of the most important books in the history of constitutional law in Europe, *The English Constitution,* in which he attempted to 'discover' what made the English system so 'special'. In order to do that, he devised the very well-known formula of the 'efficient secret'. Bagehot identified it as 'the close union, the nearly complete fusion, of the executive and legislative powers'.[2] While the fusion described by Bagehot in these lines is a horizontal one connecting two different powers existing at the same level (focusing on the frame of government), I am going to argue that the secret of the European Constitution can be identified in a vertical fusion connecting national and supranational legal orders, a fusion that makes the EU an 'interlaced' (i.e. complex) legal system.

1 It is necessary to recall what Bagehot meant by 'efficient': 'No one can approach to an understanding of the English institutions, or of others which, being the growth of many centuries, exercise a wide sway over mixed populations, unless he divide them into two classes. In such constitutions there are two parts (not indeed separable with microscopic accuracy, for the genius of great affairs abhors nicety of division: first, those which excite and preserve the reverence of the population – the dignified parts, if I may so call them; and next, the efficient parts – those by which it, in fact, works and rules. There are two great objects which every constitution must attain to be successful, which every old and celebrated one must have wonderfully achieved: every constitution must first gain authority, and then use authority; it must first win the loyalty and confidence of mankind, and then employ that homage in the work of government. There are indeed practical men who reject the dignified parts of government. They say, we want only to attain results, to do business: a constitution is a collection of political means for political ends, and if you admit that any part of a constitution does no business, or that a simpler machine would do equally well what it does, you admit that this part of the constitution, however dignified or awful it may be, is nevertheless in truth useless. And other reasoners, who distrust this bare philosophy, have propounded subtle arguments to prove that these dignified parts of old governments are cardinal components of the essential apparatus, great pivots of substantial utility; and so they manufactured fallacies which the plainer school have well exposed. But both schools are in error. The dignified parts of government are those which bring it force – which attract its motive power. The efficient parts only employ that power', W. Bagehot, *The English Constitution*, Oxford: Oxford University Press, 1867, reprinted in 2001, p. 44.

2 Bagehot, *The English Constitution*, p. 48.

DOI: 10.4324/9781003056522-1

It is not a coincidence that this book started with the citation of a work devoted to the English legal system that is characterised, as is well known, by the absence of a written constitution. In order to explain the specificity of the European Constitution, this work aims to analyse the latest constitutional trends of the European integration process in light of the idea of constitutional complexity by arguing that the efficient secret of the European Constitution can be found in what I call the constitutional synallagma.[3] This synallagma is understood as the whole of the principles, practices and rules that circulate uninterruptedly from one constitutional level to another in a twofold direction (from top to bottom and vice versa) and that permits the genesis and reshaping of the structural principles of EU law. The use of the term synallagma should not necessarily lead one to think that the relationship between EU law and national law should be understood as a contract. Although the study of Compact Theory[4] may be useful in following the latest developments in European constitutionalism,[5] it is not the purpose of this book to apply this theory to European constitutional law.

This volume tries to offer a fresh view on the EU constitutionalisation process by presenting three main points: the idea of constitutional complexity; the tension between constitutional evolutionism and constitutional constructivism in the process of European integration; and the functional nature of conflicts in the evolution of the EU.

This first part of the book is divided into two parts: in the first chapter I briefly introduce the general debate on the notion and the nature of the European Constitution, attempting, in a first moment, to define some basic concepts that will be employed during the research (i.e. 'constitution', 'constitutionalism' and 'constitutionalisation' at EU level) and, in a second moment, to map the literature in this field.

As we will see, despite the number of publications in this field, this debate is still under-theorised, and this explains why the next chapter (Chapter 2) will deal with two 'constitutional theories', i.e. with two intellectual reconstructions aimed at catching what makes the EU Constitution special. Then, in the second chapter,

3 The word synallagma comes from the Greek term 'synallássein' ('to exchange, negotiate with': sýn- 'with-' and allássein 'to change'). Although this concept has been widely employed in contract theory, for the purpose of this work I will limit myself to the etymologic level without endorsing a contractual theory for the reading of the EU constitutional dynamics.

4 Former US Vice President John Calhoun was the champion of the Compact Theory. J.C. Calhoun, 'South Carolina Exposition and Protest', 1828, https://clockworkconservative.wordpress.com/freedom/primary-documents/south-carolina-exposition-and-protest/; J.C. Calhoun, 'To General Hamilton on the subject of State Interposition', 1832, https://archive.org/stream/correspondenceof00calhrich/correspondenceof00calhrich_djvu.txt; J.C. Calhoun, 'A Discourse on the Government and Constitution of the United States', 1851, www.constitution.org; L.M. Bassani, 'John C. Calhoun: Nullification, Secession, Constitution', 2014, www.abbevilleinstitute.org/review/john-c-calhoun-nullification-secession-constitution/

5 Cf. S.J. Boom, 'The European Union After the Maastricht Decision: Will Germany be the Virginia of Europe', *American Journal of Comparative Law*, 1995, pp. 177 et seq. See also: T. Dumbrovsky, 'Federal Solution to the EU Internal Sovereignty Conundrum: The European Doctrine of the Czech Constitutional Court and the U.S. Compact Theory', in L. Tichy and T. Dumbrovsky (eds.), *Sovereignty and Competences of the European Union*, Prague: Charles University, 2010, pp. 80 et seq.; R. Schütze, 'Federalism as Constitutional Pluralism: "Letter from America"', in M. Avbelj and J. Komárek (eds.), *Constitutional Pluralism in the European Union and Beyond*, Oxford: Hart, 2012, pp. 185 et seq.

I introduce my understanding of constitutional complexity by conceiving it as one of the possible constitutional theories of EU integration. I describe the EU as a complex system that is characterised by some precise features: non-reducibility, unpredictability, non-determinism and non-reversibility.

The perspective I adopt is that of the constitutional lawyer who is aware of some possible alternative readings of European integration but who, at the same time, conceives constitutionalism as a plausible, at least, key concept for understanding the latest trends of the EU integration process.

1.2 When concepts matter: what do we mean by 'constitutionalisation', 'constitution' and 'constitutionalism' at EU level?

Since EU law is for many reasons 'particular' compared to national law, it is important to specify what constitution/constitutionalisation and constitutionalism mean for the purpose of this book before introducing the idea of constitutional complexity.

Normally by the formula 'constitutionalisation' of the EU legal order, scholars[6] mean the progressive shift of EU law from the perspective of an international organisation to that of a federal state.[7] A different meaning of the constitutionalisation process of the EU legal order can be found with regard to the progressive 'humanisation' (i.e. the progressive affirmation of the human rights issue at supranational level) of the law of the common market.[8]

In this respect, a great contribution was made by the European Convention for the Protection of Human Rights and Fundamental Freedoms (ECHR)[9] since it was crucial for the genesis of Article 6 of the EU Treaty (TEU) and for the dialogue between the European Court of Human Rights (ECtHR) and the Court of Justice of the European Union (ECJ).[10] This does not exclude tensions and misunderstandings between the two European systems, as *Opinion 2/13* confirms.[11]

6 For example, M. Cartabia and J.H.H. Weiler, *L'Italia in Europa*, Bologna: Mulino, 2000, pp. 73 et seq. About the ambiguity of the notion of constitutionalisation in EU law, see: F. Snyder, 'The Unfinished Constitution of the European Union', in J.H.H. Weiler and M. Wind (eds.), *European Constitutionalism beyond the State*, Cambridge: Cambridge University Press, 2003.

7 E. Stein, 'Lawyers, Judges, and the Making of a Transnational Constitution', *American Journal of International Law*, 1981, pp. 1 et seq.

8 On this process, see K. Lenaerts, 'Fundamental rights in the European Union', *European Law Review*, 2000, pp. 575 et seq.

9 On the interplay between ECHR and EU law, see X. Groussot, *General Principles of Community Law*, Groningen: Europa Law Publishing, 2006, pp. 63 et seq.

10 On this see S. Douglas-Scott, 'A Tale of Two Courts: Luxembourg, Strasbourg and the Growing European Human Rights Acquis', *Common Market Law Review*, 2006, pp. 629 et seq. Now, thanks to the entry into force of the Reform Treaty, the EU has acquired an international legal personality, and its accession to the ECHR system will be possible (although the process will be very long, as it implies the revision of the system of the European Convention itself).

11 ECJ, Opinion 2/13, ECLI:EU:C:2014:2454.

Another important step can be found in the proclamation of the Charter of Fundamental Rights of the EU,[12] which happened more than 20 years ago and brought new blood to the debate about the writing of a European Constitution[13] and the possibility of a Bill of Rights at EU level.[14] Although this document was not immediately binding from a *stricto sensu* legal point of view, its proclamation encouraged an important debate among scholars, especially among the constitutional lawyers of Continental Europe.

Obviously, some authors have kept these two concepts together, as is the case with Weiler,[15] but as we shall see in the book, the coexistence of these two meanings of constitutionalisation does not exclude possible conflicts between them.

By European constitutional law, one can thus mean both the *corpus of fundamental principles*[16] devised by the ECJ in attempting to transform Europe[17] (this set of principles can also be understood as the European Constitution) and a field of studies that emerged after the ideal turning point represented by the Charter of Fundamental Rights of the EU.

12 For a commentary, see K. Feus (ed.), *The EU Charter of Fundamental Rights. Text and commentaries, Constitution for Europe*, Federal Trust Series 1, London: Logan Page, 2000; G. Braibant, *La Charte des droits fondamentaux de l'Union européenne. Témoignage et commentaires*, Paris: Seuil, 2001; UK House of Commons, Human Rights in the EU: The Charter of Fundamental Rights, Research Paper 00/32, March 20, 2000; see also the special issues of the following journals: *Revue Universelle des Droits de l'Homme*, Vol. 12, Issues 1 and 2 (with contributions from Benoit-Rohmer, Jacqué, Fischbach, Dietmar, Wachsmann, Simon, Sudre, De Schutter and Tulkens) and *Maastricht Journal of European and Comparative Law*, Vol. 8, Issue 1, 2001 (with contributions from Wouters, Willem, Verhey, Gijzen, Lemmens, Besselink, de Witte, de Smijter and Lenaerts, van Ooik and Curtin); *European Review of Public Law*, Vol. 13, No. 3, 2001. For a complete bibliography on the Nice Charter, see www.arena.uio.no/cidel/cwatch/bibliography.html; A.J. Menéndez, 'Chartering Europe: The Charter of Fundamental Rights of the European Union', Arena Working Paper, No. 1/13, www.arena.uio.no/publications/wp01_13.htm

For a very interesting introduction to the idea of a European constitutional law, see S. Douglas-Scott, *Constitutional law of the European Union*, Harlow: Longman, 2002 (especially pp. 3–44 and 515–530).

13 See the image by C. Pinelli, *Pinelli, Il momento della scrittura Contributo al dibattito sulla Costituzione europea,* Bologna: Il Mulino, 2002.

14 D. Grimm, 'Il significato della stesura di un catalogo europeo dei diritti fondamentali nell'ottica della critica dell'ipotesi di una Costituzione europea', in G. Zagrebelsky (ed.), *Diritti e Costituzione nell'Unione Europea*, Rome and Bari: Laterza, 2003, pp. 15 et seq.; F. Mayer, 'La Charte européenne des droits fondamentaux et la Constitution européenne', *Revue trimestrielle de droit européen*, 2003, pp. 194–195; V. Skouris, 'La protezione dei diritti fondamentali nell'Unione europea nella prospettiva dell'adozione di una Costituzione europea', in L.S. Rossi (ed.), *Il progetto di Trattato-Costituzione, verso una nuova architettura dell'Unione europea*, Bologna: Il Mulino, 2004, pp. 254 et seq.

15 J.H.H. Weiler, 'The transformation of Europe', *Yale Law Journal*, 1991, pp. 2403 et seq.

16 On constitutionalisation as a creation, development and impact of general principles of the EU law legal order, see Groussot, *General*, p. 3.

17 See Weiler, 'The Transformation of Europe'.

After the failure of the French and Dutch referenda on the Constitutional Treaty (CT), the majority of scholars have supported the thesis of the definitive failure of any constitutional ambition for the EU.

As I will try to demonstrate in this volume, all of these scholars (whom we could term the 'discontents' of EU constitutionalism by borrowing – and adapting – the title of a very famous book by Joseph Stiglitz[18]) share some points:

1 They tend to underestimate the current constitutional dynamics already existing at EU level.
2 They consider the tradition of the (Continental) nation-state constitutionalism as the obligatory reference for any constitutional enterprise at the supranational level. In this sense, they basically tend to project the historical experience of the nation-state constitutionalism at the supranational level when studying the EU. However, in this way they result in making a particular constitutional experience (nation-state constitutionalism) the universal and very idea of constitutionalism.
3 They share a bias concerning the role to be played by judges in a context like the EU (characterised by the absence of checks and balances like those present at domestic level), and in this respect they can be seen as an expression of a sort of 'political constitutionalism'[19] present at EU level.

Some of these points have been challenged by authors such as Maduro. Indeed, he contextualised the activities of judicial actors, stressing that they are part of a political bargaining process. According to Maduro, the 'motives behind [judicial] transactions may vary greatly. Judicial criteria are not simply a result of judicial drafting but of a complex process of supply and demand of law in which the broader legal community participates'.[20] In this sense, judicial actors contribute to the development of a new legal order, which is the outcome of coordination between national and supranational levels. They also offer interconnections and links between different legal cultures, mediating values (interpretation is derived from the Latin *interpretia*,[21] i.e. intermediation among values) and comparing experiences – as has been the case, for instance, with the proportionality principle. In order to define the impact of judicial actors on the evolution of the European Union, one may use the

18 J. Stiglitz, *Globalization and its Discontents*, New York: Norton, 2002. See also the English title of a very famous book by S. Freud, *Das Unbehagen in der Kultur* (1930), which was translated into English as: S. Freud, *Civilization and Its Discontents*, New York: Norton, 2010.

19 On political constitutionalism see: R. Bellamy, *Political Constitutionalism*, Cambridge: Cambridge University Press, 2007.

20 M. Poiares Maduro, 'Contrapunctual Europe's Constitutional Pluralism in Action', in N. Walker (ed.), *Sovereignty in Transition*, Oxford: Hart, 2003, pp. 501 et seq., p. 514.

21 L. Bigliazzi Geri, *L' interpretazione. Appunti delle lezioni di teoria generale del diritto*, Milan: Giuffrè, 1994, p. 3.

notion of *cultural sources of law*,[22] which are not the result of an activity purposely aimed at the creation of law. The acceptance of such sources is based on the idea that the law is not only the pursuance of the sovereign's will (the king, the people or the parliament), 'but responds to the need for rationally determined justice'.[23]

As we will see in Chapter 3 of this volume, the ECJ's interpretative rulings in this context have served as cultural sources of law and played a fundamental role in pushing forward the process of European integration, while political sources (directives, regulations) were often locked within intergovernmental mechanisms. More precisely, courts play a fundamental role in the exchange of constitutional materials between the different levels/poles of the European system, contributing to what I call constitutional synallagma in this volume.

When looking at the primary and secondary sources of EU law (and at the case law of the ECJ, of course), it is possible to infer at least four different meanings of European constitutional law, as Monica Claes[24] has pointed out.

According to Claes, by European constitutional law one could mean: 1) the national constitutional law of the European States[25] – understood, for instance, as the Western European constitutional tradition;[26] 2) that portion of national constitutional law referring to supranational integration (for instance, those constitutional provisions that are used to explain the authority of EU law); 3) that portion of EU law provided with a constitutional status or 4) a sort of 'composite constitutional law', created by the interaction between the national and supranational levels.[27]

If the first two meanings given to this formula focus on national constitutional law, the third looks at the structural principles of EU law devised by the 'genius' of the ECJ (direct effect,[28] primacy,[29] *Francovich* doctrine[30]). These principles contribute to the autonomy and speciality of EU law,[31] understood as autonomy from the logic of public international law and from the domestic legal orders.[32] At the same time, provisions like those governing the mission and powers of the supranational institutions and devoted to the horizontal and vertical separation of powers in the EU – and codified in the Treaties – can be traced back to this

22 A. Pizzorusso, *Sistemi giuridici comparati*, Milan: Giuffrè, 1998, pp. 263–264

23 A. Pizzorusso, 'Fonti politiche e fonti culturali del diritto', in *Studi in onore di T Liebman*, I, Milan: Giuffrè, 1979, pp. 32 et seq.

24 M. Claes, 'The Emergence of a European Constitution: European and National Law in a European Constitutional Space', Paper Presented at the III EUNACON Workshop, University of Maastricht, 19–20 May 2011 (on file with author).

25 Claes, 'The Emergence of a European Constitution', p. 4.

26 Claes, 'The Emergence of a European Constitution', p. 4.

27 Building on L. Besselink, *A Composite European Constitution/Een Samengestelde Europese Constitutie*, Groningen: Europa Law Publishing, 2007.

28 ECJ, 26/62, *Van Gend en Loos*, [1963] ECR 1963, 3.

29 ECJ, 6/64, *Costa/Enel*, [1964] ECR. 1141

30 ECJ, C-6/90 e C-9/90, *Francovich and Bonifaci v. Italy*, [1991] ECR. *I-5357*.

31 R. Barents, *The Autonomy of Community Law*, The Hague: Kluwer Law International, 2004.

32 Claes, 'The Emergence of a European Constitution', pp. 4–5.

concept of European constitutional law.[33] Finally, we could mean by European constitutional law the set of principles that were developed by the ECJ but are now codified in the Charter of Fundamental Rights of the EU.

The fourth meaning dwells on the interaction between national and supranational levels, emphasising those provisions that refer to the fundamental principles of the other level, the best example of which is given by Article 6.3 of the TEU.[34]

As we will see, this kind of provision creates a composite scenario, a multidimensional and pluralistic constitutional frame where no level has a clear predominance over the other (because of the absence of a univocal 'supremacy clause').[35]

The idea of European constitutional law that I am going to adopt in this work relies on the third and fourth meanings recalled by Monica Claes. However, as will be clear in the next chapters, it is impossible to limit our attention to the wording of the EU Treaties when investigating the constitutional dynamics of the EU.

As in other contexts, in fact, a fundamental role is played even by those phenomena (soft law, policies) that from a formal point of view do not belong to the legal level.[36] These phenomena may perform a supplementary function with regard to the formal provisions.[37]

The present work starts from a clear premise: a European Constitution already exists, and if we want to define it, we could say, quoting Monica Claes again, that it should be understood as

> the set of EU norms, rules and principles constituting the polity and its legal order, establishing the institutions, attributing competences to the EU and dividing them among its institutions, governing the relationship between the EU and its Member States, limiting the exercise of its competences and guaranteeing the rights of the individuals governed under it.[38]

33 On the connection between frame of government and form of Union see: J. Bast and A. Bogdandy, 'The European Union's Vertical Order of Competences: The Current Law and Proposals for its Reform', *Common Market Law Review*, 2002, 39, pp. 227 et seq.

34 Article 6, p. 3: 'Fundamental rights, as guaranteed by the European Convention for the Protection of Human Rights and Fundamental Freedoms and as they result from the constitutional traditions common to the Member States, shall constitute general principles of the Union's law'.

35 Claes, 'The Emergence of a European Constitution', p. 7.

36 G. de Búrca, 'The Constitutional Challenge of New Governance', *European Law Review*, 2003, pp. 814 et seq.

37 This is not strange at all since something similar has happened even in other contexts, such as Canada and Switzerland (think of the importance of the *Social Union Framework Agreement* (SUFA) in Canada, for instance). For a comparison, see G. Martinico, 'Constitutional Failure or Constitutional Odyssey? What Can We Learn from Canada and Switzerland', *Perspectives on Federalism*, 2011, pp. E51 et seq.

38 Claes, 'The Emergence of a European Constitution', p. 4.

This corpus is composed of both unwritten and written principles, sometimes codified in the EU Treaties, the Charter of Fundamental Rights of the EU and sometimes in the national constitutions (as the idea of common constitutional traditions shows[39]), or in the case law of the ECJ (as the Declaration concerning primacy confirms[40]).

From this definition, it is clear that EU constitutional law is not an exhaustive phenomenon; it does not aim to replace (completely, at least) national constitutionalism. On the contrary, EU constitutionalism needs the constitutional materials of the Member States in order to perform its rationalising function[41] (the constitution, in this sense, remains the 'shape of the power'[42]). In fact, all these fundamental principles composing European constitutional law (present at both national and supranational levels) aim to shape both supranational and state powers.[43]

This point has been developed by Maduro, among others,[44] who radically challenges the argument of those who deny the existence or the possibility of a supranational constitutionalism by making a distinction between the idea of constitutionalism as such and state constitutionalism, which is understood as a particular historical experience and not as the only paradigm of constitutionalism.

Maduro does not even argue that supranational constitutionalism is constitutionalism as such but stresses that the interaction between these two constitutionalisms

39 A. Pizzorusso, 'Common Constitutional Traditions as Constitutional Law of Europe?' *STALS Research Paper*, No. 1/2008, www.stals.santannapisa.it/sites/default/files/stals_Pizzorusso_0.pdf

40 '17. Declaration concerning primacy.
The Conference recalls that, in accordance with well settled case law of the Court of Justice of the European Union, the Treaties and the law adopted by the Union on the basis of the Treaties have primacy over the law of Member States, under the conditions laid down by the said case law.
The Conference has also decided to attach as an Annex to this Final Act the Opinion of the Council Legal Service on the primacy of EC law as set out in 11197/07 (JUR 260): Opinion of the Council Legal Service of 22 June 2007. It results from the case-law of the Court of Justice that primacy of EC law is a cornerstone principle of Community law. According to the Court, this principle is inherent to the specific nature of the European Community. At the time of the first judgment of this established case law (Costa/ENEL, 15 July 1964, Case 6/64) there was no mention of primacy in the treaty. It is still the case today. The fact that the principle of primacy will not be included in the future treaty shall not in any way change the existence of the principle and the existing case-law of the Court of Justice'.

41 Adapting the idea of rationalisation employed by B. Mirkine-Guetzévitch in *Les nouvelles tendances du droit constitutionnel*, Paris: Marcel Girard, 1931.

42 F. Rubio Llorente, *La forma de poder. Estudios sobre la Constitución*, Madrid: Centro de Estudios Politicos y Constitucionales, 1997.

43 The classic example is given by the fundamental rights, but even the intergenerational equilibrium might be seen as another example of fundamental good shared by the national and supranational levels.

44 M. Poiares Maduro, 'The Three Claims of Constitutional Pluralism', Paper Presented at the Centro de Estudios Politicos y Constitucionales, Madrid, March 2011 (on file with author).

(i.e. the state-national and the supranational) might represent an approach to the ideals of constitutionalism:

> In other words, the constitutionalism of the European Union cannot be the simple product of a circular reasoning that would require the power claimed by the Union to be subject to constitutional control and then use the latter to legitimize the power being claimed. A deeper justification and legitimacy of European constitutionalism must be derived from its constitutional added value with respect to national constitutionalism. This is why the former can be opposed to the latter. European constitutionalism brings us closer to the ideals of constitutionalism. It is not, in itself, a closer representation of constitutionalism than national constitutionalism, but their interplay is. This is what constitutional pluralism argues and therein lays its thicker normative claim, one that relates constitutional pluralism and constitutionalism in general.[45]

This distinction is particularly useful to challenge the criticism advanced by Krisch,[46] by those who do not admit distinctions within that particular historical experience that is state constitutionalism[47] and by those who hold against supranational constitutionalism the absence of those features that can be found in the development of domestic constitutionalism.[48]

In this respect, EU constitutionalism – with state constitutionalism – contributes to that steady attempt to shape the power (now articulated on more levels or

45 Poiares Maduro, 'The Three Claims', pp. 13–14.

46 N. Krisch, *Beyond Constitutionalism. The Pluralist Structure of Postnational Law*, Oxford: Oxford University Press, 2010. See also M. Avbelj, 'EU Constitutional Swan Song', 2009, https://papers.ssrn.com/sol3/papers.cfm?abstract_id=1497030

47 M. Luciani, 'Costituzionalismo irenico e costituzionalismo polemico', 2006, www.rivistaaic.it/old_site_aic/materiali/anticipazioni/costituzionalismo_irenico/index.html

48 'The European Union is not a state and – as far as we can see – is not on an evolutionary track to statehood. Etatism is misleading anyway. The argument of the famous Maastricht ruling of the German Constitutional Court that the Union is neither a federal state (*Bundesstaat*) nor a federation of states (*Staatenbund*), but something in between, an association of states (*Staatenverbund*), goes in the wrong direction. The word "state" (*Staat*) is what all these variants of concepts have in common. But the Union is a unique political entity which is not only a postnational, but also a post-statist entity. Any constitution of Europe therefore has to be a constitution without a state', H. Brunkhorst, 'A polity without a state? European constitutionalism between evolution and revolution', in E.O. Eriksen, J.E. Fossum, and A.J. Menendez (eds.), *Developing a Constitution for Europe*, London-New York: Routledge, 2004, pp. 90–108, p. 103. Against this background, state constitutionalism does not disappear, since by constitutional pluralism he means the relation among constitutional orders: 'In other words, constitutional pluralism would not identify European constitutionalism itself but the nature of its relationship with other constitutional orders (national and, possibly, international)', Poiares Maduro, 'The three claims', p. 2.

poles, as we will see later) in order to protect some constitutional goods deemed as fundamental by all these levels.[49]

1.3 Dealing with the literature: what about the 'efficient secret' of the European Constitution? Some attempts at classification

After having recalled the meaning of some 'polysemic' words for the purpose of this work, it is time to have a look at how the academic debate has managed these concepts over the years.

The common core of the massive body of literature regarding the notion of the European Constitution undoubtedly rests on the idea of diversity, conceived as the ultimate value that is to be preserved in all the phases of the EU integration process. Confirmation of the correctness of this approach can be found in the continuous reference to the notion of diversity contained in the Preamble of the Charter of Fundamental Rights of the EU:

> The Union contributes to the preservation and to the development of these common values while respecting the diversity of the cultures and traditions of the peoples of Europe as well as the national identities of the Member States and the organisation of their public authorities at national, regional and local levels; it seeks to promote balanced and sustainable development and ensures free movement of persons, services, goods and capital, and the freedom of establishment.

In these lines, the EU is described as suspended on cultural and historical diversities that are conceived as a factor of spiritual richness rather than a danger for the common path. This 'tension' is highlighted in the main works devoted to European integration that find a common core (leaving their different starting perspectives out of consideration) in the acceptance of this phenomenon as *novum*.

The reflections of the most important scholars stress this aspect using different formulas: from the notion of *constitutional tolerance*[50] to that of *cosmopolitan communitarianism*.[51] According to Weiler, the main feature of Europe[52] is the capability to mix a high level of legal integration with the preservation of and respect for the different political identities and the sovereignty of the Member States. The interpretation adopted in order to summarise this combination is that

49 An author who has recently emphasised the functional nature of European constitutionalism is T. Isiksel, *Europe's Functional Constitution: A Theory of Constitutionalism Beyond the State*, Oxford: Oxford University Press, 2016.

50 J.H.H. Weiler, 'European Democracy and the Principle of Constitutional Tolerance: The Soul of Europe', in F. Cerutti and E. Rudolph (eds.), *A Soul for Europe*, Vol. I, Leuven: Peeters, 2001, pp. 33 et seq.

51 R. Bellamy and R. Warleigh, 'Cementing the Union: The Role of European Citizenship', in F. Cerutti and E. Rudolph (eds.), *A Soul for Europe*, I, Leuven: Peeters, 2001.

52 Weiler, 'European Democracy', p. 35.

of *constitutional tolerance*, which corresponds to the spirit of the European people's voluntary acceptance of a binding discipline that was not pronounced in their name (the authority, in this case, not being founded on the existence of a European *demos*). Bellamy and Warleigh also focus their reflection on diversity in their notion of *cosmopolitan communitarianism*, a synthesis of the communitarian and cosmopolitan perspectives on citizenship. Trying to overcome the weaknesses of the other visions, the authors stress the multilevel nature of the EU, defining it as 'a multitrack polity, involving co-operation between actors with different values and concerns'.[53] Against this background, the identities are multiple rather than one-dimensional because the citizens of the Union are simultaneously members of several communities.

In several works, Neil Walker[54] has attempted to 'map' the major positions present in the debate, providing an interesting schematisation that I will use in this part of the chapter to classify the vast body of literature already published on this issue. Walker identifies four groups of theoretical strands: *constitutional scepticism*, *constitutional serialism*, *constitutional processualism*, and *constitutional historical contextualism*.[55]

Within *constitutional scepticism*, Walker distinguished between deep and contingent scepticism. The former 'simply holds that the EU is just not the kind of entity that is worthy of characterisation in constitutional terms'.[56] The latter – defined as 'contingent scepticism' –

> holds that while we should not rule out the possibility of a "truly" constitutional status for the EU, and so should not entirely dismiss the prospect of a constitutional moment, no such status is yet appropriate and no such moment has yet arrived.[57]

In another piece,[58] Walker considers Antje Wiener sceptical,[59] but her scepticism is due to reasons of approach (which is contrary to the reductionist positions of the constitutional law scholars) that should not necessarily, for Walker, imply the denial of a written constitution. The opposite of this approach would be represented by the *constitutional historical contextualist* view, according to which 'the gradual development of a constitutional register of debate and self-interpretation

53 Bellamy and Warleigh, 'Cementing', p. 69.

54 For instance, N. Walker, 'After the Constitutional Moment', 2003, www.le.ac.uk/la/celi/moment.pdf

55 Walker, 'After'.

56 Walker, 'After'. Walker quotes D. Grimm, 'Does Europe need a constitution?' *European Law Journal*, 1995, pp. 282 et seq.

57 Walker, 'After'.

58 N. Walker, 'Reconstituting European Integration in Theory and Practice: A Comment on Antje Wiener', *Jean Monnet Working Paper*, No. 9/03, 2003, https://jeanmonnetprogram.org/archive/papers/03/030901-07.html

59 A. Wiener, 'Towards a Transnational Nomos. The Role of Institutions in the Process of Constitutionalization', *Jean Monnet Working Paper*, No. 9/03, 2003, https://jeanmonnetprogram.org/archive/papers/03/030901-06.pdf

by the ECJ and, gradually, by other European institutions over the past 30 years, provides abundant evidence that the EU already has a constitutional heritage'.[60] The third approach identified by Walker is that of *constitutional serialism*, according to which 'European constitutional development is best characterised as an iterative series of constitutional events rather than as a long process of normal politics interrupted by one or very few constitutional moments'.[61] Finally, there is the *constitutional processualism* approach, according to which:

> Constitutional discourse and practice within the European Union should not be seen exclusively or even mainly as a matter of Treaties and self-styled constitutional documents. Rather, the test of constitutional relevance should be functional rather than formal, and any activity and any form of reflection that is concerned with the overall legitimacy of the European juridico-political order should be seen in terms of a constitutional register.[62]

Obviously, each approach considers the Constitutional Treaty in a different perspective, as the following table attempts to sum up:

Constitutional approaches	*Key concepts*	*Authors*	*How they consider the Constitutional Treaty*
Constitutional scepticism	According to this approach, the EU lacks that 'sense of common attachment necessary to make decisions which are seriously committed to and capable of addressing matters of common interest and are broadly perceived as so doing'.[63]	Grimm[64]	The Constitutional Treaty is seen as an example of false constitutionalism, 'a text which illegitimately frames an essentially state-derivative legal configuration in autonomous and original terms, rather than an event which recognises or brings into being a new pouvoir constituant for the European Union'.[65]

60 Walker, 'After'. The classic example is provided by J.H.H. Weiler, 'In Defence of the Status Quo: Europe's Constitutional *Sonderweg*', in J.H.H. Weiler and M. Wind (eds.), *European Constitutionalism Beyond the State*, Cambridge: Cambridge University Press, 2003, pp. 7 et seq.

61 Walker, 'After'. Walker mentions B. de Witte, 'The Closest Thing to a Constitutional Conversation in Europe: The Semi-Permanent Treaty Revision Process', in P. Beaumont, C. Lyons, and N. Walker (eds.), *Convergence and Divergence in European Public Law*, Oxford: Hart, 2002, pp. 39 et seq.; see also U. Haltern, 'Pathos and Patina: The Failure and Promise of Constitutionalism in the European Imagination', *European Law Journal*, 2003, pp. 14 et seq.

62 Walker, 'After'. Walker quotes G. de Búrca, 'The Constitutional Challenge of New Governance in the European Union', *European Law Review*, 2003, pp. 814 et seq.

63 Walker, 'After'.

64 Grimm, 'Does Europe Need a Constitution?' pp. 282 et seq.

65 Walker, 'After'.

Constitutional approaches	*Key concepts*	*Authors*	*How they consider the Constitutional Treaty*
Constitutional historical contextualism	According to the historical contextualist, the constitutional moment would imply a clear-cut discontinuity and transformation upon 'a qualitative change within constitutional discourse'.[66]	Weiler[67]	'The Constitutional Treaty is seen predominantly as an exercise in documentation'.[68]
Constitutional serialism	'The idea of a defining constitutional moment clearly distinguished from the past and stably framing a constitutional future, is comprehensively challenged'.[69]	De Witte;[70] Haltern[71]	The Constitutional Treaty is seen as a part of the European 'tragic cycle of constitutional inflation',[72] the latest expression of that semi-permanent Treaty revision process that characterises the EU.[73]
Constitutional processualism	'Processes and mechanisms which are given little direct recognition within the Treaty structure, such as comitology or OMC or partnership agreements or other "new" forms of governance . . . [can be seen] as vital constitutional processes which are in danger of being obscured by the focus on surface activity'.[74]	De Búrca[75]	'The drafters of the Constitutional Treaty have drawn uncritically on the state template, giving undue attention to matters such as a Bill of Rights, the horizontal division of power between federal-level institutions, the vertical division of powers between "federal" and "state" institutions, external relations, etc., in a way which may fail to grasp the sui generis quality of the EU order'.[76]

66 Walker, 'After'.
67 Weiler, 'Europe's Constitutional Sonderweg', pp. 15 et seq.
68 Walker, 'After'.
69 Walker, 'After'.
70 de Witte, 'The Closest Thing to'.
71 Haltern, 'Pathos', pp. 14 et seq.
72 Walker, 'After'.
73 de Witte, 'The Closest Thing', pp. 39 et seq.
74 Walker, 'After'.
75 de Búrca, 'The Constitutional Challenge', pp. 814 et seq.
76 Walker, 'After'.

Among the authors who stress the current existence of a European Constitution, we can distinguish between those who identify the Constitution in the EU Treaties and in the ECJ's case law[77] and other scholars who conceive of the Constitution as the result of the never-ending dialectic between national and supranational principles. As we will see in Chapter 2, this is precisely the case of Pernice[78] and supporters of the multilevel constitutionalism approach.

It is almost impossible to give a complete precise overview in this research field, and the schematisation proposed by Neil Walker is just one of the possible attempts at classifying such a scholarly variety. There are other possible classifications of the debate.

Within a first group of scholars we may recall those labelled by Walker as 'sceptical' (we could call them 'negationists' in order not to confuse them with those authors like Ian Ward[79] who define themselves as sceptical but with remarkable differentiations). Among them, we could then distinguish different views, starting from the supporters of the no *demos* thesis (Grimm) and moving to those whom, referring to another classification, Pinelli defines as the supporters of the thesis according to which 'a constitution without a state cannot exist'.[80] It is possible, then, to identify another (more traditional) classification that distinguishes two groups of scholars interested in the European Constitution.

The first group comprises those scholars[81] who deny the possibility of a Constitution for Europe due to the lack of a European people. These authors conceive the Constitution as an expression of the people (seen as one of the three classic elements of the State by Bodin[82]). According to this view, without a European State and without a European people, it is impossible to have a proper constitution. This opinion shows the importance of the State for the constitutionalist perspective, but it is completely inadequate for the understanding of the latest trends of constitutional law. Sovereignty is in crisis (or perhaps in transition[83]), and undoubtedly globalisation has reduced the margins for isolated action by state actors. The second group of scholars, instead, admits the possibility of a Constitution without a State, also in light of the experience of the mediaeval legal orders.[84] Among these

77 Weiler, 'In Defence', pp. 7 et seq.

78 I. Pernice, 'Multilevel Constitutionalism and the Treaty of Amsterdam: European Constitution-Making Revisited?' *Common Market Law Review*, 1999, pp. 703 et seq.; I. Pernice, 'Multilevel Constitutionalism in the European Union', *WHI Paper*, No. 5/02, www.rewi.hu-berlin.de/WHI/papers/whipapers502/constitutionalism.pdf

79 I. Ward, *A Critical Introduction to European Law*, London: Butterworths, 1996, VII.

80 C. Pinelli, 'La Carta Europea dei diritti e il processo di "costituzionalizzazione» del diritto europeo"', in A. Pizzorusso, R. Romboli, A. Ruggeri, A. Saitta, and G. Silvestri (eds.), *Riflessi della Carta Europea dei diritti sulla giustizia e la giurisprudenza costituzionale: Italia e Spagna al confronto*, Milan: Giuffrè, 2003, pp. 55–78.

81 Grimm, 'Does Europe Need a Constitution?' pp. 282 et seq.

82 J. Bodin, *On Sovereignty*, edited by J.H. Franklin, Cambridge: Cambridge University Press, 1992.

83 See N. Walker (ed.), *Sovereignty in Transition*, Oxford: Hart, 2003.

84 M. Dogliani, 'Può la Costituzione europea non essere una Costituzione in senso moderno?' 2003, www.costituzionalismo.it/puo-la-costituzione-europea-non-essere-una-costituzione-in-senso-moderno/

authors we can identify two different points of view: conservative and progressive. Authors like Weiler, for example, belong to the first strand because they argue the current existence of a European Constitution that is represented by the Treaties and the principles of the case law of the European Court of Justice (principle of direct effect,[85] primacy[86]).[87] There are instead some authors who deny the current existence of a Constitution for Europe but do not radically deny the possibility of having one in the future. However, in order to achieve the goal-Constitution, it would be necessary to change the status quo, so in this respect these authors can be understood as 'progressive.[88]

The 'conservative' conception has to be framed in the light of Weiler's particular view of Europe and in light of the connected negative conception of the pseudo-constituent process started in Nice and Brussels with the two Conventions. According to Weiler, the Constitution already exists and the real problem is different, since the democratic deficit has to be overcome by insisting on the Treaties and by making more transparent the decisional modalities within the EU. The theory of multilevel constitutionalism (Pernice), as we will see, believes in the current existence of a European Constitution, but Pernice does not reduce the Constitution to the EU level alone. This theory implies an awareness of the incomplete nature of the European order. Among the supporters of the thesis of the current existence of a European Constitution, there are those whom Walker would call *historical contextualism constitutionalists* and whom Brand would call supporters of the *constitutionalisation/transformation thesis*.[89] Within the second group, it is useful to recall another difference, pointed out by Brand,[90] between those authors according to whom a formal constitution 'will do too much' (Weiler, who is afraid that a formalisation of the European Constitution might jeopardise the secret of the material European Constitution: constitutional tolerance[91]) and those according to whom a formal Constitution 'will do too little' (among these authors Brand recalls Ward and Haltern[92]).

Moreover, we can also distinguish between the scholars interested in studying the European Constitution as a mere set of norms (principles and rules) and the supporters of a constitutional theory of European integration. By constitutional

85 ECJ, 26/62, *Van Gend v. Loos*, [1963] ECR. 3.
86 ECJ, 6/64, *Costa v. Enel*, [1964] ECR. 1141.
87 Weiler, 'In Defence', pp. 7–24.
88 J. Habermas, 'Remarks on Dieter Grimm's Does Europe Need a Constitution?' *European Law Journal*, 1995, pp. 303 et seq.
89 M. Brand, 'Formalising European Constitutionalism; Potential Added Value or "Death by Constitution"', in K. Inglis and A. Ott (eds.), *The Constitution for Europe and an Enlarging Union: Unity in Diversity?* Groningen: Europa Law Publishing, 2005, pp. 3 et seq.
90 Brand, 'Formalising European Constitutionalism'.
91 Weiler, 'In Defence', pp. 15 et seq.
92 U. Haltern, 'Europe Goes Camper – The EU Charter of Fundamental Rights from a Consumerist Perspective', 2001, www.europeansources.info/record/europe-goes-camper-the-eu-charter-of-fundamental-rights-from-a-consumerist-perspective/ and Haltern, 'Pathos', pp. 14 et seq.

theory of European integration, I do not refer to what Ward[93] means when writing about an EU legal theory. I mean an intellectual effort that does not limit itself to the analysis of the legal data but attempts to catch –using the formula proposed by Bagehot[94] – 'the efficient secret' of the European Constitution and to read, as far as possible, the whole of the European dynamics. Theories such as multilevel constitutionalism and constitutional pluralism aim at studying the efficient secret of the European Constitution by going beyond the mere description of the legal and institutional evolutions of the main political actors of the EU.

These theories aim at overcoming an evident paradox present in the debate on the European Constitution and captured in these words by Maduro:

> It has become consensual to recognize that the European Union is governed by a form of constitutional law. But, to a large extent, the constitution of Europe has developed without a constitutional theory. There has been an important doctrinal effort in the dogmatics of European constitutional law, highlighting how constitutional concepts have been integrated into the law of the European Union and dominate its organization of power. At the same time, however, the constitutional theorization of the European Union has been limited, to a large extent, to a discussion on whether it deserves or not the constitutional label. More recently and following, in particular, the work of Joseph Weiler, there has been an increased discussion on the nature of European constitutionalism. But even this discussion appears more often as an upgrade on two old questions: Does Europe have a constitution? Does Europe need a constitution? Rarely do we see any work on the constitutional consequences of different constitutional conceptions of the European Union: what theories of fundamental rights, separation of powers or judicial review ought to dominate EU constitutional law? If European constitutionalism changes constitutionalism itself how does that impact on those aspects of a theory of constitutional law?[95]

By 'constitutional theory', Maduro means a theory that can explain the reasons and the added value of supranational constitutionalism[96] ('European' or 'EU constitutionalism' if compared with state constitutionalism).

When looking at the debate, one can realise that multilevel constitutionalism and constitutional pluralism have been presented as the most likely approaches to turn into a real, fully fledged constitutional theory, which is why the first part of

93 Ward, *A Critical Introduction*, VII.

94 Bagehot, *The English Constitution*, p. 48.

95 Poiares Maduro, 'The Three Claims', p. 1.

96 Poiares Maduro, 'The Three Claims': 'This does not imply that its constitutionalism is the same as that of the States or even has the same comprehensive social ambition. It only requires demonstrating that the European Union has, in certain respects, a stronger constitutional added value with respect to State constitutionalism and that it may be opposed to it'.

the next chapter will deal with them. As I will try to show, these two approaches present differences (as the respective inventors claim) but also analogies that will be shown in Chapter 3.

Constitutional complexity is indebted to these two approaches (sharing with them the idea of constitution as the outcome of an interaction among levels/poles[97]) but also presents some important peculiarities, as I will stress when dealing with the issue of constitutional conflicts, which will be treated in this book as a window of opportunity for the change of the system rather than as an expression of mere disorder that should be neutralised.

1.4 The persistent terminological ambiguity with reference to European constitutional law

If the academic debate shows the great polysemy of constitutional language when applied to EU law, a similar ambiguity can be found in the case law of the ECJ. The last few years have been characterised by interesting elements of continuity even after the failure of the Constitutional Treaty. On the one hand, the EU Court of Justice has not abandoned constitutional terminology to define its legal system. On the other hand, those terminological ambiguities regarding the concept of constitutionalisation that we identified earlier can still be found in the case law of the Luxembourg Court. As anticipated, in fact, the two meanings of constitutionalisation identified in the work can sometimes come into conflict. This is what has happened in decisions such as *Melloni*[98] or *Opinion 2/13*.[99] *Melloni* will be discussed specifically in Chapter 5, while in this final section of this chapter I will compare *Opinion 2/13* with the *Kadi* saga. At first glance, in both *Kadi* and *Opinion 2/13*, the Court of Justice used constitutional language to a great extent, adopting legal reasoning with a similar structure.

These rulings have much in common despite the outcome reached by the Court. While Kadi demonstrates the positive effect that the autonomy doctrine can have on the protection of fundamental rights beyond the state sphere, *Opinion 2/13* is rightly seen as an infamous confirmation of the inadequacy of the Court's approach. It is worth analysing them together. In order to compare the

97 This is also present in other theories, for instance, that of constitutional synthesis: 'In essence, constitutional synthesis refers to a process in which already established constitutional states integrate through constitutional law.
This is a process where participant states establish a supranational political community (in the European instance, the three original Communities) in which they become integrated without losing their institutional structure and identity', J.E. Fossum and A.J. Menéndez, 'The Theory of Constitutional Synthesis. A Constitutional Theory for a Democratic European Union', *ARENA Working Paper*, No. 15/2010, www.sv.uio.no/arena/english/research/publications/arena-publications/workingpapers/2010/wp15-10.pdf

98 ECJ, C-399/11, *Melloni*, EU:C:2013:107.

99 ECJ, Opinion 2/13 ECLI:EU:C:2014:2454.

legal reasoning followed by the ECJ in *Kadi* I and in *Opinion 2/13* I will insist on the following factors:

1 The key role played by the concept of autonomy in both the decisions;
2 The effort made by the ECJ to underline the continuity between these decisions and its foundational case law;
3 The constitutional jargon employed in the texts of these decisions;
4 The identification, in both cases, of an untouchable core of values that may not be jeopardised;
5 The polemical and unilateral (in De Búrca's words, 'chauvinist and parochial'[100]) spirit of these decisions.

However, in spite of this, the outcome was radically different as regards the protection of fundamental rights. In *Opinion 2/13*, in fact, the reasons of primacy and autonomy (constitutionalisation as federalisation) prevailed over those of the protection of rights (constitutionalisation as humanisation).

1.4.1 The **Kadi** *saga*

The *sui generis* narrative created by foundational decisions like *Van Gend en Loos*[101] and *Costa*[102] responds to the need for a demarcation from the rest of international law without the need to further label (at least, not immediately) its nature as 'constitutional' and without the effort to determine the very peculiar content of this new legal order.

Almost unanimously, *Kadi* I has been seen as a perfect representation of the jurisprudential boldness of the ECJ, as it was very rich in 'constitutional intimations'[103] and 'constitutional symbolism'.[104] *Kadi* I also recalled the idea of a community based on the rule of law and, more concretely, that of a complete and coherent system of judicial protection[105] (all elements retaken from the

100 G. de Búrca 'The European Court of Justice and the International Legal Order After Kadi', *Harvard International Law Journal*, 2010, pp. 1 et seq.

101 ECJ, 26/62, *Van Gend en Loos*, [1963] ECR 1963, 3.

102 ECJ, 6/64, *Costa/Enel*, [1964] ECR. 1141

103 N. Walker, 'Opening or Closure? The Constitutional Intimations of the ECJ', in L. Azoulai and M. Poiares Maduro (eds.), *The past and the future of EU law. The Classics of EU law on the 50th Anniversary of the Rome Treaty*, Oxford: Hart, 2010, pp. 333 et seq., p. 333.

104 Walker, 'Opening or Closure?' p. 333

105 See the contributions by K. Lenaerts, 'The Basic Constitutional Charter of a Community Based on the Rule of Law', in L. Azoulai and M. Poiares Maduro (eds.), *The past and the future of EU law. The Classics of EU law on the 50th Anniversary of the Rome Treaty*, Oxford: Hart, 2010; J.-P. Jacqué, 'Les Verts v The European Parliament', in L. Azoulai and M. Poiares Maduro (eds.), *The past and the future of EU law. The Classics of EU law on the 50th Anniversary of the Rome Treaty*, Oxford: Hart, 2010; A. Alemanno, 'What Has Been, and What Could Be, Thirty Years After Les Verts/European Parliament', in L. Azoulai and M. Poiares Maduro (eds.), *The Past and the Future of EU Law. The Classics of EU Law on the 50th Anniversary of the Rome Treaty*, Oxford: Hart, 2010.

Les Verts doctrine[106]). These references marked the continuity with the case law of the foundation of Community law,[107] in particular with *Van Gend en Loos*, as Gattini aptly pointed out:

> On the one hand, one cannot but welcome the unbending commitment of the European Court of Justice to the respect of fundamental human rights, but on the other hand the relatively high price, in terms of coherence and unity of the international legal system, that had to be paid in order to arrive at the conclusion of the invalidity of the contested Regulation, is worrying. Of course, one might argue that the ECJ was all too willing to pay that price, and that it could have even felt it as no price at all, but as a golden opportunity to bring a step further the proclaimed 'constitutionalization' and autonomy of the Community legal system. The Kadi judgment is a direct, if late, offspring of the van Gend en Loos and Costa/Enel jurisprudence, and, without wanting to sound too rhetorical, one might even venture to say that similarly to those decisions it will be a landmark in the history of EC law.[108]

In this section, I shall focus on the *Kadi* saga by showing its 'added value' in the history of EU law.

The *Kadi* saga responds to a double logic: on the one hand, it develops from a strong perception of EU law autonomy, while on the other hand it reflects the idea of the existence of a mature system in terms of fundamental rights protection. These ideas of autonomy and maturity have been used by the ECJ as a fundamental premise to justify its intervention in a rather sensitive case from a legal (and geopolitical) point of view. Indeed, at first sight, the *Kadi* saga seems to feature a progressive 'appropriation' of a question that was originally presented as an issue regulated by an external set of norms belonging to public international law (i.e. one can perceive in this saga the progressive efforts made by the Court of Justice at 'internalising' the legal questions at stake).

In *Kadi* I, the former Court of First Instance admitted the possibility of reviewing the regulation that implemented the UN resolution only in case of violation of *jus cogens*, that is to say a corpus of norms originally alien to the body of EU law.[109] This was a consequence of the approach chosen by the Court of First Instance, which adopted as point of reference a set of norms that do not belong to

106 ECJ, 294/83, *Parti Ecologiste 'Les Verts' v Parliament*, [1986] ECR 1365.

107 F. Mayer, 'Van Gend en Loos: The Foundation of a Community of Law', L. Azoulai and M. Poiares Maduro (eds.), *The Past and the Future of EU Law. The Classics of EU Law on the 50th Anniversary of the Rome Treaty*, Oxford: Hart, 2010, 16 et seq.

108 A. Gattini, 'Joined Cases C – 402/05 P & 415/05 P. Yassin Abdullah Kadi, Al Barakaat International Foundation v. Council and Commission, judgment of the Grand Chamber of 3 September 2008', *Common Market Law Review*, 2009, pp. 213 et seq., p. 224.

109 T-315/01 Kadi v. Council and Commission, [2005] ECR II-3649, par. 226: 'None the less, the Court is empowered to check, indirectly, the lawfulness of the resolutions of the Security Council in question with regard to jus cogens, understood as a body of higher rules of public international law binding on all subjects of international law, including the bodies of the United Nations, and from which no derogation is possible'. See also par. 213–215.

the EU legal order understood *stricto sensu*, i.e. norms of international law. On the contrary, moving to the Opinion of Advocate General Maduro in *Kadi* I,[110] one can realise that his point of departure was very different, since he focused on stressing the potential violation by the UN resolution of some norms peculiar to EU law. By following a similar line *Kadi* I of the Court of Justice constantly referred to the autonomy of EU law,[111] but the Court went even further on that occasion. Indeed, the issue of the autonomy of EU law was more emphasised, as the Court neglected what was an essential step in the Opinion of the Advocate General: the analysis of the question from the viewpoint of former Article 307 TEC.[112]

Starting from former Article 307 TEC, the Advocate General in *Kadi* I attempted to stress that no obligations envisaged therein can be interpreted 'so as to silence the general principles of Community law and deprive individuals of their fundamental rights'.[113] Coherent with this reconstruction, it was fundamental to find the

110 Joined Cases C-402/05 P and C-415/05 P, *Kadi and Al Barakaat*, Opinion of Advocate General Poiares Maduro [2008] ECR I-6351, especially at par. 34: 'The implication that the present case concerns a "political question", in respect of which even the most humble degree of judicial interference would be inappropriate, is, in my view, untenable. The claim that a measure is necessary for the maintenance of international peace and security cannot operate so as to silence the general principles of Community law and deprive individuals of their fundamental rights. This does not detract from the importance of the interest in maintaining international peace and security; it simply means that it remains the duty of the courts to assess the lawfulness of measures that may conflict with other interests that are equally of great importance and with the protection of which the courts are entrusted'.

111 See for instance par. 282 of *Kadi* I of the Court of Justice: 'It is also to be recalled that an international agreement cannot affect the allocation of powers fixed by the Treaties or, consequently, the autonomy of the Community legal system, observance of which is ensured by the Court by virtue of the exclusive jurisdiction conferred on it by Article 220 EC, jurisdiction that the Court has, moreover, already held to form part of the very foundations of the Community (see, to that effect, Opinion 1/91 [1991] ECR I-6079, paragraphs 35 and 71, and Case C-459/03 *Commission* v *Ireland* [2006] ECR I-4635, paragraph 123 and case-law cited)'.

112 Former Article 307 TEC (now Article 351 TFEU) read: 'The rights and obligations arising from agreements concluded before 1 January 1958 or, for acceding States, before the date of their accession, between one or more Member States on the one hand, and one or more third countries on the other, shall not be affected by the provisions of this Treaty.

To the extent that such agreements are not compatible with this Treaty, the Member State or States concerned shall take all appropriate steps to eliminate the incompatibilities established. Member States shall, where necessary, assist each other to this end and shall, where appropriate, adopt a common attitude.

In applying the agreements referred to in the first paragraph, Member States shall take into account the fact that the advantages accorded under this Treaty by each Member State form an integral part of the establishment of the Community and are thereby inseparably linked with the creation of common institutions, the conferring of powers upon them and the granting of the same advantages by all the other Member States'. On this see: N. Lavranos, 'Revisiting Article 307 EC: The Untouchable Core of Fundamental European Constitutional Law Values', in F. Fontanelli, G. Martinico and P. Carrozza, (eds.), *Shaping Rule of Law Through Dialogue: International and Supranational Experiences*, Groningen: Europa Law Publishing 2010, pp. 119 et seq.

113 Joined Cases C-402/05 P and C-415/05 P, *Kadi and Al Barakaat*, Opinion of Advocate General Poiares Maduro [2008] ECR I-6351, par. 34.

right way for the European order to interact with the international legal order's obligations and judges.

It is not a coincidence that the Advocate General devoted several lines of his Opinion to recall the importance of judicial deference in the relationship between the Court of Justice and other judges.

This deference, though, must find a limit in the possible risk for the fundamental values of the EU legal order: 'Consequently, in situations where the Community's fundamental values are in the balance, the Court may be required to reassess, and possibly annul, measures adopted by the Community institutions, even when those measures reflect the wishes of the Security Council'.[114]

In the Advocate General's own words, these values represent 'the constitutional framework created by the Treaty'.[115] In its reasoning, the ECJ seemed to pay more attention to the peculiar nature of the EU legal order than to its relationship with international law. This can be noticed by looking at the use of the idea of autonomy employed in the decision. Thus, one could say that the Court of Justice's initial assumptions were more unilateral, since they were centred not around the terms of the relationship between international and EU law, but rather around the constitutional and peculiar nature of EU law. This is also proved by the fact that the Court of Justice missed the opportunity to clarify the scope of Article 307, for example, specifying 'its position on the consequences if the "appropriate steps" of Member States remain unsuccessful'.[116]

In sum, in *Kadi* I the Court of Justice disregarded former Article 307 TEC, following a precise argumentative strategy: the need to contextualise the question of the relationship between international and Community law within the boundaries of its own legal order. It could then give the question an 'internal answer' and insist on the values of its own 'order'.[117]

This also explains why the *Kadi* saga is a *summa* of many of the traditional arguments employed in the 'Classics' of the Court of Justice[118] (*Van Gend en Loos, Costa/Enel,*[119] *Les Verts,*[120] *Opinion 1/91*[121] etc.).

114 Joined Cases C-402/05 P and C-415/05 P, *Kadi and Al Barakaat*, Opinion of Advocate General Poiares Maduro [2008] ECR I-6351, par. 44.

115 Moreover, 'the relationship between international law and the Community legal order is governed by the Community legal order itself, and international law can permeate that legal order only under the conditions set by the constitutional principles of the Community', Joined Cases C-402/05 P and C-415/05 P, *Kadi and Al Barakaat*, Opinion of Advocate General Poiares Maduro [2008] ECR I-6351, par. 24.

116 Gattini, 'Joined Cases', p. 235.

117 M. Simoncini, 'Risk Regulation Approach to EU Policy Against Terrorism in the Light of the ECJ / CFI Jurisprudence', *German Law Journal*, 2009, pp. 1526 et seq.

118 Azoulai and Poiares Maduro (eds.), *The Past*.

119 ECJ, C-6/64, *Costa/Enel*, [1964] ECR 1141.

120 ECJ, C- 294/83, *Parti Ecologiste 'Les Verts' v Parliament*, [1986] ECR 1365.

121 ECJ, Opinion 1/91, *Draft Agreement Relating to the Creation of the European Economic Area* [1991] ECR I-6079.

I think that *Kadi* II[122] can be read coherently with *Kadi* I of the ECJ, although the two decisions differ for some reasons, first of all for the language employed by the Luxembourg Court in *Kadi* II.

Indeed, it is evident from initial analysis that *Kadi* II does not present the powerful rhetoric contained in *Kadi* I. The adjective 'constitutional' was employed 9 times in *Kadi* I, while 'constitutional' is recalled just twice in *Kadi* II, and it should be stressed that in the first of these two citations,[123] the ECJ was summing up the decision held in 2008. Another evident difference in the terminology employed by the ECJ is the absence of the word 'autonomy' in *Kadi* II. These remarks might lead to considering *Kadi* II as different from *Kadi* I, but when looking at the substance of the decision, it is possible to find strong continuity.[124]

In *Kadi* II, the Court rejected the argument according to which the challenged regulation enjoyed immunity from judicial review. It did so by relying on its previous decision and borrowing the same reasoning, since 'there has been no change in those factors which could justify reconsideration of that position' (par. 66). As a consequence, all EU acts must be reviewed for compliance with fundamental rights (par. 67). It also confirmed that the intensity of the review, in principle, must be full, thus standing by its precedent. The ECJ also showed not to suffer from the pressure coming from an international context and academic circles, as it was not afraid of the possible impact of this decision over similar delisting cases. It constructed the controversy as a 'domestic' case for at least two reasons: firstly, because the issue concerned an EU act, and secondly, because it was about a possible violation of some fundamental rights protected by the EU legal order.

Thus, the ECJ confirmed the approach followed in *Kadi* I and the idea of autonomy stemming from that decision. In conclusion, the first way to read *Kadi* II by the ECJ is therefore the asymmetry existing between the form of this decision (which seems to abandon the bombastic approach used in *Kadi* I) and the substance of the judgement that maintains its approach towards public international law. Despite the different terminology employed, if one goes beyond form and looks at the substance, one can see that the confirmation of the idea 'in principle full review' confirms the strong claims of *Kadi* I.

In order to do so, the ECJ even defended the core of the decision taken by the General Court (former Court of First Instance) in *Kadi* II.[125] On that occasion, the

122 ECJ, Joined Cases C-584/10 P, C-593/10 P and C-595/10 P, *Commission, Council, United Kingdom v. Yassin Abdullah Kadi*, [2008] ECR I-06351

123 ECJ, Joined Cases C-584/10 P, C-593/10 P and C-595/10 P, *Commission, Council, United Kingdom v. Yassin Abdullah Kadi*, [2008] ECR I-06351, par. 21–22.

124 *Contra* see N. Lavranos and M. Vatsov, 'Kadi II: Backtracking from Kadi I?' in M. Avbelj, F. Fontanelli, and G. Martinico (eds.), *Kadi on Trial: A Multifaceted Analysis of the Kadi judgment*, Abingdon: Routledge, 2014, pp. 101 et seq.

125 T-85/09 *Kadi v. Commission* [2010] ECR II-5177.

General Court had agreed to revise its previous decision and to comply with the revolutionary decision of the Court of Justice, serving as a 'loyal soldier', despite the many doubts it had about the decision of the ECJ.[126]

This is evident in those passages where the General Court wanted to recall the decisions of other courts or tribunals that had shared the original position of the former Court of First Instance.[127]

In *Kadi* II, the ECJ defended the core of the decision of the General Court, endorsing the idea according to which the EU presents an untouchable nucleus of principles that may not be jeopardised by international law, not even by the UN Charter.[128]

1.4.2 Reading the Kadi saga in context

In this section, I seek to show that *Kadi* II belongs to a new generation of decisions in which the ECJ does not merely proclaim EU law autonomy from both national and international laws but sets out to identify a constitutional core of principles whose violation justifies its intervention even in cases of dubious jurisdiction.

As Rosas and Armati pointed out,

> in Kadi, the ECJ confirmed and made more explicit a tendency discernible in previous case-law according to which the EU constitutional order consists of some core principles which may prevail over provisions of the Treaties and thus of written primary law.[129]

126 T-85/09 *Kadi v. Commission* [2010] ECR II-5177, see par. 121.

127 T-85/09 *Kadi v Commission* [2010] ECR II-5177: '122. It should be observed, as an ancillary point, that, although some higher national courts have adopted a rather similar approach to that taken by this Court in its judgment in Kadi (see, to that effect, the decision of the Tribunal fédéral de Lausanne (Switzerland) of 14 November 2007 in Case 1A.45/2007 Youssef Mustapha Nada v Secrétariat d'État pour l'Économie and the judgment of the House of Lords (United Kingdom) in Al-Jedda v. Secretary of State for Defence [2007] UKHL 58, which is currently the subject of an action pending before the European Court of Human Rights (Case No 227021/08 Al-Jedda v United Kingdom), others have tended to follow the approach taken by the Court of Justice, holding the Sanctions Committee's system of designation to be incompatible with the fundamental right to effective review before an independent and impartial court (see, to that effect, the judgment of the Federal Court of Canada of 4 June 2009 in Abdelrazik v Canada (Minister of Foreign Affairs) 2009 FC 580, cited at paragraph 69 of the UK Supreme Court judgment in Ahmed and Others)'.

128 At the same time, the ECJ recognised that the General Court had erred in law in paragraphs 138 to 140 and 142 to 149 but also confirmed that these errors did not vitiate the validity of the decision under appeal

129 A. Rosas and L. Armati, *EU Constitutional Law. An Introduction*, Oxford: Hart, 2011, p. 43. On constitutional identity in EU law see also ECJ, C-156/21, *Hungary v. European Parliament and Council of the European Union*, https://eur-lex.europa.eu/legal-content/EN/TXT/?uri=CELEX:62021CN0156, par. 232.

This is evident from the wording of *Kadi* I, whereby the Court of Justice maintained that

> Article 307 EC may in no circumstances permit any challenge to the principles that form part of the very foundations of the Community legal order, which include the principles of liberty, democracy and respect for human rights and fundamental freedoms enshrined in Article 6(1) EU as a foundation of the Union.
>
> (par. 304)

When doing so, the Court of Justice acts as many Constitutional Courts do: in fact, in these cases the ECJ selects a group of principles that may not be jeopardised because their violation would imply the denial of the axiological bases on which the EU legal order is founded. At the national level, constitutional law scholars refer to this set of principles in different ways – 'Republican form' ('forma repubblicana'[130]) in Italy, eternity clause ('Ewigkeitsklause'[131]) in Germany[132] – but in the concrete task of identifying the principles that may be traced back to such an untouchable core, a primary role has always been played by constitutional judges.

This has happened with particular regard to human rights, the language of which has been codified by national constitutions *grosso modo* since the end of World War II.

This codification of rights has made those norms aimed at protecting rights constitutional principles, and the rights protected by such constitutional principles have become fundamental rights, i.e. meta-norms of many contemporary legal orders.

> Fundamental rights are to be understood as encompassing those selective and substantive criteria which, together with others, enable judgments of 'validity': the recognition of belonging to a legal order, legitimacy, compatibility of institutional behaviour and norms within a given legal-political system.[133]

Other evidence of this approach may be found in the case law of the ECJ. For instance, in some cases the ECJ has acknowledged the existence of a group of rights that cannot be subjected to any form of balancing, i.e. absolute rights.

130 Article 139 of the Italian Constitution.

131 Article 79 paragraph (3) of the Basic Law (Grundgesetz-GG) for the Federal Republic of Germany.

132 For an overview of these clauses see: F. Palermo, *La forma di stato dell'Unione europea. Per una teoria costituzionale dell'integrazione sovranazionale*, Padua: Cedam 2005.

133 G. Palombella, 'From Human Rights to Fundamental Rights. Consequences of a conceptual distinction', *EUI Working Paper LAW*, No. 2006/34, 2006, http://cadmus.eui.eu/bitstream/handle/1814/6400/LAW-2006-34.pdf;jsessionid=57A331FDFF3245D221C04E57E8469D36?sequence=1

An example of this way to proceed is *Schmidberger*,[134] in which the Court of Justice distinguished between two groups of fundamental rights: absolute rights (which admit no restrictions) and other fundamental rights. Concerning the second category of rights, the Court of Justice admitted the necessity to evaluate, through a case-by-case approach, the proportionality of their possible restrictions.[135] By doing so, the Luxembourg Court paved the way for the creation of a hierarchy of principles (and rights).

Many scholars were sure that another decision like *Kadi I* was hardly possible, but the ECJ reiterated its message to the international community, confirming the boldness of the Court.[136]

This leads me to my last point. *Kadi* I (but the same applies to *Kadi* II) has been accused of being conducive to systemic conflicts, of being 'blind' from a diplomatic point of view.[137]

However, when accepting the point that in *Kadi* I and II the ECJ assumed a constitutional approach, these considerations lose appeal and the conclusion repeated by the ECJ becomes coherent with the premises of the decision (the existence of a strong axiological core in EU law). In this sense, one should look at *Kadi* II as an emblematic judgement that goes beyond the particular situation of Mr. Kadi. A confirmation is given by the choice of the Court to face the question front-on in spite of the occurred delisting of *Kadi*[138] and of the very different approach suggested by Advocate General Bot. Probably the ECJ thought it necessary to send a strong message to the UN, just to make clear the foundation of a future convergence. It would not be the first time in the history of the EU, and even on a comparative level it is possible to detect similar decisions rendered by domestic courts. There they either insist on the need to preserve constitutional rights at the

134 ECJ, C-112/00 Schmidberger [2003] ECR I-5659.

135 'Thus, unlike other fundamental rights enshrined in that Convention, such as the right to life or the prohibition of torture and inhuman or degrading treatment or punishment, which admit of no restriction, neither the freedom of expression nor the freedom of assembly guaranteed by the ECHR appears to be absolute but must be viewed in relation to its social purpose. Consequently, the exercise of those rights may be restricted, provided that the restrictions in fact correspond to objectives of general interest and do not, taking account of the aim of the restrictions, constitute disproportionate and unacceptable interference, impairing the very substance of the rights guaranteed', ECJ, C- 112/00 Schmidberger [2003] ECR I-5659, par. 80.

136 Compare, for a different approach, the decision of the ECJ with the Opinion given by AG Bot to *Kadi* II.

137 On this debate see: J. Larik, 'Two Ships in the Night or in the Same Boat Together: How the ECJ Squared the Circle and Foreshadowed Lisbon in Its Kadi Judgment', *Yearbook of Polish European Studies*, 2010, pp. 149 et seq.

138 One might argue that the Court has deliberately chosen not to exercise its discretionary power to discontinue the case for having become 'devoid of purpose' in light of Article 149 of the Rules of Procedure, for instance. On this see the considerations made by F. Fontanelli, 'Kadieu: Connecting the Dots – from Resolution 1267 to Judgment C-584/10 P: The Coming of Age of Judicial Review', in M. Avbelj, F. Fontanelli, and G. Martinico (eds.), *Kadi on Trial: A Multifaceted Analysis of the Kadi Judgment*, Abingdon: Routledge, 2014, pp. 7 et seq.

domestic level in order to 'justify' the breach of some international obligations (as in *Kadi*),[139] or they allow the supranational intervention in a State domain (like in *Rottmann*[140] or *Zambrano*[141]) on the basis of the necessary preservation of those homogeneity clauses through which the federal Constitution limits the fundamental charters of its Member States.[142]

1.4.3 Opinion 2/13: the problematic relationship between autonomy and fundamental rights

Opinion 2/13 was triggered by the European Commission in light of Article 218.11 TFEU.[143] On that occasion, the ECJ concluded that

> the agreement on the accession of the European Union to the European Convention for the Protection of Human Rights and Fundamental Freedoms is not compatible with Article 6.2 TEU or with Protocol (No 8) relating to Article 6.2 of the Treaty on European Union on the accession of the Union to the European Convention on the Protection of Human Rights and Fundamental Freedoms.

With reference to the consequences of this Opinion, Article 218.11 TFEU reads that 'where the opinion of the Court is adverse, the agreement envisaged may not enter into force unless it is amended or the Treaties [of the EU] are revised'. Other authors have tried to present some additional options to overcome this impasse,

139 For instance, Madras High Court, Novartis Novartis v. Union of India & Others., Judgment of 6 Aug. 2007, https://indiankanoon.org/doc/266062/: 'We have borne in mind the object which the Amending Act wanted to achieve namely, . . . to provide easy access to the citizens of this country to life saving drugs and to discharge the [legislature's] Constitutional obligation of providing good health care to it's [sic] citizens. (Ibidem. par. 19)'. On this see: E. George and W. Downs, 'National Courts, Domestic Democracy, and the Evolution of International Law', *European Journal of International Law*, 2009, pp. 72 et seq. More recently (on 1 April 2013), even the Supreme Court of India ruled on the case, http://supremecourtofindia.nic.in/outtoday/patent.pdf

140 ECJ, C-135/08, *Rottmann*, [2010] ECR I-01449.

141 ECJ, C-34/09, Ruiz Zambrano, EU:C:2011:124. For a parallelism between Zambrano and Kadi see: D. Sarmiento, 'The EU's Constitutional Core', in A. Saiz Arnaiz and C. Alcoberro Llivina (eds.), *National Constitutional Identity and European Integration*, Antwerp: Intersentia, 2013, pp. 177 et seq.; G. Martinico and A.M. Russo, 'Is the European Union a Militant Democracy? The Perspective of the Court of Justice in Zambrano and Kadi', *European Public Law*, 2015, pp. 659 et seq.

142 For instance, Article 28 of the Basic Law (Grundgesetz-GG) for the Federal Republic of Germany. On this see: Palermo, *La forma di stato.*

143 Article 218.11 TFEU: 'A Member State, the European Parliament, the Council or the Commission may obtain the opinion of the Court of Justice as to whether an agreement envisaged is compatible with the Treaties. Where the opinion of the Court is adverse, the agreement envisaged may not enter into force unless it is amended or the Treaties are revised'.

suggesting the possibility of interpretative declarations[144] or, even, the adoption of a *Notwithstanding Protocol* (hypothesis that seems to me very problematic[145]). There is no need to recall the details of this very long Opinion,[146] the essence of which can be found in the last eight to nine page, as Douglas Scott[147] pointed out. Rather, I shall focus on the legal reasoning followed by the ECJ. As we will see, the reasoning of the Court resembles that of *Kadi* I.[148]

In a nutshell, the ECJ concluded that the Agreement conflicted with the EU Treaties for the following reasons:

1 Relationship between Article 53 of the Charter of Fundamental Rights[149] and Article 53 of the ECHR.[150] In this sense, the Agreement was not compatible with the EU Treaties because 'there is no provision in the agreement envisaged to ensure such coordination'.[151]

144 P.J. Kuijper, 'Reaction to Leonard Besselink's ACELG Blog', 2015, https://acelg.blogactiv.eu/2015/01/06/reaction-to-leonard-besselinks%E2%80%99s-acelg-blog/

145 L. Besselink, 'Acceding to the ECHR Notwithstanding the Court of Justice Opinion 2/13', 2014, http://verfassungsblog.de/acceding-echr-notwithstanding-court-justice-opinion-213-2/: 'Seeking inspiration in clauses of national constitutions of some of the Member States that provide a constitutional way out of constitutional divergences for the sake of further European integration, I propose solving the matter with a "Notwithstanding Protocol". It should read: "The Union shall accede to the European Convention for the Protection of Human Rights and Fundamental Freedoms, notwithstanding Article 6(2) Treaty on European Union, Protocol (No 8) relating to Article 6(2) of the Treaty on European Union and Opinion 2/13 of the Court of Justice of 18 December 2014." In this manner the Treaties have been amended fully in accordance with the requirements of the Court as well as Article 218 (11) of the TFEU. All of the several objections of the Court are covered by such a Protocol'.

146 On Opinion 2/13 see, at least, R. Alonso Garcia, 'Análisis crítico del veto judicial de la UE al CEDH en el Dictamen 2/13, de 18 de diciembre de 2014, 2015', *WP IDEIR*, 2015, 26, www.ucm.es/data/cont/docs/595-2015-11-25-Binder1.pdf; F. Fabbrini and J. Larik, 'The Past, Present and Future of the Relation between the European Court of Justice and the European Court of Human Rights', *Yearbook of European Law*, 2016, pp. 1 et seq.

147 S. Douglas-Scott, 'Opinion 2/13 on EU accession to the ECHR: A Christmas Bombshell from the European Court of Justice', 2014, http://verfassungsblog.de/opinion-213-eu-accession-echr-christmas-bombshell-european-court-justice-2/

148 'Much of the Court's Opinion considers the arguments made by EU Institutions and Member States. Indeed, only just over one quarter of the judgement, about 8 web pages, actually sets out the Court's own position on compatibility of accession with EU law', Douglas-Scott, Opinion 2/13.

149 Article 53 CFREU: 'Nothing in this Charter shall be interpreted as restricting or adversely affecting human rights and fundamental freedoms as recognised, in their respective fields of application, by Union law and international law and by international agreements to which the Union or all the Member States are party, including the European Convention for the Protection of Human Rights and Fundamental Freedoms, and by the Member States' constitutions'.

150 Article 53 ECHR: 'Nothing in this Convention shall be construed as limiting or derogating from any of the human rights and fundamental'.

151 Opinion 2/13, par. 190.

2 Principle of mutual trust,[152] being the accession, as designed by the Agreement, a menace for the equilibrium inspiring the European horizontal cooperation.
3 Protocol n. 16 of the ECHR, which is not part of the Agreement but could call into question the direct relationship between the ECJ and national judges.[153]
4 The possibility of bypassing Article 344 TFEU: there is the risk that Member States can resort to the ECtHR bringing to Strasbourg issues connected with EU law or with a potential impact over the interpretation and validity of EU law.[154]

152 'In so far as the ECHR would, in requiring the EU and the Member States to be considered Contracting Parties not only in their relations with Contracting Parties which are not Member States of the EU but also in their relations with each other, including where such relations are governed by EU law, require a Member State to check that another Member State has observed fundamental rights, even though EU law imposes an obligation of mutual trust between those Member States, accession is liable to upset the underlying balance of the EU and undermine the autonomy of EU law. However, the agreement envisaged contains no provision to prevent such a development', Opinion 2/13, par. 194–195.

153 'In the third place, it must be pointed out that Protocol No 16 permits the highest courts and tribunals of the Member States to request the ECtHR to give advisory opinions on questions of principle relating to the interpretation or application of the rights and freedoms guaranteed by the ECHR or the protocols thereto, even though EU law requires those same courts or tribunals to submit a request to that end to the Court of Justice for a preliminary ruling under Article 267 TFEU. It is indeed the case that the agreement envisaged does not provide for the accession of the EU as such to Protocol No 16 and that the latter was signed on 2 October 2013, that is to say, after the agreement reached by the negotiators in relation to the draft accession instruments, namely on 5 April 2013; nevertheless, since the ECHR would form an integral part of EU law, the mechanism established by that protocol could – notably where the issue concerns rights guaranteed by the Charter corresponding to those secured by the ECHR – affect the autonomy and effectiveness of the preliminary ruling procedure provided for in Article 267 TFEU. In particular, it cannot be ruled out that a request for an advisory opinion made pursuant to Protocol No 16 by a court or tribunal of a Member State that has acceded to that protocol could trigger the procedure for the prior involvement of the Court of Justice, thus creating a risk that the preliminary ruling procedure provided for in Article 267 TFEU might be circumvented, a procedure which, as has been noted in paragraph 176 of this Opinion, is the keystone of the judicial system established by the Treaties.

By failing to make any provision in respect of the relationship between the mechanism established by Protocol No 16 and the preliminary ruling procedure provided for in Article 267 TFEU, the agreement envisaged is liable adversely to affect the autonomy and effectiveness of the latter procedure', Opinion 2/13, par. 196–199.

154 'Consequently, the fact that Member States or the EU are able to submit an application to the ECtHR is liable in itself to undermine the objective of Article 344 TFEU and, moreover, goes against the very nature of EU law, which, as noted in paragraph 193 of this Opinion, requires that relations between the Member States be governed by EU law to the exclusion, if EU law so requires, of any other law. In those circumstances, only the express exclusion of the ECtHR's jurisdiction under Article 33 of the ECHR over disputes between Member States or between Member States and the EU in relation to the application of the ECHR within the scope ratione materiae of EU law would be compatible with Article 344 TFEU', Opinion 2/13, par. 212–213.

5 The corresponding mechanism that might lead to the breach of the distribution of competences between the Union and its Member States.[155]

6 The so-called prior intervention, established in order to preserve the ECJ's monopoly over EU law norms and that, at the end of the day, was perceived as dangerous for its own interpretative monopoly. This gave the ECtHR the possibility of interpreting the case law of the Luxembourg Court, allowing, in this way, Strasbourg to have a sort of 'meta-interpretative' function (as said in par. 239, 'to permit the ECtHR to rule on such a question would be tantamount to conferring on it jurisdiction to interpret the case-law of the Court of Justice'). Moreover, the Agreement also 'excludes the possibility of bringing a matter before the Court of Justice in order for it to rule on a question of interpretation of secondary law by means of the prior involvement procedure'.[156]

155 'A decision on the apportionment as between the EU and its Member States of responsibility for an act or omission constituting a violation of the ECHR established by the ECtHR is also one that is based on an assessment of the rules of EU law governing the division of powers between the EU and its Member States and the attributability of that act or omission. Accordingly, to permit the ECtHR to adopt such a decision would also risk adversely affecting the division of powers between the EU and its Member States. That conclusion is not affected by the fact that the ECtHR would have to give its decision solely on the basis of the reasons given by the respondent and the co-respondent. Contrary to the submissions of some of the Member States that participated in the present procedure and of the Commission, it is not clear from reading Article 3(7) of the draft agreement and paragraph 62 of the draft explanatory report that the reasons to be given by the respondent and co-respondent must be given by them jointly. In any event, even it is assumed that a request for the apportionment of responsibility is based on an agreement between the co-respondent and the respondent, that in itself would not be sufficient to rule out any adverse effect on the autonomy of EU law. The question of the apportionment of responsibility must be resolved solely in accordance with the relevant rules of EU law and be subject to review, if necessary, by the Court of Justice, which has exclusive jurisdiction to ensure that any agreement between co-respondent and respondent respects those rules. To permit the ECtHR to confirm any agreement that may exist between the EU and its Member States on the sharing of responsibility would be tantamount to allowing it to take the place of the Court of Justice in order to settle a question that falls within the latter's exclusive jurisdiction. Having regard to the foregoing, it must be held that the arrangements for the operation of the co-respondent mechanism laid down by the agreement envisaged do not ensure that the specific characteristics of the EU and EU law are preserved', Opinion 2/13, par. 230–234.

156 Opinion 2/13, par 243. 'The interpretation of a provision of EU law, including of secondary law, requires, in principle, a decision of the Court of Justice where that provision is open to more than one plausible interpretation. If the Court of Justice were not allowed to provide the definitive interpretation of secondary law, and if the ECtHR, in considering whether that law is consistent with the ECHR, had itself to provide a particular interpretation from among the plausible options, there would most certainly be a breach of the principle that the Court of Justice has exclusive jurisdiction over the definitive interpretation of EU law. Accordingly, limiting the scope of the prior involvement procedure, in the case of secondary law, solely to questions of validity adversely affects the competences of the EU and the powers of the Court of Justice in that it does not allow the Court to provide a definitive interpretation of secondary law in the light of the rights guaranteed by the ECHR', Opinion 2/13, par. 245–247.

7 Jurisdiction of the ECtHR in the area of the Common Foreign and Security Policy. Here one can clearly see the 'envy' of the ECJ, which does not accept that the ECtHR (a body that is external to the EU judiciary) can have jurisdiction in an area belonging to EU law but where the Luxembourg Court itself does not have competence.[157]

To understand *Opinion 2/13*, it is necessary to look at the premises used by the ECJ from the very first lines of its text. As in *Kadi*, in this Opinion the ECJ makes reference to its most important decisions, trying to emphasise the continuity between the Opinion and its glorious jurisprudence: from *Van Gend en Loos* to *Kadi*, also recalling some (more) recent (but already well known) decisions, like *Melki*[158] and *Melloni*,[159] among others. In this sense, there is a decision that is crucial to getting the logic followed by the ECJ: *Haegeman.*[160]

According to the *Haegeman* doctrine, the agreements concluded by the European Communities' institutions (and now by the EU) benefit from a kind of 'automatic treaty incorporation'[161] into EU law, since the provisions of these agreements 'form an integral part of Community law'.[162]

This mechanism has allowed, over the years, the ECJ to transform itself into the 'gatekeeper'[163] of the effects of the international agreements concluded by the EU, giving the Court the possibility of opening or closing the doors of the direct effects in EU law. In other words, once they are concluded, they are part of the interpretative garden of the Luxembourg Court.

Now, this approach can perhaps work with those international agreements that are not 'provided' with an authentic interpreter, but actually one of the main features of the ECHR is the presence of an interpreter of the Convention. This perspective explains how the Luxembourg Court has read the issues behind the accession as a question of judicial politics and why, in defending the autonomy of its legal order, the Court has also protected its interpretative monopoly. It is not the first time, in fact, that the ECJ has presented itself as a jealous judge, worried about not losing the interpretative monopoly of EU law and its direct relationship with national judges.[164]

157 'The Court has already had occasion to find that jurisdiction to carry out a judicial review of acts, actions or omissions on the part of the EU, including in the light of fundamental rights, cannot be conferred exclusively on an international court which is outside the institutional and judicial framework of the EU', Opinion 2/13, par. 256.

158 Joint cases C 188/10 and C 189/10, *Melki*, ECR. 2010 p. I-5667.

159 ECJ, C-399/11, *Melloni*, EU:C:2013:107

160 ECJ, 181/73, *Haegeman*, 81/73, Rec. 1974,449. 228.

161 On this see M. Mendez, 'The Legal Effect of Community Agreements: Maximalist Treaty Enforcement and Judicial Avoidance Techniques', *European Journal of International Law*, 2010, pp. 83 et seq.

162 ECJ, 181/73, *Haegeman* [1974] ECR 449.

163 F. Snyder, 'The Gatekeepers: The European Courts and WTO Law', *Common Market Law Review*, 2003, pp. 313 et seq.

164 ECJ, C-459/03, *European Commission v. Ireland* [2006] ECR I-4635. N. Lavranos, *Jurisdictional Competition. Selected Cases in International and European Law*, Groningen: Europa Law Publishing, 2009.

If seen this way, *Opinion 2* is consistent with its previous case law (*Mox Plant*, *Melki*, *Melloni*) because what the ECJ did was: 1) prevent Member States from using the ECHR and the case law of the ECtHR in order to avoid complying with supranational obligations; 2) prevent the ECtHR from affecting the interpretative monopoly of the ECJ, taking into account the number of corresponding provisions in the Charter of Fundamental Rights and the ECHR; 3) raise some specific points (like that concerning the limited jurisdiction of the ECJ in the area of the Common Foreign and Security Policy, CFSP) that can be connected to the concern of guaranteeing its interpretative monopoly.[165]

As it did in *Kadi* I, the ECJ first identified the pillars of its autonomy, understanding them as the untouchable core of its legal system, without agreeing to renounce what makes its legal system special. See for instance par. 159 et seq.,[166] where, after having recalled the conditions to be met by the accession,[167] the ECJ regained the rhetoric of the *sui generis* nature of the EU legal order and then moved to the 'specific characteristics arising from the very nature of EU law' (par. 165). The ECJ started by recalling the principle of EU law autonomy, making

165 Similarly, Alonso Garcia, 'Análisis crítico del veto judicial'.

166 Thus, first of all, having provided that the EU is to accede to the ECHR, Article 6(2) TEU makes clear at the outset, in the second sentence, that 'such accession shall not affect the Union's competences as defined in the Treaties'. Next, Protocol No 8 EU, which has the same legal value as the Treaties, provides in particular that the accession agreement is to make provision for preserving the specific characteristics of the EU and EU law and ensure that accession does not affect the competences of the EU or the powers of its institutions, or the situation of Member States in relation to the ECHR, or indeed Article 344 TFEU. Lastly, by the Declaration on Article 6(2) of the Treaty on European Union, the Intergovernmental Conference that adopted the Treaty of Lisbon agreed that accession must be arranged in such a way as to preserve the specific features of EU law'

Opinion 2/13, par. 160–162.

167 Article 6.2 TEU. See also Protocol 8 relating to Article 6.2 of the Treaty on European Union on the Accession of the Union to the European Convention on the Protection of Human Rights and Fundamental Freedoms. Article 1: 'The agreement relating to the accession of the Union to the European Convention on the Protection of Human Rights and Fundamental Freedoms (hereinafter referred to as the "European Convention") provided for in Article 6(2) of the Treaty on European Union shall make provision for preserving the specific characteristics of the Union and Union law, in particular with regard to: (a) the specific arrangements for the Union's possible participation in the control bodies of the European Convention; (b) the mechanisms necessary to ensure that proceedings by non-Member States and individual applications are correctly addressed to Member States and/or the Union as appropriate'. Article 2: 'The agreement referred to in Article 1 shall ensure that accession of the Union shall not affect the competences of the Union or the powers of its institutions. It shall ensure that nothing therein affects the situation of Member States in relation to the European Convention, in particular in relation to the Protocols thereto, measures taken by Member States derogating from the European Convention in accordance with Article 15 thereof and reservations to the European Convention made by Member States in accordance with Article 57 thereof'. Article 3: 'Nothing in the agreement referred to in Article 1 shall affect Article 344 of the Treaty on the Functioning of the European Union'.

it the premise of its discourse, then moved to the existence of an untouchable core of principles that may not be jeopardised:

> In particular, as the Court of Justice has noted many times, EU law is characterised by the fact that it stems from an **independent source of law, the Treaties**, by its primacy over the laws of the Member States . . . . These essential characteristics of EU law have given rise to a **structured network of principles, rules and mutually interdependent legal relations** linking the EU and its Member States, and its Member States with each other, which are now engaged, as is recalled in the second paragraph of Article 1 TEU, in a 'process of creating an ever closer union among the peoples of Europe'. This legal structure is based on the fundamental premiss that each Member State shares with all the other Member States, and recognises that they share with it, a set of common values on which the EU is founded, as stated in Article 2 TEU.
> (emphasis added)

In a second moment, the ECJ listed the factors composing this untouchable core:

> That premiss implies and justifies the existence of **mutual trust** between the Member States that those values will be recognised and, therefore, that the law of the EU that implements them will be respected. Also at the heart of that legal structure are the **fundamental rights recognised by the Charter** (which, under Article 6(1) TEU, has the same legal value as the Treaties), respect for those rights being a condition of the lawfulness of EU acts, so that measures incompatible with those rights are not acceptable in the EU . . . . **The autonomy enjoyed by EU law in relation to the laws of the Member States and in relation to international law requires that the interpretation of those fundamental rights be ensured within the framework of the structure and objectives of the EU . . . .** As regards the structure of the EU, it must be emphasised that not only are the institutions, bodies, offices and agencies of the EU required to respect the Charter but so too are the Member States when they are implementing EU law . . . . The pursuit of the EU's objectives, as set out in Article 3 TEU, is entrusted to a series of **fundamental provisions, such as those providing for the free movement of goods, services, capital and persons, citizenship of the Union, the area of freedom, security and justice, and competition policy.** Those provisions, which are part of the framework of a system that is specific to the EU, are structured in such a way as to contribute – each within its specific field and with its own particular characteristics – to the implementation of the process of integration that is the *raison d'être* of the EU itself. Similarly, the Member States are obliged, by reason, inter alia, of the **principle of sincere cooperation** set out in the first subparagraph of Article 4(3) TEU, to ensure, in their respective territories, the application of and respect for EU law. In addition, pursuant to the second subparagraph of Article 4(3) TEU, the Member States are to take any appropriate measure, general or particular, to ensure

> **fulfilment of the obligations arising out of the Treaties or resulting from the acts of the institutions of the EU.**
>
> (emphasis added)

Among these factors, a special role is played by the direct relationship existing between national judges and the Luxembourg Court, thanks to the preliminary ruling mechanism:

> **In order to ensure that the specific characteristics and the autonomy of that legal order are preserved, the Treaties have established a judicial system intended to ensure consistency and uniformity in the interpretation of EU law.** In that context, it is for the national courts and tribunals and for the Court of Justice to ensure the full application of EU law in all Member States and to ensure judicial protection of an individual's rights under that law . . . . **In particular, the judicial system as thus conceived has as its keystone the preliminary ruling procedure provided for in Article 267 TFEU**, which, by setting up a dialogue between one court and another, specifically between the Court of Justice and the courts and tribunals of the Member States, has the object of securing uniform interpretation of EU law. . ., thereby serving to ensure its consistency, its full effect and its autonomy as well as, ultimately, the particular nature of the law established by the Treaties.
>
> (emphasis added)

Finally, the protection of fundamental rights is also seen as part of the untouchable core, but it does not seem to be a premise of the reasoning of the Court. On the contrary, fundamental rights – as guaranteed by the EU Charter – are somehow made functional to the EU law architecture, as one can infer from the following line:

> **Fundamental rights, as recognised in particular by the Charter, must therefore be interpreted and applied within the EU in accordance with the constitutional framework** referred to in paragraphs 155 to 176 above.
>
> (emphasis added)

As in *Kadi I*, one can find in *Opinion 2/13* the following key elements in the legal reasoning of the Luxembourg Court: 1) the instrumental use of autonomy; 2) the persistent recalling of its precedents; 3) emphasis on the existence of an untouchable core of principles; 4) the constitutional jargon and 5) a unilateral and polemical approach. The word autonomy was employed 16 times throughout the text of the Opinion and the constitutional jargon was also recalled by the ECJ without forgetting that *Kadi* was mentioned five times.

Perhaps the toughest point made by the ECJ was that concerning its limited jurisdiction in the area of CFSP, since it makes the accession to the ECHR very hard, as it is necessary to amend the EU Treaties to overcome it and nowadays

Member States seem to have other priorities. Moreover, this point makes *Opinion 2/13* very different from *Kadi* in terms of outcome. While *Kadi*, at the end of the day, made the protection of fundamental rights an essential point of its concept of autonomy, here, between autonomy and possible increase of the fundamental rights protection, the ECJ seems to consider the former as the prevailing interest (although in its decision the protection of fundamental rights is part of the untouchable core identified in par. 169 of the Opinion). This point has been made clear by Kuijper. In his own words:

> All the beautiful words of the Court on this subject cannot hide that here the emperor is naked. The Court has no jurisdiction except in two well-circumscribed cases and that is it. That the Court in Strasbourg will have something to say about upholding fundamental rights in the CFSP can only be welcome news. Just as it has always been welcome news that in countries, where there is no constitutional review of the laws passed by Parliament in the light of the bill of rights (as in the Netherlands), there is at least the Court in Strasbourg that will uphold a minimum level of human rights in these countries. I fail to see why that would not be the case for the CFSP, in a situation where there is no constitutional review in part of CFSP 'law' and why the Court of Justice should not be able to live with that, if the Supreme Courts of some Member States have been able to live with that.[168]

It is impossible not to agree with those lines and not to recognise that, in *Opinion 2*, the logic 'thou shalt have no other courts before me'[169] has prevailed, unless one does not want to conceive of this Opinion as a sort of blackmail to oblige Member States to reinforce the protection of fundamental rights by giving more jurisdiction to the Luxembourg Court.

1.5 Concluding on fundamental rights in EU law

Those who criticise *Kadi* I and II may have forgotten the importance that conflicts have traditionally had in the development of the EU legal order. It is sufficient to think of the genesis of Article 6 of the TEU – codifying the human rights commitment of the EU – to find proof of this.

Indeed, this Article was the by-product of a long confrontation between Constitutional Courts and the Court of Justice, started in the 1970s after the delivery of *Internationale Handelsgesellschaft*,[170] which triggered the reaction of the national

168 Kuijper, 'Reaction'.

169 W. Michl, 'Thou Shalt Have no Other Courts Before Me', 2015, http://verfassungsblog.de/thou-shalt-no-courts/

170 ECJ, 11/70, *Internationale Handelsgesellschaft* [1970] ECR 1125 whereby the Court of Justice stated: 'the validity of a Community measure or its effect within a Member State cannot

constitutional guardians with the well-known *Solange*[171] and counter-limits[172] doctrines. Without entering the debate on the similarities (and differences[173]) existing between *Kadi* and *Solange*,[174] the *Solange* and the counter-limits doctrines are a perfect example of the importance of constitutional conflicts for the development of the EU legal order. They represented a potential crisis of the European process that actually served as a turning point, opening a new season in the case law of the ECJ and the Constitutional Courts.

As we will see in Chapter 5, conflicts belong to the life of constitutional polities. In this sense, *Kadi* is the manifestation (at its best) of the 'polemical' spirit of European constitutional law: it is likely that, even after *Kadi*, conflicts – as expressions of interpretative disagreement – will not magically disappear. Perhaps the *Kadi* saga will pave the way for a new season of contestation and, hopefully, for an improved protection of fundamental rights at the international level. The *Schrems*[175] case shares the same spirit (and indeed *Kadi* was mentioned in the text of the judgement[176]). On that occasion, the ECJ declared Decision 2000/520 invalid since it breached, among other things, 'the essence of the fundamental right to respect for private life, as guaranteed by Article 7 of the Charter)' (par. 94). As said, Kadi was mentioned at par. 60, recalling

> the Court's settled case-law should be recalled according to which the European Union is a union based on the rule of law in which all acts of its institutions are subject to review of their compatibility with, in particular, the Treaties, general principles of law and fundamental rights.

be affected by allegations that it runs counter to either fundamental rights as formulated by the constitution of that State or the principles of a national constitutional structure', par. 3.

171 BVerfGE 37, 271 (Solange I); English translation at [1974] 2 CMLR 540; 73, 339 (Solange II); English translation at [1987] 3 CMLR 225. See also *BVerfGE* 89, 155, *BVerfGE* 102, 147.

172 This formula has been introduced in the Italian scholarly debate by P. Barile, 'Ancora su diritto comunitario e diritto interno', in *Studi per il XX anniversario dell'Assemblea costituente*, VI, Florence: Vallecchi 1969, 33 et seq., p. 49. For this doctrine see: Corte Costituzionale, Decision No. 183 of 18 December 1973; see also Decision No. 170 of 5 June 1984 and Decision No. 232 of 13 April 1989.

173 'The difference, however, is that the ECJ, in its own understanding, is not such an international supervisory body [a human rights supervisory body] but a juridical body analogous to a domestic court', Gattini, 'Joined Cases', pp. 234–235.

174 See the chapter by A. Tzanakopoulos, 'The Solange Argument as a Justification for Disobeying the Security Council in the Kadi Judgments', in M. Avbelj, F. Fontanelli, and G. Martinico (eds.), *Kadi on Trial: A Multifaceted Analysis of the Kadi Judgment*, Abingdon: Routledge, 2014, pp. 121 et seq.

175 ECJ, C 362/14 *Maximillian Schrems v. Data Protection Commissioner*, ECLI:EU:C:2015:650. See also ECJ, C-311/18 – *Facebook Ireland e Schrems*, ECLI:EU:C:2020:559.

176 ECJ, C 362/14 *Maximillian Schrems v. Data Protection Commissioner*, ECLI:EU:C:2015:650, par. 60.

As Sarmiento pointed out, *Schrems* tells us that 'privacy is a super-fundamental right that reigns supreme above all other rights',[177] and together with other decisions, it gives us the impression of a court that is very eager to protect fundamental rights and to use the Charter of Fundamental Rights.[178]

It is much more difficult to trace *Opinion 2/13* back to this trend, since therein the ECJ focused on the idea of autonomy, creating uncertainty on the 'place' of fundamental rights within the identity of the EU as a constitutional subject. Moreover, in a declaration released in the plenary session of the FIDE conference the then-President of the ECJ said that 'the Court is not a human rights court: it is the Supreme Court of the Union'.[179] These are the words of a Court that is not comfortable with its own Bill for Rights, with the Charter of Fundamental Rights of the EU (whose scope of application is still unclear after decisions like *Fransson* and *Siragusa*).[180] This factor is not secondary at all; on the contrary, it is very telling about the recent difficulties encountered by the ECJ. In this sense, the Opinion can be seen as part of a broader crisis of values that put the application of Article 6 into question. Moreover, this Opinion can be read in conjunction with other decisions of many national courts opposing the activism of the ECtHR (in this sense, I agree with those colleagues who argued that the word 'autonomy' in *Opinion 2* should be understood as equivalent to 'sovereignty'[181]).

177 D. Sarmiento, 'What Schrems, Delvigne and Celaj Tell us about the State of Fundamental Rights in the EU', 2015, http://verfassungsblog.de/author/daniel-sarmiento/

178 ECJ, C-92/09 and C-93/09, *Volker und Markus Schecke e Eifert* [2010] ECR I-11063, C-293/12, *Digital Rights Ireland*: 'The Court is proving to be an active guarantor of fundamental rights when it comes to the scrutiny of EU action. When the Court faces general or individual EU acts, it is generally applying a high standard of fundamental rights protection, certainly a higher one than the one it seems to be using for Member States. Thus the judgments in Markus Schecke, Test Achats, Digital Rigths Ireland or, more recently, Schrems. These cases, like many others, concern the validity of EU acts in light of the Charter, and there the Court has proved to be enthusiastic to develop a robust and intensive degree of fundamental rights scrutiny', Sarmiento, 'What Schrems'.

179 Reported by L. Besselink, 'The ECJ as the European "Supreme Court": Setting Aside Citizens' Rights for EU Law Supremacy', 2014, http://verfassungsblog.de/ecj-european-supreme-court-setting-aside-citizens-rights-eu-law-supremacy/

180 ECJ, C-617/10, *Åklagaren v. Hans Åkerberg Fransson*, 2013, EU:C:2013:105, ECJ, C-206/13 *Siragusa*, 2014, EU:C:2014:126. See F. Fontanelli, 'Implementation of EU Law through Domestic Measures after Fransson: The Court of Justice Buys Time and Non-preclusion, Troubles Loom Large', *European Law Review*, 2014, pp. 682 et seq.

181 'Structurally, the ECJ seems to understand autonomy in a similar way as national constitutional courts conceive of sovereignty: EU law should reign supreme in its jurisdiction and any encroachment by another authority must be put under the ECJ's check. This comes in the form of various instruments safeguarding the ECJ a place, which is quite unparalleled to that of any constitutional court of the parties to the Convention. It shall be remembered that the ECJ asked for these safeguards in a "discussion paper", by which it became involved in the drafting process of the Accession Agreement in a way unthinkable in any European constitutional system', J. Komárek, 'It's a Stupid Autonomy', 2014, http://verfassungsblog.de/its-a-stupid-autonomy-2/

Against this background, there are the words pronounced by the former President of the ECtHR, Spielmann, who recalled that the victims of this situation will be the citizens of the EU:

> Let us not forget, however, that the principal victims will be those citizens whom this opinion (no. 2/13) deprives of the right to have acts of the European Union subjected to the same external scrutiny as regards respect for human rights as that which applies to each member State.[182]

Without any doubt, this Opinion is the product of a Court that does not know how to handle the axiological part of its constitution (the Charter of Fundamental Rights) and understands the ECHR as a source of problems rather than an added value. This has a clear consequence on what we could call the case law of the EU constitutional identity, with an approach that could appear schizophrenic but is tremendously coherent if seen from the perspective of a court that has always been interested in protecting the autonomy of its own legal system.

Opinion 2/13 is one of the best examples of how the two concepts of constitutionalisation recalled at the beginning of this book (constitutionalisation as humanisation and constitutionalisation as federalisation) can collide. The emphasis on autonomy in Kadi was functional to the argument according to which the protection of fundamental rights had to be improved, while in *Opinion 2/13* it was evident that the ECJ considered the protection of fundamental rights as a variable that may not jeopardise the *sui generis* nature of the EU integration process.

The negotiation on the EU accession recently restarted,[183] and hopefully soon *Opinion 2/13* will be forgotten. Something happened after *Opinion 2/13*, and the case law of the ECJ has tried to overcome a rigid reading of the concept of mutual trust.[184] This is evident from cases such as Căldăraru[185] and, more recently, decisions such as CONSOB.[186]

182 D. Spielmann, 'Foreword', in *Annual Report 2014*, 2015, www.echr.coe.int/Documents/Annual_Report_2014_ENG.pdf

183 'The EU's accession to the European Convention on Human Rights Joint statement on behalf of the Council of Europe and the European Commission' 2020, www.coe.int/en/web/human-rights-rule-of-law/-/the-eu-s-accession-to-the-european-convention-on-human-rights

184 On the latest developments in the field of the European arrest warrant see L. Mancano, 'You'll Never Work Alone: A Systemic Assessment of the European Arrest Warrant and Judicial Independence', *Common Market Law Review*, 2021, pp. 683 et seq.

185 ECJ, C-404/15 and C-659/15 *Pál Aranyosi e Robert Căldăraru*, 2016, PPU ECLI:EU:C:2016:198. On this decision see: L. Mancano, 'The Right to Liberty in European Union Law and Mutual Recognition in Criminal Matters', *Cambridge Yearbook of European Law*, 2016, pp. 215 et seq. L. Mancano, *The European Union and Deprivation of Liberty: A Legislative and Judicial Analysis from the Perspective of the Individual*, Oxford: Hart, 2020, pp. 99 et seq.

186 ECJ, C-481/19 – Consob, ECLI:EU:C:2021:84. In CONSOB the ECJ has shown to be ready to improve the protection of core values such as the fair trial and how important the case law of the ECtHR is for his activity.

1.6 Final remarks

In this chapter, I introduced the objective of the book and presented my three main claims: the EU can be defined as a complex constitutional system; there is a tension between constitutional evolutionism and constitutional constructivism in the process of European integration; constitutional conflicts may have a systemic function in the evolution of the EU. I also recalled the debate on the ambiguity of certain notions such as constitution and constitutionalisation in European studies, looking at the period of the Conventions and beyond. In the last part, I have made it clear how different concepts of constitutionalisation can sometimes collide, comparing the Kadi saga to *Opinion 2/13*.

In Chapter 2, I shall clarify in what sense the EU can be called a complex constitutional system, while in Chapter 3, I shall develop the point about the relationship between evolutionism and constructivism, concluding, in this way, the conceptual part of the book.

2 Dealing with constitutional theories of European integration

2.1 Plan of the chapter

After having tried to map the huge debate on the notion and nature of the European Constitution and having clarified what is meant by constitution, constitutionalism and constitutionalisation for the purpose of this work, it is time to move on to the analysis of some of the constitutional theories of European integration.

In this chapter I am going to deal with constitutional pluralism and multilevel constitutionalism. These are not exhaustive of the range of constitutional theories present in the international debate[1] but, for sure, are those most diffused and celebrated.

I will try to show the common element connecting them: the idea of non-exclusivity of state constitutionalism and that of interaction as the essence of the European constitutional dynamics.

After this, I will move to my own proposal: constitutional complexity. Constitutional complexity presents points of contact with both multilevel constitutionalism and constitutional pluralism. Constitutional complexity and these two constitutional theories understand constitutional conflicts differently and also differ in how to conceive the relation between order and disorder.

2.2 Multilevel constitutionalism

The idea of cooperation between actors characterised by different values and concerns is supported by those theories that emphasise the interpenetration between constitutional entities as the real engine of the EU's progressive constitutionalisation. Multilevel constitutionalism[2] is exactly that: a vision that captures the dynamic aspect of integration between legal orders and stresses the idea of complementarity between national and supranational levels. According to Pernice – the

1 For instance: J.E. Fossum and A.J. Menéndez, *The Constitution's gift. A constitutional theory for a democratic European Union*, Langham, MD: Rowman and Littlefield, 2010. I will devote some lines to their theory when dealing with the issue of the evolutionary nature of EU constitutionalisation.

2 I. Pernice, 'Multilevel Constitutionalism and the Treaty of Amsterdam: European Constitution-Making Revisited?' *Common Market Law Review*, 1999, pp. 703 et seq.

DOI: 10.4324/9781003056522-2

inventor of this concept – it is possible to conceive of the European Constitution as a process rather than a specific document.[3]

This Constitution is the result of a steady coordination of two legal orders: national and supranational. From a dynamic point of view, this interplay (as Pernice said, the national and supranational legal systems are 'closely interwoven and interdependent', so one cannot be read and fully understood without regard to the other)[4] is well represented by Article 6 of the Treaty of the European Union (TEU), which refers to the national constitutional traditions as a part of the European legal order.

This idea of interpenetration between levels deserves attention, since the 'national level' is far from being homogeneous (because of the several differences existing between the Member States' legal orders). Starting from the idea that compatibility between constitutional levels facilitates coordination, one can argue that – from a theoretical point of view – whereas the European Constitution is the result of the coordination between legal orders, the outcome of this process will depend on the national legal order taken as a parameter of coordination.

Due to the Member States' different legal traditions, such an interaction between these two levels cannot be described as typical: on the contrary, different kinds of coordination can be observed. A good example of such a horizontal diversity is represented by the coordination between national administrative legal systems and the supranational principles of European administrative law.

There have been different reactions to the supranational principle of proportionality, due to the characteristics of the various national orders: 'resistance' in the UK, 'adaptation' in Italy and 'mutation' in Germany.[5]

Why am I dwelling on this point? Because what seems to be neglected in Pernice's reasoning is the concrete consequence of the horizontal diversity that characterises the national constitutions.

Another weakness of this approach is its disregard for the international level, in spite of frequent reference to the international covenants of fundamental rights made by the EU documents and by ECJ case law.[6] The exclusion of the international level implies a lack of consideration of the European Convention on Human Rights, which was instead fundamental in the legal reasoning of the ECJ in cases such as *Rutili*,[7] *Ert*[8] and *Hauer*.[9]

3 F. Mayer and I. Pernice, 'La costituzione integrata dell'Europa', in G. Zagrebelsky (ed.), *Diritti e Costituzione nell'Unione Europea*, Rome and Bari: Laterza, pp. 43 et seq., p. 49.

4 I. Pernice, 'Multilevel Constitutionalism in the European Union', *European Law Review*, 2002, pp. 511 et seq.

5 D.U. Galetta, 'Il principio di proporzionalità comunitario e il suo effetto di spill over negli ordinamenti nazionali', *Nuove Autonomie*, 2005, pp. 541 et seq.

6 Although the author seems to 'touch on' this level in some papers: for example, I. Pernice and R. Kanitz, 'Fundamental Rights and Multilevel Constitutionalism in Europe', *WHI paper*, No. 7/2004, 2004, www.rewi.hu-berlin.de/de/lf/oe/whi/publikationen/whi-papers/2004/whi-paper0704.pdf

7 ECJ, 36/75, *Roland Rutili v. Ministre de l'intérieur*, [1975] *ECR. 1219*.

8 ECJ, C-260/89, *Elliniki Radiophonia Tiléorassi AE and Panellinia Omospondia Syllogon Prossopikou v. Dimotiki Etairia Pliroforissis and Sotirios Kouvelas and Nicolaos Avdellas and others, [1991]* ECR. I-2925.

9 ECJ, C-44/79, *Liselotte Hauer v. Land Rheinland-Pfalz*, [1979] ECR. 3727.

Returning to the ambiguities of Pernice's view, Leonard Besselink[10] criticises the notion of multilevel constitutionalism on the following grounds. First of all, according to Besselink, 'thinking in terms of "levels" . . . involves inescapably the concept of hierarchy', because levels imply 'by definition the existence of "higher" and "lower" levels, super-ordination and sub-ordination, superiority and inferiority'.[11] Secondly, 'even if the dynamics between the "levels" are emphasised – the higher level influences the lower one and the lower one tries to influence the higher one – the implicit point of departure is that these are separate levels'. In a nutshell, the author contests the fact that Pernice describes the 'levels' as autonomous legal orders. On the contrary, by 'composite constitution', Besselink means a constitution 'whose component parts mutually assume one another's existence, both *de facto* and *de iure*'.[12]

In Besselink's perspective, the 'levels' are seen as incomplete and interlaced and the heteronomy of the European Constitution seems to prevail. Indeed, limiting our attention to the Treaties does not fully grasp the importance that sources formally outside EU law – *stricto sensu* understood – have had for the development of European constitutional law (such as the national constitutional traditions and the European Convention on Human Rights). The idea of mutual relationship is therefore central in this perspective.

After having explained the grounds of his criticism of the notion of multilevel constitutionalism, Besselink moves on to deal with the burning issue of primacy. Does the primacy principle represent a counter-argument to the idea of composite constitution? Does primacy imply a hierarchical vision of the relationship between legal orders? Given the absence of a perfect impermeability between the EU and national constitutions, the primacy principle as a rule of precedence is construed as a norm conceived with the purpose of solving conflicts.

The relation between the EU and Member States is not a two-level 'junction', since they do not operate on different levels. On the contrary, they meet 'each other on the same level' (in this way, Besselink once again opposes the idea of a multilevel constitutionalism). Furthermore, Besselink argues that the hierarchical approach is not adequate to explain the relationship between the EU and national constitutions, by reason of the increasing sensitivity (at least at that time) shown by the ECJ with regard to the significance of national constitutional identities. Evidence of this is provided by the comparison between the *Internationale Hadesgeselschaft* doctrine and the ECJ case law in the field of human rights (see, for example, *Omega*[13] or *Dynamic Medien*[14]).

The example is not coincidental, because the field of human rights represents the best example of EU law's constitutional heteronomy, and

> the content of human rights norms within EU Law is largely derived from constitutional sources outside the EU sources in a strict sense: from the point

10 L. Besselink, *A Composite European Constitution/Een Samengestelde Europese Constitutie*, Groningen: Europa Law Publishing, 2007.

11 L. Besselink, *A Composite*, p. 6.

12 L. Besselink, *A Composite*, p. 6.

13 ECJ, C-36/02, *Omega*, [2004] ECR I-9609.

14 ECJ, C-244/06, *Dynamic Medien*, [2008] ECR I-505.

of view of content, the protection of human rights by the EU institutions is heteronomous.[15]

Concluding this section and reviewing the debate, we can therefore say that the ultra-state dimension of such a constitutional entity implies the absence of the classic cultural and constitutional homogeneity that characterised the usual national constitutional dimension. The European Constitution is thus conceived as a *monstrum compositum*, composed of constitutional principles developed at the European level and complemented by (common) national constitutional principles.[16] In this sense, one could conclude that in such a context national laws as well as European law partake in defining European constitutional law. Against this background, multilevel constitutionalism offers a strong but static basis for the identification of the essence of the European Constitution, understood as an interplay among levels; it acknowledges the diversification of the national legal systems towards EU integration but does not care to clarify the implications of such a diversification in the coordination. In short, multilevel constitutionalism does not pay attention to the national constitutional variety (the horizontal diversity I stressed earlier) or to the possible existence of conflicts among levels, an issue partly solved by looking at more recent works by Mayer, for instance.[17]

The same descriptive nature seems to characterise the 'multilevel governance' theory, although scholars have challenged this point by claiming that multilevel constitutionalism would surreptitiously advocate a German reading of the European integration process[18] and suggesting a federal outcome of the supranational process.[19]

In my view, multilevel constitutionalism suffers from a *deficit* of normativity that does not permit us to accept this point.

This is confirmed by the fact that it does not present (unlike other theories/approaches) a set of solutions to deal with the issue of constitutional conflicts.[20]

However, this does not mean that multilevel constitutionalism conceives conflicts as 'positive' or that it believes in the impossibility of constitutional conflicts

15 Besselink, *A Composite*, p. 15.

16 See, among others: M. Claes, *The National Courts' Mandate in the European Constitution*, Oxford: Hart, 2006.

17 F. Mayer and M. Wendel, 'Multilevel Constitutionalism and Constitutional Pluralism Querelle Allemande or Querelle d'Allemande?' in M. Avbelj and J. Komárek (eds.), *Constitutional Pluralism in the European Union and Beyond*, Oxford: Hart, 2012, pp. 127 et seq. F. Mayer, 'Rashomon in Karlsruhe: A Reflection on Democracy and Identity in the European Union', *International Journal of Constitutional Law*, 2011, pp. 757 et seq.

18 Probably this kind of criticism can be directed to authors like Bogdandy. See, for instance, the approach endorsed in the editions of the impressive volume: *Principles of European Constitutional Law*, published by Hart (Oxford) and edited with J. Bast in 2006 and 2009.

19 L. Azoulai, 'The Force and Forms of European Legal Integration', *EUI Law Working Paper*, No. 2011/06, 2011, http://cadmus.eui.eu/bitstream/handle/1814/16894/LAW_2011_06.pdf?sequence= 1

20 F. Mayer, 'The European Constitution and the Courts: Adjudicating European Constitutional Law in a Multilevel System', *WHI Paper*, No. 15/03, 2003, https://www.rewi.hu-berlin.de/de/lf/oe/whi/publikationen/whi-papers/2003/whi-paper1503.pdf

(according to Luciani,[21] it would be characterised by a sort of 'irenic' approach), based on an optimistic vision of the relation among levels.

2.3 Constitutional pluralism

The view of constitutional pluralism[22] seems to pay much more attention to the importance of judicial actors and to the burning issue of constitutional conflicts. This can be seen especially when looking at the idea of contrapuntal law proposed by Miguel Poiares Maduro[23] or at the writings by Mattias Kumm.[24] Both these positions then can be traced back to that of constitutional pluralism as expressed by Neil MacCormick[25] and Neil Walker.[26]

Let's start from what Maduro means by constitutional pluralism, recalling how his view represents just one of the different understandings of this formula, which has been frequently accused of being an 'oxymoron' or a construction characterised by a 'post-modern flavour'.[27]

21 M. Luciani, 'Costituzionalismo irenico e costituzionalismo polemico', 2006, www.rivistaaic.it/old_site_aic/materiali/anticipazioni/costituzionalismo_irenico/index.html

22 On constitutional pluralism, see: N. Walker, 'The Idea of Constitutional Pluralism', *Modern Law Review*, 2002, pp. 317 et seq.; M. Poiares Maduro, 'Contrapunctual Europe's Constitutional Pluralism in Action', in N. Walker (ed.), *Sovereignty in Transition*, Oxford: Hart, 2003, 501 et seq.; M. Poiares Maduro, 'Interpreting European Law: Judicial Adjudication in a Context of Constitutional Pluralism', *European Journal of Legal Studies*, 2007, http://ejls.eu/index.php?mode=htmlarticle&filename=./issues/2007-12/MaduroUK.htm. For a comparison between the different visions of constitutional pluralism, see K. Jaklic, *Constitutional Pluralism in the EU*, Oxford: Oxford University Press, 2014. A. Avbelj and J. Komárek (eds.), *Constitutional Pluralism in the European Union and Beyond*, Oxford: Hart, 2012; M. Avbelj, G. Davies, *Research Handbook on Legal Pluralism and EU Law*, Cheltenham: Edward Elgar, 2018; T. Flynn, *The Triangular Constitution Constitutional Pluralism in Ireland, the EU and the ECHR*, Oxford: Hart, 2019; A. Avbelj and J. Komárek (eds.), 'Four Visions of Constitutional Pluralism', *EUI Working Paper*, No. 28/2001, https://cadmus.eui.eu/handle/1814/9372. For a different concept of pluralism conceived as in opposition to that of constitutionalism, see N. Krisch, 'Europe's Constitutional Monstrosity', *Oxford Journal of Legal Studies*, 2005, 321 et seq. See also Douglas-Scott, *Constitutional Law*, pp. 523 et seq.

23 M. Poiares Maduro, 'Contrapunctual', pp. 501 et seq.

24 M. Kumm, 'The Jurisprudence of Constitutional Conflict: Constitutional Supremacy in Europe before and after the Constitutional Treaty', *European Law Journal*, 2005, pp. 262 et seq.

25 N. MacCormick, 'Beyond the Sovereign State', *Modern Law Review*, 1993, pp. 1 et seq.

26 Especially in N. Walker, 'The Idea of Constitutional Pluralism', *Modern Law Review*, 2002, pp. 317 et seq.

27 'By post-modern, I mean all that is fluid and fragmented. And that is what pluralism tries to reflect, the reality of a fragmented law which is always in flux. Perhaps it is more realistic, if the reality of law is more like that, and not at all like the modern constitutional ideal. But there may be a risk in that step. Lawyers have probably been the last to embrace postmodernism. First were the architects, then philosophers, linguists, etc., and a minority of academic lawyers have been the last to embrace it, and perhaps they have done it with a risk to their social role, because they may not be compatible. We renounce an ideal of constitutional law if we embrace the post-modern view of law which is reflected in radical pluralism, not only in the European Union but also in state constitutional law', J. Baquero Cruz, in 'Four Visions of Constitutional Pluralism', *EUI Working Paper* 28/2001, https://cadmus.eui.eu/handle/1814/9372, p. 7.

In a broad sense, 'constitutional pluralism' refers to (at least) five different phenomena:

1 Plurality (Maduro uses 'plurality' and not *pluralism* in this case) of constitutional sources;
2 Pluralism of jurisdictions or 'constitutional poles';
3 Interpretative pluralism;
4 Pluralism of powers;
5 Pluralism of polities.[28]

With particular reference to the supranational constitutional theory, by 'constitutional pluralism' one can mean two different scholarly positions[29] that should be sub-distinguished from the theory of systemic pluralism of Krisch.

All these three scholarly positions (Maduro, Kumm, Krisch) are indebted to the thought of Neil MacCormick but differ on the question of authority and on the conception of 'constitutionalism' (conceived, for instance, by Nico Krisch as hierarchical and holistic, i.e. non-open[30]).

28 'The first one is a plurality of constitutional sources and we see that in the EU European constitutional law is drawn from different constitutional sources, not from a single constitutional document, and those sources are national and European. The second one is a pluralism of jurisdictions or of different constitutional sites. This is particularly the case regarding constitutional adjudication, it is linked to the more well known aspect of European constitutional pluralism: the Kompetenz-Kompetenz question, which Matej and Jan have worked on. The third one is an interpretative pluralism if you want. It is a pluralism which is based not only on different sources but on competing interpretations of the same source by institutions that are not organized in a hierarchical manner . . . . The fourth expression of pluralism is a pluralism of powers. We increasingly have new forms of public and private power that challenge traditional legal dogmatic categories and raise constitutional questions because they affect the mechanisms of accountability linked to those legal categories. I see this as part of this new constitutional pluralism. And the fifth pluralism is a pluralism of polities. This has two consequences or two dimensions. The first one is that political pluralism in the EU is expressed in a more radical form because different political views of the constitution are supported not simply by different political groups but by different political communities. It is a more radical form of political pluralism than what you normally have at the level of a single political community', Avbelj and Komárek, 'Four Visions', p. 6.

29 In his book, Jaklic identifies four types of constitutional pluralism, namely 'epistemic pluralism', 'substantive pluralism', 'interpretative and participatory pluralism' and 'institutional pluralism'. He also includes Weiler in the second group, while the thought of Weiler in this book is understood as different from this theoretical approach.

30 'Pluralism's openness may bring with it certain risks, but it also has significant advantages over more rigidly constitutionalized structures, especially as regards the processes of adaptation and change so pervasive in postnational politics. It also has important strengths in democratic terms not only because it gives contestation greater space but also because it reflects social indecision about which polity should govern transboundary issues. National, regional, and global polities often compete here, all with strong normative grounding and significant loyalties. Pluralism, unlike constitutionalism, does not need to decide hierarchies between them; it can grant them space for competition, mutual accommodation, and perhaps eventual settlement. Pluralism's institutional openness thus corresponds with the openness and fluidity of postnational society in a way constitutionalism, tailored to less heterogeneous societies, does not', N. Krisch, *Beyond Constitutionalism: The Pluralist Structure of Postnational Law*, Oxford: Oxford University Press, 2010, p. 26.

The reflections of MacCormick, included in his work *Beyond the Sovereign State*[31] and then developed in *Questioning Sovereignty*,[32] started from the relative autonomy of the European institutional system and from the impossibility of reading the relation between EU and national law in purely hierarchical terms.[33] Another important premise is represented by the criticism of the obsession with sovereignty that characterises all the traditional interpretations of the EU integration process,[34] which result in reading the integration process from a monocular perspective.[35] On the contrary, according to MacCormick, the national and supranational systems should be defined as 'interacting systems, one of which constitutes in its own context and over the relevant range of topics a source of valid law superior to other sources recognised in each of the member state systems'.[36]

Usually, these reflections are recalled when defining constitutional pluralism, a situation characterised by a coexistence of different constitutional poles, each of them claiming authority and superiority over the other constitutional poles.

According to MacCormick, a correct reading of the European dynamics should give up this hierarchical approach by taking into account the diversity of the viewpoints (what Menéndez terms 'the plural but equal standpoints thesis'[37]) that characterise the coexistence of actors operating on different constitutional poles: a diversity of viewpoints (provided with equal weight and dignity according to the Scottish philosopher) that has practical consequences since it results in the explosion of true constitutional conflicts.

On the issue of the practical consequences of a context like this on the activity of the interpreters, MacCormick changed his mind, giving birth to two positions that are irreconcilable according to many.

31 MacCormick, 'Beyond the Sovereign State'.

32 N. MacCormick, *Questioning Sovereignty: Law, State, and Nation in the European Commonwealth*, Oxford: Oxford University Press, 1999.

33 MacCormick, *Questioning Sovereignty*, p. 117.

34 'The legal picture that confronts us seems too complex to be satisfactorily solved either way in terms of habit-of-obedience sovereignty. And so, except if you imprison yourself within one particular point of view, one particular perspective, you are bound to find the kind of sovereign command view of things implausible when you confront something like the European Community and the kind of problems of validity, invalidity, challenges to validity, which cases like the Factortame case in Community Law show or, in European Human Rights Law, a case like the Sunday Times case in its different way shows. Instead of committing oneself to a monocular vision dictated by sovereignty theory, one can embrace the possibility of acknowledging differences of perspective, differences of point of view', N. MacCormick, 'Beyond the Sovereign State', p. 5.

35 'One thing which it is necessary for jurisprudence or the philosophy of law to do in the present state of affairs is to guard against taking a narrow one-state or Community-only perspective, a monocular view of these things. The difficulty about sovereignty theory is that it seems to point inevitably in that direction', MacCormick, 'Beyond the Sovereign State', p. 5.

36 MacCormick, *Questioning Sovereignty*, p. 117.

37 A.J. Menéndez, 'From Constitutional Pluralism to a Pluralistic Constitution? Constitutional Synthesis as a MacCormickian Constitutional Theory of European Integration', *ARENA Working Paper*, No. 01/2011, 17, www.sv.uio.no/arena/english/research/publications/arena-publications/workingpapers/working-papers2011/wp-01-11.pdf

In a first moment, MacCormick seemed to conclude by accepting somehow the constitutional conflicts as inevitable in a truly pluralist system, getting to the position defined by Menéndez as 'the legal stability beyond sovereignty thesis',[38] according to which constitutional pluralism is possible thanks to the fact that it does not depend on the will of a unique sovereign.

This implied, somehow, the acceptance of the conflicting consequences of this unstable equilibrium among constitutional poles as a natural consequence of constitutional pluralism.[39]

Such a conclusion has been considered as paradoxical by some authors, since it would result in betraying the pluralistic premises and it would abandon itself to a reconstruction that acknowledges, de facto, the existence of two hierarchical and incoherent monisms, conceiving national and EU law as two parallel lines that do not share a common legal frame able to solve the issue of conflicts:[40]

> The answer is surprising because it denies the premise on which it was based. The premise was that there was no hierarchy between the EU and national law. But if there is no such hierarchy, the national court ought to accommodate EU law as if it were equal to national law. If there is no such hierarchy, the ECJ ought to accommodate national law as if it were its equal. Lack of hierarchy means equality. Instead, MacCormick's pluralism advises the courts to maintain two inconsistent monisms, EU monism and national monism. But this affirms the hierarchy and does not deny it. MacCormick's suggestion that each court is finally authoritative in its own domain affirms both hierarchies at the same time and adds that there is no reason to regret the incoherence.[41]

With these words, Eleftheriadis defined the conclusions reached by MacCormick as characterised by a sort of 'double monism'.[42]

38 Menéndez, 'From Constitutional Pluralism', p. 17.

39 'It follows also that the interpretive power of the highest decision-making authorities of the different systems must be, as to each system, ultimate. It is for the ECJ to interpret in the last resort and in a finally authoritative way the norms of Community law. But equally, it must be for the highest constitutional tribunal of each member state to interpret its constitutional and other norms, and hence to interpret the interaction of the validity of EC law with higher level norms of validity in the given state system', MacCormick, *Questioning Sovereignty*, p. 118.

40 'In MacCormick's view, there was thus no common legal framework that could have decided the conflict – the two views were (on a fundamental level) irreconcilably opposed; the two levels of law ran in parallel without subordination or external coordination', N. Krisch, 'Who Is Afraid of Radical Pluralism?' *Ratio Juris*, 2011, pp. 386 et seq.

41 P. Eleftheriadis, 'Pluralism and Integrity', *Ratio Juris*, 2010, pp. 365 et seq., p. 371.

42 'Radical pluralism takes a different view. It suggests that we may affirm the two conflicting monisms, EU monism and domestic monism, at the same time. These two monisms are in competition at least in areas that fall under the scope of EU law. MacCormick urges us not to make a choice between them and this is what MacCormick means by the term "radical" pluralism. It is radical because it suggests that there is no legal resolution to this conflict and "that is all that is to be said as a matter of law" (MacCormick 1999, 119). Nevertheless, the result is not a pluralist result. One way of seeing this is by asking. "Which legal order is now the pluralist?" If we do not make a choice between the competing claims, we are left with the decision of each court, i.e. two

The conclusions of the 'first' MacCormick – grouped under the formula 'radical pluralism' – were rethought in the late nineties, and scholars interested in his thought have written about a sort of shift from a 'radical pluralism' to a 'moderate pluralism', also called 'pluralism under international law', according to which: 'the obligations of international law set conditions upon the validity of state and of Community constitutions and interpretations thereof and hence impose a framework on the interactive but not hierarchical relations between systems'.[43]

The main difference between the first and the second MacCormick has been explained well by Carbonell and reveals that the rationale for this shift has been represented by the risk of constitutional conflicts:[44]

> Both types of pluralism stress that Member States and Community legal orders have independent validity rules and that there is no hierarchical relation among them, but an interactive one, and that each system has its own decision-making final authorities. They only differ in the nature of the relations between the states and Community law, on the one hand, and international law, on the other. According to pluralism under international law, international law set conditions or a framework for the interaction between states and Community law systems, while radical pluralism considers these conditions only a third perspective, but not a hierarchically superior obligation. A consequence of this difference is that under radical pluralism there are legal problems that cannot be solved.[45]

monisms. If we are within the national jurisdiction, then national monism is correct. If we are within the EU jurisdiction and institutions, EU monism is correct. So there are hierarchies in both legal orders. None of them is pluralist. There are two inconsistent hierarchies and we accept them both, depending where we happen to be. This is a surprising affirmation of national monism (and given how preliminary references work, with the case returning to the national court for decision, it seems that this view undermines quite seriously the idea of the value and effect of EU law). I shall call this view "double monism" ', Eleftheriadis, 'Pluralism and Integrity', p. 373. However, at the same time, he also adds: 'There is, however, a different reading of radical pluralism. It is possible that we interpret it to mean something else. It may be that when MacCormick says that relations between states and the EU are "interacting systems of law" without "an all-purpose superiority of one system over another" he means this: courts may help themselves to either of these two monisms. In other words, it is open to them to endorse either a solution derived from national law or a solution derived from EU law. This would be pluralism proper, because the answer would be entirely open-ended. It would be dependent on plural solutions. So the national system may be now taken to have become pluralist – since it does not actually take the official monism seriously. Some days we would be choosing national monism, whereas on other days we choose European monism', Eleftheriadis, 'Pluralism and Integrity', pp. 373–374.

43 MacCormick, *Questioning Sovereignty*, p. 118.

44 'Too quickly runs out of legal solutions and leaves legal actors and their addressees with a superfluity of legal answers that imperils the value of predictability and legal certainty. The resolution of constitutional conflicts under the model of radical pluralism, following MacCormick, is eventually a matter for circumspection and for political as much as legal judgment and is as such less attractive as the solutions offered by "pluralism under international law" to which he subscribes now', M. Avbelj, 'Questioning EU Constitutionalisms', *German Law Journal*, 2008, pp. 1 et seq., p. 14, note 61.

45 F. Carbonell, 'Coherence and Post-Sovereign Legal Argumentation', in J.A. Menéndez and J.E. Fossum, *The Post-Sovereign Constellation: Law and Democracy in Neil MacCormick's Legal and Political Theory*, 2008, https://www.sv.uio.no/arena/, pp. 109 et seq., pp. 147–148.

Even this shift has originated an extensive discussion on its consistency with the original premise of MacCormick's thought: while according to some authors it was a moment of clarification that has made his thought more linear and coherent,[46] others argued that it represented a return to dualism[47] or, even, to its contrary, monism.[48]

The ambiguities presented by the Scottish author before the issue of how to manage constitutional conflicts have had an impact on the work of the other pluralists.

Before the issue of constitutional conflicts, the movements of constitutional pluralists differ; for instance, one can find a distinction between a descriptive constitutional pluralism (Walker[49]) – that limits itself to the description of a constitutional context as pluralist due to the coexistence of different constitutional poles – and a normative/prescriptive constitutional pluralism (Maduro,[50] Kumm[51]), which would go beyond trying to neutralise conflicts.

Besides these two forms of constitutional pluralism, another scholarly position exists: I am referring to what Krisch defines as 'systemic pluralism', which denies that constitutionalism and pluralism can be reconciled. The only point of contact between systemic pluralism à la Krisch and the constitutional pluralisms is the common reference to the work of MacCormick.

A brief clarification on this section: while systemic pluralism is not particularly interesting to the goal of this volume (since it is not a constitutional theory at all), I will limit my attention to Maduro's view of constitutional pluralism.

46 'It seems to me that this is a change of critical importance, which increases, not diminishes, the coherence between MacCormick's overall legal-theoretical project and his European constitutional theory; while drastically re-formulating the first premise of European constitutional pluralism. The original "radical" constitutional pluralism of MacCormick was right to point out that legal monism, the claim that there is a need to reduce law to a system observed from one, and only one, legal viewpoint, is a rather flawed theory, if it stems from a prescriptivist conception of law, because the insistence on a mythical single sovereign is no solution to the key problems in legal theory, or, for that matter, in European constitutional law. However, this does not do away with the normative force of the regulatory ideal of the legal system', Menéndez, 'From Constitutional Pluralism', p. 20.

47 'In other words, MacCormick's pluralism under international law is in the end a version of dualism. EU law is accepted by the member state under the terms of mutual respect that it shows to international law. So we have made no progress at all. This is not a pluralist alternative, but a dualist one (something to which I will return to later because I think dualism is what MacCormick is really supporting)', Eleftheriadis, 'Pluralism and Integrity', p. 375.

48 '"Pluralism under international law", as he termed it, is in fact a monist conception, but one that assigns EU law and domestic constitutional law equal positions and does not subordinate one to the other as a matter of principle', Krisch, 'Who is Afraid', pp. 388 et seq.

49 For a description of the dimensions of constitutional pluralism, see N. Walker, 'The Idea of Constitutional Pluralism', *Modern Law Review*, 2002, pp. 317 et seq.

50 Poiares Maduro, 'Contrapuntal Law', pp. 501 et seq.

51 Kumm, 'The Jurisprudence'.

This is because Kumm's reflections on the EU, for instance, are part of a broader theory on cosmopolitan constitutionalism that goes beyond the constitutional state of the Union.

Something similar applies to the last reflections offered by Neil Walker, whose pluralism is the most descriptive one among those recalled, and whose interests go beyond the EU arena (i.e. the global dimension).[52]

Finally, Maduro's thought is probably the most intriguing but also the most ambiguous of the three, and this will offer us an interesting element of distinction between complexity and constitutional pluralism.

By 'constitutional pluralism', Maduro refers to a 'process' of interaction between constitutional poles:

> In other words, constitutional pluralism would not identify European constitutionalism itself but the nature of its relationship with other constitutional orders (national and, possibly, international).[53]

Here one can immediately notice the terminological ambiguity of this theory.

A good example of this ambiguity is given by the definition of 'constitutional pluralism': if, from a theoretical point of view, Maduro has stressed that his position cannot be reduced to monism – for instance, in a famous exchange with Alexander Somek[54] – his definition of pluralism does not say anything about the outcome of this process. Starting from this, Pavlos Eleftheriadis, in an article entitled 'Pluralism and integrity',[55] pointed out that in his writings on 'contrapuntal law'[56] Maduro has written about a 'European legal order',[57] to be understood as a product of the interaction between constitutional orders.[58] As said, moving from the description of such a situation to a possible solution of the conflict caused by constitutional heterogeneity, Maduro tries to identify some procedural (that is, *prima facie* neutral from an axiological point of view) principles that should

52 For example, N. Walker, 'Taking Constitutionalism Beyond the State', *Political Studies*, 2008, pp. 519 et seq.

53 Poiares Maduro, 'The Three Claims', p. 2.

54 A. Somek, 'Monism: A Tale of the Undead', in M. Avbelj and J. Komárek (eds.), *Constitutional Pluralism in the European Union and Beyond*, Oxford: Hart, 2012, pp. 343 et seq.

55 Eleftheriadis, 'Pluralism and Integrity', pp. 365 et seq.

56 Poiares Maduro, 'Contrapuntal Law'.

57 Eleftheriadis, 'Pluralism and Integrity', p. 387.

58 'In other words, the broader European legal order imposes obligations of coherence across the whole range of national courts, irrespective of national differences in jurisdiction and procedure. It is clear that the leading role in this scheme of coherence will inevitably be played by the ECJ, which alone has an overview of EU law. It is easy to see that this is not a doctrine of pluralism at all. It is a doctrine of unity', Eleftheriadis, 'Pluralism and Integrity', p. 387.

govern the behaviour of the actors involved in the constitutional-pluralistic background. According to Maduro:

> These meta-methodological principles aim to secure those values in a context where you do not have an ultimate authoritative source to do that. But certainly, I do not see it necessarily as a post-modern project. To the contrary, since my conception of constitutionalism is deeply embedded by a concern with the rationalisation of the democratic process.[59]

The system these authors describe in fact does not present itself as merely plural but also as characterised by a strong constitutional pluralism, and the need for interpretive uniformity against the danger of axiological fragmentation is the real challenge for actors in this system. Another important difference between constitutional pluralism and multilevel constitutionalism is given by the conception of the role of the judges in this context: Pernice's pattern seems not to pay sufficient attention to the gap between the letter of each level's fundamental charter and its material enforcement by the courts, thus presenting another ambiguity.

This is evident with regard to the principle of primacy, which was extracted from the spirit[60] (and not from the letter) of the Treaties, but it is also confirmed by the national constitutional experience where the national Constitutional Courts have identified, for example, some impenetrable barriers to European integration despite the absence of an explicit constitutional provision limiting European integration itself (see the Italian doctrine of counter-limits [*controlimiti*] of the Italian *Corte Costituzionale*[61]).

On the contrary, the view of constitutional pluralism (especially Maduro's vision) gives due consideration to the role that judicial interactions have had in building and supporting such a pluralistic constitutional structure. Maduro acknowledges that the decisions of courts have a crucial role in the context he describes but, at the same time, the judicial actors are pieces of a bigger puzzle because 'the language of courts in defining what the law is does not become their exclusive property. It is taken over and used by a broader legal community with meanings that may be different from those originally intended'.[62] In other words, the courts play a fundamental systemic function and the judicial dialogue is a

59 M. Poiares Maduro in Avbelj and Komárek (eds.), 'Four Visions'.

60 ECJ, 26/62, *Van Gend en Loos*, [1963] ECR 1963, 3.

61 This formula was introduced into the Italian scholarly debate by Paolo Barile: P. Barile, 'Ancora su diritto comunitario e diritto interno', in *Studi per il XX anniversario dell'Assemblea costituente*, VI, Florence: Vallecchi, 1969, pp. 49 et seq.

62 And then: 'courts may sometimes end up saying more than they wanted to say or being interpreted more broadly than they wanted to be interpreted. Judicial decisions are not the property of courts but of the legal community and this includes other legal actors whose preferences for judicial activity may vary from those of courts', Poiares Maduro, 'Contrapuntal Law', p. 514. On the political implications of the judicial decisions, see: M. Shapiro, *Law and Politics in the Supreme Court: New Approaches to Political Jurisprudence*, New York: The Free Press of Glencoe, 1964; C. Sunstein, *Legal Reasoning and Political Conflict*, Oxford: Oxford University Press, 1996. With regard to the ECJ, see J.H.H. Weiler, 'The Transformation of Europe', *Yale Law Journal*, 1991, pp. 2403 et seq.

privileged perspective for studying the relationship between legal orders without exhausting the subject.

Going beyond its descriptive value, Maduro's view on constitutional pluralism presents a strong normative character since it does not limit itself to describing what constitutional pluralism is but attempts to provide some solutions for a better coordination among judges: pluralism,[63] consistency and vertical and horizontal coherence,[64] universalisability[65] and the principle of the institutional choices[66] are at the heart of his view. All of these principles should contribute to defining judicial power as a rational and interactive power and exalting the systemic role of the courts themselves in a context of integrated and pluralistic constitutionalism.

Some authors have challenged this reconstruction: according to Komárek, for instance, the principle of universalisability could lead to an anti-pluralistic outcome of this process and be conducive to a frustration of the pluralist principle,[67] while Eleftheriadis recalled that by 'pluralism' Maduro means both one of the principles of contrapuntal law and the result of the application of the other principles.[68]

If it is very clear that constitutional pluralism cannot be reduced to monism from a theoretical point of view, it is not clear what outcome/result one envisages at the end of the process: is it a new and broader European legal order?

Starting from this ambiguity, authors such as Eleftheriadis have argued that, in the end, constitutional pluralism would lead to what he calls an amalgamation between the national and supranational legal orders, a unitary legal order:

> There is much to be gained from a pluralist conception of the EU legal order. But, to take full advantage of this legal pluralism we need to discover forms of reducing or managing the potential conflicts between legal orders while promoting communication between them and requiring courts to conceive of their decisions and the conflicts of interests at hand in the light of a broader European legal order – one which arises from the discourse between EU and national legal orders. The European legal order should be conceived of as integrating the claims of validity of both national and EU constitutional law.[69]

63 According to Maduro, pluralism is mutual respect for the identity of the other legal orders and promotion of the broadest and most equal participation achievable.

64 In his own words: 'When national courts apply EU law they must do so in such a manner as to make to these decisions taken by the European Court of Justice but also by other national courts', Poiares Maduro, 'Contrapuntal Law', p. 528.

65 According to Maduro, every judge in the multilevel system should be obliged to argue and justify his or her decisions so that the national courts have to justify their decisions 'in a manner that could be universalisable', Poiares Maduro, 'Contrapuntal Law', p. 530.

66 The institutions of each legal order must 'be fully aware of the institutional choices involved in any request for action in a pluralist legal community', Poiares Maduro, 'Contrapuntal Law', p. 530.

67 J. Komárek, 'European Constitutionalism and the European Arrest Warrant: In Search of the Limits of "Contrapuntal Principles" ', *Common Market Law Review*, 2007, pp. 9 et seq.

68 Eleftheriadis, 'Pluralism and Integrity', pp. 385 et seq.

69 Poiares Maduro, 'Contrapuntal Law', p. 524.

The essence of Eleftheriadis' criticism is in the presumed theoretical betrayal carried out by Maduro: while MacCormick conceived national and supra-national laws 'as rival orders that may overlap, Maduro advises us to merge them as a "broader European legal order" under the principles of "contrapuntal law" '.[70]

Actually, Maduro does not seem to advocate a 'fusion' between constitutional poles, but there is surely a certain ambiguity in his terminology that might suggest such a consequence.

A similar observation may be made with regard to Mattias Kumm's works, especially paying attention to his principle of best fit:

> But how should national courts go about making a positive choice between competing conflict rules, assuming that the adoption of both NCS (National Constitutional Supremacy) and ECS (European Constitutional Supremacy) fulfills the threshold criterion of fit that defined the limits the court's institutional role? Is there anything to guide the choice of national courts? Judges dealing with constitutional conflicts cannot look either to their respective national constitution or to the Constitutional Charter of the European Union as their ultimate point of reference without committing a petitio principi. Does that mean that their choice is necessarily legally unguided? . . . Instead of being constrained by neither national nor European constitutional law, when choosing the right rule, national courts ought to seek guidance from both. The task of national courts is to construct an adequate relationship between the national and the European legal order on the basis of the best interpretation of the principles underlying them both. The right conflict rule or set of conflict rules for a national judge to adopt is the one that is best calculated to produce the best solutions to realise the ideals underlying legal practice in the European Union and its Member States. Just as the constraints that judges face are not appropriately defined exclusively by reference to a rule of recognition, the resources that are available to guide their decision-making are not ultimately defined by an ultimate legal rule, but by legal practice seen as a whole. The relevant question is, therefore: what is the interpretation of the relationship between national constitutions and the EU constitution that best fits and justifies legal practices in the European Union, seen as a whole? Or alternatively: what makes national and European constitutional practice in Europe appear in its best light?[71]

Balancing and systemic interpretation: this is the core of Kumm's proposal. The solution proposed, even the language employed, opens the door for criticism based on a presumed monist flavour of this proposal (the reference to 'the whole', for instance).

70 Eleftheriadis, 'Pluralism and Integrity', p. 386.
71 Kumm, 'The Jurisprudence of Constitutional Conflict', p. 286.

According to Kumm, EU law should in principle prevail over national law (Kumm conceives a presumption of applicability of EU law) except when there is a risk that some countervailing principles (protection of fundamental rights, democracy) provided with greater weight[72] may be jeopardised.

Kumm's view presents a strong German flavour, being shaped on the dialectic between the German Constitutional Court and the ECJ (from *Solange*[73] onwards) and on a sort of a priori superior democratic legitimacy of the national level given the democratic *deficit* existing at supranational level.[74]

Concluding this reconstructive part of the chapter, one can see how both views – multilevel constitutionalism and constitutional pluralism – go beyond the no *demos* debate[75] when describing the constitutional dynamics of European integration.

These theories conceive the European Constitution as the outcome of the relationship existing between constitutional levels or poles. At the same time, while multilevel constitutionalism does not seem to pay attention to the horizontal diversity present at national level and to the issue of the constitutional conflicts, these elements are at the heart of the constitutional pluralists' vision. Moreover, especially when referring to the works of Maduro and Kumm, constitutional pluralism is also characterised by a strong normative position aimed at neutralising possible constitutional conflicts. I return to this point in the final part of the volume when I stress the systematic role that constitutional conflicts might play in the complex

72 'My question is about your argument that in principle EU law should prevail unless countervailing principles have greater weight. You mention three exceptions, and their ground seems to be the greater democratic pedigree of national law. Assuming that this is the case, I wonder whether you can balance these principles as you do. On the one hand you have the rule of law, with predictability, the ability to know in advance who is going to decide and according to which rules. And you unsettle that on the grounds that national law is more democratic. This is problematic, because you cannot have democracy without the rule of law. If you accept this kind of balancing, you may end up damaging the rule of law in the European Union, and also in national systems because the European dimension of the rule of law is part of the national rule of law. And you do not improve democracy on the European level or on the national level. You just preserve what you take to be superior national constitutional law. So how do you deal with the heterogeneity of these two values? Can you really balance them in any meaningful way', Baquero Cruz, in M. Avbelj and J. Komárek, 'Four Visions', p. 29.

73 *BVerfGE* 37, S. 271, https://www.servat.unibe.ch/dfr/bv037271.html

74 'Kumm accurately shows that the arguments in favour of NCS are related to the a priori superior democratic legitimacy of the national legal orders and national constitutions in contrast to the European legal order. Kumm puts it in the following terms: 'if the laws passed at the level of the European legal order are characterised by the fact that the procedure in which they were enacted suffers from significant democratic defects, why should those laws trump even the constitutions of the Member States?'

D. Baez Seara.

'The Practice of European Constitutional Pluralism, 2010, http://eui.academia.edu; See also M. Goldoni, 'Constitutional Pluralism and the Politics of the European Common Good', www.juragentium.org/topics/rights/en/goldoni.htm

75 See the debate between Habermas and Grimm on this point: D. Grimm, 'Does Europe Need a Constitution?' *European Law Journal*, 1995, pp. 282 et seq.; J. Habermas, 'Remarks on Dieter Grimm's Does Europe Need a Constitution?' *European Law Journal*, 1995, pp. 303 et seq.

legal order. In the Preface to this second edition of the volume, I recalled that constitutional pluralism has been under siege, as it were a wrong concept that would inevitably lead to the disintegration of the EU. Suffice it to recall the reaction of some academics who signed a petition after the decision of the German Constitutional Court (BVG) on the European Central Bank's Public Sector Purchase Program (PSPP) of 5 May 2020.[76]

There, constitutional pluralism and national identity have been targeted as indirectly responsible for the decision of the German Constitutional Court:

> We also write to challenge those versions of scholarship on constitutional pluralism and constitutional identity that would defend the authority of the BVerfG or any national court to make such a ruling and that helped (even if unintentionally) encourage it to do so . . . . Of course, most constitutional pluralists didn't have in mind that national courts would engage in such brazen disregard for the authority of the CJEU. They assumed that head-to-head conflicts could be avoided or worked out through dialogue and accommodation. The crisis created by the BVerfG's Weiss judgment reminds us of a painful truth that many constitutional pluralists tried to wish away – that sometimes direct conflicts will occur.[77]

Indeed, the PSPP judgement of the BVG found the Court of Justice decision in the *Weiss and others* case[78] to be ultra vires and thus considered the German constitutional organs not bound by any of the relevant effects. This decision has triggered a very interesting debate on legal journals and blogs.

At the same time, as convincingly argued by Bobić,[79] the decision of the BVG by no means can be traced back to constitutional pluralism.

76 German Constitutional Court, 5 May 2020–2 BvR 859/15–2 BvR 1651/15–2 BvR 2006/15–2 BvR 980/16. For some comments see M. Poiares Maduro, 'Some Preliminary Remarks on the PSPP Decision of the German Constitutional Court', 2020, https://verfassungsblog.de/some-preliminary-remarks-on-the-pspp-decision-of-the-german-constitutional-court; M. Avbelj, 'The Right Question About the FCC Ultra Vires Decision', 2020, https://verfassungsblog.de/the-right-question-about-the-fcc-ultra-vires-decision; T. Marzal, 'Is the BVerfG PSPP Decision "Simply Not Comprehensible"? A Critique of the Judgment's Reasoning on Proportionality', 2020, https://verfassungsblog.de/is-the-bverfg-pspp-decision-simply-not-comprehensible/; M. Dani, J. Mendes, A.J. Menendez, M. Wilkinson, H. Schepel, and E. Chiti, 'At the End of the Law. A Moment of Truth for the Eurozone and the EU', 2020, https://verfassungsblog.de/at-the-end-of-the-law; A. Baraggia, G. Martinico, 'Who is the Master of the Treaties? The Compact Theory in Karlsruhe', 2020, www.diritticomparati.it/who-is-the-master-of-the-treaties-the-compact-theory-in-karlsruhe/

77 R.D. Kelemen, P. Eeckhout, F. Fabbrini, L. Pech, and R. Uitz 'National Courts Cannot Override CJEU Judgments a Joint Statement in Defense of the EU Legal Order', 2020, https://verfassungsblog.de/national-courts-cannot-override-cjeu-judgments/

78 ECJ, C-493/17, *Weiss and others* [2018] ECLI:EU:C:2018:1000.

79 A. Bobić, 'Constructive Versus Destructive Conflict: Taking Stock of the Recent Constitutional Jurisprudence in the EU', *Cambridge Yearbook of European Legal Studies*, 2020, pp. 60 et seq.

Moreover, constitutional pluralists have been accused of offering arguments to autocrats and justifying violations of the values set out in Article 2.[80] Avbelj powerfully rejected these accusations by showing that this criticism

> due to its truncated, exclusively positivist understanding of constitutional pluralism, it has failed to take into account pluralism's normative core. The latter presents itself an antipode to authoritarianism, which means that autocratic regimes simply cannot credibly avail themselves of the theory of constitutional pluralism to justify their authoritarian actions.[81]

Concluding on constitutional pluralism, it is interesting to note that it has been going through a kind of self-rethinking. Walker in this respect wrote an important article in 2016 in which he reflected on the constitutional pluralism, revisiting it.[82] Afterwards, Bobić explained why 'constitutional pluralism is not dead';[83] in that article and in more recent works we can see an interesting move in the universe of constitutional pluralism, according to which it seems to me that over recent years constitutional pluralists started distinguishing between good ('constructive'[84]) and bad conflicts. This is not a detail; until ten years ago, the obsession with coherence would have led many constitutional pluralists to deny the potential importance that conflicts might have in re-adjusting the system. In her own words, constitutional pluralism 'rests on the premise of regarding law as a dynamic, incrementally developing creature, constitutional conflict is no exceptional event, and represents an important element of the system's functioning'.[85] Another interesting element is the reference made to complexity by Walker in his 2016 article. He defines complexity as 'as a neutral, pre-theoretical description of something that is made up of different elements linked in a close or complicated way'.[86] This definition corresponds to one of the meanings of this word employed in this book. All of these recent scholarly developments make constitutional pluralism closer to what I called constitutional complexity some years ago and in the first edition of this volume, with some important differences, that we will recall again throughout the book.

80 R.D. Kelemen and L. Pech, 'Why Autocrats Love Constitutional Identity and Constitutional Pluralism. Lessons from Hungary and Poland', *Reconnect Working Paper*, 2018, https://reconnect-europe.eu/wp-content/uploads/2018/10/RECONNECT-WorkingPaper2-Kelemen-Pech-LP-KO.pdf

81 M. Avbelj, 'Constitutional Pluralism and Authoritarianism', *German Law Journal*, 2020, pp. 1023 et seq., p. 1031.

82 N. Walker, 'Constitutional Pluralism Revisited', *European Law Journal*, 2016, pp. 333 et seq.

83 A Bobić, 'Constitutional Pluralism Is Not Dead: An Analysis of Interactions Between the European Court of Justice and Constitutional Courts of Member States', *German Law Journal*, 2017, pp. 1395 et seq.

84 Bobić, 'Constructive'.

85 Bobić, 'Constructive', p. 61. Neil Walker's take on the relationship between federalism and constitutional pluralism seems more nuanced, Walker, 'Constitutional Pluralism Revisited', pp. 342–347.

86 Walker, 'Constitutional Pluralism Revisited', p. 333.

2.4 Complexity as 'the efficient secret' of the European Constitution

After having recalled the main aspect of these two constitutional theories, it is time to introduce the idea of constitutional complexity.

The adopted notion of complexity stems from a comparison of the different meanings of this word as used in several disciplines (law, physics, mathematics, psychology, philosophy) and regains the etymological sense of this concept (complexity from Latin *complexus* = interlaced). By applying the idea of complexity developed by Morin to the supranational context, I argue that the European legal order is a complex entity that shares some features with complex systems in natural sciences. The *mot-problème*[87] 'complexity' is used in several ways. Millard, for instance, recalls at least four different meanings of the word complex.[88] Complex, in fact, is often used as a synonym of 'complicated', and in this sense an antinomy may be understood as complex, given its difficulty in being solved because of the legal abundance caused by the coexistence of so many legislators in the EU and of the consequent difficult manageability of the several materials, languages and meanings present in the multilevel system. Secondly, complexity may refer 'à la situation d'un objet fragmentée, découpée. L'ensemble social n'est pas simple, au sens d'une théorie des ensembles: il résulte de l'addition ou de l'interaction entre une pluralité d'ensembles partiels, eux-mêmes sans doute s'entremêlés'.[89] Thirdly, complex is understood as non-aprioristic/pragmatic; in this respect, a reason is complex when it is not possible to infer choices and decisions from general, clear and abstract principles that were defined aprioristically. Finally, complexity is meant as interdependency of objects with regard to their relative autonomy: in this work, I focus on the relative autonomy of the legal orders (national, supranational and international) in the multilevel system.

From a preliminary and general comparison between the different meanings of 'complexity', as used in several disciplines,[90] it is possible to 'extract' a common

87 E. Morin, *Introduzione al pensiero complesso,* Milan: Sperling & Kupfer, 1993; E. Morin, *Conoscenza della conoscenza,* Milan: Feltrinelli, 1989. On Morin: M. Sandri, 'La complessità: verità acquisite e falsi miti', *Kéiron*, 2001, pp. 98 et seq. On Europe as a complex system, see E. Morin, *Pensare l'Europa*, Milan: Feltrinelli, 1988.

88 E. Millard, 'Eléments pour une approche analytique de la complexité', in M. Doat, J. Le Goff, and P. Pédrot (eds.), *Droit et complexité (Pour une nouvelle intelligence du droit vivant)*, Rennes: Presses Universitaires de Rennes, 2007, pp. 141 et seq.

89 Millard, 'Eléments', p. 143.

90 'Complexity theory is simply a mess. There are plenty of publications on it and it has gained a place in whatever discipline that comes to mind: philosophy, sociology, computational science, neurobiology, aesthetics, anthropology and, of course, economics. Because complexity theory is so complex, it is easy to find skeptics on the one hand or almost fanatical supporters on the other. The first step in taking complexity theory seriously should be to give it an exact definition. Unfortunately, a clear definition of complexity theory does not exist: according to the physician Seth Miller there are 45 definitions of complexity (Horgan, 1997; Rosser, 2009), but there are many characteristics which are recognized and accepted by scholars involved in this field of research', G. Becchio, 'Carl Menger and Complexity', Paper Presented at the Center for the History of

meaning of complexity as a bilateral and active relationship between diversities. This definition is very broad, but it also has two merits: it regains the etymological sense of this concept and, at the same time, it acknowledges the importance of a multidisciplinary approach to 'capture' the hidden dimension of the European process.

The notion of complexity does not deny the importance of diversity, but it permits, in my opinion, a distinction of the European phenomenon from the experiences of, for example, the multinational States. In this sense, I would like to link my reasoning to Weiler's reflections,[91] which stress the difference between Europe (where the States accept the law of another institutional actor with an autonomous act of subordination and without the need for a reference to a common name of a people) and other cases (Weiler gives the example of Canada). Complexity accurately describes the multilevel situation where the legal orders are not only distinguishable but also 'interlaced'.

All the disciplines have dealt with complexity as a general category and have attempted to apply it to several fields of knowledge. I am convinced that it is possible to extract a common notion of complexity from these different disciplines. My belief is confirmed by the fact that complexity is not only a particular concept but a general category that has caused a fundamental shift in the history of social and experimental sciences.[92] The notion of complexity is the result of a crisis of the certainties of modern thought and expresses the relativity and the problematic nature of truth. It is important to distinguish the notion of

---

Political Economy, Duke University, 4 December 2009, https://fdocuments.in/document/history-of-political-economy-lunch-seminar-center-for-the-history-staffwrkshoppapers2009-2010.html

91 J.H.H. Weiler, 'In Defence of the Status Quo: Europe's Constitutional Sonderweg', in J.H.H. Weiler and M. Wind (eds.), *European Constitutionalism beyond the State*, Cambridge University Press, 2003, pp. 7 et seq.

92 In mathematics, a number is defined as compound (conceived as complex) when it is formed by a real number plus (or minus) an imaginary number (example: 3+2i is a compound number). In sociology, 'the complexity is the dilation of possibilities of experience and action of the subjects, caused by an evolutionary trend which increases the functional differentiation, the specification and autonomy of the primary subsystems of the social system, of the economy, of science, of policy, of family and personal relations', D. Zolo, 'L'analisi sistemica del Welfare State', in D. Zolo (ed.), *Complessità e democrazia*, Turin: Giappichelli, 1987, p. 106. For Jung, complex is 'a structured and active set of representations, thoughts and remembrances partially or fully unconscious and with strong affective potential'; entry '*Complesso*', in U. Galimberti (ed.).Dizionario di psicologia, 1992, pp. 196–197. Among Jung's works on this topic: C.G. Jung, 'Considerazioni generali sulla teoria dei complessi' (1934) in *Opere*, 1976, Vol. III. For the mediaeval logicians a complex term is composed of different words (example: 'white man' or 'rational animal') while *incomplexum* means *isolated*; entry: 'Complesso', N. Abbagnano (ed.), *Dizionario di filosofia*, Turin: UTET, 1968, p. 134. For a physicist, a system is complex if it is characterized by the following features: *non-reducibility* to its parts, *unpredictability* of its dynamics, *non-reversibility* and *non-determinability*, I. Prigogine and I. Stengers, *La nuova alleanza*, Turin: Einaudi, 1999. For a jurist, an act is complex if it is the result of the expression of the wills of many subjects who have the same aim; their wills lose their individuality in this interpenetration. In this sense 'complex' is different from 'collective', L. Bigliazzi Geri, U. Breccia, F.D. Busnelli, and U. Natoli, *Diritto civile*, Vol. I Tomo II, Turin: UTET, 2000, pp. 546–547.

complexity from other concepts: as recalled, complex does not just mean complicated or composed of several elements. In a complex system, the collective behaviour is not determinable from the behaviour of its components. One of the most important scholars of complexity, Edgar Morin,[93] also distinguishes complexity from completeness. According to him, on the one hand, the thought of complexity aims at multidimensional knowledge, but on the other hand it knows that it cannot aspire to complete knowledge. This category is obviously polysemous if related to the different disciplines, but what I am now interested in stressing is the common element of these definitions: complexity as a *relational phenomenon* among *elements characterised by diversity* (conceived as the opposite of identical in the Aristotelian sense).[94] Starting with the physical meaning of complexity, it is possible to identify the following features commonly accepted in the other disciplines:

- Non-reversibility;
- Non-reducibility;
- Unpredictability;
- Non-determinability (rectius, non-determinism).

I am going to use these four features in order to read the structure of the European Constitution. As said at the beginning of this work, constitutional complexity can be employed to provide the following research question with an answer: what is the 'efficient secret' of the European Constitution?

2.4.1 Non-reversibility

For a complex system, non-reversibility is the impossibility of returning to the status quo spontaneously and precisely. Unlike reversible processes, in fact, where it is possible to return from the final condition to the starting condition, complex systems are non-reversible due to the non-linearity of the evolution.[95]

93 E. Morin, *Introduzione al pensiero complesso*.

94 In the history of philosophy, there are three main definitions of identity: identity as convention (F. Waismann), identity as unity of substance (Aristotle) and identity as substitutability (G. Liebniz). For an overview of these opinions: N. Abbagnano (ed.), *Dizionario di filosofia*, Turin: UTET, 1960, pp. 446 et seq.

95 'The Newtonian world was also "reversible." This means that "time exists merely as a parameter for gauging the interval between events. Past and future have no real significance. Nothing actually happens (Davies, 1989, p. 14). This is a particularly interesting feature that defies common sense, but made perfect sense in the Newtonian world. The Newtonian world is therefore a "clean machine," like a clockwork. Interestingly, it reflects the same static view of the world before Newton, which was considered a perfect, pre-ordained, Godgiven hierarchical order: Nothing actually happens, because the Laws of Nature are the Laws of God, and these Laws are perfect, therefore no change occurs, is necessary, or even possible', C. Montuori, 'Foreword: Edgar Morin's Path of Complexity', in E. Morin (ed.), *On Complexity. Advances in Systems Theory, Complexity, and the Human Sciences*, Cresskill, NJ: Hampton Press, 2008, pp. I et seq., p. XXX.

The EU journey has not been a linear process because of functional predominance and State resistance. Article 267 TFEU provides for the ECJ's jurisdiction to give preliminary rulings at national judges' request. Over time, thanks to such a provision, the Luxembourg Court has had a fundamental role in the EU integration process. It has allowed the ECJ to reshape the original legal materials of EU law by extracting national constitutional elements from the domestic legal orders and exchanging arguments with national judges.

Of course, EU law is just one of the factors to which national judges owe loyalty. They also have a similar, crucial role in the application of the ECHR and international law.

However, what is special about EU law is the preliminary ruling mechanism. It makes the relationship between national judges and the ECJ a powerful one.

When carrying out such an enterprise, the ECJ has benefited from the collaboration of national judges. The preliminary ruling mechanism has played a fundamental role in this respect by giving 'voice' to national interpreters.

This has made the preliminary ruling mechanism a privileged instrument for that constitutional *do ut des*, that constitutional synallagma between levels that I described as the efficient secret of the European Constitution.

In a second moment, the political legal sources (by revisions of the EU Treaties, constitutional amendments) attempted to adapt themselves to such interpretations. Today it is probably impossible to return to the initial condition because all the systems involved in the coordination have evolved and changed, thanks to mutual implications and influences. More generally, once in the EU, all of the Member States have acquired a set of duties and (legal, economic and political) obligations that has affected in a decisive manner their sovereignty. One could challenge such a conclusion, relying on one of the most important novelties introduced by the Lisbon Treaty: Article 50 TEU,[96] governing the 'right' of withdrawal from

96 '1. Any Member State may decide to withdraw from the Union in accordance with its own constitutional requirements.

2. A Member State which decides to withdraw shall notify the European Council of its intention. In the light of the guidelines provided by the European Council, the Union shall negotiate and conclude an agreement with that State, setting out the arrangements for its withdrawal, taking account of the framework for its future relationship with the Union. That agreement shall be negotiated in accordance with Article 218(3) of the Treaty on the Functioning of the European Union. It shall be concluded on behalf of the Union by the Council, acting by a qualified majority, after obtaining the consent of the European Parliament.
3. The Treaties shall cease to apply to the State in question from the date of entry into force of the withdrawal agreement or, failing that, two years after the notification referred to in paragraph 2, unless the European Council, in agreement with the Member State concerned, unanimously decides to extend this period.
4. For the purposes of paragraphs 2 and 3, the member of the European Council or of the Council representing the withdrawing Member State shall not participate in the discussions of the European Council or Council or in decisions concerning it.
A qualified majority shall be defined in accordance with Article 238(3)(b) of the Treaty on the Functioning of the European Union.
5. If a State which has withdrawn from the Union asks to rejoin, its request shall be subject to the procedure referred to in Article 49'.

the Union (sometimes also called the 'secession clause[97]). From a technical point of view, the situation of the Member State that decides to withdraw cannot be compared to the status quo properly understood for many reasons, for instance, because the wording of the provision refers to an agreement devoted to the 'future relationship' with the EU that will represent a sort of legacy of the previous membership of the European enterprise.

The Brexit saga – and this might appear counter-intuitive – confirms that. Will Brexit imply a perfect return to the starting condition of the British legal system? I think not. The simple fact that the European Union (Withdrawal) Act 2018 also aims to save EU-derived domestic legislation while incorporating EU legislation[98] shows that the future of the UK will build upon the legacy of its European membership instead of radically denying the added value produced by these years of integration. In other words, 'Brexit does not mean that all these rights will be lost'.[99]

2.4.2 Non-reducibility

The result of the relationship between diversities does not present itself as a mere sum of the latter but is something different.

Indeed, the European Constitution is not reducible to the sum of legal provisions at various levels. I mean, for example, that it is impossible to 'find' the legal basis for the principles of supremacy and their direct effect in the letters of the Treaty or in the letters of the national constitutions. In *Van Gend en Loos*[100] and *Costa*,[101] in fact, the ECJ found the roots of such principles to be in the 'spirit' of the Treaties and, also, in the indirect will of the States signing the Treaties.[102]

A consequence of the impossibility of tracing these principles back to the wording of a univocal primacy clause,[103] for instance, has galvanised the role of the

97 P. Athanassiou, 'Withdrawal and Expulsion From the EU and EMU. Some Reflections', *Legal Working Paper Series*, No. 10/2009, 2009, www.ecb.int/pub/pdf/scplps/ecblwp10.pdf

98 European Union (Withdrawal) Act 2018; see for instance sections 2 and 3. www.legislation.gov.uk/ukpga/2018/16/contents/enacted. See also M. Simoncini, Part I: The Uncertain Application of the EU Withdrawal Act 2018. From the Great Repeal to the Contingency Plan? (2018) IACL-AIDC Blog, https://blog-iacl-aidc.org/blog/2018/8/6/part-i-the-uncertain-application-of-the-eu-withdrawal-act-2018-from-the-great-repeal-to-the-contingency-plan

99 P. Eeckout and E. Frantziou, 'Brexit and Article 50 TEU: A Constitutionalist Reading', *Common Market Law Review*, 2017, pp. 695 et seq., p. 701.

100 ECJ, 26/62, *Van Gend en Loos*, [1963] ECR 3.

101 ECJ, 6/64, *Costa v. ENEL*, [1964] ECR 1141.

102 'The European Economic Community constitutes a new legal order of international law for the benefit of which the states have limited their sovereign rights, albeit within limited fields, and the subjects of which comprise not only the member states but also their nationals', 26/62, *Van Gend en Loos*, [1963] ECR 3

103 Scholars have identified at least four different meanings of primacy/supremacy in ECJ case law. Moreover, the notion of primacy enshrined in Art I-6 of the Constitutional Treaty seems to be different from that used by the ECJ. See e.g. M. Claes, *The National Courts' Mandate in the European Constitution*, Oxford: Hart, 2006, pp. 100–101. In order to find a solution to this ambiguity, some scholars have proposed a 'law of laws'; see W.T. Eijsbouts and L. Besselink, 'Editorial: "The Law of Laws" – Overcoming Pluralism', *European Constitutional Law Review*, 2008, pp. 395 et seq.

judge. My assumption is that this context galvanises the case-by-case judicial approach to solving legal conflicts between norms. The impossibility of operating a distinction between legal orders implies the end of interpretative autonomy for these courts, showing the other side of the sovereignty crisis. The judicial dialogue and judicial interactions in general thus represent a privileged perspective for studying the relations between interacting legal orders, especially when looking at the multilevel and pluralistic structure of the European constitutional legal order.[104] These interactions create a kind of additional information that is not visible to an external observer (in this sense, one could say that in complex systems there is no Laplace's demon).[105] New properties that cannot be explained from the properties of individual elements emerge as a result of the interactions among levels/poles. Such features are usually called emergent properties and correspond to those constitutional principles that cannot be entirely reduced to the national or supranational levels. In this sense, a complex system should not be understood as a mere sum of its components, but as something characterised by an added value that is the product of all the interactions among them. The idea of emergent properties refers to those entities that '"arise" out of more fundamental entities and yet are "novel" or "irreducible" with respect to them'.[106] The emergence of these properties is frequently associated to evolutionary dynamics that shape and reshape the natural order stemming from the different types of interactions possible among actors operating at the different levels/poles.

The case law on Brexit confirms this. For example, in *Wightman*,[107] the Court of Justice recalled that:

> According to settled case-law of the Court, that autonomy of EU law with respect both to the law of the Member States and to international law is justified by the essential characteristics of the European Union and its law, relating in particular to the constitutional structure of the European Union and the very nature of that law. EU law is characterized by the fact that it stems from an independent source of law, namely the Treaties, by its primacy over the laws of the Member States, and by the direct effect of a whole series of provisions which are applicable to their nationals and to the Member States themselves. **Those characteristics have given rise to a structured network of principles, rules and mutually interdependent legal relations binding the European Union and its Member States reciprocally as well as binding its Member States to each other**
>
> (judgement of 6 March 2018, Achmea, C-284/16, EU:C:2018:158, paragraph 33 and the case law cited; emphasis added)

104 I developed these thoughts in G. Martinico, 'Judging in the Multilevel Legal Order: Exploring the Techniques of "Hidden Dialogue"', *King's Law Journal*, 2010, pp. 257 et seq.

105 I. Prigogine and I. Stengers, *Order Out of Chaos: Man's New Dialogue with Nature*, New York: Bantam, 1984.

106 T. O'Connor and H.Y. Wong, 'Emergent Properties', in E.N. Zalta (ed.), *The Stanford Encyclopaedia of Philosophy*, 2012, http://plato.stanford.edu/entries/properties-emergent/#EmeSub

107 ECJ, C-621/18, Wightman, ECLI:EU:C:2018:999.

Wightman is interesting as it also offers a confirmation of the difficult distinguishability between national and supranational legal systems and the complex nature of European law. Another example of the complex context triggered by the Europeanisation of the national system is the *Miller* I decisions of the High Court[108] and the UK Supreme Court, especially in the passages devoted to the importance of the EU integration for the genesis of a new category of rights.[109]

2.4.3 Unpredictability

It is difficult to foretell or foresee the evolution of the system by looking at the starting position. In a deterministic system, it is always possible to predict the final state if the initial state is known. In a complex adaptive system, it is not possible to predict the final state of its evolution if we know the initial state of the components.[110]

It is very difficult to foresee the result of the coordination between levels by looking only at the formal provisions: the best example is given by the 'constitutional tolerance' in those national legal orders that do not have a specific constitutional provision enabling the EU to exercise their powers within national boundaries. From looking at the original Italian Constitution (Article 11 IC), it is very hard to understand how the guardians of the constitution have permitted the erosion of competences caused by EU interferences. Article 11, in fact, 'agrees to limitations of sovereignty where they are necessary to allow for a legal system of peace and justice between nations, provided the principle of reciprocity is guaranteed'.[111] This provision was conceived for participation in the UN or other limited-power organisations but not for the EU. The latter imposes limitations of sovereignty for goals that go beyond the 'peace and justice between nations' mentioned in Article 11. The Italian Constitutional Court was forced to 'adjust' the original meaning of Article 11 in order to allow such limitations. At the same time, when looking at Article 101 ('judges are only subject to the law'[112]), it is impossible to find the legal basis of the judge's power of non-application of the national rule contrasting with EU law. In conclusion, the knowledge of the starting (legal) condition does not allow us to foresee the development of the EU order.

Bearing in mind the original provision of national constitutions, how can one explain (a posteriori) or foresee (a priori) events like, for instance, the acceptance

108 R (Miller) v. Secretary of State for Exiting the European Union [2016] EWHC 2768.

109 R (Miller) v. Secretary of State for Exiting the European Union [2017] UKSC 55 at [69].

110 'Two fundamental things make up the Newtonian world: matter and energy. Matter and energy exist in the emptiness of absolute space and time – the "sterile machine" Davies mentions. Matter is composed of atoms and even subatomic particles such as electrons and protons. Knowing the location, mass, and velocity of all the particles in the universe, it would be possible to predict the future. With progressive improvement in scientific knowledge, in other words, it was believed that eventually it would be possible to predict every event', Montuori, 'Foreword', p. XXX.

111 Italian Constitution, Article 11.

112 Italian Constitution, Article 101.

of the *Simmenthal* mandate by national Constitutional Courts? This is exactly what I mean by unpredictability in this volume.

*2.4.4 Non-determinability (*rectius, *non-determinism)*

Complex systems do not follow necessary and univocal laws according to a linear concept of the evolution based on the dialectic of cause/effect.[113]

Similarly, European integration does not follow a precise political project (the triumph of 'functionalism') and the ECJ has not assumed an imperialistic approach in its interpretative function. In this sense, it is possible to recall the famous dialectic between constitutional tolerance and judicial activism[114] in the activity of the ECJ and its effect on the consistency of ECJ case law: *Kalanke*[115] versus *Marschall*,[116] *Grant*[117] versus *P/S*.[118]

The non-determinability implies the non-manageability of constitutional complexity; in this sense, the attempt of the Constitutional Treaty is an effort to 'manage' complexity without good results. The best confirmation of this statement can be found in Article I-6, which aimed to crystallise primacy. The difficulty of this enterprise is also caused by the absence of a strong political power at the supranational level.

2.5 From complexity to constitutional synallagma: some examples

If the EU as a complex system is characterised by the interlacing of different legal orders, the constitutional synallagma is the blood of its Constitution, which runs through the veins connecting constitutional levels. By this formula, I mean the whole of the principles, practices and rules that circulate uninterruptedly from one level to another in two directions (from top to bottom and vice versa). Constitutional synallagma conforms to the definition of a new kind of law that is not reducible to the legal provisions of the Treaties or of the national legislations. I try to clarify this formula with some examples in what follows.

113 'The Newtonian world was therefore deterministic. Every event had to happen by necessity. Once set in motion, the universe unfolds following precise laws. The assumption was that fundamentally, the universe is governed by simplicity and simple rules. There is an unquestionable order to the universe, and anything we consider disorder or complexity was simply a function of our limited knowledge. Simplicity, predictability, and determinism were central to the Newtonian worldview', Montuori, 'Foreword', p. XXX.

114 See O. Pollicino, 'Legal Reasoning of the Court of Justice in the Context of the Principle of Equality between Judicial Activism and Self-Restraint', *German Law Journal*, 2004, pp. 283 et seq.

115 ECJ, C-450/93, *Kalanke v. Freie Hansestadt Bremen*, [1995] ECR I-3051.

116 ECJ, C-409/95, *Marschall v. Land Nordrhein-Westfalen*, [1997] ECR. I-6363.

117 ECJ, C-249/96, *Grant v. South West Trains Ltd.*, [1998] ECR I-2143.

118 ECJ, C-13/94, *P / S and Cornwall County Council*, [1996] ECR I-2143.

The most obvious symbol of this exchange between orders is the directive, which needs to be 'completed' by the States, but I will focus on other types of complex sources: the common constitutional traditions in their relationship with the counter-limits (*controlimiti*, quoting the language used by the Italian Constitutional Court[119]). Common constitutional traditions represent another confirmation of the interlacing of orders (as previously described) since they are the outcome of the comparison and selection of the national constitutional 'materials'. In this sense, it is curious to note the connection between the *counter-limits* and the common constitutional traditions as pointed out by some scholars.[120] The common constitutional traditions and the counter-limits are linked by means of the fundamental principles of the national legal order selected, compared and used as European sources of law by the ECJ.

Another example is related to the development of the EU principle of proportionality. The principle of proportionality was clearly 'extracted' from the German legal tradition, although the classic three-step partition (*Geeignetheit*, *Erforderlichkeit*, *Verhältnismäßigkeitsprüfung im engeren Sinne*) elaborated by the German judges is rarely respected by the ECJ.[121] The translation of the German principle in the supranational context has also been enriched by the French experience of the *bilan coûts-avantages* (cost/benefit analysis) as elaborated in the case law of the *Conseil d'État.*

Such bottom-up flows (from the national traditions to the supranational level) induced the creation of a supranational principle. As I said previously, the constitutional exchange between levels is continuous and implies a second constitutional flow, top-down, from the EU level to the national levels. Due to the diversification of the national legal orders, we can distinguish different 'spill-over' effects. Galetta[122] has identified three examples of different reactions to this top-down flow. The first case is that of the UK, where the judges refused to apply the proportionality test, preferring the so-called *Wednesbury test* until the approval of the Human Rights Act of 1998, which represented a fundamental turning point. Another example is represented by Italy, where national judges misunderstood the test of proportionality: evidence of such a situation can be found in the confusion between reasonableness and proportionality.[123] Last but not least, the German case: here the same principle of proportionality comes back after the 'supranational transformation', causing new evolutions in the judges' activity in order to adapt their case law to the supranational demands.[124]

119 Corte Costituzionale, Frontini (Case 183/73), Granital (Case 170/84) and Fragd (Case 232/89), www.cortecostituzionale.it

120 A. Ruggeri, 'Tradizioni costituzionali comuni e "controlimiti", tra teoria delle fonti e teoria dell'interpretazione', *Diritto Pubblico Comparato ed Europeo*, 2003, pp. 102 et seq.

121 ECJ, C-96/03 and C-97/03, *A. Tempelman and Coniugi T.H.J.M. van Schaijk v. Directeur van de Rijksdienst voor de keuring van Vee en Vlees*, [2005] ECR I-1895.

122 Galetta, 'Il principio', pp. 541 et seq.

123 TAR Lecce, Bari, Sez. III, from 2483/2004 to 2493/2004, www.giustizia-amministrativa.it

124 *Gundesverwaltungsgericht*, BVerwG- Federal Administrative Court, *Deutsches Verwaltungsblatt* (DVBl) 613, 1993; *Gundesverwaltungsgericht*, BVerwG- Federal Administrative Court, *Deutsches Verwaltungsblatt* (DVBl) 68 1997.

More recently, in its decision on the European Central Bank's PSPP,[125] the German Constitutional Court somehow confirmed that by questioning the way in which the CJEU had carried out the proportionality test in *Weiss*.[126] In the German Constitutional Court's words:

> The specific manner in which the CJEU applies the principle of proportionality in the case at hand renders that principle meaningless for the purposes of distinguishing, in relation to the PSPP, between monetary policy and economic policy, i.e. between the exclusive monetary policy competence conferred upon the EU (Art. 3(1) lit. c TFEU) and the limited conferral upon the EU of the competence to coordinate general economic policies, with the Member States retaining the competence for economic policy at large.
>
> (Art. 4(1) TEU; Art. 5(1) TFEU)[127]

This judgement is very telling of the unexpected consequences of such a scenario. Indeed, the risk of collision when handling these 'shared' sources (indeed, general principles could be defined as 'multi-sourced equivalent norms')[128] is evident, as we will see in the second part of the book.

2.6 The idea of a complex 'order'

Studies on complexity in law can hardly renounce the idea of 'order'. In her masterpiece, Delmas Marty employed the idea of a 'pluralisme ordonné'[129] in order to explain the uncertain equilibrium to be achieved between unity and respect for diversity in the 'internationalisation du droit'.

When dealing with the daunting task of defining what she meant by 'pluralisme ordonné', the French scholar used the following words:

> Ordonner le multiple sans le réduire à l'identique, admettre le pluralisme sans renoncer à un droit commun, à une commune mesure du juste et de

125 2BvR859/15, www.bundesverfassungsgericht.de/SharedDocs/Entscheidungen/EN/2020/05/rs20200505_2bvr085915en.html;jsessionid=F892FE5330900A9A29FDCBEF992814FE.2_cid392

126 ECJ, C-493/17, *Weiss and Others* [2018] ECLI:EU:C:2018:1000. On this see: O. Scarcello, 'Proportionality in the PSPP and Weiss Judgments: Comparing Two Conceptions of the Unity of Public Law', *European Journal of Legal Studies*, 2021, pp. 45 et seq. On proportionality and national law see: G. Martinico and M. Simoncini, 'An Italian Perspective on the Principle of Proportionality', in S. Vogenauer and S. Weatherill (eds.), *General Principles of Law European and Comparative Perspectives*, Oxford: Hart, 2017, pp. 221 et seq.; M. Simoncini, 'La regolazione del rischio e il sistema degli standard. Elementi per una teoria dell'azione amministrativa attraverso i casi del terrorismo e dell'ambiente', Naples: Editoriale Scientifica, 2010, pp. 206–207.

127 2BvR859/15, par. 127, www.bundesverfassungsgericht.de/SharedDocs/Entscheidungen/EN/2020/05/rs20200505_2bvr085915en.html;jsessionid=F892FE5330900A9A29FDCBEF992814FE.2_cid392. On this see: Marzal, "Is the BVerfG'.

128 For this concept in international law see: T. Broude and Y. Shany (eds.), *Multi-Sourced Equivalent Norms in International Law*, Oxford: Hart, 2011.

129 M. Delmas Marty, *Le pluralisme ordonné. Les forces imaginantes du droit*, Paris: Ed. du Seuil, 2006.

> l'injuste, peut dès lors sembler un objectif inaccessible, un exercice, peut-être divertissant pour l'esprit, mais pratiquement vain . . . Transposées dans le champ juridique, les deux opérations semblent pourtant conduire à une double impasse, car la fusion (les dix mille êtres "mêlant leurs souffles") annonce une unité juridique qui semble utopique, voire inquiétante; tandis que la séparation ("l'un a grandi seul du multiple") suppose une autonomie parfaite qui n'existe plus. De l'une à l'autre, les pratiques oscillent en réalité entre un désordre de plus en plus anarchique et une hégémonie de moins en moins masquée. Pour sortir de l'impasse, il faut abandonner tout à la fois l'utopie de l'unité et l'illusion de l'autonomie, afin d'explorer l'hypothèse d'un processus d'engendrement réciproque entre l'un et le multiple que l'on pourrait nommer, pour marquer le mouvement, "pluralisme ordonné".[130]

Such a conception represents an evident reaction to the presumed legal monopoly of state law and against the vision of order as hierarchical holism, and an exaltation of the idea of law as interaction.[131]

Delmas Marty's pluralism cannot be traced back to those groups of scholars termed 'pluralists'.

The only 'pluralist' who seems to be interested in her reflections is Nico Krisch, who cannot be defined, as we know, as a constitutional pluralist.[132]

Indeed, the pluralism proposed by Delmas Marty is the product of a very extensive and thoughtful reflection upon the changing landscape of public international

130 ' – Des mots pourtant si commodes, comme « ordre » ou « système », « hiérarchie » ou « autonomie » – peinent à traduire les phénomènes d'indétermination, d'incohérence et d'instabilité qui accompagnent l'internationalisation du droit : indétermination, car les processus d'intégration, en devenant interactifs, se diversifient et se libèrent du principe de hiérarchie; incohérence quand les niveaux d'organisation se fragmentent, avec la multiplication d'organisations internationales de plus en plus sectorielles (droits de l'homme, du commerce, de l'environnement); enfin instabilité, dès lors que les écarts entre les vitesses d'intégration produisent des dysfonctionnements, d'un ensemble à l'autre ou, dans le même ensemble, d'un acteur à l'autre (on se souvient du débat à propos de la directive européenne anticipant sur la mise en oeuvre du protocole de Kyoto sur les gaz à effet de serre [GES]). Pour tenter d'échapper à la fois au désordre du monde (séparation radicale et relativisme absolu) et à l'ordre qui serait imposé par le plus fort au nom d'un universalisme de surplomb (fusion totale de type hégémonique), il faut donc chercher une issue par-delà relatif et universel. Autrement dit, explorer les voies et moyens d'un droit qui réussirait à ordonner la complexité sans la supprimer, apprenant à la transformer en un « pluralisme ordonné »', Delmas Marty, *Le pluralisme*, p. 28.

131 'On observe en effet que les interactions provoquent des mouvements d'intégration, mais aussi de désintégration de l'ordre juridique; tandis que les changements de niveau entre les divers espaces – national, régional et mondial – se traduisent par des mouvements d'expansion, mais aussi de repli; enfin, les changements de vitesse peuvent faciliter une synchronisation progressive ou conduire à une désynchronisation des rythmes, comme on le voit, au niveau mondial, entre droit du commerce et droit des droits de l'homme.' Delmas Marty, *Le pluralisme*, p. 256.

132 Krisch, 'Who Is Afraid'.

law, where the EU is just a piece of a broader puzzle, i.e. fragmentation and 'legal pluralism'.[133]

Nevertheless, her studies are important for the purpose of this work since they represent a sort of meeting point between the idea of pluralism and that of complexity,[134] and also because of her changing idea of order.

Whereas in the first English translation of her works she had employed a literal translation of the French 'pluralisme ordonné', in her book she employs the term 'ordering pluralism' in order to give readers the idea of a process,[135] or a work in progress, of a steady transformation whose point of arrival we do not yet know.

Her 'pluralisme ordonné' is a sort of a third way between two forms of pluralism, respectively the 'pluralisme de separation' (pluralism of separation) and 'pluralisme de fusion' (pluralism of fusion):

> 'Ordered' pluralism (pluralisme ordonné) is not to be confused with the pluralism of separation, nor with the pluralism of fusion. Rather, it oscillates from one to the other, in a process of making differences compatible [une sorte de 'mise en compatibilite' des differences]. It is not a matter of an established order but of the instability that results from the interaction which engenders trends both toward integration and toward disintegration, but also of expansion and of the falling back of one normative level to another, at speeds which vary for each normative ensemble, even within a single ensemble.[136]

133 'From the viewpoint of tradition in France, or any continental European state, the term "legal pluralism" seems to be a kind of monster – a chimera, if you will. That is because the 2 words that make up the term usually carry opposite meanings:

- "Pluralism" implies differences, dispersion, and free movement, interaction and evolution; in contrast,
- "Legal" leads us to think in terms of a unified, hierarchical, static structure.

But the world is not static, and so we must take up the challenge of overcoming this contradiction. We must change our minds just as our legal history changed. It changed at the end of World War II, when a European legal order emerged, and then again since the end of Cold War, when the so-called globalisation of law accelerated', M. Delmas Marty, 'Coping With Legal Pluralism: French & American Approaches to the Transnational Legal World', part 1, 2010, www.intlawgrrls.com/2010/01/coping-with-legal-pluralism-french.html

134 See her works on complexity: M. Delmas Marty, 'La tragédie des 3 C', in Préface in M. Doat, J. Le Goff, and P. Pédrot (eds.), *Droit et complexité (Pour une nouvelle intelligence du droit vivant)*, Rennes: Presses Universitaires de Rennes, 2007, pp. 7 et seq., Université de Rennes, 2007, pp. 7–12.

135 'I use "ordering," rather than "ordered," pluralism in order to stress the movement rather than the model, the process rather than the result', M. Delmas Marty, 'Coping With Legal Pluralism'.

136 M. Delmas Marty, 'Comparative Legal Studies and Internationalization of Law', *Working Paper*, 2005, www.college-de-france.fr/media/en-mireille-delmas-marty/UPL46493_mdm_pt3_pluralism_2004_2005_RevD.pdf

As Calbucci suggested,[137] against this background 'order' should be understood as the whole of interactions (that is why, especially in the French version of her books, she relies on the idea of 'complexity') among 'ensembles juridiques':[138] in this sense, order is above all the product of this interaction between interdependent legal systems. In her view, in fact, 'transformations of international law require a reappraisal of the compartmentalised vision of law in favour of a certain level of interdependence'.[139]

According to Delmas Marty,

> the pluralism of separations does not impose isolation and does not exclude interactions, but it limits them to horizontal processes, without hierarchy, by the interaction of crossed influences, by the intersections one might say to mark the reciprocity of one ensemble to another, of one institution to another, even of one Supreme Court to another.[140]

On the contrary, pluralism of fusion would be conducive to hegemony.

Her idea of 'pluralisme ordonné' should lead to 'neither utopian fusion nor illusory autonomy'; it should be conceived as a way of

> creating a common legal area by progressive adjustments that preserve diversity. Since an immutable world order is impossible, the imaginative forces of law must be called upon to invent a flexible process of harmonisation that leaves room for believing we can agree on – and protect – common values.[141]

The idea of order endorsed by the author is a dynamic one, something that should not be seen as immutable and closed but open, interactive and changeable.

Despite the fact that the idea of order has a certain importance for the purpose of her work (an element confirmed by the title of her book, the 'pluralisme ordonné'), from these words a certain 'caution' when employing the word 'order'[142]

137 A. Calbucci, 'La complessità del diritto e il diritto della complessità', in A. Calbucci (ed.), *La complessità del diritto dalla demagogia della semplificazione alla pedagogia della complessità in campo giuridico*, Naples: Guida, 2008, pp. 11–32, 31.

138 M. Delmas Marty, 'Le pluralisme ordonné et les interactions entre ensembles juridiques', 2006, n° 14, https://ieim.uqam.ca/IMG/pdf/article_Dalloz.pdf

139 M. Delmas Marty, 'Comparative Law and International Law: Methods for Ordering Pluralism', *University of Tokyo J Law and Politics*, 2006, https://saudeglobaldotorg1.files.wordpress.com/2015/08/comp-and-int-law-final-21.pdf

140 Delmas Marty, 'Comparative Law and International Law'.

141 See the presentation by Delmas Marty, 'Ordering Pluralism'.

142 While the last chapter of her English book is entitled 'In the Land of Organised Clouds?', in the last chapter of her French book, Delmas Marty wrote about an 'ordre en formation' specifying the consequences of the (partial at least) abandonment of the idea of hierarchical order: 'L'expansion selon le modèle de la pyramide conduit vers un ordre de type fusionnel, qui reste conçu comme une structure simple, ordonnée autour du principe de hiérarchie. Doublement simple, parce que l'ordre juridique (au sens de processus d'engendrement des normes) est prédéterminé par le principe de hiérarchie et parce que la cohérence est garantie par une corrélation, en quelque sorte « naturelle », entre l'intégration normative, les niveaux d'organisation et les

seems to emerge and this is confirmed by some 'interventions' in law blogs where she concluded that:

> Scrutiny of legal pluralism in the transnational legal world reveals not a well established global legal order, but rather interactions between national and international systems that play out in apparently contradictory, nonlinear, disorderly movements. It is a world in which new processes, extremely complex, continue to evolve. Legal systems seem to change form almost as soon as they take shape, long before we have had the time to determine their outlines. This contemporary reality departs from the hierarchical pyramid-of-law metaphor advanced decades ago by the jurist Hans Kelsen. I suggest that we replace the image of the static pyramid for that of dynamic clouds. The cloud metaphor aptly represents the continuity of formation and deformation ongoing in Europe. It applies too at the global level, where individual experience and interests represent fragments of an ever-changing sky.[143]

I would call this set of interactions/intersections[144] described by Delmas Marty as 'order',[145] and what I plan to do in the next chapter is to link such a dynamic, complex concept of order with the idea of 'evolutionary constitutionalism'.[146]

---

vitesses de transformation. Satisfaisant en apparence aux conditions d'une sécurité juridique qui suppose la prévisibilité des normes, ce modèle est politiquement redoutable, car il contredit ouvertement la souveraineté des États et risque en outre de légitimer, sous prétexte de favoriser l'émergence d'un ordre mondial, un processus d'intégration de type hégémonique. En revanche, l'expansion selon le modèle du réseau, à première vue plus facile à accepter en termes de souveraineté nationale, reste équivoque en ce sens qu'elle peut conduire à deux types d'ordre juridique, selon que l'expansion privilégie les interactions horizontales (internationales ou transnationales, qui s'organisent entre acteurs publics ou privés) ou les combine avec des interactions verticales (par harmonisation ou par unification). Le premier modèle s'ordonnerait exclusivement par le jeu d'interactions horizontales. Complexe, dans la mesure où la structure est interactive, il relève d'un ordre dont les mouvements seraient spontanément corrélés, donc d'un ordre autorégulé, comme prétend l'être l'ultralibéralisme au risque de favoriser des formes d'hégémonie plus souterraines au profit des pouvoirs économiques privés. Mais un ordre véritablement pluraliste appelle, comme on l'a vu, une conception que l'on pourrait nommer « hypercomplexe », car elle doit à la fois combiner interactions horizontales et verticales et corréler cette intégration à géométrie variable avec les autres mouvements, à plusieurs niveaux et à plusieurs vitesses', Delmas Marty, *Le pluralisme ordonné*, pp. 278–280.

143 M. Delmas Marty, 'Where and When Transnational Law Develops', 2010, www.intlawgrrls.com/2010/01/where-and-when-transnational-law.html

144 Delmas Marty clearly identified three processes of interaction: 'Coordination through cross-references', 'Harmonisation by approximation' and 'Unification by hybridisation'. Needless to say that since these were inferred by looking at a broader context (the new landscape of public international law), I will not rely on this tripartition.

145 Whose essence would be that exchange between constitutional materials grouped under the formula 'constitutional synallagma'.

146 There is an increasing and indeed multidisciplinary literature on the connection between complexity, evolution and order. For instance, see E.L. Khalil and K.E. Boulding (eds.), *Evolution, Order and Complexity*, Abingdon: Routledge, 1996.

How can we conceive this order? And how should we conceive the relation between conflicts (disorder) and order against this background.

Walker suggested the presence of a 'global disorder of normative orders'.[147] I would say that the EU is a case of 'order of disorders', and to explain my position I will rely on Hayek's work and, namely, his distinctions between constructivism and evolutionism and between κόσμος (spontaneous/natural order) and τάξις (constructed/artificial order).

In other words, trying to develop this idea of order as interaction/intersection and adapting it to the EU legal context, I will try to present this as an evolutionary type of order and to clarify the role played by constitutional conflicts in this context.[148]

As mentioned at the end of the first chapter, constitutional conflicts appear as elements of disturbance along the path towards legal coherence, which is why (normative) constitutional pluralists claim to neutralise them. My idea is that constitutional conflicts are physiological and that they can play a systemic role, favouring the changing nature of the EU legal order.

In other words, constitutional conflicts are functional to the development (not to be understood in a deterministic manner) of the EU legal order.

As Le Goff put it when writing about the relation between complexity and labour law: 'Comme si s'on optait pour la technique homéopathique de lutte contre le mal par le mal lui-même, le désordre devenant paradoxalement vecteur d'ordre'.[149]

How can we understand the relation between order and disorder in complex systems? How does 'order' develop in this context?

> Organization without disorder leads to a sterile, homogenous system where no change and innovation is possible. Complete disorder without order precludes organization. Only with the interaction of order and disorder is an

147 N. Walker, 'Beyond Boundary Disputes and Basic Grids: Mapping the Global Disorder of Normative Orders', *International Journal of Constitutional Law*, 2008, pp. 373 et seq.: 'pluralism proposes a kind of "non-order" of orders, in which no general steering mechanism is available to frame the relations between orders . . . it is important to conceptualize and understand the emerging configuration as a (candidate-neutral) disorder of orders'. See also G. Itzcovich, 'Legal Order, Legal Pluralism, Fundamental Principles: Europe and Its Law in Three Concepts', *European Law Journal*, 2012, pp. 358 et seq.: 'Another theoretical consequence of the authoritativeness of distinct and competing claims to authority is the confusion, the "legal dis-order" that ensues from the need to take them all seriously. Since external reasons must be evaluated in order to decide this kind of conflict, the legal order ceases to regulate in an exclusive way its transformation and application over time. It no longer makes much sense to conceptualise the legal order as being a consistent system of norms: at the most, it seems to be a precarious equilibrium, on the edge of a void, between momentarily converging authorities. Thus, consistency is projected outside the legal order, in the "principles of political morality" and in the "common values" – sort of Byzantine sky that can no longer hide the fact that the law of integration has stopped to regulate its own transformation', p. 374.

148 On the idea of law in Hayek, see A. Ogus, 'Law and Spontaneous Order: Hayek's Contribution to Legal Theory', *Journal of Law and Society*, 1989, pp. 393 et seq.; E. Angner, *Hayek and Natural Law*, Abingdon: Routledge, 2007.

149 J. Le Goff, 'Le droit du travail, terre d'élection de la complexité', in M. Doat, J. Le Goff, and P. Pédrot (eds.), *Droit et complexité. Pour une nouvelle intelligence du droit vivant*, Rennes: PUR, 2007, p. 106.

> organization possible that remains open to change, growth, and possibilities . . . . Disorder was viewed as a function of human ignorance, something that would, eventually, with better knowledge, be integrated in the larger master-plan . . . . Rather than seeing order as fundamental and unchanging, we are now seeing an ongoing process of order-disorder-interaction-organization that is the hallmark of self-organization . . . . As Taylor (2001, p. 121) writes, 'disorder does not simply destroy order, structure, and organization, but is also a condition of their formation and reformation'. The interaction of order and disorder can be generative of new forms of organization, and any order is the result of an ongoing process, not of pre-established forms.[150]

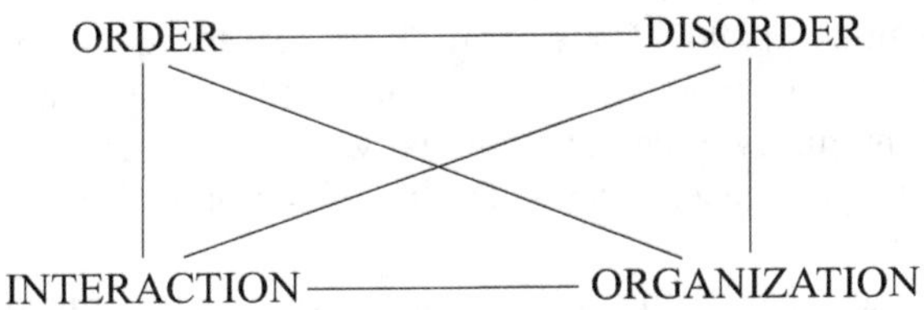

Source: C. Montuori, 'Foreword: Edgar Morin's Path of Complexity', in E. Morin, *On Complexity: Advances in Systems Theory, Complexity, and the Human Sciences*, Cresskill, NJ: Hampton Press, 2008, pp. I et seq., p. XXXIII.[151]

Order and disorder thus interact, favouring the emergence of social changes and the renovation of the organisation.

In the next chapters, I will try to present constitutional conflicts as a window of opportunity for legal change in EU law without implying a rationalistic understanding of order and development.

On the contrary, consistently with the tradition of complexity studies (and even with a certain branch of political science scholars[152]), conflicts (as a form of disorder) are conceived as factors of constitutional, in our case, transformation.

Finally, like some complex systems in natural sciences, the European legal order is adaptive; it reflects 'an ability to adapt through the emergent characteristic of self-organization, which comes from the inter-dependency of their individuals or agents, a.k.a. sub-systems'.[153] In other words, the European legal order develops through non-constructivist dynamics.

150 Montuori, 'Foreword', p. XXXIV.

151 'In Newton's world, Order reigned, and what we perceived as Disorder was simply the result of our human ignorance. We simply were not yet aware of the Laws governing the phenomena we called disordered, confused, ambiguous. This is also the Laplacean universe, where virtual omniscience is the ideal. With Clausius and the second law of thermodynamics, we find that Order and Organization move toward Disorder. With Darwin, and the new developments in physics, Morin proposes a key tetragram that shows how the interactions of order and disorder lie at the heart of organization', Montuori, 'Foreword', p. XXXIV.

152 J. Knight, *Institutions and Social Conflict*, Cambridge: Cambridge University Press, 1992.

153 M. Schneider and M. Somers, 'Organizations as Complex Adaptive Systems: Implications of Complexity Theory for Leadership Research', *The Leadership Quarterly*, 2006, pp. 351–365, p. 355.

From a theoretical point of view, one could question the connection between Hayek's thought and the theory of complexity, but there is a growing scholarship[154] (especially in the field of history of economic thought) that has pointed out some common elements between these two theoretical trends. They share an evident anti-constructivism, anti-reductionism and anti-determinism,[155] the 'passion' for the theme of uncertainty.[156] Moreover, 'complexity and spontaneous order are linked in the Austrian paradigm by 'a process of systematic, ordered change in either the formal or informal rule structures by which people attempt to achieve their purposes' (Vaughn, *Austrian economics in America: the migration of a tradition*, Cambridge, New York: Cambridge University Press 1994, 125)'.[157]

They also do not understand development in either a rationalistic manner or a progressive manner. In 1967, Hayek himself wrote a piece on complexity.[158]

Indeed, the kind of spontaneous order conceived by Hayek is also complex.[159] When developing his own idea of complexity, Hayek stressed the importance of non-linearity and path dependency in the life of complex phenomena:

> The basic idea, then, is that a large number of variables may interact in complex ways, such that they give rise to patterns that constitute 'wholes' that are distinctive complex phenomena, which have properties that are not reducible to the particular properties of each element.[160]

154 The literature is enormous. For instance: E. Kilpatrick Jr, 'Complexity, Spontaneous Order, and Friedrich Hayek: Are Spontaneous Order and Complexity Essentially the Same Thing?' *Complexity*, 2011, pp. 16 et seq.; L. Dobuzinskis, 'The Complexities of Spontaneous Order', *Critical Review: A Journal of Politics and Society*, 1989, pp. 241 et seq.

155 In 1967 in his article on complexity, Hayek devoted a section of that work to the 'ambiguity of the claims of determinism', A. Hayek, 'The Theory of Complex Phenomena', now published in his *Studies in Philosophy, Politics and Economics*, University of Chicago Press, 1967, p. 66.

156 This point has been stressed in Menger's thought by Becchio (G. Becchio, 'Carl Menger and the Second Edition of His Principles', 2010, http://econ.as.nyu.edu/docs/IO/14399/Becchio_20100201.pdf).

157 Becchio, 'Carl Menger'

158 A. Hayek, 'The Theory of Complex Phenomena', published in his *Studies in Philosophy, Politics and Economics,* University of Chicago Press, 1967, pp. 22–42. In this connection, see also J.B. Rosser, 'How Complex Are the Austrians?' in R. Koppl, S. Horwitz, and P. Desrochers (eds.), *What Is So Austrian About Austrian Economics? Advances in Austrian Economics*, Bingley: Emerald Publishing Limited, 2010, pp. 165 et seq.

159 'Although spontaneous orders also may be complex, they need not be. Crucial to Hayek's analysis of economic and social orders is that they are not only spontaneous, but also complex. Indeed, although most readings of Hayek stress the idea of a spontaneous order, I believe Hayek's great contribution to social and political theory is the notion of an organized complexity, and it is this idea that poses the biggest challenge for expediency as the aim of social policy. Hayek's analysis of social complexity, especially the complexity of economic systems, points to eight elements, which remain part of current analyses of complexity', G. Gaus, 'Social Complexity and Evolved Moral Principles', in P. McNamara (ed.), *Liberalism, Conservatism, and Hayek's Idea of Spontaneous Order*, London: Palgrave Macmillan, 2007, pp. 149 et seq., also available electronically at: www.gaus.biz/Gaus-SocialComplexity.pdf

160 Gaus, 'Social Complexity'.

As we can see, non-linearity, non-reducibility, anti-constructivism[161] and non-(complete at least) predictability[162] and dynamism[163] are indeed crucial concepts in Hayek's understanding of spontaneous order. As recalled, the idea of emergent properties is frequently associated with that of evolutionism. If this is true, constructivism and complexity cannot be reconciled in my view, since the former implies the possibility of domesticating complex processes by reducing them to 'human design'.

In this sense, constitutional complexity can provide 'an analogical foundation for that new paradigm of legal theory',[164] and in this particular field it can describe how the authority of EU law impacts on the domestic constitutional systems and how the constitutional systems react by challenging a complete unification. Since unpredictability is one of the basic features of a complex system, it is impossible within the logic of constitutional complexity to foresee the evolution of the EU system.

In this respect, complexity appears as a neutral reading, since it does not advocate this or that institutional result as the natural or necessary end of the integration process.

At the same time, and this is another difference from constitutional pluralism, it does not exclude the possibility that federal systems can be to a certain extent compared to the EU.[165]

161 'Because of the complexity of the system, there is "no global controller that can exploit all opportunities or interactions." This brings us to the very heart of Hayek's economics: global planners cannot secure and employ sufficient information to direct individuals to employ their capital and labor in a way that will tend to a social optimum. This was the crux of Hayek's position in the socialist calculation debate', Gaus, 'Social Complexity'.

162 Here we can find a slight difference as pointed out by Gaus: 'Complex systems often display micro unpredictability with some range of macro predictability (this is closely tied to emergent properties, point [ii]). This is crucial in understanding Hayek's conception of social complexity. It was no part of Hayek's intention to argue that economies or societies are too complex to predict, or that we could not possess a predictive social science. His claim, rather, was that in complex systems the only successful predictions will be "pattern predictions," not predictions of specific states of the system at particular times. That is, we can predict a certain "range of possibilities" for the system or, we might say, parameters within which the system will settle. Thus Hayek insisted that theories of complex phenomena were testable as they predict a range of possible system states. However, because of the nonlinearity of the relations in the system, there is no unique solution; only predictions of ranges of possibilities are feasible', Gaus, 'Social Complexity'.

163 'Complex systems such as the economy are characterized by constant novelty. We need to remember that Hayek, like the Austrian school of economics in general, insisted on the importance of dynamic and unknown factors in economic life. "The solution of the economic problem of society . . . is always a voyage of exploration into the unknown, an attempt to discover new ways of doing things better than they have been done before." Although mainstream economics generally has been critical of this emphasis on the novelty of entrepreneurship in Austrian economics, understanding the differing effects of predictable and unpredictable developments has been the core of rational expectations theory', Gaus, 'Social Complexity'.

164 J. Ruhl, 'Complexity Theory as a Paradigm for the Dynamical Law-and-Society System', *Duke Law Journal*, 1995–96, pp. 851 et seq. On complexity and legal system as applied to computer science see: V. Frosini, *Ordine e disordine nel diritto*, Naples: Guida, 1979.

165 Bobić, 'Constructive Versus Destructive Conflict', pp. 64–65.

Multinational federalisms[166] are particularly helpful, with their emphasis on asymmetry that can play a key role in favouring adaptiveness, but also the experience of American pre-Civil War federalism is very useful in order to understand the current state of the EU integration process, as Schütze pointed out.[167] In doing so, he emphasised the role of the Supreme Court and other US courts in the determining the meaning of the formula 'We the people' as used in the US Constitution's Preamble,[168] in a context in which there was no unitary or homogeneous *demos* at the beginning. Similar comparative considerations apply to the burning issue of the scope of implementation of the Charter of Fundamental Rights of the EU, as suggested by Torres Pérez.[169] After all, comparing two entities does not necessarily imply that they are identical; comparison is also about discovering differences, and there are important books on federalism that have marked the history of European studies.[170] In some respects, moreover, especially if one does not accept Krosigk's criticism[171] of Friedrich, one could also argue that the supranational process can be studied from the perspective of the federalising process,[172]

166 A. Gagnon and J. Tully (eds.), *Multinational Democracies*, Cambridge: Cambridge University Press, 2001; M. Seymour and A. Gagnon (eds.), *Multinational Federalism, Problems and Prospects. Comparative Territorial Politics*, London: Palgrave, 2012.

167 E. Morgan, *Inventing the People: The Rise of Popular Sovereignty in England and America*, New York: WW Norton & Company 1988, p. 15.

168 R. Schütze, 'Federalism as Constitutional Pluralism', pp. 185–186.

169 A. Torres Pérez, 'Rights and Powers in the European Union: Towards a Charter that is Fully Applicable to the Member States?' *Cambridge Yearbook of European Legal Studies*, 2020, pp. 279 et seq. The clarification of the scope of the *Ruiz Zambrano* doctrine and an active use of the Charter of Fundamental Rights in this area must be at the heart of the Court of Justice's agenda and could make a fundamental contribution to unlocking the federal potential of the European integration process. This is, however, food for another book. See the considerations made by AG Sharpston: AG Sharpston in C-34/09 *Ruiz Zambrano* [2011] ECLI:EU:C:2010:560, par. 172–173.

170 Just to give some examples: P: Hay, *Federalism and Supranational Organizations. Patterns for New Legal Structures*, Urbana: University of Illinois Press, 1966; E. Stein, 'Treaty-Based Federalism, A.D. 1979: A Gloss on Covey T. Oliver at the Hague Academy', *University of Pennsylvania Law Review*, 1979, pp. 897 et seq.; E. Stein, *Thoughts from a Bridge: A Retrospective of Writings on New Europe and American Federalism*, Ann Arbor: University of Michigan Press, 2000; E. Stein, 'Lawyers, Judges and the Making of a Transnational Constitution', *American Journal of International Law*, 1981, pp. 1 et seq.; M. Cappelletti, M. Seccombe, J. Weiler (eds.), *Integration Through Law: Europe and the American Federal Experience*, I, Berlin: W. De Gruyter, 1986; K. Lenaerts, 'Constitutionalism and the Many Faces of Federalism', *American Journal of Comparative Law*, 1990, pp. 205 et seq.; R. Schütze, *From Dual to Cooperative Federalism. The Changing Structure of European Law*, Oxford: Oxford University Press, 2009. Apart from Stein's 1981 essay and Lenaerts' 1990 article, all other authors are not mentioned by Bobić.

171 F. von Krosigk, 'A Reconsideration of Federalism in the Scope of the Present Discussion on European Integration', *Journal of Common Market Studies*, 1970, pp. 197 et seq.

172 C.J. Friedrich, *Trends of Federalism in Theory and Practice*, London: Pall Mall, 1968. There is, however, an important difference between the concept of federalising process and complexity: they both describe a process of interaction, they are both interested in the dynamics of the system rather than in its static, but, as etymology again suggests, federalism puts a greater emphasis on the *foedus*, that is, the pact, the integrative moment and on the idea of governing differences

especially in a comparative perspective.[173] Finally, neglecting the importance of this strand of studies would exclude an important contribution to the construction of the EU. Indeed, as suggested by Avbelj: 'The comparative American constitutional experience was thus taken over as a mindset, as an intellectual pattern underlying the EU constitutional narrative which has won a dominant position in the legal construction of European integration'.[174] Another feature of constitutional complexity is that it inevitably galvanises the importance of comparative law from a methodological point of view, not only in the construction of the general principles of EU that are indebted to the national constitutional materials and that are the main vehicles of what I have called the constitutional synallagma. Comparative law is also essential to understand the reasons behind the decision to trigger constitutional conflicts or to raise resistance to EU law primacy, as we will see in Chapter 5.

without crushing them as suggested by K.G. Wheare, *Federal Government*, Oxford: Oxford University Press, 1953.

173 The present author has done so elsewhere. For instance, in G. Martinico, 'Reading the Others: American Legal Scholars and the Unfolding European Integration', *European Journal of Law Reform*, 2008, pp. 35 et seq.

174 M. Avbelj, 'The Pitfalls of (Comparative) Constitutionalism for European Integration', *Eric Stein Working Paper*, 2008, http://papers.ssrn.com/sol3/papers.cfm?abstract_id=1334216

3 Constructivism, evolutionism and (mega) constitutional politics in the EU from 1992 to 2010

3.1 Plan of the chapter

As said at the beginning of this work, the rejection of the Constitutional Treaty and the adoption of the Lisbon Treaty (also known as Reform Treaty) have been read by scholars[1] as confirmation of the impossibility of the EU developing its constitutional ambitions. This conclusion can be challenged for both theoretical and empirical reasons (the latter stemming from the actual comparison with other legal experiences), as I have tried to prove elsewhere.[2] While I do not wish to enter into this debate in this book, this chapter examines the years from 1992 to 2010, in light of the dichotomy of constructivism/evolutionism, trying to present different rounds of constitutional politics at EU level as a (frustrated) attempt at dominating (and reducing) the constitutional complexity of the EU.

I have already defined what I mean by European Constitution (Chapter 1) after an *excursus* on the main theoretical views on the idea and nature of the European Constitution (or Basic Law, according to the terminology employed by other scholars[3]). Following that, I have tried to explain in Chapter 2 why these kinds of constitutional dynamics can be defined as an expression of constitutional complexity, by insisting on non-reductionism as part of the complexity message.

Constructivism and complexity cannot be reconciled in my view; they are antithetical since the former implies the possibility of domesticating complex processes by reducing them to 'human design' and controlling them. I will insist

1 For instance: M. Avbelj, 'EU Constitutional Swan Song', 2009, https://papers.ssrn.com/sol3/papers.cfm?abstract_id=1497030

2 For the employment of the comparative argument see: G. Martinico, 'Constitutional Failure or Constitutional Odyssey? What Can We Learn From Canada and Switzerland', *Perspectives on Federalism*, 2011, pp. 51 et seq. For the theoretical reasons that lead me to question this conclusion, see: G. Martinico, *Lo spirito polemico del diritto europeo Studio sulle ambizioni costituzionali dell'Unione*, Rome: Aracne, 2011.

3 L. Besselink, 'The Notion and Nature of the European Constitution After the Reform Treaty', 2007, http://papers.ssrn.com/sol3/papers.cfm?abstract_id=1086189

DOI: 10.4324/9781003056522-3

on one of the most interesting provisions introduced over the years to control the evolutionary dynamics of EU constitutionalisation: I will treat very different phenomena as case studies, trying to present them as connected by the same 'logic' and introducing, in this escalation, Article 4.2 TEU as an example of this trend. This provision, at first glance, might be read as a confirmation of the irreducible complexity of EU law but actually, from a historical point of view, it can be seen as the last link in a chain of constructivist constitutional politics that, since 1992, have characterised the constitutional narrative of the EU. Also, it is inspired by an evident attempt at 'neutralising' constitutional conflicts but, as we will see, in my view this plan is far from being workable.

3.2 Constitutional constructivism versus constitutional evolutionism

At first glance, the rejection of the CT by the majority of the French and Dutch voters, and the Irish 'No' to the Reform Treaty (RT), gave the impression of an inescapable constitutional crisis for Europe. Although the RT does not include any reference to the word 'constitution', the substantive continuity between this document and the Constitutional Treaty is evident. As some scholars have stressed, a 'constitutional substance' had been 'rescued' despite the elimination of some 'dirty words' such as 'Constitution', 'Law', and 'Minister' from the text of the Lisbon Treaty.[4] From this point of view, as Corthaut points out, 'the Reform Treaty looks more like the (evil?) twin of the Constitutional Treaty than its distant cousin'.[5] Ziller[6] argues that the possible major changes (the primacy clause's disappearance, for example[7]) were just functional to overcome the risk of the Member States' refusal. Despite this substantive relative continuity, other authors have stressed the sense of disappointment that would characterise the document, defining it as a 'Postconstitutional Treaty'.[8]

According to such scholarship, the RT cannot be regarded as a Constitution since it limits itself to reflecting the problems without solving them: it seems to

4 J. Ziller, *Il nuovo Trattato europeo*, Bologna: Il Mulino, 2008, p. 127.

5 T. Corthaut, 'Plus ça change, plus c'est la même chose? A Comparison With the Constitutional Treaty', *Maastricht Journal of European and Comparative Law*, 2008, pp. 21 et seq., p. 34.

6 Ziller, *Il nuovo Trattato*, pp. 27 et seq.

7 However, as we know, Declaration n. 17 concerning primacy was annexed to the Final Act of the Intergovernmental Conference, which adopted the Treaty of Lisbon, signed on 13 December 2007, https://eur-lex.europa.eu/legal-content/EN/TXT/?uri=CELEX%3A12008E%2FAFI%2FDCL%2F17

8 According to Somek: 'A postconstitutional ordering, by contrast, cannot settle contested issues, for it cannot find sufficient support for a clear solution. A postconstitutional norm does not speak with one voice. It is a document recording the adjournment of an ongoing debate. Maybe this is addressed by those talking about the Union's alleged lack of a *pouvoir constituant*. Ideally, a constitution is about channelling political dealings, not about postponing their resolution.' A. Somek, 'Postconstitutional Treaty', *German Law Journal*, 2007, pp. 1121 et seq., pp. 1126–1127.

suffer the social forces rather than lead them. This point is crucial because a very similar criticism was expressed by Bast with regard to the CT. In his own words:

> Wading through the complete text – some 474 pages of reading material in the Official Journal – one experiences how far away the Constitutional Treaty is from the ideal of a concise, expressive constitutional document. This is not, or at least not primarily, an editorial deficiency. The structure and length of the constitutional text reflect the unsolved problems involved with fostering unity . . . . The tension between – only partially 'correct' – self-description (Part I) and normative reality (Part III) cannot, for the most part, be resolved by jurisprudence, but by constitutional politics. This confers on the Constitutional Treaty the status of a reflexive constitution. Such a constitution makes normative demands of itself, without (yet) fully accounting for them.[9]

The real issue thus concerns the nature of a potential Constitution for Europe: what kind of Constitution would it be? Would the idea of a Constitution as such be applicable to the European Union experience? Besselink makes a very good contribution to the debate on the notion and the nature of a Constitution for Europe.[10] In his view, the notion of Constitution itself as applied to the EU results in an ambiguous picture, with that of a fundamental law (*Grundgesetz* rather than *Verfassung*) being more suitable.

This seems to imply a sceptical approach to the issue of the European Constitution's formalisation, conceived as a real constitutional moment. Besselink also reaches this conclusion after having distinguished between two categories of constitution: revolutionary and evolutionary. In his own words, 'these revolutionary constitutions tend to have a blueprint character, wishing to invent the design for a future which is different from the past . . . . Old fashioned historic constitutions are, to the contrary, evolutionary in character'.[11] When observing the evolutionary/historical constitutions, one realises that 'codification, consolidation and adaptation are more predominant motives than modification. The constitution reflects historical movements outside itself'.[12] The semi-permanent treaty revision process[13] makes the attempt to transpose the idea of Constitution into a supranational level very difficult. The Constitution, in fact, should be the fundamental charter, that is, a document characterised by a certain degree of resistance and continuity. Against this background, the European Treaties seem unable to lead social forces: they can only 'reflect the historical movements',[14] thus seeming mere 'snap-shot

9 J. Bast, 'The Constitutional Treaty as a Reflexive Constitution', *German Law Journal*, 2005, pp. 1433 et seq., pp. 1438 and 1449.

10 Besselink, 'The Notion'.

11 Besselink, 'The Notion'.

12 Besselink, 'The Notion'.

13 B. de Witte, 'The Closest Thing to a Constitutional Conversation in Europe: The Semi-Permanent Treaty Revision Process', in P. Beaumont, C. Lyons, and N. Walker (eds.), *Convergence and Divergence in European Public Law*, Oxford: Hart, 2002, pp. 39 et seq.

14 Besselink, 'The Notion'.

constitutions'. This is precisely what Besselink argues, writing that 'a formal EU "constitution", if ever realized, would only be a momentary reflection, no more than a snap-shot';[15] hence the comparison with a *Grundgesetz*.

All these views emphasise what we could call the need for a 'written dimension' in the European constitutional experience and they neglect the current constitutional dynamics already existing in the EU. Another reason to continue trusting in the existence of a European constitutional law (or, better, in its subject, the European Constitution) is the existence of a copious case law of the Court of Justice of the EU, where the expression 'constitution' is frequently used with regard to the Treaties.[16] This idea of Constitution mentioned by the critics of the Constitutional Treaty and by that body of literature that defines itself as 'pluralism' (distinguishing itself from what some authors mean by 'constitutional pluralism'[17]) implies a 'constructivist' nature in every 'real' constitutional moment. By constructivism, that is, 'a conception which assumes that all social institutions are, and ought to be, the product of deliberate design'.[18] The dualistic structure of Hayek's thought links the idea of constructivism to that of order, which can be conceived in two different ways: order[19] as κόσμος (spontaneous order) and order as τάξις (constructed order). According to many continental authors,[20] to be binding and normative (and not merely descriptive), constitutions are supposed to be 'constructivist', since they are directed at the achievement of an ideal society characterised by those values deemed fundamental. For example, the concept of

15 Besselink, 'The Notion'.

16 The first case is *Les Verts*: ECJ, C-294/83, *Parti ecologiste 'Les Verts' v. European Parliament* [1986] ECR 1339, par. 23: 'It must first be emphasized in this regard that the European Economic Community is a community based on the rule of law, inasmuch as neither its member states nor its institutions can avoid a review of the question whether the measures adopted by them are in conformity with the basic constitutional charter, the treaty'. But see also ECJ, Opinion 1/91 on the EEA Agreement [1991] ECR I-6079: 'The European Economic Area is to be established on the basis of an international treaty which merely creates rights and obligations as between the Contracting Parties and provides for no transfer of sovereign rights to the inter-governmental institutions which it sets up. In contrast, the EEC Treaty, albeit concluded in the form of an international agreement, none the less constitutes the constitutional charter of a Community based on the rule of law'. ECJ, C-402/05 P, *Kadi v. Council and Commission*, ERC, 2008 I-0635: '[The] European Community is based on the rule of law, inasmuch as neither its Member States nor its institutions can avoid review of the question whether their acts are in conformity with the basic constitutional charter, the EC Treaty, which established a complete system of legal remedies and procedures designed to enable the Court of Justice to review the legality of acts of the institutions'. For an account of the constitutional mission carried out by the ECJ over the years, see L. Azoulai and M. Poiares. Maduro (eds.), *The Past and the Future of EU Law*, Oxford: Hart, 2010.

17 N. Krisch, *Beyond Constitutionalism: The Pluralist Structure of Postnational Law*, Oxford: Oxford University Press, 2010.

18 A. Hayek, *Law, Legislation and Liberty, vol. 1, Rules and Order*, Abingdon: Routledge, 1973, p. 5.

19 'the situation where one author could argue with regard to a given phenomenon that it was artificial because it was the result of human action, while another might describe the same phenomenon as natural because it was evidently not the result of human design', Hayek, *Law*, p. 20.

20 On the development of legal doctrine in Europe (and beyond) see: A. Bogdandy, 'The Past and Promise of Doctrinal Constructivism: A Strategy for Responding to the Challenges Facing Constitutional Scholarship in Europe', *International Journal of Constitutional Law*, 2009, pp. 364 et seq.

constitution (and constitutionalism) inferred from Article 16 of the Declaration of the Rights of Man and of the Citizen[21] is to pursue the division of powers and the protection of rights, strive for change and address the social forces that lead to a common goal.

The constructivism that seems to accompany modern (continental, at least) constitutionalism seems to be oriented towards the *political sources of law*, which are the conclusive result of a debate where opposing political forces struggle to influence the manifestation of states' wills, represented by the *loi* (*legge*, *ley*, statute).[22] In contrast, cultural sources are inferred from the experience of the past (customs, judicial precedent) or from the rational analysis of legal phenomena (the role of scholars, for example). The *loi* resulting from political sources of law is an act (generally) characterised by abstractness and generality, and in this sense, laws are the product of a rational legislator moved by a clear intent to build coherence, unity and order conceived as τάξις (constructed order). From this perspective, the (second) European Convention gave us the illusion of a strong and constructivist will at a supranational level, which has miserably failed. The consequence of this failure could have been the absence of legitimacy and unity, or, in other words, fragmentation, disorder and obscurity.

In my opinion, all of the abovementioned sceptical theories have a common core: they ignore the possibility that a factual (as opposed to formal) constitution can be the gradual outcome of long-lasting judicial activity that is affected by an evolving cultural background. That is why, according to other scholars,[23] these theories overlook the importance of the rationalising task performed by the judges, and that judicial interactions can be effective in providing pluralistic and multilevel systems with a reliable structure, at least in procedural terms.

As has been said earlier, I think that the dichotomy evolutionism/constructivism might be useful as an approach to reading those years (1992–2010) of constitutional politics at EU level. As, for instance, Peters once wrote, 'the European Constitution was not "given" in a specific constitutional moment by a single authority. There was no single event which created a European Constitution, but only an accumulation of steps of diverse legal character'.[24] The EU has historically followed a pattern of evolutionary constitutionalism, whereas the debate of that period was dominated by (and obsessed with) the idea of giving this process a constructivist flavour, by creating something that could resemble the continental idea of constitution (that is, a revolutionary constitution).

21 Declaration of the Rights of Man and of the Citizen, Article 16: 'A society in which the observance of the law is not assured, nor the separation of powers defined, has no constitution at all'.

22 A. Pizzorusso, 'Fonti politiche e fonti culturali del diritto', in *Studi in onore di T. Liebman*, I, Milan: Giuffrè, 1979, 327 et seq.

23 M. Poiares Maduro, 'Contrapunctual Europe's Constitutional Pluralism in Action', in N. Walker (ed.), *Sovereignty in Transition*, Oxford: Hart, 2003, pp. 501 et seq.

24 A. Peters, 'The Constitutionalisation of the European Union – Without the Constitutional Treaty', in S.P. Riekmann and W. Wessels (eds.), *The Making of a European Constitution: Dynamics and Limits of the Convention Experience*, Wiesbaden: VS Verlag für Sozialwissenschaften/GWV Fachverlage GmbH, 2006, pp. 35 et seq., pp. 51–52.

This leads us to three fundamental questions that have been present throughout the history of constitutional thought: should we consider the constitution as a moment of rupture with the past? Should we consider 'constitution' and 'revolution' as two necessarily connected elements?[25] What is the role for the constituent power? According to many discontents of the EU, it would not be possible to argue for the current existence of an EU Constitution because of the absence of a real constituent power to be read as the direct expression of a fully fledged European general will and *demos*.[26]

The literature on the importance of the constituent power is huge but, limiting this section to what is necessary for the purpose of the book, here I endorse the view according to which the constituent power is a legal-historical *fictio*[27] behind which there is a normative claim. In other words, behind the correspondence between constitution and constituent power there is the necessity to conceive the constitution as the product of the will of a pre-existing political entity (the people). Such a political entity 'serves' as a source of legitimacy for the constitution, helping us to conceive the constitution as the product of a democratic process.[28]

The fiction of the constituent power is necessary in order to justify and legitimise the rupture with the past and the new constitutional design present in the fundamental charter.

Another confirmation of the fact that we are describing a historical-legal *fictio* is given by an argument supported by established scholars: usually, the constitutions and the revolutions behind them (understood in a technical sense, as the break of a chain of validity à la Kelsen[29]) have been a product of the action of élite.[30]

25 G. Ferrara, 'Costituzione e rivoluzione. Riflessioni sul Beruf del costituzionalista', 2010, https://www.costituzionalismo.it/costituzione-e-rivoluzione-riflessioni-sul-beruf-del-costituzionalista/

26 For instance, D. Grimm, 'Does Europe Need a Constitution?' *European Law Journal*, 1995, pp. 282 et seq.

27 'Who is the constituent power and what is its role in the formation of constitutions? Sieye's answer is plain on both counts: the constituent power is the people, who through their representatives create a constitution. This is not a normative claim about the rights of the people or about how constitutions should be created; it is explicitly descriptive of how and why they are formed. When the discourse moves from the descriptive to the normative, it changes and becomes the claim that the constituent power in modern societies should be the people, for democracy is tied to the people and the legitimacy of legal authority depends on a democratic foundation', D.J. Galligan, 'The Paradox of Constitutionalism or the Potential of Constitutional Theory?' *Oxford Journal of Legal Studies*, 2008, pp. 343 et seq., p. 353.

28 Galligan, 'The Paradox', pp. 354 et seq.

29 H. Kelsen, *General Theory of Law and State*, New York: Russell and Russell, 1945, pp. 115–122; H. Kelsen, *The Pure Theory of Law*, Berkeley and Los Angeles: University of California Press, 1970, pp. 208–214. On Kelsen and revolution see: G. Maher, 'Analytical Jurisprudence and Revolution', 1981, http://ru.juridicas.unam.mx/xmlui/handle/123456789/17146

30 'Here we encounter a major concern with the idea of the constituent power: Loughlin and others assume it must be the people. That the people should be responsible for their constitution is now a principle of democratic societies. In reality, the constituent power is not often exercised by the people in any true sense, but instead by a few. The tendency of rulers and their apologists, from the Roman Republic on, to claim to act in the name of the people, is misleading and quite different from the people ruling themselves. Constituent power can be defined as the people; but it is then

If we look closely at the seasons of the European Conventions, we can realise how that period was characterised by the attempt to provide the EU with all the clichés present in the continental idea of a constituent process (a constituent actor, a constituent assembly in charge of writing a document expression of the will of the people and so on). In this respect, it might be useful to recall what Weiler wrote on the lack of a constituent power in the European constitutional process:

> To judge by the renewed popularity of the idea of a Constitution for Europe one might get the impression that right now Europe is in some kind of constitutional desert. And now we have a European Philadelphia busy preparing yet another document in which the word 'constitution' is almost certain to figure. If a formal constitution is to be the European Promised Land, I think I will join Moses and stick to the desert. In this chapter I will explain this preference. The idea of a constitution is presented as indispensably part and parcel of a legitimating reform package of an enlarged Europe. It is not, of course, an original idea and can be traced back at least to Spinelli's Draft Treaty for European Union. Whether one can have a Europe which would respect the current constitutional acquis and embed it in a formal constitution adopted through a European constituent power and, at the same time, not become a federal state in all but name is very doubtful. I think it is a chimera. But the very idea of a formalized constitution requires some serious critical reflection. What appears to be progressive may in fact be regressive. This new fad of a new constitution for Europe may, in fact, be leading us away from the Promised Land into a familiar and boring desert. Put differently, the constitutional discipline which Europe demands of its constitutional actors – the Union itself, the Member States and state organs, European citizens and others – is in most respects indistinguishable from that which you would find in advanced federal states. But there remains one huge difference: Europe's constitutional principles, even if materially similar, are rooted in a framework which is altogether different. In federations, whether American or Australian, German or Canadian, the institutions of a federal state are situated in a constitutional framework which presupposes the existence of a 'constitutional demos', a single pouvoir constituant made up of the citizens of the federation in whose sovereignty, as a constituent power, and by whose supreme authority the specific constitutional arrangement is rooted.[31]

---

a normative stipulation as to what should be the case rather than what is', Galligan, 'The Paradox of Constitutionalism', pp. 354–355.

31 J.H.H. Weiler, 'In Defence of the Status Quo: Europe's Constitutional *Sonderweg*,' in J.H.H. Weiler and M. Wind (eds.), *European Constitutionalism Beyond the State*, Cambridge: Cambridge University Press, 2003, pp. 7 et seq., pp. 7–8.

The obsession with constituent power and the constitutional moment has led to the description of the United Kingdom as the only example in Europe[32] of evolutionary constitutionalism (i.e. not revolutionary). However, actually many other experiences, provided with written constitutions, are in a problematic relationship with the 'constituent power': the German and French case (1958) are two other examples of this problematic trend.[33] Many other EU Member States also do not have a document formally termed 'constitution' (Sweden, the Netherlands). Another example is represented by the Eastern Europe countries, which are characterised by atypical constituent processes that have been influenced by the international community.

Another weakness of this approach – consisting of making this category a fundamental element of any constitutional process – is the fact that it proves too much, since it is always possible, by making an intellectual effort, to find a constituent power that might be traced back to that idea of revolution mentioned previously. In this respect, it is sufficient here to recall the scholarship that conceives the Court of Justice of the EU as the heroic protagonist of that turning point represented by *Van Gend en Loos*[34] and those authors who conceive the Maastricht Treaty as a moment of constitutional rupture.[35]

Obviously, here I do not want to question the importance that this concept has had and will have in the future in the history of constitutional thought, first of all because of the noble nature of that normative claim present behind the idea of constituent power,[36] which is fully consistent with the very nature of constitutionalism understood as a philosophical movement. However, it is important to bear

32 M. Luciani, 'Costituzionalismo irenico e costituzionalismo polemico', 2006,

33 C. Möllers, '"We Are (Afraid of) the People": Constituent Power in German Constitutionalism', in M. Loughlin and N. Walker (eds.), *The Paradox of Constitutionalism Constituent Power and Constitutional Form,* Oxford: Oxford University Press, 2008, pp. 87 et seq.

34 On these theories see: K. Alter, *The European Court's Political Power: Selected Essays*, Oxford: Oxford University Press, 2009, pp. 34–35.

35 In a more nuanced way see J.H.H. Weiler: 'My claim is that the 1992 eruption was preceded by two deeper, and hence far less visible, profound mutations of the very foundational strata of the Community, each taking place in a rather distinct period in the Community's evolution. The importance of these earlier subterranean mutations is both empirical and cognitive. Empirically, the 1992 capsule was both shaped by, and is significant because of, the earlier Community mutations. Cognitively, we cannot understand the 1992 eruption and the potential of its shockwaves without a prior understanding of the deeper mutations that conditioned it', J.H.H. Weiler, 'The Transformation of Europe', *Yale Law Journal*, 1991, pp. 2403 et seq., p. 2407.

36 'The more basic standard suggested by the idea of constituent power relates to the two conceptually separate if institutionally intertwined facets of self-government, or "democracy" broadly conceived. The first relates to the "self" dimension of self-government: it concerns the idea that authority should be duly authorized – that it should possess an authentic democratic pedigree. That is to say, those who are "constituted" as the subjects of constitutional authority should also be its "constituent" authors. The second relates to the governmental dimension: it suggests that, as "government" refers to a wide-ranging and ongoing set of political practices rather than a simple and discrete decision, the realization of a democratically responsive system of government requires more than the affirmation of an appropriate popular pedigree', N. Walker, 'Post-Constituent Constitutionalism? The Case of the European Union', in N. Walker and M. Loughlin (eds.), *The Paradox of Constitutionalism Constituent Power and Constitutional Form*, Oxford: Oxford University Press, 2008, pp. 247 et seq., p. 248.

in mind that it is a fiction that even critics of the Burkean-evolutionary tradition have, despite their words, been forced to renounce, at least in part.[37]

At the EU level, the issue of the constituent power has been treated by Neil Walker,[38] who distinguishes in this respect four possible scenarios:

> Arising from the different combination of answers given to the prior 'why' and 'whether' questions, four basic positions on the issue of EU specific constituent power can be identified. First, it is possible to maintain that constituent power is not a necessary feature of European constitutionalism, or at least that its absence does not significantly diminish European constitutionalism, and therefore that the 'whether' question simply does not arise. The basic hypothesis, which is one of redundancy, may be termed non-constituent constitutionalism. Second, it is possible to hold that constituent power is a necessary or a desirable feature of any constitutional project, that it is not present in the EU context, and neither is it possible to envisage its generation in the future. The basic hypothesis here is one of miscategorization: the attachment of the constitutional label to the European enterprise is a simple 'category error', constitutional scepticism. Third, it might be agreed that constituent power is indeed a necessary or desirable feature of European constitutionalism, whilst claiming, contrary to the constitutional sceptics, that it is already properly identified and more or less fully realized in the emergent constitutional form. This basic hypothesis is that of maturity, framing a position that may be termed constitutional vindication. Finally, it may be claimed (contrary to the redundancy argument) that constituent power remains a necessary feature of European constitutionalism, that (contrary to the maturity thesis) it has not yet been realized, but that (contrary to the sceptics) this constituent power is capable of being developed in the future. The basic hypothesis here is one of constructivism, and the position it frames is post-constituent constitutionalism.[39]

Walker challenged the argument of 'non-constituent constitutionalism' for several reasons: the contradiction with the tradition of the national constitutionalism, its alleged constitutional scepticism and its conception of the EU as a *sui generis* entity that is satisfied with the indirect legitimation of the EU.[40]

37 See, for instance, Ackerman's criticisms addressed to the 'Burkeans' and the answers of the latter to the former in the American debate. B. Ackerman, 'Constitutional Politics/Constitutional Law', *Yale Law Journal*, 1989, pp. 453 et seq., pp. 473 et seq. *Contra* see: E. Moglen, 'The Incomplete Burkean: B. Ackerman's Foundation for Constitutional History', 1993, http://moglen.law.columbia.edu/publications/burkean.ps

38 Walker, 'Post Constituent'.

39 Walker, 'Post Constituent', pp. 251–252.

40 'The common vulnerability of the various species of non-constituent constitutionalism is exposed if we move to the second stage of the redundancy argument: underlying most positions within the horizon of non-constituent constitutionalism is a continued reliance on the indirect pedigree of national constitutional authority and democratic origins', Walker, 'Post Constituent', p. 254.

In replying to these observations, it should be said, first of all, that evolutionary constitutionalism, which renounces the idea of 'constituent power', is not in contrast with the tradition of national constitutionalism. On the contrary, as said, there are many national constitutional traditions that exist in a problematic relation with the notion of constituent power (not only that of the United Kingdom[41]).

Moreover, the classic idea of constituent power has lost many of its 'contours': the role of the international community, in fact, has played a fundamental role in reshaping or shaping many constituent processes in recent decades, and this hardly implies that all the processes can be traced back to the concept of the constituent power as an act of the sovereign people.[42]

Thirdly, what Walker calls 'non-constituent constitutionalism' is not accompanied (necessarily at least) by a constitutional scepticism. This is because many other legal orders that share some similar difficulties to those of the EU can be labelled unequivocally as constitutional, for instance Canada, which has experienced a 'constitutional odyssey',[43] or Switzerland, which has suffered from a semi-permanent constitutional revision.

This does not imply the impossibility of comparing the EU with other legal experiences or the necessity of concluding that the EU does not have a fully fledged constitution. Of course, even the idea of evolutionary constitutionalism

41 Loughlin questions the French origin of the idea of constituent power by tracing back its first expression to the English Leveller movement: 'The concept of constituent power provides the key to unlock the mysteries of modern constitutional arrangements in Britain. Although the concept received its first clear expression by the Levellers in the 1640s, their claims raised a series of fundamental questions that those seeking to manage the unfolding English revolution felt it necessary to repress', M. Loughlin, 'Constituent Power Subverted: From English Constitutional Argument to British Constitutional Practice', in M. Loughlin and N. Walker (eds.), *The Paradox of Constitutionalism Constituent Power and Constitutional Form*, Oxford: Oxford University Press, 2008; M. Loughlin and N. Walker (eds.), *The Paradox of Constitutionalism Constituent Power and Constitutional Form*, Oxford: Oxford University Press, 2008, p. 27 et seq.

42 On this phenomenon see: A. Lollini and F. Palermo, 'Comparative Law and the "Proceduralization" of Constitution-Building Processes', in J. Raue and P. Sutter (eds.), *Facets and Practices of State-Building*, Leiden and Boston MA: Brill/Martinus Nijoff, 2009, pp. 301 et seq.

43 P.H. Russell, *Constitutional Odyssey: Can Canadians Become a Sovereign People*? Toronto: University of Toronto Press, 1992; P.H. Russell, 'The End of Mega Constitutional Politics in Canada?' *PS: Political Science and Politics*, 1993, pp. 33 et seq.; R.S. Kay, 'Book Review Essay: Canada's Constitutional Cul de Sac', *American Review of Canadian Studies*, 2005, pp. 705 et seq.; M. Simpson, *Peter Russell: Constitutional Odyssey: Can Canadians Become a Sovereign People?* 3rd edition, Toronto: University of Toronto Press, 2004', 2006, www.academia.edu/35372457/Book_Review_Peter_Russell_Constitutional_Odyssey_3rd_ed_

As a matter of clarification, it is better to specify what I mean by 'constitutional odyssey'. By this formula, I refer to cases of tension between the 'constitutional form' (i.e. the texts or texts representing the constitutional document in a given legal order) and its constitutional substance (i.e. the set of principles governing the equilibrium between powers in the frame of government and in the form of State – i.e. the relationship between centre and periphery – and the protection of fundamental rights). Canada and Switzerland represent two different examples of constitutional odyssey: while in Canada the tension between the constitutional form and the constitutional substance has produced a long series of failed attempts at amending the constitutional charter, in other cases (the Swiss case is the best example of this) this tension has produced a continuous series of revisions of the formal constitution. On this comparison see: Martinico, 'Constitutional Failure'.

can be criticised, for instance for its ambiguity. In fact, in the English debate two great concepts of evolutionary constitutionalism can be found: the first is the classical concept that can be found in Burke, for instance, and insists on the value of customs and traditions. A second conception can be found in authors like Griffith, for instance, who understands as peculiar to the English legal system the absence of a higher law and the centrality of the ordinary political process[44] following a model that relies on parliamentary sovereignty.[45] Moreover, more recently this alleged absence of a higher law has been questioned by some scholars and even in some judgements of the UK Courts. *Thoburn v. Sunderland*,[46] for instance, demonstrates the existence of a sort of 'higher law', even in the English context or, more famously, the *Miller* judgement[47] and the prorogation judgement[48] of the Supreme Court of the United Kingdom.[49] Finally, in Burke (and Spencer[50]), the idea of evolutionary constitutionalism can be connected to a certain degree of

44 'The constitution of the United Kingdom lives on, changing from day to day, for the constitution is no more and no less than what happens. Everything that happens is constitutional. And if nothing happened, that would be constitutional also', J.A.G. Griffith, 'The Political Constitution', *Modern Law Review*, 1979, pp. 1, p. 19.

45 See the reflections of W. Bagehot on the 'fusion' between the legislative and the executive in the English legal order; *The English Constitution*, Oxford: Oxford University Press, 1867, reprinted in 2001, p. 44. I am indebted to Marco Goldoni for these considerations.

46 Thoburn v. Sunderland City Council [2002] EWHC, 195.

47 R (Miller) v. Secretary of State for Exiting the European Union [2017] UKSC 55

48 R (Miller) v. The Prime Minister and Cherry v. Advocate General for Scotland ([2019] UKSC 41 [2019] UKSC 41.

49 In this judgment, Laws LJ recognised the existence of a constitutional group of statutes and acts that included the European Communities Act 1972:

'In the present state of its maturity the common law has come to recognise that there exist rights which should properly be classified as constitutional or fundamental. We should recognise a hierarchy of Acts of Parliament: as it were "ordinary" statutes and "constitutional" statutes. The two categories must be distinguished on a principled basis. In my opinion a constitutional statute is one which (a) conditions the legal relationship between citizen and State in some general, overarching manner, or (b) enlarges or diminishes the scope of what we would now regard as fundamental constitutional rights. (a) and (b) are of necessity closely related: it is difficult to think of an instance of (a) that is not also an instance of (b)'.

The Magna Charta, the Bill of Rights of 1689, the Acts of Union of 1707, the Reform Acts, the Human Rights Act of 1998, the Scotland Act of 1998, the Government of Wales Act of 1998 and the European Communities Act of 1972 all belong to the category of 'constitutional' statutes. Looking at the judges' reasoning, it is possible to appreciate a further effort to reconcile the primacy of EU law (now vested with constitutional status) with parliamentary sovereignty. According to this judgment, in fact, the EU law's primacy is based on the Parliament's self-limitation; in other words, the legal basis of the UK's relationship with the EU rests on national provisions, not on EU law:

'There is nothing in the [European Communities Act] which allows the Court of Justice, or any other institutions of the EU, to touch or qualify the conditions of Parliament's legislative supremacy in the United Kingdom. Not because the legislature chose not to allow it; because by our law it could not allow it'.

50 For some considerations on the constitutional implications of the thought of these authors see: C. McIlwain, *Constitutionalism: Ancient and Modern*, Clark NJ: The Lawbook Exchange, 2005.

'organicism', while in Hayek the idea of evolution is strongly connected to his concept of liberty and market.[51]

A caveat is necessary: within the scope of this book, the idea of constitutional evolution is not necessarily linked to organicist theses. Something similar can be said with regard to the concept of law employed by Hayek in his works. As recalled by some authors, in the attempt to understand what Hayek meant by his definition of the judge as 'an institution of a spontaneous order',[52] we cannot avoid finding in this definition a sort of mechanical conception of the judicial function, a conception, however, that does not belong to all the universe of evolutionary constitutionalism.

Because of the ambiguity of the evolutionary tradition, in order to read the supranational integration in constitutional terms, some authors have advocated a sort of third way, that of 'constitutional synthesis',[53] which would be in the middle between the evolutionary and the revolutionary understandings of constitutionalism.

51 'The central failure of Hayek's failure, however, lies in his identification of complex systems with systems of liberal content maximizing individual freedom. They both sustain that the function of law is the protection of expectations so that social life can be less complex', G. Vasconcelos Vilaça, 'From Hayek's Spontaneous Orders to Luhmann's Autopoietic Systems', *Studies in Emergent Order*, 2010, pp. 50 et seq., p. 50.

52 'Hayek claims that only a system restricted almost exclusively to rules of just conduct can constitute a spontaneous order. In case of conflict, courts adjudicate the issue by judging the particulars of that case. According to Hayek (1982: I 72, 119), judges would then merely discover the existing law, never creating it. That is why Hayek preferred the common law over the civil law tradition. When adjudicating disputes, judges do not start from a rule posited by the legislator but from experience and tradition, searching to apply such general principles that survived time to potentially unlimited new situations. Ultimately, to Hayek (ibidem: 94), the judge is "an institution of a spontaneous order", precisely because when deciding he simply restores the order that nobody created but persists anyway', Vasconcelos Vilaça, 'From Hayek's Spontaneous Orders to Luhmann's Autopoietic Systems', pp. 57 et seq.

53 'The constitutional law which frames and contributes to steer this process is neither revolutionarily established in a "Philadelphean" constitutional moment, nor the outgrowth or cumulation of "Burkean" constitutional conventions and partial constitutional decisions *à la anglaise*. On the contrary, constitutional synthesis is characterised by the central structuring and legitimising role played by the constitutions of the participating states (seconded to a new role as part of the collective constitutional law of the new polity), or what is the same, by the regulatory ideal of a common constitutional law, which is progressively recognised as the constitution of the new polity, and whose normative consequences are fleshed out and specified as the process goes further. To put it differently, instead of a revolutionary act of constitution making or the slow growth of constitutional conventions, constitutional synthesis is launched by an act which implies the secondment of national constitutions to the role of common constitutional law. This makes synthetic founding much more economical in political resources than revolutionary founding, at the same time that it is much quicker than evolutionary founding', J.E. Fossum and A.J. Menéndez, 'The Theory of Constitutional Synthesis: A Constitutional Theory for a Democratic European Union', *ARENA Working Paper*, 15/2010. 2010, www.sv.uio.no/arena/english/research/publications/arena-working-papers/2019/wp-2-19.pdf. This paper has been included in their book: J.E. Fossum and A.J. Menéndez, *The Constitution's Gift: A Constitutional Theory for a Democratic European Union*, Lanham MD: Rowman and Littlefield, London 2010, pp. 38 et seq.

It is a very fascinating attempt that to my view, however, is based on a misunderstanding. According to Fossum and Menéndez:

> Constitutional synthesis is different from evolutionary constitutionalism in the sense that there is always an agent (be it the legislature or the judiciary) behind the process of fleshing out the concrete implications of the regulatory ideal of a common constitutional law.[54]

However, the figure of the *agent* is not per se excluded by the evolutionary theories; on the contrary, Hayek, for instance, distinguished between 'action' and human 'design',[55] and in regaining this distinction one could argue that only the latter is deeply present in the very idea of constructivism.

According to this scheme, the action and the role of the agent would not be excluded from the constitutional dynamics, but these actions are not performed with the intent of producing a legal change. It is sufficient to think of how usually scholars interested in sources of law explain the origin of customary law that emerges from the repetition of some conducts that are not characterised by the specific intent to produce an *erga omnes* effect[56] but, rather, that can be justified in light of other contingent reasons. Looking at this example, it is possible to find relevance in the distinction between the mere will behind the realisation of a certain conduct and the further intent to produce through that conduct a pattern of action for the other members of the society (and this also explains the insufficiency of mere *diuturnitas*[57] in the genesis of customary law).[58] In light of the

54 'Constitutional conventions may be distinguished in European Community law, but the process of concretisation of solidarity in social security arrangements, or on the protection of fundamental rights is one which has been undertaken, respectively, by the European legislature (with the Council of Ministers having the last legislative word) and by the European Court of Justice', Fossum and Menéndez, 'The Theory of Constitutional Synthesis'.

55 'Spontaneous orders are the result of human action but are not the result of deliberate design (Hayek 1973: 37). Stated another way, a spontaneous order is an unintended consequence of the nonetheless purposeful action of multiple individuals. This is what distinguishes spontaneous orders from what Hayek characterizes as made orders. Made orders, which may also be described as artificial orders, organizations or τάξις are deliberately constructed by an individual or group of individuals. Think a corporation or a marching band. Grown orders or spontaneous orders are different. If an order is like a sentence, then a spontaneous order is like a sentence with no author. It is as if the words, aware of the rules of grammar, arranged themselves into a meaningful structure that conveyed a sentiment that no individual word in the sentence intended to convey. A spontaneous order is a side effect not the goal of individual human action', N.P. Martin and V. Henry Storr, 'On Perverse Emergent', *Studies in Emergent Order*, 2008, pp. 73–91, pp. 76 et seq.

56 A. Pizzorusso, *Fonti del diritto*, Bologna-Roma: Zanichelli-Il Foro italiano, 2011, p. 169.

57 P. Calamandrei, 'Appunti sulla sentenza come fatto giuridico 1932', in *Opere giuridiche*, I, Naples: Morano, 1965, pp. 270 et seq. On this see: A. Pizzorusso, 'La produzione normativa in tempi di globalizzazione', 2008, www.associazionedeicostituzionalisti.it

58 For a different view on this: G. Postema, 'Nature as First Custom: Hayek on the Evolution of Social Rules', 2009, http://papers.ssrn.com/sol3/papers.cfm?abstract_id=1505430

above, I prefer the evolutionary model to understand the supranational integration, considering its nature of a logical (and not historical) category.[59]

A similar conclusion had been reached, some time ago, by Anne Peters, who described the consistency of the European integration with the evolutionary model in the following terms:

> That idea of constitutional evolution is a highly suitable explanation for the legal events on the European level. They may be characterized as 'creeping constitutionalisation' in contrast to 'constitutional engineering'. In terms of political theory, it is an evolutionary, not a revolutionary occurrence: Constitution by evolution. It is difficult to pinpoint a precise moment in which the Union was transformed from a non-constitutional entity into a constitutionalised polity. However, given the density of constitutional features within the body of European law as it stands now, that issue seems less important. The concept of constitutionalisation implies by necessity that this process is a continuing one. The existence of a European Constitution does not rule out that this constitution may be further developed. On the premise that European constitutional law existed before the adoption of the Constitutional Treaty of 2004, that Treaty could in theory have been created in normative discontinuity to the existing law. But the option of 'revolutionary', original, disruptive mode of constitution making was not chosen by the relevant actors. Instead, the Constitutional Treaty came into being by means of legal evolution in normative continuity to the existing law.[60]

The evolutionary understanding of the European Constitution does not exclude the possibility that the core of fundamental principles essential to the functioning of the EU can be further developed, changing it either according to the dynamics followed during the period of the Conventions or through other paths.

Finally, another criticism of the evolutionary reconstruction of the EU's constitutionalisation involves a sort of mathematical argument: since the majority of the national constitutional traditions has not followed the evolutionary constitutional pattern, this would imply the necessity of concluding that the EU (here conceived by these authors as a sort of sum of the national constitutional experiences) cannot

59 D. Chalmers, 'Constituent Power and the Pluralist Ethic', in M. Loughlin and N. Walker (eds.), *The Paradox of Constitutionalism Constituent Power and Constitutional Form*, Oxford: Oxford University Press, 2008; M. Loughlin and N. Walker (eds.), *The Paradox of Constitutionalism Constituent Power and Constitutional Form*, Oxford: Oxford University Press, 2008, pp. 291 et seq., p. 295.

60 Peters, 'The Constitutionalisation of the European Union', p. 47. Peters also wrote that 'the Constitutional Treaty is formally an amendment of the EC and EU Treaties (cf. also Article IV-438 TCE on "succession and legal continuity"). The revision procedure of Article 48 TEU has basically governed this amendment process. So although the Constitutional Treaty does not – legally speaking – constitute a revolutionary break with the preceding European Constitution, it still is in political terms a mile-stone – even without ratification'. I partly disagree, as we will see when dealing with the season of the European Conventions.

be explained through the evolutionary lens.[61] This argument is very weak for various different reasons, but here I will limit myself to the most evident one: the EU, its general principles, its law and policies cannot be seen as a mere sum of the national legal experiences. Arguing the contrary would mean not taking into account the case law of the Court of Justice of the EU[62] and reducing supranationalism to mere intergovernmentalism.[63]

3.3 The discontents of European constitutionalism and their relations with constitutional constructivism

What I would like to do in this section is to present the alternative conception to the evolutionary understanding of the constitutionalisation processes. I am referring to the conception that usually has been considered as the only way possible by both the discontents and the supporters of the season of the Conventions: the constructivist option. According to Fossum and Menéndez:

> In conclusion, what the Laeken process is a clear indicator of (and here is the first constitutional lesson we would like to draw) is the fact that any constitution-making process, even if relying on the democratic legitimacy of national constitutions, cannot proceed according to an exclusive logic of evolutionary constitutionalism. Consequently, any normative model of constitution-making portrays a process of overt and intentional constitutionalisation, which is designed so as to equip the constitution with the necessary democratic legitimacy, which can then be irradiated to the whole legal order, on account of the hierarchical superiority of constitutional norms. In that sense, the model stands in contrast to the processes of evolutionary constitutionalism, where the material constitution emerges through a slow process in which legislative and judicial decisions cumulate over time so as to establish a new legal order, or to actually change the contents of the material constitution.[64]

61 For example, Luciani, 'Costituzionalismo Irenico'.

62 See, for instance, the Opinion of the Advocate General Trstenjak to the Audiolux case C-101/08, *Audiolux*, [2009] ECR I-9823: 'In principle, a distinction can be drawn between general principles of Community law in the narrow sense, namely those which are developed exclusively from the spirit and system of the EC Treaty and relate to specific points of Community law, and those general principles which are common to the legal and constitutional orders of the Member States. Whereas the first category of general principles can be derived directly from primary Community law, the Court essentially uses a critical legal comparison in order to determine the second category, which does not, however, amount to using the lowest common denominator method. Nor is it regarded as necessary for the legal principles developed in this way in their specific expression at Community level always to be present at the same time in all the legal orders under comparison', par. 69.

63 On the idea of supranationalism see: P. Hay, *Federalism and Supranational Organisations*, Urbana and. London: University of Illinois Press, 1966; J.H.H. Weiler, 'The Dual Character of Supranationalism', *Yearbook of European Law*, 1981, pp. 267 et seq.

64 J.E. Fossum and A.J. Menéndez 'Democratic Constitution-Making: Reflections on the European Experiment', *ARENA Working Paper Working Paper*, No. 18/2005, http://econpapers.repec.org/paper/erparenax/p0198.htm

Constructivism and holism emerge from these lines, written by scholars who seem to see in the season of the Conventions the democratic redemption of the EU.

These kinds of reflections can be inferred from the importance of the French Revolution in legal and political history, and this explains why constructivism is frequently associated with the preference for the political sources of law. Political sources of law are the result of an activity purposely aimed at the creation of law, and their acceptance is based on the idea that the law is only the pursuance of the sovereign's will (the king, the people or the parliament), while the idea of cultural sources of law 'responds to the need for rationally determined justice'.[65]

According to this scheme, I will try to show how the latest rounds of constitutional politics in the EU have been characterised by a strong constructivist flavour and that they can be read in continuity with those attempted hijacks of the *acquis communautaire* described in the 1990s by Deirdre Curtin.[66] This representation is shared by those who argue that the EU will fail in its constitutional ambitions for non-contingent but structural reasons (reasons that go beyond the good or bad result achieved by the Conventions). This representation is also the product of a rather questionable idea of constitutionalism, characterised, according to the words of one of the most famous 'pluralists', Nico Krisch,[67] by a holistic flavour that will result in crushing the axiological diversity characterising the postnational law. In Avbelj's words:

> Constitutionalism was believed to be capable of reinforcing the process of integration and making its overall legal as well as socio-political construction stronger . . . . Drawing on the conventional meaning of constitutionalism, its proponents have found it almost perfectly tailored for a desired rupture with the EU's international law past, for ensuring stability, unity and order, based on the rule of law and respect for human rights; for bringing progress in form of an ever closer and deeper integration and, thanks to its normative allure, for mobilizing the member states and their people in favour of the integration's cause. Yet, as we know, the expectations about the integration furthering potentials of constitutionalism, about its capacity to make the integration de facto stronger, have eventually proven to be too high and unrealistic.[68]

65 A. Pizzorusso, *Sistemi giuridici comparati*, Milan: Giuffrè, 1998, pp. 263–264. See also: Pizzorusso, 'Fonti politiche', pp. 327 et seq.

66 D. Curtin, 'The Constitutional Structure of the Union: A Europe of Bits and Pieces', *Common Market Law Review*, 1993, pp. 17 et seq., p. 21.

67 Krisch, *Beyond Constitutionalism*. On this see: G. Martinico, 'Constitutionalism, Resistance, and Openness: Comparative Law Reflections on Constitutionalism in Postnational Governance', *Yearbook of European Law*, 2016, pp. 318 et seq.

68 Avbelj, 'EU Constitutional Swan Song'.

In these lines, constitutionalism is perceived as a guided and constructivist process, revolutionary (because it implies a 'desired rupture' with the past) and aimed at constructing 'order' and 'unity', a conception of order as something closed and impermeable. All these features would be missing in the European context.

All these scholarly positions – the pluralists à la Krisch, even those who conceived the Conventions as a potential moment of reception for the EU – share a common core. They underestimate the rationalising function performed by the tribunals; all these views tend to extract the alleged essence of constitutionalism, looking at that historical and particular experience represented by nation-state constitutionalism. In short, they tend to make a particular historical and legal experience a sort of general and universal pattern that should be applied to the EU.

All these views start from a sort of presumption: the presumption of exclusivity of nation-state constitutionalism. This point has already been challenged by many authors; in this respect, the theory of complexity shares the points made, among others, by Pernice and Maduro, who have tried to present national and European constitutionalism as two complementary elements. This implies that the emergence of EU constitutionalism does not need and will not lead to the exhaustion of nation-state constitutionalism, since these two forms of constitutionalism are both expressions of the very idea of constitutionalism.[69]

According to this scheme, the existence of an EU constitutionalism does not imply incompatibility with and the death of national constitutionalism. Complexity shares this point, the two (or more) levels at stake being fundamental for that constitutional exchange at the heart of the constitutional synallagma.

3.4 The (attempted) hijack of the *acquis communautaire*

In this section of the chapter I shall pay attention, in a first moment, to some recent and less recent attempts to hijack the *acquis communautaire* (the set of Protocols annexed to the Maastricht Treaty, references included in the Charter of Fundamental Rights of the EU – EUCFR – Article 6.3 TEU, Article 4.2 TEU etc.), while, in a second moment, I shall focus on the novelties introduced by the Lisbon Treaty and on the EUCFR and its explanations. This excursus will present Article 4.2 TEU as the 'apex' of a crescendo that started with the introduction of the *Grogan* and *Barber* Protocols in 1992.

In this narrative, a crucial role has been played by the proclamation of the EUCFR, a document containing a number of clauses referring to the necessity of taking into account the 'national laws and practices' in the interpretation of the Charter, insofar as fundamental rights that are also guaranteed at national level are concerned. This is a very heterogeneous group of phenomena and one could

69 Poiares Maduro, 'The Three Claims', pp. 13–14.

wonder what they share. As anticipated, all these 'events' may be seen as attempts to 'hijack' the *acquis communautaire* and share at least a triple intent:

1. First of all, to contain the interpretive 'creativity' of the Court of Justice of the EU (ECJ) – which has been a source *of constitutional disagreement* between the EU and the Member States over the years – by putting a sort of immobilising device on the Court. In this respect, conventionally 1992 is considered as the end of the period of 'benign neglect' described by Eric Stein.[70]
2. At the same time, there has been an attempt to deliver the keys of the European integration process to political actors of the multilevel system by these provisions (therefore the image of the 'hijack' employed by Curtin). In this sense, rather than permitting the EU constitutionalisation to adapt itself through the cultural sources of law (including the ECJ's decisions), it is better to give the political actors the 'control' of the EU integration process. In this respect, 1992 is the beginning of the semi-permanent Treaty revision process described by Bruno de Witte.[71] Let me clarify what I mean by 'delivering the keys' to the political actors in the multilevel legal system, as this is an important issue. Taking into account the 'dual' nature of European integration (today still suspended between 'supranationalism' and 'intergovernmentalism'), two groups of provisions have been introduced since 1992. The first is represented by those provisions aimed at strengthening the position of the 'supranational' actors (I am referring to the progressive empowerment of the European Parliament), which respond to the idea of involving and favouring the supranational nature of the EU integration. Secondly, at the same time, provisions aimed at 'defending' the constitutional structure and the sovereignty of Member States have been included in the new Treaties. This second set of provisions responds to the legacy of the intergovernmental origin of the EU enterprise.
3. All the provisions are, more in general, an attempt to 'domesticate' the EU's constitutionalisation and to 'reduce' the implications of constitutional complexity by trying to create a change of paradigm, by planning a constitutional 'agenda' for the EU (by abandoning the idea of 'order as κόσμος' and employing that of order as τάξις). This is evident especially in the latest rounds of mega-constitutional politics, which tried to give the EU a continental constituent process (I am referring to the rhetorical use of words like 'Convention').

As we will see, these attempts have hardly worked since, contrary to the expectations created, neither the role of the ECJ nor the emergence of new conflicts have decreased over the years.

70 E. Stein, 'Lawyers, Judges and the Making of a Transnational Constitution', *American Journal of International Law*, 1981, pp. 1 et seq.

71 de Witte, 'The Closest Thing', pp. 39 et seq.

The struggle for τάξις

3.5 The Maastricht Treaty as a turning point in the relationship between the ECJ and national governments

All scholars interested in EU law know the famous words by which Eric Stein described the 'golden age' of the ECJ and the preconditions of its judicial activism:

> Tucked away in the fairyland Duchy of Luxembourg and blessed, until recently, with benign neglect by the powers that be and the mass media, the Court of Justice of the European Communities has fashioned a constitutional framework for a federal-type structure in Europe.[72]

The ECJ was thus 'blessed' by the lack of attention of the Member States and thus was able to drive European integration by its interpretive judgements, aided by the lucky alliance with the national judges.[73] This narrative has been relativised by some recent historical and sociological studies, which have benefited from access to the archives of the EU institutions.[74] These are very important studies but the centrality of the ECJ in those years of integration cannot be questioned.

With its judgements, the ECJ played a fundamental role in pushing forward the reasons for integration while the political sources (directives, regulations) were sometimes stopped by the traps of the intergovernmental mechanisms. How can we explain its success? Because the interpretive judgements of the ECJ are flexible sources, more adaptable to the changing aims of 'functionalism' and less 'exposed' to the attention of national governments.

Through its judgements, the ECJ has acted as a 'federator',[75] favouring the emancipation (and autonomy) of EC law from the classical public international law and the emergence of some constitutional issues (like the fundamental rights' protection) in the multilevel arena,[76] following a model of evolutionary

72 Stein, 'Lawyers, Judges and the Making of a Transnational Constitution'.

73 This does not mean that the ECJ was completely free from national pressure in that period. See the comments on the historical decisions of the ECJ in M. Poiares Maduro and L. Azoulai (eds.), *The Past and Future of EU Law: The Classics of EU Law Revisited on the 50th Anniversary of the Rome Treaty*, Oxford: Hart, 2010.

74 A. Cohen and A. Vauchez, 'The Social Construction of Law: The European Court of Justice and its Legal Revolution Revisited', *Annual Review of Law and Social Sciences*, 2011, pp. 417 et seq.; M. Rasmussen, 'The Origins of a Legal Revolution – The Early History of the European Court of Justice', *Journal of European Integration History*, 2008, pp. 77 et seq.

75 D. Starr-Deelen and B. Deelen, 'The European Court of Justice as a Federator', *Publius*, 1996, pp. 81 et seq.

76 I have discussed the polysemy of the word 'constitutionalisation' in EU law elsewhere; see: G. Martinico, 'From the Constitution for Europe to the Reform Treaty: A Literature Survey on European Constitutional Law', *Perspectives on Federalism*, 2009, pp. E-13 et seq.

constitutionalism.[77] Of course, the Luxembourg Court has never acted in a vacuum; on the contrary, the Member States, jealous of their sovereignty or simply worried about their constitutional structure, have always attempted to interfere with the interpretative activity of the ECJ in order to preserve their sphere of autonomy.

Having recalled that, it is curious to note that after 1991 the Court limited itself to operations of 'decisions enforcement' of its previous judicial acquisitions (the primacy,[78] direct effect[79] and *Francovich*[80] doctrines), probably because the Member States had finally started paying greater attention to its work. Member States, aware of the supranational danger posed by the ECJ, attempted to 'block' its legal route (see the conclusions of the summit of Edinburgh, in 1992,[81] for example). Curiously, it was from 1992 that the semi-permanent process of Treaty revisions described by de Witte[82] began giving new energy to the political side of integration and consequently to the political sources of law and political actors. The new importance of such actors and of the political formulas is testified to by the strategy of Conventions introduced with the Charter of Nice experience and by the fundamental rule of proceedings: the vote for consensus.

Before entering the section of the chapter devoted to the history of constitutional politics in the EU, it is necessary to say that in my view all the phenomena taken into account in this section can be read in light of two factors. The first is the 'constructivist' flavour of what Curtin termed the attempted hijack of the *acquis communautaire*, embodied by the attempt at making European integration an order (ταξις, *constructed* order) understood as the product of a political design (constructivism). Secondly, all of these episodes can be understood as a reaction endorsed by the Member States to the ECJ's activism ('ECJ-aversion').

Starting from 1992, the Maastricht Treaty has been described as a turning point in the narrative of European integration:

> However political and legal, especially judicial, developments surrounding the adoption of the Treaty of Maastricht (ToM) caused a significant blow to the vision of integration espoused by the classical constitutional narrative. In 1993 the Treaty of Maastricht introduced the (in)famous three-pillared temple structure of the European Union, consisting of the pre-existing Community pillar and of two, so called, intergovernmental pillars of the EU, namely

77 See: Peters, 'The Constitutionalisation of the European Union'.

78 ECJ, C-6/64, *Costa v. ENEL* [1964] ECR 1141.

79 ECJ, C-26/62, *Van Gend en Loos* [1963] ECR 3.

80 ECJ, Joined Cases C-6/90 and C-9/90, *Andrea Francovich and Others v. Italian Republic* [1991] ECR I-5357.

81 J.H.H. Weiler, 'Journey to an Unknown Destination: A Retrospective and Prospective of the European Court of Justice in the Arena of Political Integration', *Journal of Common Market Studies*, 1993, pp. 417 et seq.

82 de Witte, 'The Closest Thing'.

> the Common Foreign and Security Policy (CFSP) and the Justice and Home Affairs (JHA). Moreover, it introduced a set of protocols and declarations that granted some Member States exemption from the acquis communautaire of the Community pillar.[83]

This set of protocols and declarations was described by Curtin[84] as an attempt to 'hijack' the *acquis communautaire* and, in this jungle of sources of hard and soft law, the *Danish Second Home*, the *Grogan* and the *Barber* Protocols deserve special attention.

The *Danish Second Home* Protocol refers to that set of derogations from the *acquis communautaire* contained in Protocol no. 1 annexed to the Treaty, according to which, 'notwithstanding the provisions of this Treaty, Denmark may maintain the existing legislation on the acquisition of second homes'. This Protocol originates from the fact that Danish legislation prohibited the acquisition of second homes in Denmark by non-Danish people. On this basis Denmark insisted on introducing such a Protocol that, de facto, represented a derogation of the principles of non-discrimination on the basis of nationality, the freedom to provide services and the free movement of capital established by the Treaties. The Protocol also represented a response to the *Cowan*[85] and *Commission v. Greece*[86] judgements given by the ECJ in 1989. In the latter case, the Court had held the 'restrictions applied by a Member State to nationals of other Member States in regard to the acquisition and enjoyment of rights in immovable property are contrary to Articles 48, 52 and 59 of the Treaty'.[87] These judgements were seen as dangerous precedents jeopardising the scope of national sovereignty in this field.

More famous is the *Grogan* Protocol (no. 17), according to which

> nothing in the Treaty on European Union or in the Treaties establishing the European Communities, or in the Treaties or Acts modifying or supplementing those Treaties, shall affect the application in Ireland of Article 40.3.3 of the Constitution of Ireland.

This Protocol originated from the very well-known *Grogan* judgement given in a preliminary ruling mechanism, where the ECJ held that 'medical termination of pregnancy, performed in accordance with the law of the State in which it is carried out, constitutes a service within the meaning of Article 60 of the Treaty'.[88]

83 M. Avbelj, 'Questioning EU Constitutionalism', *German Law Journal*, 2008, pp. 1 et seq., p. 8.

84 Curtin, 'The Constitutional Structure', p. 21.

85 ECJ, C-186/87, *Cowan v. Trésor public* [1989] ECR 195.

86 ECJ, C-305/87, *Commission v. Greece* [1989] ECR 1461.

87 ECJ, C-305/87, *Commission v. Greece* [1989] ECR 1461.

88 The case before the national judge was brought by the Society for the Protection of Unborn Children Ireland Ltd (SPUC) against Stephen Grogan and other people who had distributed information concerning abortion services in other EC States. Among other things, the Irish High Court

This judicial saga induced Ireland to insist on the introduction of Protocol no. 17.[89]

Curtin has duly pointed out the danger of such a Protocol since it potentially gave all the Member States the possibility to obtain a document like this, requiring respect for a particular provision of the national constitution.

> This spectre of a Pandora's box which has been opened is of course profoundly disintegrative and strikes at the heart of the very uniqueness of Community law, as well as the image that has been carefully cultivated since the early 1970s that the Community takes its human rights protection seriously.[90]

Finally, the famous *Barber* Protocol (no. 2) laid down a derogation – not geographically limited this time – to the *acquis communautaire*.

> For the purposes of Article 119 of this Treaty, benefits under occupational social security schemes shall not be considered as remuneration if and in so far as they

---

asked the ECJ whether a 'Member State can prohibit the distribution of specific information about the identity, location and means of communication with a specified clinic or clinics in another Member State where abortions are performed'. After having defined the medical termination of pregnancy as a service, the ECJ said: 'The provision of information on an economic activity is not to be regarded as a provision of services within the meaning of Article 60 of the Treaty where the information is not distributed on behalf of an economic operator but constitutes merely a manifestation of freedom of expression.

As a result, it is not contrary to Community law for a Member State in which medical termination of pregnancy is forbidden to prohibit students associations from distributing information about the identity and location of clinics in another Member State where voluntary termination of pregnancy is lawfully carried out and the means of communicating with those clinics, where the clinics in question have no involvement in the distribution of the said information', ECJ, C-159/90, *Society for the Protection of Unborn Children Ireland (SPUC) v. Grogan and others* [1991] ECR I-4685. In this way, the ECJ attempted to avoid a clash with the national constitution of Ireland.

Later, in a similar case, in order to avoid conflict with the ECJ, the Irish Supreme Court preferred not to take EC law into consideration, arguing that 'apart from the practical time scale difficulties of obtaining a ruling by way of preliminary ruling from the Court of Justice of the European Community, pursuant to Article 177 of the Treaty, in time for the due resolution of the problems arising in this case, it is consistent with the jurisprudence of the Court that there being a ground on which the case can be decided without reference to European law, but under Irish law only, that method should be employed', *The Attorney General (Plaintiff) v. X. and Others* [1992] 1 IR 1. In a previous decision (*S.P.U.C. v. Grogan* [1989] IR 753), the Irish Supreme Court had menaced: 'If and when a decision of the Court of Justice of the European Communities rules that some aspect of European Community law affects the activities of the defendants impugned in this case, the consequence of that decision on these constitutionally guaranteed rights and their protection by the courts will then fall to be considered by these courts'. Clearly, this passage represented a sort of warning sent to the ECJ.

89 Another important decision on abortion was given by the European Court of Human Rights; see Application no. 25579/05, *A, B, C v. Ireland* [2010] ECHR http://cmiskp.echr.coe.int/tkp197/view.asp?action=html&documentId=878721&portal=hbkm&source=externalbydocnumber&table=F69A27FD8FB86142BF01C1166DEA398649

90 Curtin, 'The Constitutional Structure', p. 49.

> are attributable to periods of employment prior to 17 May 1990, except in the case of workers or those claiming under them who have before that date initiated legal proceedings or introduced an equivalent claim under the applicable national law.

By this Protocol, Member States (pushed by the UK and the Netherlands) 'interpreted' in an authoritative way the consequences of the contested judgement of the ECJ in *Barber*,[91] a judgement that had a considerable impact on national legislation. In order to contain the retroactive effects of this decision (exploiting the ambiguity of the ECJ in this respect[92]), the Protocol was approved.

3.6 *Pupino*: a frustrated attempt to limit the interpreter?

As indicated at the beginning of this chapter, these constructivist attempts have rarely worked, and the next example will offer a good illustration of this. More recently, in fact, another attempt to limit the ECJ in its interpretive activity has been frustrated by the Court. One of the other legacies of the Maastricht Treaty was the three-pillar structure: within this system, the first pillar presented a degree of integration that cannot be compared with that present in the other two new pillars, called intergovernmental pillars. In order to 'preserve' the State's sovereignty and contain the judicial activism of the ECJ, Article 34(2)(b) TEU was introduced, according to which

> the Council may . . . (b) adopt framework decisions for the purpose of approximation of the laws and regulations of the Member States. Framework decisions shall be binding upon the Member States as to the result to be achieved but shall leave to the national authorities the choice of form and methods. They shall not entail direct effect.

Since direct effect is, with the principle of primacy, one of the structural principles of EC law, and since it is the most famous outcome of judicial creativity of the ECJ, Article 34 (2)(b) was conceived with the specific intention of limiting the ECJ. However, this effort failed miserably, since in *Pupino* the ECJ, de

91 In this case, the ECJ said that 'it is contrary to Article 119 of the Treaty for a man made compulsorily redundant to be entitled to claim only a deferred pension payable at the normal retirement age when a woman in the same position is entitled to an immediate retirement pension as a result of the application of an age condition that varies according to sex in the same way as is provided for by the national statutory pension scheme. The application of the principle of equal pay must be ensured in respect of each element of remuneration and not only on the basis of a comprehensive assessment of the consideration paid to workers', ECJ, C-262/88, *Douglas Harvey Barber v. Guardian Royal Exchange Assurance Group* [1989] ECR I-01889.

92 The ECJ judgment said that 'the direct effect of Article 119 of the Treaty may not be relied upon in order to claim entitlement to a pension, with effect from a date prior to that of this judgment, except in the case of workers or those claiming under them who have before that date initiated legal proceedings or raised an equivalent claim under the applicable national law', *Barber v. Guardian Royal Exchange Assurance Group*. For the different readings of this passage in the literature on employment law, see Curtin, 'The Constitutional Structure', p. 51.

facto, placed directives (which may be provided with direct effect) and frame-decisions on equal footing.[93] The Court concluded its reasoning by stressing that the principle of consistent interpretation is binding in relation to framework decisions adopted in the context of (at that time) Title VI of the TEU. It pointed out, however, that the obligation on the national court to refer to the content of a framework decision when interpreting the relevant rules of its national law is limited by the general principles of law, especially those of legal certainty and non-retroactivity.

Commenting on *Pupino*, some scholars have spoken of the third pillar's attempted 'supranationalisation' or 'constitutionalisation',[94] while other authors have correctly pointed out that the principle of direct effect has not been extended to the framework decision (as it would have been in contrast with the wording of Article 34 of the TEU). The Court has 'only' extended the duty of consistent interpretation – which is a form of 'indirect' effect[95] – to framework decisions. In other words, as Piqani[96] pointed out, the ECJ performed a sort of scission between direct effect and primacy, in the attempt to avoid a clash with the letter of the EU Treaty. Obviously, the lack of direct effect itself with regard to the framework decisions and the limited jurisdiction of the ECJ – according to Article 35 of the TEU – provided the principle of consistent interpretation with a very peculiar role in this pillar. In any case, what is interesting here is to see how in this way the ECJ anticipated the innovations later introduced by the Reform Treaty – i.e. the extension of some features of EC law to EU law – and announced in the (failed) Constitutional Treaty, confirming itself as a key actor in the European integration process.

93 In the Pupino case, reference was made to the ECJ by the Florence Tribunal in criminal proceedings against Maria Pupino. The ECJ was asked to rule on the following question: 'Are Articles 2, 3 and 8 of Council Framework Decision 220 of 15 March 2001 on the standing of victims in criminal proceedings to be interpreted as precluding national legislation such as that in Articles 392(1a) and 398(5a) of the Italian Code of Criminal Procedure, which do not provide that, in respect of offences other than sexual offences or those with a sexual background, the testimony of witnesses who are minors under 16 may be heard at the stage of the preliminary enquiries, in a Special Inquiry (*incidente probatorio*) and under special arrangements, for example for the recording of testimony using audio-visual and sound recording equipment?' The ECJ held that children could be classified as vulnerable victims, giving them the right to the special out-of-court hearing, stressing, at the same time, that the granting of such a right would have to be considered in light of the system of criminal procedure and that the right to fair trial should not be violated.

94 On this concept: C. Lebeck, 'Sliding Towards Supranationalism? The Constitutional Status of EU Framework Decisions after *Pupino*', *German Law Journal*, 2007, pp. 501.

95 M. Fletcher, 'Extending 'Indirect Effect' to the Third Pillar: The Significance of *Pupino*', *European Law Review*, 2005, pp. 862 et seq.

96 See D. Piqani, 'Supremacy of European Law Revisited: New Developments in the Context of the Treaty Establishing a Constitution for Europe', 2007, www.enelsyn.gr/papers/w4/Paper%20by%20Darinka%20Piqani.pdf. On the relationship between primacy and direct effect, see also M. Claes, *The National Courts' Mandate in the European Constitution*, Oxford: Hart, 2006, 589; E. Spaventa, 'Opening Pandora's Box: Some Reflections on the Constitutional Effects of the Ruling in *Pupino*', *European Constitutional Law Review*, 2007, pp. 5 et seq.

3.7 The season of the conventions and its products

Before analysing the novelties introduced by the Lisbon Treaty, it is better to devote a few lines to the process that led (after the Dutch and French referenda) to the conclusion of the Reform Treaty.

The latest phase of the EU constitutionalisation process has been dominated throughout by the attempt to provide the EU with a constituent process with all the clichés present in the continental tradition (for instance, the idea of a Convention resembling a constituent assembly). In this respect, the EUCFR has represented a turning point. This is not just in terms of contents[97] since it represents a codification of many principles already taken into account by the ECJ in its case law or already codified in other international conventions from which the ECJ has taken inspiration over the years. It is also important for the attention created around the EU among continental European scholars interested in constitutional law (traditionally committed to more domestic themes of investigation) and for the procedure followed in its preparation. The latter is due to the introduction of the so-called conventional method, then adopted even in the draft of the Constitutional Treaty. In this sense, the Convention has represented a rupture in the traditional European 'constitutional politics':

> Legal and political science scholars have for a long time propounded the notion that the EU has a constitution, even though both this notion and its connotations remain disputed. The European constitution resulted from a gradual process of interaction – between primary norms and the case law that interpreted them. The European Court of Justice (ECJ) acted as the leading 'constitutionalizing actor' by extracting constitutional principles from a body of law that also encompassed national constitutions. In parallel, Intergovernmental Conferences (IGCs) were largely treated as episodes of Treaty reform. The intellectual hegemony of 'liberal intergovernmentalism' in the explanation of Treaty changes, and its emphasis on a model of preference aggregation that came closer to the model of normal pluralistic politics (Moravcsik 1991, 1998), had the effect of removing their consideration from the prism of 'constitutional polities'. The Convention on the Future of Europe has subtly modified this landscape. Nominally at least, the Convention has expressed a larger constitutional ambition, the most evident trait of which is the naming of its product a draft constitution.[98]

Another 'rift' caused by the conventional method derives from the language adopted in that particular phase: the decision to name this body 'Convention' made the comparison with the US federalising process evident and recalled the American analogy.

97 See F. Rubio Llorente, 'A Charter of Dubious Utility', *International Journal of Constitutional Law*, 2003, pp. 405 et seq.

98 C. Closa, 'The Convention Method and the Transformation of EU Constitutional Politics', in E.O. Eriksen, J.E. Fossum, and A.J. Menendez (eds.), *Developing a Constitution for Europe*, Abingdon: Routledge, 2004, pp. 184 et seq.

Hoffmann, in his works on the Convention, attempted to summarise the novelties introduced by the conventional method, by reading the activity of the second Convention in light of three features: *socialisation*,[99] *institutional involvement*[100] and *consensus rule*.[101] Other authors, like Karlsson, have insisted on the partial innovativeness introduced by the conventional method, since 'it has not done much to increase the quality of responsiveness and accountability in EU treaty reform. The main problems from a democratic viewpoint are therefore left unresolved'.[102] At the end of this spectrum of views, one could also recall Magnette, who pointed out that:

> Although a number of political leaders described it as the victory of a new 'constitutional doctrine', the Laeken Declaration, which created the Convention and raised a long list of questions its members would have to address, was the result of a classical intergovernmental compromise.[103]

Elsewhere,[104] I tried to read the seasons of Conventions in light of the idea of mega-constitutional politics employed by Peter Russell in the Canadian debate. In his masterpiece *Constitutional Odyssey: Can Canadians Become a Sovereign People?*[105] Peter Russell describes the long striving for the 'patriation'[106] of the

99 'Socialisation took place in and around the Convention and led to changes in government positions because it clarified and emphasised different viewpoints and thereby highlighted the importance of certain issues during the Convention negotiations. Sebenius points out that when there is a "perceived conflict" dynamics in groups come into play that may enable negotiated results because "a powerful norm towards reciprocity operates in most groups". Socialisation in the Convention, especially compared with an IGC, was further reinforced by the group dynamics that developed as a result of different meetings at different levels with often overlapping', L. Hoffmann, 'Wanna Be Starting Something: The Impact of the Convention on the Future of Europe on Member State Positions and the Outcome of the Constitutional Treaty', *TICOM Working Paper*, No. 9/2009, 2009, http://papers.ssrn.com/sol3/papers.cfm?abstract_id=1475217

100 'The Convention membership consisted not only of government representatives but it included members of national parliaments, the European Parliament (MEPs) and the European Commission. So institutional participation led to changes in government positions because it created additional value through an increase in knowledge', Hoffmann, 'Wanna'.

101 'Consensus rule: the fact that the Convention Praesidium determined the Convention outcome by consensus means that the veto power of that member state governments was removed and the power of non-agreement was reduced if not removed. As Tsebelis and Proksch point out, the Convention Praesidium was responsible for the determination of where the consensus in the Convention laid. The lack of voting meant that conventionnels were able to voice their disagreement on individual issues but not to vote them down. The Praesidium also established that the final document was submitted to the Convention as one draft treaty, thereby presenting participants with two options: giving their consent to the document or rejecting it in its entirety', Hoffmann, 'Wanna'.

102 C. Karlsson, 'The Convention Method Revisited: Does It Have a Future and Does It Matter?' *European Law Journal*, 2010, pp. 717 et seq., p. 734. See also: C. Karlsson, 'Deliberation at the European Convention: The Final Verdict', *European Law Journal*, 2008, pp. 604 et seq.

103 P. Magnette, 'In the Name of Simplification: Coping With Constitutional Conflicts in the Convention on the Future of Europe', *European Law Journal*, 2005, pp. 432 et seq.

104 Martinico, 'Constitutional Failure or Constitutional Odyssey?'

105 Russell, *Constitutional Odyssey*; Russell, 'The End of Mega Constitutional Politics in Canada?'.

106 'The word "patriation", a genuine Canadian invention, refers to Canada's final "bringing home" of its constitution from Westminster, with full patriotic fanfare, on 17 April 1982. Although

constitution, the constitutional failures of the Meech Lake and Charlottetown accords and the difficulty of recovering Quebec after the constitutional rupture of 1980. By 'constitutional odyssey', Russell refers to at least two different historical events that can be logically distinguished, although they present themselves as historically connected: firstly, the struggle to 'bring the constitution home' after the formal independence of Canada from the United Kingdom; secondly, the attempt to heal the constitutional rupture with Quebec after the approval of the Constitution Act of 1982, decided without the consent of Quebec and with the support of the Supreme Court of Canada.[107] Although these two events are closely connected, one can understand the first as the logical cause of the second, which produced a series of (failed) attempts at modifying the Constitution and recovering Quebec. The failure of the agreements of Meech Lake (1987) and Charlottetown (1992) – the latter after a 'no' expressed by the people in a national referendum – seems to have slammed the door shut on mega-constitutional politics.

In order to explain the Canadian picture better, Russell devised the distinction between low and mega-constitutional politics:

> Virtually all constitutional democracies are constantly engaged in low level, piecemeal constitutional change, whether through formal constitutional amendments, informal political practice, or judicial interpretation. This is ordinary constitutional politics. Canada's constitutional politics fits this pattern through most of its first century after confederation in 1867. When constitutional politics moves well beyond disputing the merits of specific constitutional proposals and addresses the very nature and principles of the political community on which the constitution is based, it is a horse of a very different color. At this 'mega' level, 'precisely because of the fundamental nature of the issues in dispute-their tendency to touch citizens' sense of identity and self-worth-mega constitutional politics is exceptionally emotional and intense' (Russell 1992, 75). The constitutional question tends to dwarf all other issues in public discussions and media coverage when a country's constitutional politics is at the mega level.[108]

Russell's idea of mega-constitutional politics presents two premises: first, the idea according to which behind the constitution there is a pre-existing social entity: 'That is, it makes no sense to attempt to create a constitution – or a state – for a group

Canada enjoyed sovereignty since at least 1931, it nonetheless continued to depend on requests to the United Kingdom Parliament for making amendments to its constitution. The reason for this anomaly was clear: Canadian governments had proved unable to agree on an internal amending procedure by which legal changes to the constitution could be made at home without having recourse to Britain', D. Milne, entry: 'Patriation of the Constitution – Canada, Constitutional, Quebec, Amendments, Consent, and Governments', 2004, www.oxfordreference.com/view/10.1093/oi/authority.20110803100310612

107 Re: objection by Quebec to resolution to amend the constitution, 1982, 2 SCR, 793, also known as the Quebec Veto Reference.

108 Russell, 'The End of Mega Constitutional Politics in Canada?'.

of people who do not share some minimum commonalities'.[109] The second premise refers to the rise of popular participation in the constitution-making process and to the idea of a constitution as an act of the people, the real sovereign entity. As Russell pointed out, mega-constitutional politics is not exclusive to Canada. It can be found in other legal experiences as well,[110] and that is why some scholars have recovered this distinction and attempted to apply it to the supranational level to describe the different phases of the process of semi-permanent revision of the EU Treaties that started after 1992.[111]

All the scholars interested in this phenomenon have emphasised the new communication strategy adopted by the Convention, the great announcements, the constitutional rhetoric, the publicity, a new symbolism,[112] fostered by the use of words like 'constitution', 'law' and 'minister':

> Although it was the Treaty establishing a Constitution for Europe that first gathered together these basic rules and principles in a treaty-based written constitution, its content was largely a codification (or recodification) of the existing treaties and case law; only a small number of its provisions were actually new. These provisions were partly prompted by dissatisfaction with the functioning of the EU, and were designed to improve it. However, the main difference between the Treaty establishing a Constitution for Europe and the earlier amending treaties, such as the Treaties of Maastricht, Amsterdam and Nice, lay not so much in its content as in the constitutional symbolism that it was meant to convey, with a strong emphasis on democracy and fundamental rights, and hence on European citizenship.[113]

109 Kay, 'Book Review Essay'.

110 'Mega constitutional politics is not peculiar to Canada. The United States knew this kind of politics last in the Civil War. Recently, much of eastern Europe passed through mega constitutional upheavals', Russell, 'The End of Mega Constitutional Politics in Canada?' p. 33.

111 'First, mega constitutional politics goes beyond disputing the merits of specific constitutional proposals and addresses the very nature of the political community on which the constitution is based. Mega constitutional politics, whether directed towards comprehensive constitutional change or not, is concerned with reaching agreement on the identity and fundamental principles of the body politic. The second feature of mega constitutional politics flows from the first. Precisely because of the fundamental nature of the issues in dispute – their tendency to touch citizens' sense of identity and self-worth – mega constitutional politics is exceptionally emotional and intense. When a country's constitutional politics reaches this level, the constitutional question tends to dwarf all other public concerns', J.E. Fossum, 'The Transformation of the Nation-State: Why Compare the EU and Canada?' *ARENA Working Paper*, No. 1/19, 2001, www.sv.uio.no/arena/english/research/publications/arena-working-papers/2001-2010/2002/wp02_28.htm

112 'The main novelty brought in by the Constitutional Treaty, and abandoned by the Lisbon Treaty, was precisely that constitutional symbolism, rhetoric and publicity', G. Itzcovich, 'Closer to the Citizens? European Constitutional Processes, Communication Policy and Publicity', *STALS Research Paper*, No. 6/2009, 2009, www.stals.santannapisa.it/european-politics-and-policies

113 *Raad van State*, opinion on the ICG mandate to revise the EU Treaty and the EC Treaty, 12 September 2007.

The Conventions phase reminds me of the definition of mega-constitutional politics given by Peter Russell in his works, due to its attention to the policy of big announcements, its obsession with involvement and participation (despite its elitist nature).

Mega-constitutional politics presents an emotional grasp; it talks to the soul, to the heart and even to the stomach of the people (conceiving the constitution as the product of a professed *Volksgeist* even in those cases where the existence of such a common culture is problematic and questionable). It presents itself as an identity-based concept. Mega-constitutional politics wants to involve the people; it is obsessed with this idea of popular participation. Why? Mega-constitutional politics aimed at curing a sort of original sin present in Canada's constitutional history: a sort of democratic deficit, consisting of the fact that the first Canadian Constitution was a document approved by a foreign parliament. Mega-constitutional politics attempted to achieve a sort of a posteriori legitimacy that was missing at the beginning of Canadian constitutional history. In order to do so, constitutional politics created another constitutional wound by excluding Quebec, and this created a new round of mega-constitutional politics aimed at curing this wound.

I think similar elements can be found in EU history: the Convention was conceived as an attempt to react to the democratic deficit of the Union, to present the EU as closer to the citizens, by involving them, by creating a common constitutional and rhetorical language (see also the discussion concerning the possibility of identifying some common European roots to be mentioned in the Preamble of the Constitutional Treaty,[114] which triggered a debate on the commonalities of Europeans). Another similitude appears from the end of the latest round of mega-constitutional politics in both the EU and Canada and the role played by the instrument of referendum in this respect. In the following passage, taken from a piece written by Russell, in which he describes the sense of frustration and fatigue of Canadians after the failure of the mega-constitutional political rounds; one could replace the words 'Canadians' or 'Canada' with 'Europeans' and 'European Union', such are the similarities between the two contexts:

> The recent referendum may have demonstrated that Canadians are deeply divided in their sense of identity and political justice but it has, nonetheless, left them united in their constitutional fatigue. There are no politicians of any consequence in post-referendum Canada with any stomach for resuming the effort to fashion a grand constitutional restructuring designed to strengthen national unity . . . . There are still some well-meaning intellectuals and some constitutional junkies who would like to have another kick at that can. But they will find no support from political leaders or the general public.[115]

114 For instance, the long debate on the Christian roots: J.H.H. Weiler, *Un' Europa cristiana. Un saggio esplorativo*, Milan: Rizzoli, 2003.

115 Russell, 'The End of Mega Constitutional Politics in Canada?', p. 36.

Europe seems to be suffering from a similar reaction after the 'referenda rounds' involving both the Constitutional Treaty and the Lisbon Treaty. However, again, this should not be understood as a signal of the impossibility of the constitutionalisation of the EU; rather, it seems to be a problem shared by other constitutional experiences characterised by cultural plurality and diversity.

However, despite these similarities, there are also important differences. While the Canadian attempts to modify the constitution after 1982 have been unsuccessful, since 1992 the European Union has experienced a long series of approved amendments to the original Treaties. In any case, Canada is just one of two examples that can be taken into account in this respect: another pattern of constitutional odyssey might be represented by the Swiss case, where it is possible to count two total revisions of the constitution and many partial revisions.

Dealing with 'roots': guiding the interpreter in a context of multilevel constitutionalism. The charter of fundamental rights of the European Union

3.8 Article 4.2 TEU as the apex of a constitutional crescendo

Bogdandy and Schill[116] described Article 4.2 TEU[117] as one of the most important novelties of the Lisbon Treaty, reading this provision as an exception to primacy provided for under EU law itself.[118] I will attempt to demonstrate the continuity between Article 4 TEU and other provisions of EU law adopted (Article 6.3 TEU) or proclaimed (the EUCFR) even before the Lisbon Treaty.

116 A. Bogdandy and S. Schill, 'Overcoming Absolute Primacy: Respect for National Identity Under the Lisbon Treaty', *Common Market Law*, 2011, pp. 1417 et seq.

117 Article 4 TEU: '1. In accordance with Article 5, competences not conferred upon the Union in the Treaties remain with the Member States. 2. The Union shall respect the equality of Member States before the Treaties as well as their national identities, inherent in their fundamental structures, political and constitutional, inclusive of regional and local self-government. It shall respect their essential State functions, including ensuring the territorial integrity of the State, maintaining law and order and safeguarding national security. In particular, national security remains the sole responsibility of each Member State. 3. Pursuant to the principle of sincere cooperation, the Union and the Member States shall, in full mutual respect, assist each other in carrying out tasks which flow from the Treaties. The Member States shall take any appropriate measure, general or particular, to ensure fulfilment of the obligations arising out of the Treaties or resulting from the acts of the institutions of the Union. The Member States shall facilitate the achievement of the Union's tasks and refrain from any measure which could jeopardise the attainment of the Union's objectives'.

118 'In our view, this (compared to the Maastricht Treaty) revised identity clause can help to reconceptualize the relationship between EU law and domestic constitutional law and guide the way to a more nuanced understanding beyond the categorical positions of the ECJ on the one side, which supports the doctrine of absolute primacy of EU law even over the constitutional law of Member States, and that of most domestic constitutional courts on the other, which largely follow a doctrine of relative primacy in accepting the primacy of EU law subject to certain constitutional limits', A. Bogdandy and S. Schill, 'Overcoming Absolute Primacy'.

In my view, in fact, the substance of these two provisions (Article 4.2 TUE and Article 6.3 TEU) is the same and no material change has occurred. The only relevant change that I can see consists in the 'decoupling' provided in the wording of the TEU between the concept of common constitutional traditions (now Article 6 TEU) and that of national constitutional identity (now codified in Article 4.2 TEU), while in the previous version of the TEU these two concepts were dealt with in the same place, Article 6, at its par. 2 (common constitutional traditions) and par. 3 (national identity) respectively.[119]

What is interesting to note instead – and here I agree with Bogdandy and Schill[120] – is the importance acquired by the principle of sincere cooperation in the wording of Article 4 TEU. Even before such a codification, the ECJ knew this principle well, making it autonomous from the mere internationalist principle of the *pacta*

119 Article 6.2 and 6.3 TEU (pre-Lisbon version): 'The Union shall respect fundamental rights, as guaranteed by the European Convention for the Protection of Human Rights and Fundamental Freedoms signed in Rome on 4 November 1950 and as they result from the constitutional traditions common to the Member States, as general principles of Community law. The Union shall respect the national identities of its Member States'.

As we know, the ECJ has started to show a sort of deferential respect towards the constitutional traditions and structures of the Member States: C-88/03 *Portugal v. Commission (Azores)* [2006] ECR I-7115, especially para. 62–67; C-36/02 *Omega* [2004] ECR I-9609, para. 34–5, 39–41; C-244/06 *Dynamic Medien* [2008] ECR I-505; C-208/09 *Sayn-Wittgenstein*, 2010 I-13693). Normally, these judgements are grouped together with another series of cases (C-112/00, *Schmidberger* [2003] ECR I-5659, for instance) since all these decisions would represent the leading cases of the (alleged) margin of appreciation doctrine of the ECJ. At a closer look, however, it is possible to distinguish two groups of cases, which the literature too often describes as amenable to the same argumentative model:

In this respect Article 4.2 TEU does not say anything new but limits itself to reflect this distinction.

1. In a first group of cases (like *Schmidberger*) the ECJ identified a constitutional tradition that is considered as 'common' to several Members.
2. In a second group of cases (*Omega, Dynamic Medien, Sayn Wittgenstein*), instead, the ECJ was confronted with a constitutional principle specific to a single legal system.

Arguably, only in the first scenario is the Court required to do some proper balancing. In these cases, indeed, the Court needs to balance two principles or sources belonging to the same legal order (the idea behind that is that national and supranational law share a zone where they overlap, in which the two terms of the balancing are situated). This is not the case in the second group of cases, because the ECJ cannot strike a balance between two norms that are exogenous with respect to each other (the principle of EU law and the norm deriving from the national legal order).

This reminds us of those cases of international private law where there is a national norm (the norm of collision, in this case Article 4 TEU) referring to another legal system, therefore implicating the retreat of the EU law from a zone that is to be regulated by 'foreign' law (in this case, domestic law).

Other scholars, like Pollicino (O. Pollicino, 'Strasbourg and Luxembourg at the forefront of the Enlargement of Europe: An Antithetical Judicial Approach?', in F. Fontanelli and G. Martinico (eds.), *The ECJ Under Siege*, Hyderabad: ICFAI University Press, 2009, p. 109), use the idea of 'margin of appreciation' in order to describe the national constitutional sensitivity of the ECJ, but they tend to extend the idea of the margin of appreciation even to the first group of cases (*Schmidberger*), while in my view we should limit this concept to the second group of cases.

120 Bogdandy and Schill, 'Overcoming Absolute Primacy'.

sunt servanda.[121] The ECJ recalled this principle for referring to different obligations: to give full implementation and application to the EU law,[122] to provide information to the Commission[123] and to avoid adopting measures in contrast with the EU acts coming into force.[124] The ECJ stressed its binding nature for all the Members State bodies, including national judges,[125] and, of course, for all the European institutions.[126]

Of course, this principle was already present in the wording of Article 10 TEC, but in that case the provision focused much more on the duty of loyalty of the States, while according to this new text the duty of loyalty is bilateral, involving the necessity to respect the national identities 'inherent in their fundamental structures, political and constitutional, inclusive of regional and local self-government'.[127]

As suggested elsewhere,[128] the chemistry represented by the principle of sincere cooperation and the respect for national identity might give new blood to some procedural principles traditionally neglected by the ECJ, first of all, the principle of subsidiarity. As suggested by Bogdandy and Schill, this article could 'guide the way to a more nuanced understanding beyond the categorical positions of the ECJ on the one side . . . and that of most domestic constitutional courts'. The argument presented by the authors is based on the pluralistic spirit of Article 4 TEU (which would codify the pluralistic structure and nature of EU law) and on the importance of judicial cooperation and loyalty (favoured by the second part of Article 4):

> Under such a pluralistic understanding, the answer to the question of who has the ultimate power to decide on issues of national identity is that there is no definitive answer as there is no final arbiter in a composite system of European constitutional adjudication. The ensuing potential for conflict is tamed by the mutual duty to Cooperate.[129]

As anticipated, in my view this provision as the apex of a 'crescendo', in natural continuity with the progressive 'constitutionalisation' of the EU, a process through

121 See G. Ferraiuolo, 'Leale collaborazione: un principio costituzionale supremo?' in S. Staiano (ed.), *Giurisprudenza costituzionale e principi fondamentali. Alla ricerca del nucleo duro delle costituzioni*, Turin: Giappichelli, 2006, pp. 691 et seq., p. 718.

122 ECJ, C-71/76 *Thieffry v. Council de l'ordre des avocats de la Cour de Paris* [1977] ECR 765; C-54/81 *Fromme v. BALM* [1982] ECR 449; C-68/81 *Commission v. Greece* [1989] ECR 2965.

123 ECJ, C-30/90 *Commission v. United Kingdom* [1992] ECR I-829; C-82/03 *Commission v. Italy*, [2004] ECR I-6635.

124 ECJ, *Commission v. United Kingdom* [1981] ECR 1045.

125 ECJ, C-94/00 *Roquette Frères* [2002] ECR I-9011; C-344/98 *Masterfoods and HB* [2000] ECR I-11369.

126 ECJ, C-99/02 *Commission v. Italy* [2004] ECR I-3353; C-344/01 *Germany v. Commission* [2004] ECR I-2081.

127 Article 4.2 TEU.

128 G. Martinico, 'Dating Cinderella: On Subsidiarity as a Political Safeguard of Federalism in the European Union', *European Public Law*, 2011, pp. 649.

129 Bogdandy and Schill, 'Overcoming Absolute Primacy', p. 1452.

which the EU over the years has partly overcome its purely economic nature, becoming something more, a union based on fundamental rights as acknowledged in the national constitutions.

This provision should be read as the confirmation of a long process that started after *Solange I*, a direct product of the dialectic existing between the national Constitutional Courts and the ECJ. The rapprochement between the national and the supranational legal orders is confirmed by the structural continuity between common constitutional traditions and counter-limits.[130] From a theoretical point of view, in fact, counter-limits are related to the input of the Community legal materials in the domestic legal order. The common constitutional traditions, instead, are related to the input of domestic legal materials in the European legal order. Apparently, they both follow opposite routes and are inspired by different rationales: the former by the rationale of integration, the latter by the rationale of constitutional diversification. However, as stressed by Ruggeri,[131] thanks to the hermeneutical channel represented by the preliminary ruling, the constitutional principles of the domestic legal orders arise from their origin (national level) and become common sources of EU law. These common constitutional traditions then return to their origin in a new form when they are applied by the ECJ.[132]

This progressive 'Europeanisation' of national fundamental principles can be seen – as, among others, von Bogdandy and Schill argue – as another limit to the primacy of EU law, as scholars have stressed, reading together Articles I-5 (Article 4 TEU after the Reform Treaty of Lisbon) and I-6 of the Constitutional Treaty (absent in the Reform Treaty of Lisbon). In Article 4 TEU, in fact, we can find the proof of the 'Europeanisation' of the counter-limits theory as a result of the judicial dialogue between Constitutional Courts and the ECJ. Before proceeding further, it is worth remembering that this is only one of the possible readings of this clause. Indeed, scholars have clarified the genesis of Article 4.2 TEU by exploring the *travaux préparatoires* of the second Convention and emphasising similarities and differences with Article I-5 of the Treaty establishing a Constitution for Europe. In her seminal article, Guastaferro stressed the importance of the so-called Christophersen clause:[133]

> Indeed, the current formulation of the identity clause stems from the works of the European Convention drafting the Treaty establishing a Constitution

130 On the role played by the German Constitutional Court see: M. Gonzáles Pascual, *Il tribunal constitucional alemán en la construcción del espacio europeo de los derechos*, Madrid: Civitas, 2010.

131 Ruggeri, 'Tradizioni costituzionali comuni', p. 102.

132 Emblematically, the ECJ held in *Omega*: 'The Court draws inspiration from the constitutional traditions common to the Member States and from the guidelines supplied by international treaties for the protection of human rights on which the Member States have collaborated or to which they are signatories', ECJ, C-36/02, *Omega* [2004] ECR I-9609.

133 'The "Christophersen clause" was envisaged in the first paragraph of Article I-5 of the Constitutional Treaty, devoted to the "Relations between the Union and the Member States". The second paragraph enshrined the principle of sincere cooperation, according to which the Union and the Member States shall, in full mutual respect, assist each other in carrying out the tasks of

> for Europe. In particular, the clause was conceived within working group V on 'complementary competence', which was explicitly set up to avoid the interferences between functional and sectorial competences (ie between competences based on aims and competences based on fields).[134]

She also clarified that originally the identity clause was understood as provision about competences,[135] or said, in other words, it 'was conceived as an instrument to undermine the creeping encroachment of EU powers upon sensitive areas related to national identity and sovereignty'.[136] These considerations are very helpful in contextualising Article 4.2 TEU and confirm the need for a systematic reading of this clause. Indeed, the fact that Article I-5 preceded Article I-6 – the codification of the primacy clause – has been recalled by Claes to question Bogdandy and Schill's reading of the clause and to avoid the use of Article 4.2 TEU.[137]

These considerations also help us understand the relationship between the national identity and what the provision calls the 'essential state functions'. In other words, the genesis of this provision shows that 'essentially, the drafters

---

the Constitutions. Article I-5(1), of the Constitutional Treaty stated: The union shall respect the equality of Member States before the constitution as well as their national identities, inherent in their fundamental structures, political and constitutional, inclusive of regional and local self-government. It shall respect their essential State functions, including ensuring the territorial integrity of the State, maintaining law and order and safeguarding national security', B. Guastaferro, 'Beyond the Exceptionalism of Constitutional Conflict: The Ordinary Functions of the Identity Clause', *Yearbook of European Law*, 2012, pp. 263 et seq., p. 285. See also M. Claes, 'National Identity: Trump Card or Up for Negotiation?', in A. Saiz Arnaiz and C. Alcoberro Llivina (eds.), *National Constitutional Identity and European Integration*, Antwerp: Intersentia 2013, pp. 109 et seq., p. 121: 'In comparison to the version of the Constitutional Treaty, the only change to the wording of the provision – other than that "the Constitution" has been reworded to "the Treaties" – is the addition of the final sentence concerning national security, which does not seem to add much to the preceding sentence. Yet, wording aside, what has also changed is the context: the primacy provision in the next clause has been deleted from the corpus of the Treaty and has been downgraded to a Declaration to the Treaty. While this may not decisively change the meaning of the identity clause taken on its own, the fact that the obligation imposed on the EU to respect national identities is no longer counterbalanced by the statement of primacy, does affect its stature', Claes, 'National Identity', p. 121

134 Guastaferro, 'Beyond the Exceptionalism', p. 264.

135 See also, Claes, 'National Identity', p. 119.

136 Guastaferro, 'Beyond', p. 286.

137 'Nevertheless, while Article I-5 (with the general aim of containing the competence creep and carving out a space for the Member States on which the EU was not to tread) and Article I-6 are part of this same basket and Article I-5 may have been aimed to counterbalance the primacy principle, this should not lead one to construe the national identities provision as providing a legal exception to the primacy clause. Once EU law has been validly adopted (and accordingly also based on a solid legal basis and within the competences transferred), Article I-5 does not allow for exceptions. Rather, Article I-5 was intended to help delineate the space if the EU and therefore concerns the conditions under which the EU can validly exercise its competences. Logically and legally, therefore, Article I-5 was antecedent to Article I-6 and refers to the scope of the primacy clause, more precisely to the specification in that provision that primacy applies only to 'the Constitution and law adopted by the institutions of the Union in exercising competences conferred on it', Claes, 'National Identity', at p. 119.

sought to carve out core areas of national sovereignty, as no list of Member States' exclusive powers was eventually included in the Treaties'.[138]

Here we have two main approaches to Article 4.2 TEU. While constitutional lawyers[139] have been influenced by the case law of the German Constitutional Courts, EU lawyers[140] have taken a different road by privileging an autonomous reading of Article 4.2 TEU. This distinction has huge implications on the role that Constitutional Courts should have in the interpretation of national identity.

For those who insist on the thesis according to which the other goods mentioned in Article 4.2 TEU would be emanations of national identity, Article 4.2 TEU seems to create a 'concentric circle system', where different levels of 'untouchability' of national sovereignty are indicated. In this sense, we know that essential state functions include 'ensuring the territorial integrity of the State, maintaining law and order and safeguarding national security'.[141] Within this circle, a hard nucleus, represented by national security, is identified in order to clarify that it 'remains the sole responsibility of each Member State'.[142]

My point here is that this provision does not represent a complete innovation: the model of Article 4 TEU is undoubtedly represented by Article 6 TEU (pre-Lisbon version), which efficaciously described the closeness between common constitutional traditions and national constitutional principles. As we saw, in that provision these two kinds of legal sources (common constitutional traditions[143] and national constitutional principles) were mentioned in two subsequent paragraphs, as we saw at the beginning of this chapter.

Looking at the pre-Lisbon version of Article 6, it suffices to recall the reference made in Article 6.2 to the common constitutional traditions, and the reference to the 'national identities' of its Member States in Article 6.3. It is possible to argue that, within a legal context, by the formula 'national identities', the relevant domestic players tend to mean the constitutional identities of the Member States, that is the counter-limits, as defined by national Constitutional Courts. By adopting this approach (which is, again, only one of the possible readings of this clause), in this sense one can say that Article 4 of the TEU has just expressly codified such an interpretation by referring to 'constitutional structure'.

138 Claes, 'National Identity', p. 119.

139 M. González Pascual, 'Criminal Law as an Essential Function of the State: Last Line of Resistance?' in A. Saiz Arnaiz and C. Alcoberro Llivina (eds.), *National Constitutional Identity and European Integration*, Antwerp: Intersentia, 2013, pp. 159 et seq.

140 F.X. Millet, *L'Union européenne et l'identité constitutionnelle des États membres*, Paris: LGDJ 2013, p. 153.

141 Article 4.2 TEU.

142 Article 4.2 TEU.

143 About the common constitutional traditions as sources of EC law, see: A. Pizzorusso, 'Common Constitutional Traditions in Europe as a Source of Community Law', *STALS Research Paper*, No. 1/2008, 2008, www.stals.santannapisa.it/sites/default/files/stals_Pizzorusso_0.pdf

However, contrary to what von Bogdandy and Schill[144] argue, in my view neither Article 4 TEU nor its predecessors or successors will (automatically at least) produce a more cooperative season. According to von Bogdandy and Schill:

> Also as regards procedure, Article 4(2) TEU indicates a path to overcome the hierarchical model. Although the ECJ has jurisdiction over the interpretation of Article 4(2) TEU, and thus determines the relevance under EU law of domestic constitutional law from an EU law perspective, its interpretation must be coordinated with the interpretations by national constitutional courts and their constitutional limits to protect national identity. At the same time, domestic constitutional courts have to exercise these powers in light of their European responsibility.[145]

I disagree, as in my view these *prima facie* open provisions could increase rather than decrease the risk of conflicts in the multilevel system. I shall deal with this in the chapter devoted to constitutional conflicts when describing the paradox of EU constitutionalisation, i.e. the fact that the progressive attention paid by the EU to the fundamental rights has created new causes of conflict rather than extinguishing them.

In fact, the product of this convergence gave birth to new kinds of conflicts among interpreters, conflicts due to the existence of legal sources (the principles concerning the protection fundamental rights) that are now shared by the ECJ and the national Constitutional Courts: such a scenario has produced dynamics of interpretive competition, as we will see in Chapter 5. It is sufficient to look at Article 4.2 TEU for confirmation of this: who is in charge of defining what belongs to the idea of national identity or constitutional structure of Member States? National Constitutional Courts or the ECJ?[146]

Similar considerations apply to other open provisions (i.e. provisions referring to national law in the interpretation of EU law) present in the recent product of EU constitutional politics. We will see the results produced by such a clause, and here again I am more sceptical than von Bogdandy and Schill. Here it suffices to recall the *Lissabon Urteil*,[147] in which the German Constitutional Court specified

144 Bogdandy and Schill, 'Overcoming Absolute Primacy', pp. 1418 et seq.

145 Bogdandy and Schill, 'Overcoming Absolute Primacy', pp. 1452 et seq.

146 See A. Ruggeri, 'Trattato costituzionale, europeizzazione dei "controlimiti" e tecniche di risoluzione delle antinomie tra diritto comunitario e diritto interno (profili problematici)', 2005, www.forumcostituzionale.it. See also: M. Kumm, 'The Jurisprudence of Constitutional Conflict: Constitutional Supremacy in Europe before and after the Constitutional Treaty', *European Law Journal*, 2005, pp. 262 et seq.

147 'European unification on the basis of a union of sovereign states under the Treaties may, however, not be realised in such a way that the Member States do not retain sufficient space for the political formation of the economic, cultural and social circumstances of life. This applies in particular to areas which shape the citizens' circumstances of life, in particular the private space of their own responsibility and of political and social security, which is protected by the fundamental rights, and to political decisions that particularly depend on previous understanding as regards culture,

the sensitive sectors that embody the national constitutional identity. In doing so, the German Constitutional Court made an important contribution to the definition of Article 4 of the TEU, in its problematic concept of 'national identity'. However, one can easily see the risk of proceeding in this way, namely, interpretive anarchy, a context in which each Constitutional Court can express its own view on the notion of constitutional identity while pretending to participate in a 'pluralist' interpretation.

This episode and the relevant case law (see Chapter 5) in my view confirm the risks present in a clause like Article 4.2 TEU.[148]

3.9 The Charter of Fundamental Rights of the EU

Returning to the issue of the legal clauses aimed at guiding the ECJ in interpretation, it is not a coincidence that all the products of the recent European constitutionalism are characterised by the presence of such provisions. When looking at the EUCFR (which has become binding thanks to the coming into force of the Lisbon Treaty), one can notice the several clauses of the Charter referring to 'national laws and practices' that have been introduced in order to avoid a breach of any of the national constitutions and, in this respect, these clauses should be read together with the new Article 4 TEU (previously Article 6 TEU). See, for instance, Articles 9[149] ('right to marry and right to found a family'), 10.2[150] ('freedom of thought, conscience and religion'), 14.3[151] ('right to education'), 27[152] ('workers'

history and language and which unfold in discourses in the space of a political public that is organised by party politics and Parliament. Essential areas of democratic formative action comprise, inter alia, citizenship, the civil and the military monopoly on the use of force, revenue and expenditure including external financing and all elements of encroachment that are decisive for the realisation of fundamental rights, above all as regards intensive encroachments on fundamental rights such as the deprivation of liberty in the administration of criminal law or the placement in an institution. These important areas also include cultural issues such as the disposition of language, the shaping of circumstances concerning the family and education, the ordering of the freedom of opinion, of the press and of association and the dealing with the profession of faith or ideology', *BVerfG*, cases 2 BvE 2/08, par. 249.

148 More recently, see the decision of the Czech Constitutional Court in C-399/09, which did not have to do with constitutional identity but demonstrates the permanent risks of conflicts even after the entry into force of Article 4.2 TEU.

149 EUCFR, Article 9: 'The right to marry and the right to found a family shall be guaranteed in accordance with the national laws governing the exercise of these rights'.

150 EUCFR, Article 10, 2: 'The right to conscientious objection is recognised, in accordance with the national laws governing the exercise of this right'.

151 EUCFR, Article 14, 3: 'The freedom to found educational establishments with due respect for democratic principles and the right of parents to ensure the education and teaching of their children in conformity with their religious, philosophical and pedagogical convictions shall be respected, in accordance with the national laws governing the exercise of such freedom and right'.

152 EUCFR: Article 27: 'Workers or their representatives must, at the appropriate levels, be guaranteed information and consultation in good time in the cases and under the conditions provided for by Union law and national laws and practices'.

rights to information and consultation within the undertaking'), 28[153] ('right of collective bargaining and action'), 30[154] ('protection in the event of unjustified dismissal') and 34–36 ('social security and social assistance', 'health care' and 'access to services of general economic interest').[155]

Title IV, devoted to 'Solidarity', is particularly rich in such references and perhaps that is no coincidence, since in this field the EUCFR is more innovative than in other cases (with the exceptions of the title devoted to 'Citizens' rights', for obvious reasons) compared with the ECHR.

However, these clauses represent just one of the strategies adopted to limit the efficacy of the Charter and avert the danger of a US-style 'incorporation' through the Bill of Rights.[156] Other evidence of this is the (in)famous Polish and UK 'opt out' (although it does not represent an 'opt out' properly speaking[157]). This is consistent with that constructivist trend recalled earlier, since it confirms the attempt to 'dominate' and plan the evolution of EU law and guide the activity of the judicial interpreter.

153 EUCFR, Article 28: 'Workers and employers, or their respective organisations, have, in accordance with Union law and national laws and practices, the right to negotiate and conclude collective agreements at the appropriate levels and, in cases of conflicts of interest, to take collective action to defend their interests, including strike action'.

154 EUCFR, Article 30: 'Every worker has the right to protection against unjustified dismissal, in accordance with Union law and national laws and practices'.

155 EUCFR. Article 34: '1. The Union recognises and respects the entitlement to social security benefits and social services providing protection in cases such as maternity, illness, industrial accidents, dependency or old age, and in the case of loss of employment, in accordance with the rules laid down by Union law and national laws and practices.

2. Everyone residing and moving legally within the European Union is entitled to social security benefits and social advantages in accordance with Union law and national laws and practices.

3. In order to combat social exclusion and poverty, the Union recognises and respects the right to social and housing assistance so as to ensure a decent existence for all those who lack sufficient resources, in accordance with the rules laid down by Union law and national laws and practices'.

EUCFR, Article 35: 'Everyone has the right of access to preventive health care and the right to benefit from medical treatment under the conditions established by national laws and practices. A high level of human health protection shall be ensured in the definition and implementation of all the Union's policies and activities'.

EUCFR, Article 36: 'The Union recognises and respects access to services of general economic interest as provided for in national laws and practices, in accordance with the Treaties, in order to promote the social and territorial cohesion of the Union'.

156 On these fears soon after the proclamation of the Charter see: P. Eeckhout, 'The EU Charter of Fundamental Rights and the Federal Question', *Common Market Law Review*, 2002, pp. 945 et seq.

157 'The opt-out is not an opt-out at all', C. Barnard, 'The "Opt-Out" for the UK and Poland From the Charter of Fundamental Rights: Triumph of Rhetoric Over Reality?', paper presented at the Conference 'The Lisbon Treaty and the Future of European Constitutionalism', 11–12 April 2008, EUI, Fiesole. Confirmation of this hypothesis could be found in the words of the House of Lords EU Select Committee: 'The Protocol is not an opt-out from the Charter. The Charter will apply in the UK, even if its interpretation may be affected by the terms of the Protocol. The Preamble itself of the document does not use the qualification in terms of opt-out, its goal consists of the clarification of certain aspects of the application of the Charter,' House of Lords EU Select Committee, 'The Treaty of Lisbon: An Impact Assessment'.

In order to escape the risk of being subject to such provisions, the UK and Poland insisted on signing a specific Protocol (no. 30) stating that:

1. The charter does not extend the ability of the Court of Justice of the European Union, or any court or tribunal of Poland or of the United Kingdom, to find that the laws, regulations or administrative provisions, practices or action of Poland or of the United Kingdom are inconsistent with the fundamental rights, freedoms and principles that it reaffirms.
2. In particular, and for the avoidance of doubt, nothing in Title IV of the charter creates justiciable rights applicable to Poland or the United Kingdom except in so far as Poland or the United Kingdom has provided for such rights in its national law.

It has been said, rightly, that the goal of this Protocol consisted in limiting the effect of the Charter without saying – and it would have been impossible under Article 6 of the TEU[158] – that it was not binding on the UK and Poland. How is it possible to limit the ECJ and the national judges – the most efficient allies of the Luxembourg Court, thanks to the preliminary ruling mechanism? The ECJ is the master of the principle of direct effect (a precondition of the disapplication of national acts inconsistent with EU law). Admitting the possibility to derogate from the interpretive monopoly of the ECJ (codified by Article 344 of the Treaty on the Functioning of the European Union, TFEU) would imply contesting the autonomy of EU law. Moreover, since in many parts the Charter repeats pre-existing principles, the ECJ or the national judges could refer to such principles, obtaining the same result without need to recall the formal text of the Charter.

Another textual confirmation of the possibility of reading Protocol No. 30 together with the mentioned clauses of the Charter referring to national law and practices is given by Article 2 of the Protocol, according to which

> to the extent that a provision of the Charter refers to national laws and practices, it shall only apply to Poland or the United Kingdom to the extent that the rights or principles that it contains are recognized in the law or practices of Poland or of the United Kingdom.

The ECJ clarified its view on this Protocol in the *NS* judgement, by confirming that Protocol No. 30 'does not call into question the applicability of the Charter in the United Kingdom or in Poland'.[159]

158 As we know, in fact, Article 6 TEU states: 'The Union recognises the rights, freedoms and principles set out in the Charter of Fundamental Rights of the European Union of 7 December 2000, as adapted at Strasbourg, on 12 December 2007, which shall have the same legal value as the Treaties'.

159 ECJ, C-411/10 *NS & Others v. SSHD* and C-493/10 *M.E. and Others v. Refugee Applications Commissioner, Minister for Justice, Equality and Law Reform*, [2011] ECR I-13905: 'In those circumstances, Article 1(1) of Protocol (No 30) explains Article 51 of the Charter with regard to the scope thereof and does not intend to exempt the Republic of Poland or the United Kingdom

The clearest example of the attempt to limit the jurisdiction of the ECJ and to guide constitutional interpretation in the EU, however, is given by the explanations to the EUCFR. The Charter refers to them on two occasions in the Preamble:

> In this context the Charter will be interpreted by the courts of the Union and the Member States with due regard to the explanations prepared under the authority of the Praesidium of the Convention which drafted the Charter and updated under the responsibility of the Praesidium of the European Convention.

In this sense, another relevant provision is Article 52 (7) of the Charter, reading that 'the explanations drawn up as a way of providing guidance in the interpretation of this Charter shall be given due regard by the courts of the Union and of the Member States'.[160] The mention of the explanations in the Preamble was introduced under pressure from the UK[161] and was immediately by criticised scholars[162] and by some of the former members of the first Convention.[163]

Concerning the reference contained in Article 52 of the Charter, as explained by Mr Vitorino, Chairman of Working Group II 'Incorporation of the Charter/ Accession to the ECHR' within the second Convention, it was the result of a compromise. On the one hand, the introduction of such a reference made it possible to overcome the British resistance; on the other hand, it does not give binding effect to the explanations. As Sciarabba pointed out, the content of these explanations is partial, incomplete and repetitive. In some cases, they consist of the mere repetition of the sources mentioned[164] with particular attention to the provisions of the ECHR (and the case law of the ECtHR).

Such attention to the ECHR can be explained as an attempt to coordinate the action of the two European Courts, since the future accession of the EU to the ECHR is required by Article 6.2[165] TEU after the coming into force of the Lisbon Treaty (see Chapter 1). But, at the same time, it is also a clear attempt to acknowledge the leadership in the field of fundamental rights to a court, the ECtHR, which

from the obligation to comply with the provisions of the Charter or to prevent a court of one of those Member States from ensuring compliance with those provisions' (par. 116–120).

160 On this, see V. Sciarabba, 'Le "spiegazioni" della Carta dei diritti fondamentali dell'Unione', *Diritto pubblico comparato ed europeo*, 2005, pp. 59 et seq.

161 On the British pressure and the 'Goldsmith plan', named after Lord Goldsmith, who proposed to divide the Charter into two parts, a first part characterised by a 'political' nature and non-binding from a legal point of view, and a second part that was legally binding, see Sciarabba, 'Le "spiegazioni" ', pp. 65–66.

162 Sciarabba, 'Le "spiegazioni" ', p. 62.

163 See E. Paciotti, 'Introduzione' in E. Paciotti (ed.) *La Costituzione europea. Luci e ombre*, Rome: Meltemi, 2003, pp. 12 et seq.

164 See the explanations of Articles 2, 4, 5, 6, 7, 9, 10, 11, 12, 14, 17, 47, 48, 49, 50 and 54 of the Charter in V. Sciarabba, 'Le "spiegazioni" della Carta dei diritti fondamentali dell'Unione', p. 67

165 Article 6.2 TEU: 'The Union shall accede to the European Convention for the Protection of Human Rights and Fundamental Freedoms. Such accession shall not affect the Union's competences as defined in the Treaties'.

has been historically more *respectful* of national sovereignty, with its well-known doctrine of margin of appreciation (although in the last few years some exceptions to this judicial trend have been introduced[166]). In this field, a key provision is Article 52.3 of the EUCFR:

> In so far as this Charter contains rights which correspond to rights guaranteed by the Convention for the Protection of Human Rights and Fundamental Freedoms, the meaning and scope of those rights shall be the same as those laid down by the said Convention. This provision shall not prevent Union law providing more extensive protection.

Scholars have wondered whether Article 52.3 makes the ECHR a minimum standard and whether Article 52 makes the ECtHR's case law binding. What is impressive in the explanations given for Article 52 is the enumeration of two lists of rights: the former containing the 'articles of the Charter where both the meaning and the scope are the same as the corresponding Articles of the ECHR',[167] and the latter the 'articles where the meaning is the same as the corresponding Articles of the ECHR, but where the scope is wider'.[168]

These kinds of lists seem to strengthen the idea according to which the reference to such explanations was introduced in order to limit the interpretive autonomy of the ECJ and in order to make the ECtHR the top of the European judicial 'hierarchy' in the area of rights. However, in the same explanations of Article 52.3, reference is made to the necessity of preserving the interpretive autonomy of the ECJ.[169] I will come back to this provision when discussing the well-known *Melloni* case,[170] which partly reshaped the meaning of the provision.

Thus, the destiny of the explanations is strongly related to the burning issue of the accession of the EU to the ECHR, which is supposed to clarify the

166 See W. Sadurski, 'Partnering With Strasbourg: Constitutionalisation of the European Court of Human Rights, the Accession of Central and East European States to the Council of Europe, and the Idea of Pilot Judgments', *Human Rights Law Review*, 2009, pp. 397 et seq.; Pollicino, 'Strasbourg and Luxembourg'.

167 'Articles of the Charter where both the meaning and the scope are the same as the corresponding Articles of the ECHR', https://fra.europa.eu/en/eu-charter/article/52-scope-and-interpretation-rights-and-principles

168 'Articles where the meaning is the same as the corresponding Articles of the ECHR, but where the scope is wider', https://fra.europa.eu/en/eu-charter/article/52-scope-and-interpretation-rights-and-principles

169 'Paragraph 3 is intended to ensure the necessary consistency between the Charter and the ECHR by establishing the principle that, insofar as the rights in the present Charter also correspond to rights guaranteed by the ECHR, the meaning and scope of those rights, including authorised limitations, are the same as those laid down by the ECHR. This means in particular that the legislator, in laying down limitations to those rights, must comply with the same standards as are fixed by the detailed limitation arrangements laid down in the ECHR without thereby adversely affecting the autonomy of Community law and of that of the Court of Justice of the European Communities'. https://fra.europa.eu/en/eu-charter/article/52-scope-and-interpretation-rights-and-principles

170 ECJ, C-399/11, *Melloni*, EU:C:2013:107.

relationship existing between the Strasbourg and Luxembourg Courts,[171] as we saw in Chapter 1.

The use of the case law of the ECtHR by the ECJ could be indicative of the openness of the latter court towards the former. In this sense, it seems interesting to mention the *McB* case, in which the ECJ interpreted Article 51 of the Charter in a very restrictive way, by showing great deference towards the Member States' legislation and competences.[172] This seemed to confirm the interpretation of Article 52 of the Charter, according to which the ECHR should be conceived as a minimum standard,[173] and, in doing so, the ECJ recalled the case law of the ECtHR on this matter at points 56 et seq. of the judgement. The same attention was given by the ECJ in the *Volker* case,[174] where the ECJ declared two provisions of an EU regulation conflicting with the Charter of Nice[175] to be invalid.

Returning to the main subject of this section, one can see how the explanations of the Charter were made binding – to a certain extent at least – in the attempt (once again) to hijack European integration by limiting the activism of the ECJ.

A similarly complicated picture could be noticed with regard to the relationship between the ECJ and the Constitutional Courts. The *Honeywell* case[176] seemed

171 On this see S. Douglas-Scott, 'A Tale of Two Courts: Luxembourg, Strasbourg and the Growing European Human Rights *Acquis*', *Common Market Law Review*, 2006, pp. 629 et seq. See also K. Kuhnert, '*Bosphorus*: Double Standards in European Human Rights Protection?' *Utrecht Law Review*, 2006, pp. 177 et seq., ECtHR, application No. 45036/98, *Bosphorus Hava v. Ireland*, https://www.eui.eu/Documents/DepartmentsCentres/AcademyofEuropeanLaw/CourseMaterialsHR/HR2009/DeWet/DeWetBackgroundReadingCase3.pdf

172 ECJ, C-400/10 PPU, *McB*. [2010] ECR I-08965: 'First, according to Article 51(1) of the Charter, its provisions are addressed to the Member States only when they are implementing European Union law. Under Article 51(2), the Charter does not extend the field of application of European Union law beyond the powers of the Union, and it does not 'establish any new power or task for the Union, or modify powers and tasks as defined in the Treaties'. Accordingly, the Court is called upon to interpret, in the light of the Charter, the law of the European Union within the limits of the powers conferred on it.

'It follows that, in the context of this case, the Charter should be taken into consideration solely for the purposes of interpreting Regulation No. 2201/2003, and there should be no assessment of national law as such. More specifically, the question is whether the provisions of the Charter preclude the interpretation of that regulation set out in paragraph 44 of this judgment, taking into account, in particular, the reference to national law which that interpretation involves', pp. 51–52.

173 'It follows from Article 52(3) of the Charter that, in so far as the Charter contains rights which correspond to rights guaranteed by the ECHR, their meaning and scope are to be the same as those laid down by the ECHR. However, that provision does not preclude the grant of wider protection by European Union law. Under Article 7 of the Charter, 'everyone has the right to respect for his or her private and family life, home and communications'. The wording of Article 8(1) of the ECHR is identical to that of the said Article 7, except that it uses the expression 'correspondence' instead of 'communications'. That being so, it is clear that the said Article 7 contains rights corresponding to those guaranteed by Article 8(1) of the ECHR. Article 7 of the Charter must therefore be given the same meaning and the same scope as Article 8(1) of the ECHR, as interpreted by the case law of the European Court of Human Rights (see, by analogy, Case C-450/06 Varec [2008] ECR I-581, paragraph 48)', C-400/10 PPU, *McB*.

174 ECJ, C-92/09 and C-93/09, *Volker und Markus Schecke* and *Eifert*, [2010] ECR I-11063.

175 ECJ, C-92/09 and C-93/09, *Volker und Markus Schecke* and *Eifert*, [2010] ECR I-11063.

176 2 BvR 2661/06.

to imply the overcoming of the post-*Mangold* tension between the German Constitutional Court and the ECJ after the bad signals given out with the *Lissabon Urteil.*[177] We will see later that these signals have recently produced concrete and very problematic frictions between the German Constitutional Court and the ECJ. Moreover, some Constitutional Courts have accepted the use of the preliminary ruling mechanism governed by Article 267 of the TFEU, but this does not imply the end of all the problems between Constitutional Courts and the ECJ, as cases such as *Filipiak*[178] and the *Winner Wetten*[179] show. In this respect, it is useful to recall Article 52.4 of the EUCFR, according to which 'in so far as this Charter recognizes fundamental rights as they result from the constitutional traditions common to the Member States, those rights shall be interpreted in harmony with those traditions'. I will come back to this point in the following chapters, especially in Chapter 5.

3.10 Final remarks

In this chapter I have offered a reflection upon some selected examples of Member States' interference in the interpretative activity of the ECJ, by conceiving them as attempts at giving a constructivist flavour to the EU constitutionalisation process: the set of Protocols and Declarations introduced by the Maastricht Treaty, Article 34 of the TEU, all the provisions referring to national laws and practices included in the EU Charter of Fundamental Rights, the explanations to the Charter and, finally, Article 4 of the TEU after the coming into force of the Lisbon Treaty.

Such interference might appear pathological in a properly functioning constitutional system, but actually it is possible to find analogies in many other constitutional cases.[180] The European Union is unique in this, and these interactions between the judicial and political powers confirm the non-mechanical nature of the interpretative dynamics (the judge is not the *bouche de la loi*) and the 'collective' nature of interpretation understood as an enterprise involving all the actors operating in a constitutional system. This creates disagreement, contestation and even conflicts, but it would be wrong to conceive of these conflicts as pathological. On the contrary, conflicts are natural and fundamental in the constitutional dynamics of any political entity and the EU does not deviate from this trend. The main difference from the US experience[181] is probably the vertical trajectory of

177 *BVerfG*, cases 2 BvE 2/08 cit, at par. 249.

178 ECJ, C-314/08, *Filipiak* [2009] ECR I-11049.

179 ECJ, C-409/06, *Winner Wetten* [2010] I-08015.

180 On the importance of the comparative approach in European studies, see R. Dehousse, 'Comparing National and EC Law: The Problem of Level of Analysis', *American Journal of Comparative Law*, 1994, pp. 761 et seq.

181 D. Halberstam, 'Constitutional Heterarchy: The Centrality of Conflict in the European Union and the United States', in J. Dunoff and J. Trachtman (eds.), *Ruling the World? Constitutionalism, International Law and Global Governance*, Cambridge: Cambridge University Press, 2009, pp. 326 et seq., also http://papers.ssrn.com/sol3/papers.cfm?abstract_id=1147769

these conflicts, involving national governments and the ECJ, rather than the ECJ and the other supranational bodies. However, this is understandable as the product of a different degree of integration or as a different stage of a federalising process. The analysis of the cases cited here demonstrates how these attempts to interfere with the ECJ's activity have hardly worked.

Finally, I have sought to demonstrate how this set of clauses will not produce (necessarily at least) a more cooperative season; on the contrary, conflicts will remain crucial in the development of EU law. We will see whether the complex mechanisms will achieve their purpose, but in any case, very much will depend on the interaction with the other judges operating at national and international level (i.e. national Supreme/Constitutional Courts and the ECtHR), especially with regard to the application of the clauses included in the EUCFR. In this respect, once again, the European Union will continue to suffer from its democratic deficit, since the vague nature of those provisions that are supposed to be crucial (see Article 52 of the EUCFR) in the end seems to confirm the great importance of the judiciary in the multilevel system.

4 The multiple crises of the European Union (2011–2021)

4.1 An existential crisis

Over the last years, the EU, as has been said, has encountered a series of multiple crises[1] that have also had an impact on the dialectic between constructivism and evolutionism in the process of European integration.

These crises have challenged the constitutional ambitions of the EU. In the final chapter of the first edition of this book, I had identified some elements that had to be taken into account as a potential engine of new constitutional conflicts. They were the impact of the anti-crisis measures taken by the EU and its Member States: the accession of the EU to the ECHR and threat to the EU values and the rule of law crisis. Unfortunately for the EU, all the hypotheses were confirmed by the latest developments.

Since it is not possible here to analyse all aspects of this multifaceted crisis, for the purpose of this chapter I will choose the economic crisis that exploded after 2008 as the perspective of analysis.

The importance of this perspective can be explained as follows:

1 The financial crisis has opened a season of evident decline for European mega-constitutional politics. The need to deal with contingent emergencies has led to the end of grand designs for reform (with the exception, perhaps, of Macron's vision[2]) and the emergence of a managerial approach aimed at responding in a timely manner to urgent issues.
2 It has produced a policy of austerity that has led to much criticism, causing further blame on the European Union.
3 It has made evident the limits of an – unfortunately still weak – inter-state solidarity that also exploded in the migration crisis.[3]

1 A. Menéndez, 'The Existential Crisis of the European Union', *German Law Journal*, 2013, pp. 453 et seq., p. 453.

2 See the recent launch of the Conference on the Future of Europe, https://futureu.europa.eu/

3 'Editorial Comments: From Eurocrisis to Asylum and Migration Crisis: Some Legal and Institutional Considerations About the EU's Current Struggles', *Common Market Law Review*, 2015, pp. 1437 et seq.

DOI: 10.4324/9781003056522-4

4 It confirmed the existence of a different British political agenda, which did not agree to sign the Fiscal Compact. As is well known, this difference of views (among other things) later led to Brexit.[4]
5 It fostered the emergence of sovereigntist populisms that have ended up challenging the values of the Union as set out in Article 2 TEU.
6 It marked a revival of intergovernmental dynamics and, according to some, a constitutional mutation of the Union.

Indeed, the constitutional ambitions of the EU have suffered a severe blow with the economic crisis, which has led many scholars to argue for a radical change in the structure of the European order. There is no need to recall all the debate on the genesis of the crisis as the literature on this is huge[5] and the facts are very well known. In this chapter I will instead look at how scholars interested in EU constitutional law have interpreted the series of events that has put the EU in troubled waters.

As Maduro pointed out, it is possible to identify two different 'narratives'[6] of the economic crisis: those who accuse the EU of having major responsibility for the crisis and those who blame Member States. The second strand seems to insist more on the role of the States whose irresponsible fiscal policies would have amplified the crisis.[7] According to the first group, the fault of the EU instead would consist of not having been able to correct some flaws present in the European economic architecture since 1992 (the year of the Maastricht Treaty). This economic architecture has been conceived as based on four main pillars: 1) coordination of economic policy-making between Member States; 2) coordination of fiscal policies, notably through limits on government debt and deficit; 3) a

4 On Brexit, see the multi-volume work edited by Fabbrini: F. Fabbrini, *The Law & Politics of Brexit*, Oxford: Oxford University Press, 2017; F. Fabbrini, *The Law & Politics of Brexit: Volume II, The Withdrawal Agreement*, Oxford: Oxford University Press, 2020; F. Fabbrini, *The Law & Politics of Brexit: Volume III, The Framework of New EU-UK Relations*, Oxford: Oxford University Press, 2021.

5 From a legal point of view see: X. Contiades, *Constitutions in the Global Financial Crisis: A Comparative Analysis*, Farnham: Ashgate, 2013; G. Cooper, *The Origin of Financial Crises*, New York: Vintage Books, 2008; R.M. Lastra and J.V. Louis, 'European Economic and Monetary Union: History, Trends, and Prospects', *Yearbook of European Law*, 2013, pp. 57 et seq.; K. Tuori, 'The European Financial Crisis – Constitutional Aspects and Implications', *EUI Working Papers LAW*, No. 2012/28, 2012, cadmus.eui.eu/handle/1814/24301

6 'The European Union is not only experiencing these crises, but is significantly responsible for the crises in the first place. The transformation of the institutional structure of the Union and the substantive policy choices made in the last three decades have fostered the very structural weaknesses that were turned into crises by the subprime crisis. In particular, it seems to me that the self-standing and disembedded understanding of economic freedoms, as expressions of the right to individualistic private autonomy and the creation of an asymmetric economic and monetary union, played a major role in destabilizing the Union', A. Menéndez, 'The Existential Crisis of the European Union', *German Law Journal*, 2013, pp. 453 et seq., p. 453.

7 On these two narratives see: M. Poiares Maduro, 'A New Governance for the European Union and the Euro: Democracy and Justice', *RSCAS Working Paper 2012*, https://papers.ssrn.com/sol3/papers.cfm?abstract_id=2180248

centralised monetary policy with a European Central Bank (ECB)[8] and 4) the creation of a single currency (euro).[9] Especially the persistent asymmetry between the monetary union (centralised) and the economic union (based on a mere coordination of national economic policies), the incomplete (if compared to a fully fledged federal Central Bank) mandate of the European Central Bank,[10] the limited budget of the EU and the uncertainty surrounding budgetary policies in the Union together with the weaknesses of the Stability and Growth Pact[11] have been indicated among the main anomalies of the system.[12] All these defects emerged with the explosion of the Greek crisis.[13] The Greek crisis triggered an escalation of measures that began with a Council Decision dated 10 May 2010[14] and was then followed by a series of more structured but still incremental interventions.[15]

At the beginning of March 2012, 25 European leaders signed the new Treaty on Stability, Coordination and Governance in the Economic and Monetary Union – TSCG – which represents just one of the links in a longer chain of measures adopted to fight the EU crisis. I am referring to the creation of the European Financial Stability Facility (EFSF), the European Financial Stabilisation Mechanism (EFSM), the Euro Plus Pact, the amendment of Article 136 of the TFEU, the European Stability Mechanism (ESM) and the so-called six and two packs,[16] among others.[17]

8 On the role of the ECB in the crisis see: P. Doely, 'The European Central Bank's Securities Markets Programme: Why a Necessary Response to the European Debt Crisis Should Come to an End', *Minnesota Journal of International Law*, 2013, pp. 214 et seq.; W. Buiter and W. Rahbari, 'The European Central Bank as Lender of Last Resort for Sovereigns in the Eurozone', *The Journal of Common Market Studies Annual Review of the European Union in 2011*, 2012, pp. 6 et seq.

9 C. Degryse, 'The New European Economic Governance', *Working Paper European Trade Union Institute*, No. 2012/14, 2012, www.etui.org/Publications2/Working-Papers/The-new-European-economic-governance

10 On the asymmetry between the economic and monetary policies see: M. Draghi, 'The Future of the Euro: Stability Through Change', *Die Zeit*, 29 August 2012, www.ecb.europa.eu/press/key/date/2012/html/sp120829.en.html. See also the more recent interesting perspectives offered by the so-called Banking Union: Council Regulation (EU) No 1024/2013 of 15 October 2013, 'conferring specific tasks on the European Central Bank concerning policies relating to the prudential supervision of credit institutions'.

11 On these see J.V. Louis, 'The Review of the Stability and Growth Pact', *Common Market Law Review*, 2006, 85 et seq.

12 See now P. Krugman, *End This Depression Now!* New York: W. W. Norton & Co Inc., 2012 especially chapter 10.

13 J.V. Louis, 'The Unexpected Revision of the Lisbon Treaty and the Establishment of a European Stability Mechanism', in D. Ashiagbor, N. Countouris, and I. Lianos (eds.), *The European Union After the Treaty of Lisbon*, Cambridge: Cambridge University Press, 2012, pp. 284 et seq.

14 Council Decision (2010/320/EU) of 10 May 2010.

15 M. Ruffert, 'The European Debt Crisis and European Union Law', *Common Market Law Review*, 2011, pp. 1777 et seq.; V. Paliouras, 'Why Europe Should Say No to the Proposed Framework of Economic Governance: A Legal and Policy Analysis in Light of the Establishment of the European Stability Mechanism and the Euro Plus Pact', 2011, papers.ssrn.com/sol3/papers.cfm?abstract_id=1908435

16 The so-called six pack is composed of five Regulations (Regulations n. 1173/2011, n. 1174/2011, 1175/2011, 1176/2011 and 1177/2011) and one Directive (Directive n. 2011/85). The two pack is composed of the following regulations: Regulation n. 472/2013 and 473/2013.

17 On this 'jungle' of measures see: G. Bianco, 'The New Financial Stability Mechanisms and Their (Poor) Consistency with EU Law', *EUI RSCAS Working Paper*, No. 2012/44, 2012, http://cadmus.eui.eu/handle/1814/23428

With all these measures, the EU has intended to deal with very different aspects of the crisis, trying to achieve a new integrated surveillance system for budgetary and economic policies and a new budgetary timeline. It insists on the establishment of clearer rules and of better coordination of national policies. This system has been provided with swifter sanctions.

All these measures run in parallel. Some of them are part of the EU legal order (e.g. six pack, two pack), some of them are external to it, some of them are interdependent (in some aspects, the six pack and the TSCG), some of them are not (for instance, quite roughly, while the Euro Plus Pact is more about competitiveness, the TSCG is more about austerity). This explains why some Member States participate in some of these actions without necessarily being part of the others.

The contents of all these measures have been extensively analysed by scholars,[18] and the aim of this chapter is not to offer a mere description of them. Rather, I shall explore a common element emerging from this scenario, namely the asymmetrical feature of the new European economic governance.

Within the new European economic governance, the asymmetric dimension of the EU has been amplified by two main factors: first of all, because of the instruments employed since some of the measures recently introduced have been adopted out of the EU law frame, namely via the conclusion of international agreements. This factor has permitted the creation of a set of rules shared by a group of the EU Member States in the form of a public international law treaty.

As Bruno de Witte has pointed out, this 'turn to international treaties' is not new, as even in other cases this path has been followed.[19]

The first reaction to this trend may be to interpret it as a return to intergovernmentalism and as a loss in terms of supranationalism. But, as Fabbrini pointed out, the use of differentiated agreements among members of a union is known even

18 See for instance the contributions included in B. de Witte, A. Heritier and A. Trechsel (eds.), *The Euro Crisis and the State of European Democracy: Contributions From the 2012 EUDO Dissemination Conference*, Florence: European University Institute, 2013.

19 'And yet, what happened then, and what happened later when the ESM Treaty and the Fiscal Compact were concluded by groups of Member States, seems less shocking when seen within a broader evolutionary perspective of European law. In fact, there are numerous earlier examples of international treaties concluded between groups of member states of the EU. They have concluded, ever since the 1950s, agreements in areas such as tax law, environmental protection, defence, culture and education. The most prominent example of an inter se agreement (that is: an agreement between some but not all the EU member states) was the Schengen cooperation regime, composed of a first Agreement signed in 1985, and an implementing Convention adopted in 1990. The Schengen instruments were expressly designed as interim arrangements in preparation of a final regime at the level of the European Community, rather than as a rival co-operation regime. The same was true for the Social Policy Agreement concluded, as a separate part of the Maastricht Final Act, between 11 of the then 12 member states; and for the Prüm Convention later on. In the course of the evolution of European integration, the importance of international agreements between the EU member states has declined', B. de Witte, 'Using International Law in the Euro Crisis Causes and Consequences', *ARENA Working Paper*, No. 4/2013, 2013, www.sv.uio.no/arena/english/research/publications/arena-publications/workingpapers/working-papers2013/wp4-13.pdf (last visited 21 August 2013).

in federal experiences.[20] The second main source of asymmetry in this context is connected to the contents of these measures. I shall thus turn to this subject and deal with some of the provisions included in these acts, with particular attention paid to the TSCG.

The TSCG was the solution chosen to challenge the crisis after evaluating a list of alternatives, first of all the revision of the EU Treaties, i.e. the TFEU and the TEU. Another option considered was the use of enhanced cooperation as regulated under the EU Treaties.[21] This path was suggested by some leading scholars as a way to overcome many of the EU's difficulties,[22] and still today if one takes a closer look at the draft of the TSCG, it is possible to see that the use of enhanced cooperation techniques is advocated therein (Article 10 TSCG). Two of these options (enhanced cooperation and the plan then endorsed by the political actors) present an asymmetrical nature. As mentioned, this is not the first time in which the international law instruments have been employed to face a supranational issue, even in the field of European economic governance.[23] However, scholars do not see a common strategy behind this trend; rather, this path was chosen because of the flexibility that it can offer:[24]

> Basically, in the case of the EFSF and of the ESM, EU law did not offer any suitable instruments because of the insufficiency of the EU's financial

20 'As the comparative analysis makes clear, also the US Constitution is endowed with an instrument – the "compact clause" – which allows states to pursue flexible and differentiated action within the American Union. Yet, the comparison reveals that this instrument is not subject to a specific finality and has consequently been utilized in the US for a wide variety of purposes having to do generally with interstate adjustments. In the EU context, instead, it emerges that the function of the enhanced cooperation is essentially circumscribed to ensuring multispeed integration in the EU. The identification of a clear pro-integrationist ratio in the structure of the enhanced cooperation mechanism, however, has important implications, both for the kind of cooperation that can be launched by the states and for the role of the EU institutions in policing the constraints that surround its use', F. Fabbrini, 'The Enhanced Cooperation Procedure: A Study in Multispeed Integration', *CSF Research Paper*, 2012, http://nuovo.csfederalismo.it/en/publications/research-papers/998-the-enhanced-cooperation-procedure-a-study-in-multispeed-integration-2

21 This is not an exhaustive list; authors like Beukers, for instance, identified a more complex scenario but these two options are still topical, partly at least, as the last provisions of the TSCG seem to confirm. T. Beukers, 'The Eurozone Crisis and the Legitimacy of differentiated Integration', in B. de Witte, A. Heritier and A. Trechsel (eds.), *The Euro Crisis and the State of European Democracy: Contributions from the 2012 EUDO Dissemination Conference*, Florence: European University Institute, 2013, pp. 7 et seq.

22 J.C. Piris, 'It is Time for the Euro Area to Develop Further Closer Cooperation Among its Members', *Jean Monnet Working Paper*, No. 5/2011, 2011, https://jeanmonnetprogram.org/paper/it-is-time-for-the-euro-area-to-develop-further-closer-cooperation-among-its-members/

23 For instance, the Treaty Establishing the European Stability Mechanism was signed by the Member States of the Eurozone to create the European Stability Mechanism (ESM), http://europa.eu/rapid/press-release_DOC-12-3_en.htm

24 'Separate international agreements, which do not involve an amendment of the TEU and TFEU, can define alternative requirements for their entry into force. Not only can such agreements be concluded between less than all the EU states, but they can also provide for their entry into force

> resources, a problem that can be remedied only in the long run, but not in the immediate context of the unfolding euro crisis. As for the Fiscal Compact, one could say that the states accidentally stumbled into the conclusion of a separate international agreement, for a mix of reasons including the rigidity of the TFEU amendment process, the belief (especially on the German side) in the symbolic power of a treaty, and also – admittedly – the wish to avoid going through the cumbersome and lengthy procedures of EU legislation.[25]

The TSCG is peculiar for many reasons, the most evident being the fact that it intervenes in a situation already dominated by asymmetry, adding another pattern of differentiation. For instance, besides the already existing asymmetry between Euro and non-Euro members, this second group will be differentiated, from now on, between those who signed the new Treaty and those who did not.

For instance, building on Rossi's work,[26] it is possible to argue that the TSCG has created a system characterised by various concentric circles:

- A first circle is represented by those EU Member States of the Eurozone that have ratified the TSCG (at least 'twelve Contracting Parties whose currency is the euro', according to Article 14 TSCG[27]).
- A second group is given by those States that do not belong to the Eurozone but that have ratified the TSCG.[28]
- A third circle includes those States that do not participate in the Euro Plus Pact but have ratified the TSCG.[29]

It is clear from this scenario that the TSCG is going to amplify the variable-geometry Union, emphasising the asymmetric feature of the EU economic governance.

---

even if not all the signatories are able to ratify. The Fiscal Compact offers a spectacular example of this flexibility in that it provided that the treaty would enter into force if ratified by merely 12 of the 25 signatory states, provided that those 12 are all part of the euro area. The fact that the authors of the Fiscal Compact moved decidedly away from the condition of universal ratification for its entry into force has created a 'ratification game' which is very different from that applying to amendment of the European treaties, where the rule of unanimous ratification gives a strong veto position to each individual country', de Witte, 'Using International'.

25 de Witte, 'Using International'.

26 L.S. Rossi, 'Fiscal Compact e conseguenze dell'integrazione differenziata nell'Ue', in G. Bonvicini and F. Brugnoli (eds.), *Il Fiscal Compact*, Rome: Edizioni Nuova Cultura, 2012, pp. 29 et seq.

27 Article 14.2: 'This Treaty shall enter into force on 1 January 2013, provided that twelve Contracting Parties whose currency is the euro have deposited their instrument of ratification, or on the first day of the month following the deposit of the twelfth instrument of ratification by a Contracting Party whose currency is the euro, whichever is the earlier'. The ratification process can be followed at the following link: www.consilium.europa.eu/policies/agreements/search-the-agreements-database?command=details&lang=en&aid=2012008&doclang=EN

28 For instance, Poland.

29 For instance, Hungary.

From a constitutional law viewpoint, the most important clauses are represented by Article 1, which is devoted to the aim of the Treaty, namely

> to strengthen the economic pillar of the economic and monetary Union by adopting a set of rules intended to foster budgetary discipline through a fiscal compact, to strengthen the coordination of economic policies and to improve the governance of the euro area, thereby supporting the achievement of the European Union's objectives for sustainable growth, employment, competitiveness and social cohesion.

Another relevant provision is Article 2, which concerns the relationship with EU law and reaffirming the precedence of EU law over the Treaty, a point that is present in many other parts of the Treaty. Article 3.2 provides for the necessity for the States to codify the budget rule in national law 'through provisions of binding force and permanent character, preferably constitutional, or otherwise guaranteed to be fully respected and adhered to'. It is debatable whether this last provision (Article 3.2) is inconsistent with Article 4.2 of the TEU stating the necessity to respect the national identity and constitutional structure of the EU Member States. Things are even more complex in countries whose fundamental laws are written in more than one document (see Sweden, for instance).

Another reference to EU law is included in Article 5, which requires contracting parties subject to an excessive deficit procedure to put in place 'a budgetary and economic partnership programme including a detailed description of the structural reforms'[30] to reduce the deficit. 'The content and format of such programmes shall be defined in European Union law'.[31]

Another problematic provision is Article 8, which gives the ECJ the jurisdiction to rule on the parties' compliance with the requirements of Article 3.2 of the Treaty. Is this provision compatible with the TFEU? The Preamble of the international agreement refers to Article 273 TFEU and Article 260 TFEU, but Article 273 TFEU seems to be very clear in anchoring the jurisdiction of the ECJ to the subject matter of the EU Treaties.[32] As the Court said, the extension of the competences of the Court is always possible provided that the core of the Treaties[33] is

30 Article 5 TSCG.

31 Article 5 TSCG.

32 'Professor Craig, for instance, agreed that Article 273 was sufficient to give the Court jurisdiction, but that Article 8 of the proposed treaty caused difficulties because even though the Commission would not bring a case in name, the provisions meant that it might do so in effect, and there is no provision under the EU treaties for the Commission to bring such a case', House of Commons European Scrutiny Committee, *Treaty on Stability, Coordination and Governance: Impact on the Eurozone and the Rule of Law*, 2012, www.publications.parliament.uk/pa/cm201012/cmselect/cmeuleg/1817/1817.pdf

33 On the involvement of EU institutions outside the scope of EU law, see ECJ, C-316/91 EP v. Council and C-181/91, ECR 1994 p. I-625. On the possibility of giving the ECJ a jurisdiction not referred to in the Treaties see Opinion 1/00 [2002] ECR I-3493. On this see S. Peers, 'Written Evidence', House of Lords, *Select Committee on the European Union, the Euro Area Crisis. Oral*

respected. This point, again, led the commentators to take into account the very finality of this new international agreement in order to assess its compatibility with the EU Treaties.

The TSCG aimed to get a certain degree of bindingness, which was missing in the previous instruments of the European economic governance. This also explains the concern for the role to be played by the political institutions in the new contexts. The debate about the alleged loss of power of the European Parliament is emblematic from this point of view: it might look paradoxical that now many scholars have started worrying about the role of the European Parliament for the purpose of this new Treaty, since its position is relatively stronger than it was in the past, especially if one compares the position of this institution in the TSCG to what it had in the previous Stability and Growth Pacts.

This sounds like a paradox but is not a paradox at all, since it may be explained by the new binding nature of the TSCG.[34]

In order to find the exact 'place' of EU institutions in the TSCG, it would be necessary to clarify the actual 'scope' of this new international agreement, and here again scholars are divided.

According to Peers, the new international agreement would add 'very little to the measures already set out in EU law or which have been or could be proposed as part of EU law'.[35] A confirmation of this can be found even in the words pronounced at the end of 2011 by Guy Verhofstadt: 'it is for political, symbolic

and Written Evidence, 2016, www.parliament.uk/documents/lords-committees/eu-select/euroarea-crisis/Evidencevolume.pdf

34 Indeed, according to Fasone: 'Without doubt the EP is stronger now than it was at the time of the previous regime of the Stability and Growth Pact (1997 and reformed in 2005), when the name of this institution was not even mentioned in Regulations 1466/97 and 1467/97. However, at that time, the weak enforcement of the Stability and Growth Pack did not make the lack of involvement on the part of the EP particularly problematical. On the contrary, nowadays, in principle, the mechanism does not admit derogations, except for exceptional circumstances: compared to the past, warnings and sanctions have become semi-automatic because the system is based upon the reverse qualified-majority voting (warnings and sanctions proposed by the Commission are deemed to be adopted unless the qualified-majority in the Council rejects it). Furthermore, the co-ordination of economic policy has also become binding by the embedding the European Semester within the EU legislation', C. Fasone, *Constitutional Courts Facing the Euro Crisis. Italy, Portugal and Spain in a Comparative Perspective, Max Weber Programme MWP* 2014/25, 2015, cadmus.eui.eu/bitstream/handle/1814/33859/MWP_WP_2014_25.pdf

35 'There was general agreement with Professor Peers' view of the legal aspect, and our witnesses highlighted the ways in which provisions in the proposed Treaty were effectively mirrored in existing EU Treaty and legislative obligations. It is worth considering further whether there is any significant element of the treaty which is not or could not be achieved within the existing legal framework, not least for its relevance to the ease with which the proposed treaty might in due course be integrated into the EU legal framework, as proposed in Article 16, so in effect, and there is no provision under the EU treaties for the Commission to bring such a case', House of Commons European Scrutiny Committee, *Treaty on Stability, Coordination and Governance: Impact on the Eurozone and the Rule of Law*, 2012, www.publications.parliament.uk/pa/cm201012/cmselect/cmeuleg/1817/1817.pdf

reasons that they want to do this agreement'.[36] Concerning the last provisions of the TSCG, Article 16 seems to favour the future incorporation of the TSCG in EU law, stating that

> within five years, at most, of the date of entry into force of this Treaty, . . . the necessary steps shall be taken . . . with the aim of incorporating the substance of this Treaty into the legal framework of the European Union.

This element makes the possibility of a future amendment of the EU Treaties still relevant, while another crucial aspect is represented by the abandonment of the unanimity rule for the entry into force of the TSCG[37] under Article 14: this is an important novelty that, according to many,[38] should be transplanted in the EU law context. The deadline recalled in Article 16 expired on 1 January 2018, but such an incorporation has not yet occurred.[39]

4.2 The impact over the EU constitutional system and the reaction to the pandemic

Many other authors have argued that the latest developments affect the legitimacy and democracy of the European project and represent a fracture in the history of its economic constitution[40] and, more in general, a change in its constitutional paradigm. This is the point made by Dawson and (Floris) de Witte, for instance, who argued that the anti-crisis measures have 'altered the constitutional balance upon which the Union's stability is premised',[41] its com-

36 H. Mahony, 'Doubts Increase Over Usefulness of New Fiscal Treaty', 2011, http://euobserver.com/843/114698

37 C. Closa Montero, 'Moving Away From Unanimity: Ratification of the Treaty on Stability, Coordination and Governance in the Economic and Monetary Union', *Recon Working Paper*, No. 2011/38, 2011, www.academia.edu/1439935/Moving_Away_from_Unanimity_Ratification_of_the_Treaty_on_Stability_Coordination_and_Governance_in_the_Economic_and_Monetary_Union

38 See for instance the option in: The Spinelli Group, Bertelsmann Stiftung, *The Fundamental Law of the European Union*, Gütersloh: Verlag Bertelsmann Stiftung, 2013.

39 J. Graf von Luckner, 'How to Bring It Home – The EU's Options for Incorporating the Fiscal Compact into EU Law', 2018, https://europeanlawblog.eu/2018/04/09/how-to-bring-it-home-the-eus-options-for-incorporating-the-fiscal-compact-into-eu-law/#comments

40 See also C. Joerges, 'Europe's Economic Constitution in Crisis and the Emergence of a New Constitutional Constellation', *Zentra Working Papers in Transnational Studies* No. 06 / 2012, 2012, http://papers.ssrn.com/sol3/papers.cfm?abstract_id=2179595

41 'The response to the euro-crisis destabilises the Union's substantive balance by circumventing its limited mandate in redistributive policies, which was meant to ensure that citizens have ownership and authorship over the core values that shape their society (the second section). It equally recalibrates the institutional balance by decreasing the voice of marginalised interests and representative institutions. This loss of representative influence is likely to result in greater power for national executives, with responsibilities for the initiation of, and compliance with, policy proposals shifting during the crisis towards the European Council (in the third section). Finally . . . the Union's

mitment to pluralism, and shows its inability to 'accommodate the plurality of interests that distributive conflicts engender'.[42] In their view, the crisis would cause the abandonment of the 'relative neutrality of the Union's policies'[43] due to the need to face the crisis through the adoption of an austerity path, resulting also in a breach of the system of competences. Moreover, this situation is worsened by the absence of a political arena where parliaments and citizens can participate in and discuss[44] transnational political choices. The second element is given by the reduced role of the Commission and the European Parliament in the progressive 'executivism' of the EU politics[45] in favour of the European Council.[46]

Although it is difficult not to agree with these considerations, for the purpose of this chapter it is useful to recall what other scholarships have argued about the concrete impact of these measures in order to give a more complete account of the debate. On the contrary, Bruno de Witte underlined the limited effect of the anti-crisis measures on the European architecture, describing it with the concept of 'institutional change'[47] instead of the – in his opinion more radical – concept of constitutional mutation.

---

response to the euro-crisis also threatens the spatial balance of the Union, which protects the voice of smaller and poorer Member States and their citizens from majoritarian or even hegemonic tendencies. The increased influence of the bigger, more resourceful Member States, in combination with the changes to the Union's substantive and institutional structure, leads to the loss of political autonomy for smaller and poorer Member States', M. Dawson and F. de Witte, 'Constitutional Balance in the EU After the Euro-Crisis', *Modern Law Review*, 2013, 817 et seq., pp. 817–818.

42 Dawson and de Witte, 'Constitutional Balance', p. 822.

43 Dawson and de Witte, 'Constitutional Balance', p. 823.

44 'In side-lining the national parliaments, the Union's response to the crisis has excluded a wide range of (often weak and diffuse) societal interests that have no presence in the transnational political arena', Dawson and de Witte, 'Constitutional Balance', p. 827.

45 On this process see: D. Curtin, *Executive Power in the European Union: Law, Practices and the Living Constitution*, Oxford: Oxford University Press, 2009.

46 On this see: U. Puetter, 'Europe's Deliberative Intergovernmentalism: The New Role of the Council and European Council in EU Economic Governance', *Journal of European Public Policy*, 2012, pp. 170 et seq. Finally, the creation of parallel institutions and the legal developments out of the EU Treaties also affected the institutional balance of the EU. The authors have the ESM in mind, since 'voting under the ESM is based on capital contributions. Levels of influence upon the ESM's principal decisions are therefore determined by the financial strength of the Member States, only indirectly taking into account their populations. As a result, there are significant disparities in influence when compared to normal decision-making procedures. Germany, for example, has 27 per cent of all votes in the governing board of the ESM compared to 8.5 per cent of all votes in the Council. Cyprus by contrast carries 0.2 per cent of ESM votes compared to 1.2 per cent of votes in the Council. Most decisions of the ESM are to be made by an 80 per cent qualified majority (with only the most important decisions carried by unanimity)', M. Dawson, F. de Witte, *Constitutional Balance*, pp. 837–838.

47 B. de Witte, 'Euro Crisis Responses and the EU Legal Order: Increased Institutional Variation or Constitutional Mutation?', *European Constitutional Law Review*, 2015, pp. 434 et seq., in particular p. 444.

The erosion of the equality of the Member States and of the unity of the legal system,[48] the return to intergovernmentalism,[49] the violation of the principle of legality[50] and the reduction of the financial sovereignty of the countries that have benefited from financial assistance programmes due to the well-known conditionality mechanisms[51] are the main examples of constitutional change mentioned by the authors (and criticised) by Bruno de Witte who, as mentioned, shows a preference for the concept of 'institutional variation'.

This is for several reasons: first of all, the important changes produced within the monetary union are not such, according to Bruno de Witte, as to alter the more general balance on which the integration process is based.[52]

Second, pillars of supranational law such as the principle of primacy have not been called into question by the changes introduced by the new European economic governance:

> I do not see evidence of a brutal setting aside of the rule of law in the name of political expediency, but rather a major effort to deal with urgent matters in a constitution-compatible way. Nor do I see a threat to the primacy of EU law in the fact that a number of international side agreements were concluded, since the state parties, in all of those agreements, sought to preserve the precedence of EU law, and since the main action in EMU matters is still (or again) very much embedded within the EU institutional structure.[53]

Bruno de Witte's thesis is convincing, even if the conceptual opposition of institutional change versus constitutional mutation seems excessive, since the latter is broad enough to also include non-radical changes.[54]

Looking at the reforms introduced in the new European economic governance, intergovernmentalism and increased asymmetry seem to be the main effects of the constitutional mutation induced by the crisis.

For example, for Tuori and Tuori, the crisis has not only had economic effects, but has also generated important systemic changes, favouring, for instance, the replacement of the principle of price stability with the broader one of financial stability. Tuori and Tuori's book also has the merit of clarifying what is meant by 'constitution' in this process of mutation, conceiving it not so much as a precise document as a process of change, that is, a 'multi-dimensional and multi-temporal

48 de Witte, 'Euro Crisis', p. 450.
49 de Witte, 'Euro Crisis', p. 448.
50 de Witte, 'Euro Crisis', p. 451.
51 de Witte, 'Euro Crisis', p. 452.
52 de Witte, 'Euro Crisis', p. 453.
53 de Witte, 'Euro Crisis', p. 450.
54 G. Martinico, 'Le Implicazioni Costituzionali della Crisi. Una Rassegna della Letteratura', 2016, www.federalismi.it

process of constitutionalisation, where periods of dominance of particular pace-maker constitutions are distinguishable'.[55]

Another interesting volume is the one by Scicluna, according to which the EU is currently suffering the effects of two 'twin crises of twenty-first-century EU constitutionalism',[56] referring to the crisis that followed the Dutch and French rejection of the Constitutional Treaty and the economic and financial crisis. As a result of these crises, the EU would have gone from an 'unsuccessful attempt at democratisation via politicization' to an 'unintended politicisation without democratization'.[57] In that volume, the author attempts to demonstrate 'how the integration process over burdened law in an attempt to overcome political deficiencies, with serious consequences for the EU's 'democratic deficit'[58] and to cast doubt on the ability of the so-called Integration through Law (ITL) scholarship[59] (this view is also shared by Joerges and Glinski[60]). A large part of Scicluna's book is devoted to reconstructing the debate and the context of the 'twin crises' of the EU. According to Scicluna, the European crisis would have shown a 'complex and changing relationship between law and politics in the EU, and the limits of law as an integrationist tool'[61] and, more generally, would have generated the 'EU's identity crisis'.[62] According to the author, the decline of the 'ITL scholarship' would also be a consequence of the reduced role of the courts at this stage – a fact, however, that seems to be clearly contradicted by the important case law of the crisis[63] – and of the increased prominence of technocratic actors, in which Scicluna also includes the ECB, defined, not surprisingly, in another essay, as the real 'heir to the Court of Justice'.[64]

However, this reconstruction seems problematic to me for two reasons: the legal element has not lost its importance in crisis management. The intergovernmental instruments adopted to create the TSCG and the ESM are legal as treaties of international law. Secondly, the courts have not lost their centrality, with reference

55 K. Tuori and K. Tuori, *The Eurozone Crisis: A Constitutional Analysis*, Cambridge: Cambridge University Press, 2014, pp. 10 et seq.

56 N. Scicluna, *European Union Constitutionalism in Crisis*, Abingdon: Routledge, 2015, p. 1.

57 Scicluna, *European Union*, pp. 1–2.

58 Scicluna, *European Union*, p. 1.

59 This refers to the work in several volumes edited by M. Cappelletti, M. Seccombe and J.H.H. Weiler (cur.), *Integration Through Law: Europe and the American Federal Experience*, I, Berlino-New York: de Gruyter, 1985.

60 C. Joerges and C. Glinski (eds.), *The European Crisis and the Transformation of Transnational Governance: Authoritarian Managerialism versus Democratic Governance*, Oxford: Hart, 2014.

61 Scicluna, *European Union*, p. 120.

62 Scicluna, *European Union*, p. 122.

63 For an overview see: C. Fasone, 'Constitutional Courts Facing the Euro Crisis. Italy, Portugal and Spain in a Comparative Perspective', *Max Weber Programme MWP*, No. 2014/25, 2015, cadmus.eui.eu/bitstream/handle/1814/33859/MWP_WP_2014_25.pdf

64 N. Scicluna, 'Politicization without Democratization: The Impact of the Eurozone Crisis on EU Constitutionalism', 2013, www.carloalberto.org/assets/working-papers/no.341.pdf

to both Constitutional Courts,[65] such as the Portuguese one,[66] and the Court of Justice, whose pronouncements have in turn triggered reactions at national level, I am thinking of rulings such as Pringle,[67] Gauweiler[68] and Weiss.[69] This confirms the centrality of the Court of Justice and the continuous presence of interpretative conflicts with national courts, two elements that we found in Chapter 3 regarding the evolutionary European Constitution.

What emerges from this overview confirms the halting of European mega-constitutional politics and of the attempts at constructivism (with the partial exception of the Conference on the Future of Europe) that had characterised the rounds of the semi-permanent revision of the Treaties that we analysed in Chapter 3. At the same time, the rise of the intergovernmental approach has brought about changes, however, that have not produced a radical revolution.

The pandemic was also a tremendous test for the European Union. In spite of the original ambiguity of President Lagarde,[70] the ECB has confirmed the 'whatever it takes approach',[71] 'firing its bazooka'[72] with new bond purchases to mitigate the economic consequence of the pandemic. The escape clause (so-called suspension) of the Fiscal and Growth Pact has been activated,[73] the ESM has been reshaped,[74] the European instrument for temporary Support to mitigate Unemployment Risks

65 Fasone, *Constitutional Courts.*

66 For a detailed analysis of this case law see: M. Canotilho, T. Violante, and R. Lanceiro 'Austerity Measures Under Judicial Scrutiny: The Portuguese Constitutional Case-Law', *European Constitutional Law Review*, 2015, pp. 155 et seq.

67 ECJ, C-370/12, *Pringle*, ECLI:EU:C:2012:756. See also the first comments on the Pringle case of the ECJ: (ECJ, C-370/12 *Pringle*, ECLI:EU:C:2012:756); P. Craig, 'Pringle: Legal Reasoning, Text, Purpose and Teleology', *Maastricht Journal of European and Comparative Law*, 2013, pp. 3 et seq.; B. de Witte and T. Beukers, 'The Court of Justice Approves the Creation of the European Stability Mechanism: Pringle', *Common Market Law Review*, 2013, pp. 805 et seq.

68 ECJ, C-62/14, *Gauweiler e a.*, ECLI:EU:C:2015:400.

69 ECJ, C-493/17, *Weiss e a.*, ECLI:EU:C:2018:1000.

70 Her declarations boosted another round of anti-Europeanism: 'Italy Furious at ECB's Lagarde "Not Here to Close Spreads" Comment', 13 March 2020, www.reuters.com/article/us-ecb-policy-italy-minister/italy-furious-at-ecbs-lagarde-not-here-to-close-spreads-comment-idUSKBN20Z3DW

71 'Within our mandate, the ECB is ready to do whatever it takes to preserve the euro. And believe me, it will be enough', 'Speech by Mario Draghi, President of the European Central Bank at the Global Investment Conference in London 26 July 2012', 2012, www.ecb.europa.eu/press/key/date/2012/html/sp120726.en.html

72 B. Hall in London, M. Arnold and S. Fleming, 'Coronavirus: Can the ECB's "Bazooka" Avert a Eurozone Crisis?' 23 March 2020, www.ft.com/content/a7496c30-6ab7-11ea-800d-da70cff6e4d3; T. Fairless, 'After Firing Its Bazooka, ECB Could Reload to Fight Coronavirus', 29 April 2020, www.wsj.com/articles/after-firing-its-bazooka-ecb-could-reload-to-fight-coronavirus-11588155329

73 'Statement of EU Ministers of Finance on the Stability and Growth Pact in Light of the COVID-19 Crisis', 23 March 2020, www.consilium.europa.eu/en/press/press-releases/2020/03/23/statement-of-eu-ministers-of-finance-on-the-stability-and-growth-pact-in-light-of-the-covid-19-crisis/

74 'Finance ministers agreed on the features and standardised terms for euro area countries to access the European Stability Mechanism (ESM) Pandemic Crisis Support. Member States can borrow up to 2% of their GDP to finance direct and indirect healthcare, cure and prevention related costs due to the COVID-19 pandemic', 2020, www.consilium.europa.eu/en/policies/coronavirus/timeline/

in an Emergency (SURE) was launched[75] and above all a fight for a bigger European budget to sustain the new European Recovery Fund has started. Finally, the Board of Directors of the European Investment Bank agreed to a 25 billion Euro Pan-European Guarantee Fund to respond to the COVID-19 crisis on 26 May 2020.[76] This perhaps falls a good deal short of creating a robust European solidarity, but it is a big move if compared to the status quo. Moreover, the debate on the mutualisation of sovereign debt has resumed,[77] and if the battle over the budget is well managed, it could be a game changer. It is no coincidence that some have evoked the need for a European Hamiltonian[78] (or Madisonian?[79]) moment. The tip of the iceberg was reached in the decision on the Public Sector Purchase Program (PSPP),[80] when the German Constitutional Court declared that the ECJ had acted *ultra vires* because of the way in which the Luxembourg Court had exercised the proportionality review in the *Weiss* case.[81] Even before this decision, scholars[82] had already warned about the 'bad example'[83] set by the German

75 'Report on the Comprehensive Economic Policy Response to the COVID-19 Pandemic', 9 April 2020, www.consilium.europa.eu/en/press/press-releases/2020/04/09/report-on-the-comprehensive-economic-policy-response-to-the-covid-19-pandemic/; 'The Commission's SURE Initiative Provides Funding to Member States of Up to €100 billion by Covering Part of the Costs Related to the Creation or Extension of National Short-Time Work Schemes', 'ESM Pandemic Crisis Support', 2020, www.esm.europa.eu/content/europe-response-corona-crisis

76 'EIB Board approves €25 Billion Pan-European Guarantee Fund in Response to COVID-19 crisis', 2020, www.eib.org/en/press/all/2020-126-eib-board-approves-eur-25-billion-pan-european-guarantee-fund-to-respond-to-covid-19-crisis.htm

77 A. Steinbach, 'The Mutualization of Sovereign Debt: Comparing the American Past and the European Present', *Journal of Common Market Studies*, 2015, pp. 1110 et seq.

78 S. Capooer, 'This Isn't Europe's "Hamilton" Moment', 2020, www.politico.eu/article/this-isnt-europes-hamilton-moment/; G. Calhoun, 'Europe's Hamiltonian Moment – What Is It Really?' 26 May 2020, www.forbes.com/sites/georgecalhoun/2020/05/26/europes-hamiltonian-moment–what-is-it-really/; A. Kaletsky, 'Europe's Hamiltonian Moment', 2020, www.project-syndicate.org/commentary/french-german-european-recovery-plan-proposal-by-anatole-kaletsky-2020–05

79 E. Jones, 'Not Hamilton but Madison: Diversity Makes for a Better Union', 2020, www.iiss.org/blogs/survival-blog/2020/05/europe-diversity-politics-covid-19

80 German Constitutional Court, 5 May 2020, 2 BvR 859/15–2 BvR 1651/15–2 BvR 2006/15–2 BvR 980/16. For some comments see M. Poiares Maduro, 'Some Preliminary Remarks on the PSPP Decision of the German Constitutional Court', 2020, https://verfassungsblog.de/some-preliminary-remarks-on-the-pspp-decision-of-the-german-constitutional-court; M. Avbelj, 'The Right Question About the FCC Ultra Vires Decision', 2020, https://verfassungsblog.de/the-right-question-about-the-fcc-ultra-vires-decision; T. Marzal, 'Is the BVerfG PSPP Decision "Simply Not Comprehensible"? A Critique of the Judgment's Reasoning on Proportionality', 2020, https://verfassungsblog.de/is-the-bverfg-pspp-decision-simply-not-comprehensible

81 ECJ, C-493/17, Weiss and others ECLI:EU:C:2018:1000.

82 G. Halmai, 'Abuse of Constitutional Identity: The Hungarian Constitutional Court on Interpretation of Article E) (2) of the Fundamental Law', *Review of Central and East European Law*, 2018, pp. 23 et seq.

83 O. Pollicino, 'Metaphors and Identity Based Narrative in Constitutional Adjudication: When Judicial Dominance Matters', 2019, https://blog-iacl-aidc.org/2019-posts/2019/2/27/metaphors-and identity-based-narrative-in-constitutional-adjudication-when-judicial-dominance-matters

judges, especially since in 2012, the Czech Constitutional Court[84] declared the ECJ's judgement in C-399/09 *Landtová ultra vires*.[85] The Czech case represents the first example of the application of the *ultra vires* doctrine. However, now the situation is different because of the prestige and charisma of the German Constitutional Court, and the risk of a domino effect is now very high. Indeed, the judgement found the Court of Justice decision in the *Weiss* case[86] to be *ultra vires* and thus considered the German institutions to be unbound by any of the relevant effects. This decision has triggered a very interesting debate in legal journals and blogs. In particular, the German Constitutional Court somehow questioned the way in which the ECJ had carried out the proportionality test in *Weiss*.[87] In the German Constitutional Court's words:

> The specific manner in which the CJEU applies the principle of proportionality in the case at hand renders that principle meaningless for the purposes of distinguishing, in relation to the PSPP, between monetary policy and economic policy, i.e. between the exclusive monetary policy competence conferred upon the EU (Art. 3(1) lit. c TFEU) and the limited conferral upon the EU of the competence to coordinate general economic policies, with the Member States retaining the competence for economic policy at large.
> (Art. 4(1) TEU; Art. 5(1) TFEU)[88]

In a nutshell, the German Constitutional Court gave the ECB Governing Council a three-month ultimatum to adopt 'a new decision that demonstrates in a comprehensible and substantiated manner that the monetary policy objectives pursued by the ECB are not disproportionate to the economic and fiscal policy effects resulting from the programme'.[89] While the tone of the German Constitutional

84 Czech Constitutional Court (Pl. ÚS 5/12), www.usoud.cz/en/decisions/20120131-pl-us-512-slovak-pensions/. After that, the Danish Supreme Court in Ajos also took the chance to delimit the competences of the EU. Danish Supreme Court, decision 15/2014, *Dansk Industri (DI) acting for Ajos A/S v. The estate left by A*, also analysed by M. Madsen and others, 'Legal Disintegration? The Ruling of the Danish Supreme Court in AJOS', 2017 https://verfassungsblog.de/legal-disintegration-the-ruling-of-the-danish-supreme-court-in-ajos/

Very recently, the Polish Constitutional Court also declared that interim measures imposed on it by the Luxembourg Court are unconstitutional and accused the CJEU of imposing 'ultra vires obligations', Polish Constitutional Court, decision P 7/20, https://trybunal.gov.pl/postepowanie-i-orzeczenia/wyroki/art/11589-obowiazek-panstwa-czlonkowskiego-ue-polegajacy-na-wykonywaniu-srodkow-tymczasowych-odnoszacych-sie-do-ksztaltu-ustroju-i-funkcjonowania-konstytucyjnych-organow-wladzy-sadowniczej-tego-panstwa

85 ECJ, C-399/09, *Landtová*, ECLI:EU:C:2011:415.

86 ECJ, C-493/17 Weiss and Others, ECLI:EU:C:2018:1000.

87 ECJ, C-493/17, Weiss and Others, ECLI:EU:C:2018:1000.

88 2 BvR 859/15, par. 127, www.bundesverfassungsgericht.de/SharedDocs/Entscheidungen/EN/2020/05/rs20200505_2bvr085915en.html;jsessionid=F892FE5330900A9A29FDCBEF992814FE.2_cid392. On this see: Toni Marzal, 'Is the BVerfG PSPP Decision'.

89 'Following a transitional period of no more than three months allowing for the necessary coordination with the ESCB, the Bundesbank may thus no longer participate in the implementation and

Court is shocking and perhaps also a bit arrogant, scholars have already stressed that there are many ways of overcoming the impasse.[90] Moreover, as the German Constitutional Court explicitly stated, this decision does not affect the new Pandemic Purchasing Program of the ECB.

This judgement confirms a recent trend, according to which courts have been eager to intervene despite the technicalities of the question by making a series of important decisions concerning European economic governance.[91]

Despite this decision, the ECB confirmed its intention to insist on its expansive monetary policy approach, and a press release following the judgement of the German Constitutional Court of 5 May 2020 was published on the website of the Court of Justice stating:

> In general, it is recalled that the Court of Justice has consistently held that a judgment in which the Court gives a preliminary ruling is binding on the national court for the purposes of the decision to be given in the main proceedings. In order to ensure that EU law is applied uniformly, the Court of Justice alone – which was created for that purpose by the Member States – has jurisdiction to rule that an act of an EU institution is contrary to EU law. Divergences between courts of the Member States as to the validity of such acts would indeed be liable to place in jeopardy the unity of the EU legal order and to detract from legal certainty. Like other authorities of the Member States, national courts are required to ensure that EU law takes full effect. That is the only way of ensuring the equality of Member States in the Union they created. The institution will refrain from communicating further on the matter.

---

execution of Decision (EU) 2015/774, the amending Decisions (EU) 2015/2101, (EU) 2015/2464, (EU) 2016/702 and (EU) 2017/100, and the Decision of 12 September 2019, neither by carrying out any further purchases of bonds nor by contributing to another increase of the monthly purchase volume, unless the ECB Governing Council adopts a new decision that demonstrates in a comprehensible and substantiated manner that the monetary policy objectives pursued by the ECB are not disproportionate to the economic and fiscal policy effects resulting from the programme. On the same condition, the Bundesbank must ensure that the bonds already purchased under the PSPP and held in its portfolio are sold based on a – possibly long-term – strategy coordinated with the ESCB', German Constitutional Court, 5 May 2020, 2 BvR 859/15–2 BvR 1651/15–2 BvR 2006/15–2 BvR 980/16.

90 'I don't think the ECB can and will directly comply with the German Court's judgment. To do so would open the door to multiple national legal challenges, placing it under the jurisdiction of all national high courts, with disastrous consequences for the ECB and its role under the Treaties. But, without directly addressing the German Constitutional Court demand, the ECB may adopt a new decision with a more in depth justification of the program. This justification will likely mostly pay lip service to the arguments on proportionality raised by the Constitutional Court. But that may be sufficient to provide the justification needed by German authorities, that are the actual addressees of the judgment, to say that the requirement the Court has imposed has been fulfilled by the ECB and the problem is therefore solve. Naturally, those that brought this case will argue otherwise but that will have to be done through a new case: time will be gained (and the composition of the Court will also partly change)', Poiares Maduro, 'Some Preliminary Remarks'.

91 Fasone, 'Constitutional Courts Facing'.

Scholars have asked for the activation of a procedure of infringement against Germany, which is possible under Article 258 TFEU,[92] and on 9 June 2021, the Commission sent letter of notice to Germany.[93] This move was surprising since it came only a few days after a decision of the German Constitutional Court in which the *Bundesverfassungsgericht* dismissed two applications for an order of execution that had been lodged after the BVG's judgement of 5 May 2020 on the PSPP.[94] However, the Commission announced the decision to end its infringement proceedings against Germany on 2 December 2021 in light of the German reply to the letter of formal notice.

More generally, the current phase seems to confirm the persistent weaknesses affecting European economic governance and the protagonism of the ECB[95] in this phase. In this sense, the EU's economic architecture is still paying the price for the choices made by the Maastricht Treaty.

However, after this decision of the German Constitutional Court on the PSPP, the scholarly debate has mirrored the political one. Scholars accused the German Constitutional Court of pushing for an ordoliberal understanding of the European Union.[96] Scholars have written about the end of the law;[97] others have

92 Article 258 TFEU: 'If the Commission considers that a Member State has failed to fulfil an obligation under the Treaties, it shall deliver a reasoned opinion on the matter after giving the State concerned the opportunity to submit its observations.
If the State concerned does not comply with the opinion within the period laid down by the Commission, the latter may bring the matter before the Court of Justice of the European Union', F. Fabbrini, 'Suing the BVerfG', 2020, https://verfassungsblog.de/suing-the-bverfg/#comments

93 'June Infringements Package: Key Decisions', 9 June 2021, https://ec.europa.eu/commission/presscorner/detail/en/inf_21_2743

94 German Constitutional Court, 2 BvR 1651/15, 2 BvR 2006/15.

95 N. Scicluna, 'Politicization Without Democratization: The Impact of the Eurozone Crisis on EU Constitutionalism', 2013, www.carloalberto.org/assets/working-papers/no.341.pdf; Scicluna, *European Union.*

96 'Probably the GCC, reflecting part of the German public opinion, considers perfectly legitimate the phenomenon – described by Giacché as "monetary annexation" – by which control of production within a monetary union must be given to the "more deserving" actors. Once again, a Darwinian perspective which ignores the notion that diverging yield spreads will make access to credit prohibitive to businesses situated in peripheral Member States, negating the concept of fair competition versus "more deserving" businesses situated in the stronger Member States', A. Guazzarotti, 'Very Unkind Things About the German Constitutional Court's Rebellion Against the ECJ in the Quantitative Easing Case', 2020, https://verfassungsblog.de/very-unkind-things-about-the-german-constitutional-courts-rebellion-against-the-ecj-in-the-quantitative-easing-case/. Guazzarotti referred to a book by V. Giacché, *Anschluss. L'annessione: L'unificazione della Germania e il futuro dell'Europa*, Reggio Emilia: Imprimatur, 2013. Giacché is also author of another book titled *Costituzione italiana contro trattati europei. Il conflitto inevitabile*, Reggio Emilia, 2015, where he writes of an 'unavoidable conflict' between the Italian Constitution and the EU Treaties.

97 M. Dani, J. Mendes, A.J. Menéndez, M. Wilkinson, H. Schepel, and E. Chiti, 'At the End of the Law: A Moment of Truth for the Eurozone and the EU', 2020, https://verfassungsblog.de/at-the-end-of-the-law. This approach forgets that things like these have happened even in fully fledged federal systems: A. Baraggia and G. Martinico, 'Who Is the Master of the Treaties? The Compact Theory in Karlsruhe', 2020, www.diritticomparati.it/who-is-the-master-of-the-treaties-the-compact-theory-in-karlsruhe/;

again insisted on the German-driven conspiracy.[98] In spite of this pessimism, that episode was not the end of anything.

In the light of all these considerations, scholars also reflected on the advisability of abandoning the dichotomy between intergovernmentalism and supranationalism, since it is no longer really useful for interpreting the integration process. After all, these instruments of an intergovernmental nature have accelerated the integration process and strengthened the position of the controller, the Commission, which, however, is certainly supranational in nature.[99]

There are elements of continuity (centrality of courts, persistence of conflicts, which also involve political actors) that, also in light of the lack of constructivism, seem to confirm the evolutionary dynamics of the European Constitution. The agreement on the European budget could be a turning point if confirmed, but it is probably too early to advance hypotheses.

Obviously, the fact that the elements of continuity prevail over discontinuity does not rule out the possibility that improvements can be made. Indeed, in this respect, the institutional battle fought by the European Parliament on the budget to strengthen, on the one hand, the compromise reached in the European Council and, on the other, to make the allocation of European funds conditional on respect for the rule of law,[100] has been very important.

The conditionality regulation[101] was later passed and almost immediately brought to the Court of Justice by Hungary[102] and Poland[103] for an alleged lack of an appropriate legal basis. On 16 February 2022 the ECJ delivered two

---

S.J. Boom, 'The European Union After the Maastricht Decision: Will Germany Be the Virginia of Europe', *American Journal of Comparative Law*, 1995, pp. 177 et seq.; T. Dumbrovsky, 'Federal Solution to the EU Internal Sovereignty Conundrum: The European Doctrine of the Czech Constitutional Court and the U.S. Compact Theory', in L. Tichy and T. Dumbrovsky (eds.), *Sovereignty and Competences of the European Union*, Prague: Charles University, 2010, pp. 80 et seq.; R. Schütze, 'Federalism as Constitutional Pluralism: "Letter from America"', in M. Avbelj and J. Komárek (eds.), *Constitutional Pluralism in the European Union and Beyond*, Oxford: Hart, 2012, pp. 185 et seq.

98 See the interview given by Becchi: F. Provenzani, '«La trappola della Germania per far accettare il MES all'Italia»' (Paolo Becchi), 7 May 2020, www.money.it/Piano-Germania-MES-Italia-Paolo-Becchi

99 P. Tortola and L. Vai, 'What Government for the European Union? Five Themes for Reflection and Action', *CSF- IAI WP Series*, 2015, www.iai.it/sites/default/files/iai1517.pdf

100 European Council conclusions, 17–21 July 2020, www.consilium.europa.eu/en/press/press-releases/2020/07/21/european-council-conclusions-17-21-july-2020/

101 Regulation (EU, Euratom) 2020/2092 of the European Parliament and of the Council of 16 December 2020 on a general regime of conditionality for the protection of the Union budget', https://eur-lex.europa.eu/legal-content/EN/ALL/?uri=CELEX%3A32020R2092

102 ECJ, C-156/21, *Hungary v. European Parliament and Council of the European Union*, https://eur-lex.europa.eu/legal-content/EN/TXT/?uri=CELEX:62021CN0156

103 ECJ, C-157/21, *Republic of Poland v. European Parliament and Council of the European Union*, https://eur-lex.europa.eu/legal-content/EN/TXT/?uri=CELEX:62021CN0157

decisions by dismissing these actions[104] while on 2 March 2022 the Commission published the "Guidelines on the application of the Regulation (EU, EURATOM) 2020/2092 on a general regime of conditionality for the protection of the Union budget".[105] Finally, on 5 April 2022 the President of the Commission announced that the Commission had triggered the conditionality mechanism against Hungary.

At the same time, the European Parliament and the Commission have been struggling about what to do with Poland after the astonishing judgement of the Polish Constitutional Court in which it rejected the principle of EU law primacy.[106] The origin of this institutional battle has to be found in the letter of Conclusions of the European Council of 10–11 December 2020,[107] in particular its letter c stating that:

> With a view to ensuring that these principles will be respected, the Commission intends to develop and adopt guidelines on the way it will apply the Regulation, including a methodology for carrying out its assessment. Such guidelines will be developed in close consultation with the Member States. Should an action for annulment be introduced with regard to the Regulation, the guidelines will be finalised after the judgment of the Court of Justice so as to incorporate any relevant elements stemming from such judgment. The Commission President will fully inform the European Council. Until such guidelines are finalised, the Commission will not propose measures under the Regulation.[108]

The European Parliament almost immediately urged the Commission to apply the Regulation in a resolution adopted on 25 March 2021, arguing 'that the application of the Rule of Law Conditionality Regulation cannot be subject to the adoption of guidelines'.[109]

104 ECJ, C-156/21, *Hungary v Parliament and Council*, ECLI:EU:C:2022:97 and C-157/21, *Poland v Parliament and Council*, ECLI:EU:C:2022:98.

105 https://eur-lex.europa.eu/legal-content/EN/TXT/?uri=CELEX%3A52022XC0318%2802%29

106 Polish Constitutional Court, decision K 3/21, https://trybunal.gov.pl/en/hearings/judgments/art/11662-ocena-zgodnosci-z-konstytucja-rp-wybranych-przepisow-traktatu-o-unii-europejskiej

107 European Council meeting (10 and 11 December 2020) – Conclusions, www.consilium.europa.eu/media/47296/1011-12-20-euco-conclusions-en.pdf

108 European Council meeting (10 and 11 December 2020) – Conclusions, www.consilium.europa.eu/media/47296/1011-12-20-euco-conclusions-en.pdf. There are also other ambiguous passages in the Regulation. For a detailed analysis see: N. Kirst, 'Rule of Law Conditionality: The Long-Awaited Step Towards a Solution of the Rule of Law Crisis in the European Union? *European Papers*, 2021, pp. 101 et seq.

109 European Parliament resolution of 25 March 2021 on the application of Regulation (EU, Euratom) 2020/2092, the rule-of-law conditionality mechanism, www.europarl.europa.eu/doceo/document/TA-9-2021-0103_EN.html

On 10 June 2021, another resolution was passed by the European Parliament in which it warned the Commission by stating that:

> Regrets the Commission's failure to respond to Parliament's requests by 1 June 2021 and to activate the procedure laid down in the Rule of Law Conditionality Regulation in the most obvious cases of breaches of the rule of law in the EU; instructs its President to call on the Commission, within two weeks from the date of adoption of this resolution at the latest, on the basis of Article 265 of the TFEU, to fulfil its obligations under this regulation; states that, in order to be prepared, Parliament shall, in the meantime, immediately start the necessary preparations for potential court proceedings under Article 265 of the TFEU against the Commission.[110]

These are developments that could lead to an epoch-making turning point and confirm not only the overcoming of the austerity paradigm that undoubtedly characterised the management of the (previous) economic crisis, but also the Union's commitment to respect for fundamental rights.

However, as has been pointed out, there are also problematic aspects linked to the influence that EU law has exerted in the years of the crisis on national legal systems, in particular of those Member States that have benefited from the ESM.

The so-called European Semester has in fact subordinated social objectives to economic ones, and today it seems that European social spaces have become 'adjustment variables in the EMU'.[111] Costamagna has explained better than others how supranational market law has infiltrated national social spaces and how this has led, over the years, to a progressive reduction of the margin of space of states for social policies, in particular with the emergence of budgetary constraints:

> On the one hand, budgetary constraints aimed at limiting Member States' capacity to play 'Keynes at home', forcing them, in particular, to cut down on one of the heaviest items in their budgets, i.e. social expenditure. On the other, most of the policy coordination processes touched upon, directly or indirectly, social issues.[112]

Conditionality, in particular, has played a major role in this, although there were – even before the outbreak of the pandemic – some attempts at 'socialising structural adjustment programmes'.[113]

110 European Parliament resolution on the rule of law situation in the European Union and the application of the Conditionality Regulation 2020/2092, www.europarl.europa.eu/doceo/document/B-9-2021-0319_EN.html

111 F. Costamagna, 'National Social Spaces as Adjustment Variables in the EMU: A Critical Legal Appraisal', *European Law Journal*, 2018, pp. 163 et seq.

112 Costamagna, 'National Social', p. 171.

113 Costamagna, 'National Social', p. 185.

The phenomenon of conditionality has also recently been the subject of interesting legal studies, which have offered a clear and non-ideologised view of the phenomenon, confirming its possible role as a driver of constitutional change.[114] This analysis also reveals the specificities of the Greek case, which is certainly dramatic in terms of impact, and yet not devoid of national responsibilities,[115] the dynamics of which are not fully traceable in the other national cases involved in the ESM.

In particular, the Spanish case appears very different from the Greek one and this therefore confirms the need for a serious comparative approach[116] to the national impact of conditionality.[117]

In this sense, the debate on the European Stability Mechanism is also one about the kind of democracy we have in mind. Too often, we exclude the importance of intergenerational justice, which should be taken into account as an essential element of any constitutional reflection on this topic. Suffice it to think of the exchange between Jefferson and Madison, for instance. Who owns the constitution? Who owns the Earth?[118] For those who believe in the European integration process as a constitutional phenomenon, these lines by Maduro still have a lot to say:

> The freedom to do things that the current members of the political community acquire by incurring on large budget deficits may limit the democratic freedom of deliberation for future generations. I say may, because, in effect, budget deficits may also bring benefits for future generations depending on how productively the money is employed. The democratic problem remains however: one current generation decides for another (particularly, because we cannot be certain that the current members of a political community will base their decisions on the interests of the future members of that political community instead of their own immediate needs). This can be presented as a democratic malfunction, a democratic externality in generational terms. Also, in this case, EU law can be presented as an instrument of external constitutional control on national democratic processes. EU law exercises

114 A. Baraggia, *Ordinamenti giuridici a confronto nell'era della crisi: la condizionalità economica in Europa e negli Stati nazionali*, Turin: Giappichelli, 2017.

115 V. Da Rold, Il debito greco, una lunga storia di errori', 2 July 2018, www.ilsole24ore.com/art/il-debito-greco-lunga-storia-errori-AEPQskFF

116 Baraggia, *Ordinamenti giuridici a confronto*, pp. 87 et seq.

117 V. Vita, 'The Rise of Spending Conditionality in the EU: What Can EU Learn From the U.S. Conditional Spending Doctrine and Policies?' *EUI Department of Law Research Paper*, No. 16, 2017, https://papers.ssrn.com/sol3/papers.cfm?abstract_id=3062680

118 See the powerful arguments used by Jefferson: T. Jefferson, 'To James Madison Paris', 6 September 1789, www.let.rug.nl/usa/presidents/thomas-jefferson/letters-of-thomas-jefferson/jefl81.php

> many other such forms of external constitutional discipline and reform over national democratic processes.[119]

Unfortunately, we often do not consider intergenerational balance as part of the concept of solidarity, and normally when we refer to solidarity, we mean it in a synchronic and not diachronic sense. This leads us (rightly) to a negative conclusion: the policy of austerity and other failures, such as the inability to overcome the Dublin system,[120] with regard to asylum seekers and refugees seems to make us lean towards the absence of true solidarity at the supranational level, but if we look at these issues closely it is difficult to distinguish the responsibility of the EU from those of its Member States.

4.3 Why the European Union is not (only) an ordoliberal entity

As we saw, many of the threats present when the first edition of this book came out have become reality and have progressively jeopardised the plausibility of the supranational constitutional ambitions. In this chapter I used the debate on the economic crisis as a privileged perspective to offer an analysis on the last ten years of the European integration process. The reaction to the economic crisis has for sure reinforced the intergovernmental component of the EU integration process. However, while I acknowledged that the crisis has produced some changes in the structure of the EU constitutional order, in my view these changes are not radical or capable of altering its main features.

More recently, scholars have accused colleagues interested in European constitutional law of constructing dangerous mythology and have also boldly suggested that

> it is simply impossible to claim that acknowledging to European law the condition of 'constitutional order' is either a neutral way of referring to the object of study of a legal-dogmatic discipline, or a means of promoting the transformation of European law in the semblance of democratic and social constitutionalism.[121]

In works like these, the EU today is depicted as a dangerous and undemocratic ordoliberal entity, the rejection of everything constitutionalism stands for.

119 M. Poiares Maduro, 'Passion and Reason in European Integration', 2010, https://papers.ssrn.com/sol3/papers.cfm?abstract_id=1709950

120 A. Binetti Armstrong, 'You Shall Not Pass! How the Dublin System Fueled Fortress Europe', *Chicago Journal of International Law*, 2020, pp. 332 et seq.

121 M. Dani and A. José Menéndez, 'European Constitutional Imagination: A Whig Interpretation of the Process of European Integration?' *iCourts Working Paper Series*, No. 243, 2020, https://papers.ssrn.com/sol3/papers.cfm?abstract_id=3807102&fbclid=IwAR0JL6Ho86_KZ4SFPWL-Et2jIlbZvGFhqEAaoW44ZRaPPdefWSHb9bBaL3hQ

These approaches are open to criticism from various points of view. From a terminological point of view, they often confuse ordoliberalism and neoliberalism[122] and seem to reduce the liberal tradition to the thought of Hayek, referred to as the inspirer of supranational economic federalism.[123] Secondly, they base their arguments on false dichotomies, such as that between democratic and social constitutionalism and liberal constitutionalism,[124] as if the former were not also based on liberal premises. Finally, they are often vitiated by a certain determinism that leads them to see in the European integration process a 'neo-liberal device'[125] from the very beginning.

Despite the tempting nihilism that this scholarship constantly offers, this book has other plans. My claim is to show that the EU participates in the function historically performed by constitutionalism.[126]

Careful historical studies have also shown the centrality of other schools of thought (and action), starting with French dirigisme. It is no coincidence that a few years ago Kaupa wrote about the pluralistic nature of the European economic constitution, arguing in other works that 'the European Treaties cannot be understood to conform to any specific socioeconomic paradigm or ideology in a way that would bind institutions or Member States to such a view'.[127]

Other literature has argued that describing the European integration process in purely ordoliberal terms is an 'exaggeration'[128] and illustrates in great detail the 'myths of ordoliberalism'.[129]

122 See, for instance, A. Somma, *Quando l'Europa tradì sé stessa. E come continua a tradirsi nonostante la pandemia*, Laterza, Roma-Bari, 2021.

123 On the basis of his essay: F.A. von Hayek, 'The Economic Conditions of Interstate Federalism', *New Commonwealth Quarterly*, 1939, pp. 131 et seq. 'The original constitution of Economic and Monetary Union (EMU) rested on a neoliberal approach to interstate federalism à la Hayek', H. Lokdam and M. Wilkinson, 'The European Economic Constitution in Crisis: A Conservative Transformation', *LSE Legal Studies Working Paper*, No. 03/2021, https://papers.ssrn.com/sol3/papers.cfm?abstract_id=3813816

124 M. Dani and A. Menéndez, 'È ancora possibile riconciliare costituzionalismo democratico-sociale e integrazione europea?' *DPCE Online*, 2020, pp. 289 et seq.

125 Somma, *Quando l'Europa tradì*, pp. 181 et seq.

126 In this respect, it has been argued that the EU responds to a form of functional constitutionalism: T. Isiksel, *Europe's Functional Constitution: A Theory of Constitutionalism Beyond the State*, Oxford: Oxford University Press, 2016.

127 C. Kaupa, 'The Pluralist Socio-Economic Character of the European Treaties', in G. Davies and M. Avbelj (eds.), *Research Handbook on Legal Pluralism and EU Law*, Cheltenham: Edward Elgar Publishing, 2018, pp. 257 et seq., p. 258.

128 P. Nedergaard, 'The Ordoliberalisation of the European Union?' *Journal of European Integration*, 2020, pp. 213 et seq., p. 228; A. Wigger, 'Debunking the Myth of the Ordoliberal Influence on Post-War European Integration', in J. Hien and C. Joerges (eds.), *Ordoliberalism, Law and the Rule of Economics*, Oxford: Hart, 2017, 161 ss.

129 'Ordoliberalism has been, and is, much less influential than is often assumed to be the case. And yet the importance attributed to it is itself significant because it serves to distract attention from the real forces driving policy. In particular, to focus on European (especially German) leaders' claimed commitment to ordoliberalism suggests that they are (partially at least) prisoners of rigid

Of course, it cannot be denied that ordoliberalism is an important tradition in the European context; after all, the Lisbon Treaty itself makes explicit reference to 'the social market economy'.[130] However, this importance should not lead to neglecting the other traditions that characterise the European economic constitution. The theory of constitutional complexity, with its emphasis on national diversity, reveals the 'Pluralist Character of the European Economic Constitution'[131] since it acknowledges a high level of differentiation at national level. In denying such a diversity, the supporters of a purely ordoliberal reading of the EU frequently reveal a reductionist approach, and what they propose is the application of their own constitutional tradition to the supranational arena.[132] In so doing, they demonstrate endorsement of a 'monocular view'[133] of the EU integration process.

A confirmation of this tendency to underestimate the constitutional diversity characterising national law can also be seen when reading the debate concerning the *Laval*[134] and *Viking*[135] cases. In these cases, the ECJ recognised the fundamental right to collective action as an integral part of Community law. Against this background, this right can justify restrictions on the fundamental freedom of establishment or on the freedom to provide services guaranteed under the EU Treaty, when it is exercised to protect workers and their conditions of employment. Significantly, the ECJ limited itself to declaring that collective action restricting economic freedoms is legal

> only if it pursues a legitimate aim compatible with the Treaty and is justified by overriding reasons of public interest. But even if that were the case, it would still have to be suitable for securing the attainment of the objective pursued and must not go beyond what is necessary in order to attain it.[136]

As disappointing as these rulings are, one cannot deny the difficult role of the ECJ in this area. The field of social rights is characterised by a great deal of fragmentation at the domestic level, as is also shown by the constant references to

---

belief systems, victims of forces that are almost beyond their conscious control', A. Storey, 'The Myths of Ordoliberalism', 2017, www.erc-europeanunions.eu/working-papers/

130 Article 3.3 TEU: 'The Union shall establish an internal market. It shall work for the sustainable development of Europe based on balanced economic growth and price stability, a highly competitive social market economy, aiming at full employment and social progress, and a high level of protection and improvement of the quality of the environment. It shall promote scientific and technological advance'.

131 C. Kaupa, *The Pluralist Character of the European Economic Constitution*, Oxford: Hart, 2016.

132 Somma, *Quando l'Europa tradì*, p. 181.

133 N. MacCormick, 'Beyond the Sovereign State', *Modern Law Review*, 1993, pp. 1 et seq., p. 6.

134 ECJ, C-341/05, *Laval un Partneri*, ECLI:EU:C:2007:809.

135 ECJ, C-438/05, *The International Transport Workers' Federation and the Finnish Seamen's Union*, ECLI:EU:C:2007:772.

136 ECJ, C-438/05, *The International Transport Workers' Federation and the Finnish Seamen's Union*, ECLI:EU:C:2007:772, par. 75.

'national laws and practices' that characterise the title on solidarity in the Charter of Fundamental Rights.

This explains the recourse to the principle of proportionality that is frequently used by the Court of Justice in some cases where ultimately the national court is in a better position to decide the case in the light of the guidelines offered by the Court. These are guidance cases, that is, decisions by which 'the ECJ sets parameters and provides the national court with guidelines which it must take into account in resolving the dispute'.[137] Indeed, in *Viking*:

> The Court was faced with a fundamental conflict between, on the one hand, upholding free market ideals and enabling states and private actors to take advantage of the EU enlargement to the East and, on the other hand, avoiding social dumping. The judgment is characterized by a high degree of equivocation. The ECJ gives guidelines but the scope of the referring court's intervention is ample and creative. How is the national court to decide whether there are less restrictive alternatives? And what does it mean that 'the jobs or conditions of employment at issue must not be jeopardized or be under serious threat'? The judgment awards points to each party but does not resolve the dispute and redirects the litigation to the national court.[138]

In this sense, those who have defended the ECJ argued that 'it is quite evident that the Court does not have the power to impose an equalization of social costs or to harmonize employment conditions in the Community'.[139] The point here is not so much to say that the ECJ was wrong or right in deciding *Laval* and *Viking*; what I mean is that we cannot understand these cases if we do not pay attention to the diversity that characterises the national levels in this area. It is precisely this diversity in terms of constitutional traditions that is often underestimated or ignored by supporters of a purely ordoliberal reading of the EU. It is no coincidence that in these areas the EU still bears the legacy of what Mancini called the 'social frigidity'[140] of the original Treaties.

Disappointing as it was, the *Laval* quartet[141] should also be read in the light of these considerations. However, the recent developments in EU law have also shown that they know how to go beyond the *Laval* quartet, as the judgements on

137 T. Tridimas, 'Constitutional Review of Member State Action: The Virtues and Vices of an Incomplete Jurisdiction', *International Journal of Constitutional Law*, 2011, pp. 737 et seq.

138 Tridimas, 'Constitutional Review', pp. 744–745.

139 L. Azoulai, 'The Court of Justice and the Social Market Economy: The Emergence of an Ideal and the Conditions for its Realization', *Common Market Law Review*, 2008, pp. 1335 et seq., p. 1353.

140 Somma traces all evil back to the concept of governance, which would have allowed the Union to enter areas that belong to the States: A. Somma, 'Verso il postdiritto? Fine della storia e spoliticizzazione dell'ordine economico', *Politica del diritto*, 2018, pp. 79 et seq., p. 98.

141 ECJ, C-341/05 *Laval un Partneri* [2007] ECR I-11767; C-346/06 *Rüffert* [2008] ECR I-1989; C-319/06 *Commission vs. Luxembourg* [2008] ECR I-4323, -438/05 *The International Transport Workers' Federation and the Finnish Seamen's Union* [2007] ECR I10779.

holidays, for example, confirm.[142] The Commission's recent activism[143] on the social pillar says a lot about the weight it would like to give to more solidarity-based dynamics,[144] and the European Parliament's firm resolution on the right to disconnect[145] also points in that direction.[146]

Moreover, we should also mention judgements that seem to leave behind the approach of limited solidarity that characterised the well-known *Dano*[147] judgement and look at a different scenario, as underlined by recent studies on EU social citizenship.[148] I am referring to *Saint Prix*,[149] *Florea Gusa*,[150] *Tarola*[151] and *CG*.[152] So, there is no shortage of encouraging signs, although it very much remains to be done. Moreover, more recently the Court of Justice has been using the Charter to require national judges to disapply national norms in conflict with provisions included in the title on solidarity, namely Article 31.[153] Other provisions of the Charter have been at the centre of a series of interesting exchanges between national constitutional judges and the Court of Justice, as in the case of Article 34.[154]

Finally, and this is a crucial point, the purely ordoliberal view of the integration process fails to explain what one could call here the added value of European law

142 C-762/18, *Varhoven kasatsionen sad na Republika Bulgaria*; C-609/17 and C-610/17, *Terveys-ja sosiaalialan neuvottelujärjestö (TSN)*, 2019.

143 P. Vesan and F. Corti, 'The Return of the Commission Social Entrepreneurship Before and After the Covid-19 Pandemic', *Journal of European Integration*, 2021, pp. 1 et seq.

144 On solidarity in EU law F. Croci, *Solidarietà tra stati membri dell'Unione europea e governance*, Turin: Giappichelli, 2020.

145 P9_TA(2021)0021. The right to disconnect. European Parliament resolution of 21 January 2021 with recommendations to the Commission on the right to disconnect (2019/2181(INL)), www.europarl.europa.eu/doceo/document/TA-9-2021-0021_EN.pdf

146 G. Bronzini, 'Il senso di Ursula per la solidarietà: verso un welfare paneuropeo?' 2021, www.questionegiustizia.it/data/doc/2859/bronzini-il-senso-di-ursula-per-la-solidarieta.pdf

147 ECJ, C-333/13, *Elisabeta Dano e Florin Dano contro Jobcenter Leipzig*, EU:C:2014:2358. In this decision, the ECJ argued that the relevant EU law norms 'must be interpreted as not precluding legislation of a Member State under which nationals of other Member States are excluded from entitlement to certain "special non-contributory cash benefits" within the meaning of Article 70(2) of Regulation No 883/2004, although those benefits are granted to nationals of the host Member State who are in the same situation, in so far as those nationals of other Member States do not have a right of residence under Directive 2004/38 in the host Member State'.

148 A. Nato, *La cittadinanza sociale ai tempi della crisi economica*, Rome: Cacucci, 2020, pp. 244–245.

149 ECJ. C-507/12, *Jessy Saint Prix contro Secretary of State for Work and Pensions*, EU:C:2014:2007.

150 ECJ, C-442/16, *Florea Gusa contro Minister for Social Protection*, EU:C:2017:1004.

151 ECJ; C-483/17, *Neculai Tarola contro Minister for Social Protection*, EU:C:2019:309.

152 ECJ, C-709/20, *The Department for Communities in Northern Ireland*, ECLI:EU:C:2021:602.

153 ECJ, C-569/16, *Bauer*, ECLI:EU:C:2018:871. ECJ, C-619/16, *Max-Planck-Gesellschaft zur Förderung der Wissenschaften eV/Tetsuji Shimizu*, ECLI:EU:C:2018:872.

154 ECJ, O.D. and Others vs. Istituto nazionale della previdenza sociale (INPS), ECLI:EU:C:2021:659. On this decision see: D. Gallo, 'Op-Ed: Migrants' Social Rights in the Dialogue Between the CJEU and the Italian Constitutional Court: Long Live Article 267 TFEU!' 2021, https://eulawlive.com/op-ed-migrants-social-rights-in-the-dialogue-between-the-cjeu-and-the-italian-constitutional-court-long-live-article-267-tfeu-by-daniele-gallo/

to the protection of fundamental rights, real shared constitutional goods in a complex system. It is no coincidence that this literature devotes very few pages to the added value that EU law gives to the protection of fundamental rights.[155] In this literature, Union law is seen as a source of inequality.[156] The irony in that is that a large part of anti-discrimination law is of EU derivation, such as the important case law on sex discrimination.[157]

These theories also frequently define the EU citizen as a consumer or entrepreneur,[158] but it would suffice here to cite judgements such as *Zambrano*,[159] *Rendón Marín*[160] e *Chavez-Vilchez*[161] to challenge this conclusion, in particular these last two, in which the potential of the Charter of Fundamental Rights of the EU acquired an explicit role in the judicial legal reasoning.

EU law is frequently depicted as the arm of liberalist globalisation, but this reconstruction forgets the role that the EU is playing in taming globalisation. It is sufficient to recall the case law of the Court of Justice in the field of privacy and data protection against Google and Facebook, for instance, and based on Articles 7 and 8 of the Charter of Fundamental Rights.[162]

This literature starts from the right premises, for example the need to complete the process of European integration, the right criticism of the alleged neutrality of the language of numbers that often serves to present as neutral what is not, shifting the discourse from the level of merit to that of method.[163] Finally, they also emphasise the need not to exclude recourse to other disciplines[164] in legal analysis in order to avoid a decontextualised and naïve reading of what is going on at supranational level. However, it seems to me that these premises sometimes

155 Somma, *Quando l'Europa tradì*, pp. 111 et seq. He emblematically devoted fewer than ten pages to the topic of fundamental rights.

156 Somma, *Quando l'Europa tradì*, pp. 111 et seq.

157 O. Pollicino, *Discriminazione sulla base del sesso e trattamento preferenziale nel diritto comunitario: un profilo giurisprudenziale alla ricerca del nucleo duro del new legal order*, Milan: Giuffrè 2005.

158 M. La Torre, Editoriale, 'Ordines. Per un sapere interdisciplinare sulle istituzioni europee', 2017, www.ordines.it/editoriale-di-massimo-la-torre-5/

159 ECJ, C-34/09, *Ruiz Zambrano* EU:C:2011:124.

160 ECJ, C-165/14, *Rendón Marín*, EU:C:2016:675.

161 ECJ, C-133/15, *Chavez-Vilchez and Others*, EU:C:2017:354.

162 ECJ, C-362/14, *Schrems*, ECLI:EU:C:2015:650; ECJ, C-311/18, *Facebook Ireland e Schrems*, ECLI:EU:C:2020:559; ECJ, C-131/12, Google Spain e Google, ECLI:EU:C:2014:317; ECJ, C-18/18 *Glawischnig-Piesczek c. Facebook Ireland Limited*, ECLI:EU:C:2019:821; ECJ, C-131/12, *Google Spain SL and Google Inc. v. Agencia Española de Protección de Datos (AEPD)*, ECLI:EU:C:2014:317.

163 M. Dani, 'Numeri e principio democratico: due concezioni a confronto nel diritto pubblico europeo', in A. Guazzarotti, C. Bergonzini and S. Borelli (eds.), *La legge dei numeri. Governance economica europea e marginalizzazione dei diritti*, Naples: Jovene, pp. 101 et seq.; V.A. Schmidt, *Europe's Crisis of Legitimacy: Governing by Rules and Ruling by Numbers in the Eurozone*, Cambridge University Press: Cambridge, 2020.

164 O. Chessa, *La costituzione della moneta. Concorrenza, indipendenza della banca centrale, pareggio di bilancio*, 2016, Naples: Jovene, 2016, p. 4.

lead to exaggerated conclusions and do not grasp the complexity of the EU constitutional system.

For instance, talking about the function performed by constitutionalism, more recently, authors have also used the formula 'authoritarian constitutionalism'[165] to define the EU. I think this theorisation really risks stretching the concept of constitutionalism too much. It is true that even authoritarian regimes may be equipped with documents called constitutions,[166] but in these cases there will be constitutions without constitutionalism and these fundamental laws will be instruments of government only.

After this historical overview, the next chapter will analyse the role played by the courts in a complex system such as the EU.

165 M. Wilkinson, 'Authoritarian Liberalism as Authoritarian Constitutionalism', in H. Alviar García and G. Frankenberg (eds.), *Authoritarian Constitutionalism. Comparative Analysis and Critique*, Cheltenham: Edward Elgar, 2019, pp. 317 et seq.

166 T. Ginsburg and A. Simpser (eds.), *Constitutions in Authoritarian Regimes*, Cambridge: Cambridge University Press, 2014.

5 Complexity in action

From the structure to the actors

5.1 Plan of the chapter

After having explored the meaning and the potential of constitutional complexity when applied to EU law, it is time to move from the structure of this complex legal order to the consequences that such a structure has on the actors operating at the different levels/poles.

The general idea is that in an order that is characterised by shared legal norms (i.e. common constitutional traditions, some of the general principles of EU law), that are the product of the constitutional synallagma, interpreters cannot work in an isolated manner (what Delmas Mary calls the 'l'isolement impossible'[1]); on the contrary, they have to interact with the other actors operating at different levels.

Constitutional pluralism has emphasised this aspect, but the cooperative spirit inspiring the principles of contrapuntal law,[2] for instance, captures just a part of the phenomenon.

'Interactions' may cover a broader range of actions (cooperative, competitive, conflicting), with cooperation being just one of these.

In this chapter I will try to present some of these kinds of interactions produced by the EU constitutionalisation process.

In order to do that, I shall focus on judges, employing a viewpoint on national judges that play a fundamental role in the multilevel legal system, as we will see.

In Chapter 2, I attempted to describe a 'complex' legal order as an 'entity' characterised by the following features: *non-reducibility*, *unpredictability*, *non-reversibility* and *non-determinability*.

This context favours the emergence of particular antinomies provided with some particular features:

- **First type of complex antinomy.** An antinomy may be defined as complex when it is due to the interlacement described earlier and by the consequent

1 M. Delmas Marty, *Delmas Marty, Le pluralisme ordonné. Les forces imaginantes du droit*, Paris: Ed. du Seuil, 2006, p. 39.

2 M. Poiares Maduro, 'Contrapunctual Europe's Constitutional Pluralism in Action', in N. Walker (ed.), *Sovereignty in Transition*, Oxford: Hart, 2003, pp. 501 et seq.

DOI: 10.4324/9781003056522-5

non-distinguishability among the different levels. According to this definition, one could say that an antinomy is complex if it cannot be resolved by looking at the relations between legal orders. For instance, starting from the assumption of the prevalence of order A over order B, we cannot say that norm x always prevails over norm y because x belongs to the order A while norm y succumbs because it belongs to order B. This occurs because in an integrated and interlaced system x and y could belong to both legal orders, A and B.

- **Second type of complex antinomy.** The absence of univocal norms of collision influences the 'reducibility' and the 'resolvability' of the constitutional conflict in a multi-layered system. Looking at this scenario, European constitutional law suffers from the absence of an unambiguous *primacy* clause. These antinomies can be resolved only on a case-by-case basis and not by an unequivocal solution offered by the existence of a precise rule for collision norms, such as a clear and undisputed supremacy clause. This occurs because in a context like this a provision that, *prima facie*, seems to belong to the national level could actually be the repetition of another norm existing at international or supranational level.

This is a pretty rough but useful bipartition, and I shall start from this distinction when dealing with the issue of constitutional conflicts in this chapter.

What are the consequences of this on the role of national judges? A consequence of the impossibility of tracing these principles back to the wording of a univocal primacy clause has galvanised their role. My assumption is that this context galvanises the case-by-case judicial approach to solving legal conflicts between rules. The impossibility of operating a distinction between legal orders implies the end of interpretative autonomy for these courts. The judicial side thus represents a privileged perspective for studying the relations between interacting legal orders, especially when looking at the multilevel and pluralistic structure of the European constitutional legal order.

This chapter is structured as follows: firstly, I shall describe the multiple loyalties characterising the position of judges in a complex legal system, then I shall present some of the consequences of these situations on the universe of judicial interactions possible in a complex legal order.

Finally, great room will be devoted to the issue of conflicts: contrary to what many constitutional theories argue, conflicts are not negative per se, but they might have a positive function in a complex legal order.

In order to provide this intuition with a theoretical framework, I am going to 'apply' the theory of Chantal Mouffe to these judicial interactions.

One might ask whether Chantal Mouffe's concept of agonistic pluralism is applicable to interactions between courts. I think it is. The argument that courts operate according to radically different dynamics than political actors does not take into account the copious literature on judicial politics.[3] Frequently,

3 B.Z. Tamanaha, 'The Several Meanings of "Politics" in Judicial Politics Studies: Why "Ideological Influence" Is Not "Partisanship" ', *Emory Law Journal*, 2012, pp. 759 et seq. T. Pavone and R.D.

courts – especially supreme and Constitutional Courts – can operate as veto players.[4] I believe I was among the first to propose the extension of Chantal Mouffe's conceptual apparatus[5] to the courts, and more recently other studies have developed in a similar direction.[6]

The last part of the chapter deals with some problematic and recent cases of conflicts that might contribute to the change of the complex legal order in the future.

5.2 Multiple loyalties and complexity in action: how hard it is being a judge in a complex legal order

In a complex legal system, actors present multiple loyalties, since they act at the same time as national and supranational actors.

In order to explore this aspect, I shall focus on the particular issue of multiples loyalties of the judges by examining some selected cases taken from national and supranational case law.

I decided to focus on multiple loyalties because they give a pretty realistic idea of how judges have to operate in an interlaced context presenting sources common to different levels.

It also demonstrates that the mere convergence does not produce (automatically at least) the end of interpretative conflicts, with judicial cooperation being just one of the options for judges in such a complex legal order.

As we know, national judges play a fundamental role in the multilevel system, being at the same time the guardians of the application of national law and the first defenders of the *Simmenthal* doctrine:[7] this is indeed one of the confirmations of the complex structure of the European legal order. Since in this context national and supranational levels share 'legal materials' (common constitutional traditions or general principles of European law are inferred from national legal principles), their judges present multiple loyalties: they have to be loyal to the ECJ and to their Constitutional Court at the same time. I think we can describe this situation by using the formula 'dual loyalty'.

Kelemen, 'The Evolving Judicial Politics of European Integration: The European Court of Justice and National Courts Revisited', *European Law Journal*, 2019, pp. 352 et seq.

4 S. Brouard and C. Hönnige, 'Constitutional Courts as Veto Players: Lessons from the United States, France and Germany', *European Journal of Political Research*, 2017, pp. 529 et seq.

5 Another caveat is important: the application of Mouffe's conceptual apparatus to judicial interactions does not imply the adoption of a populist understanding of politics. Moreover, in-depth studies have underlined the tensions that exist within Mouffe's thought. See D. Michelsen, 'Agonistic Democracy and Constitutionalism in the Age of Populism', *European Journal of Political Theory*, 2019, pp. 1 et seq.

6 D. Michelsen, 'Agonistic Democracy and Constitutionalism in the Age of Populism', *European Journal of Political Theory*, 2019, pp. 1 et seq.; R. Mieńkowska-Norkiene, 'The Political Impact of the Case Law of the Court of Justice of the European Union', *European Constitutional Law Review*, 2021, pp. 1 et seq.

7 ECJ, 106/77 *Simmenthal* [1977] ECR 1-62.

It is necessary here to make a clarification: in politics and political philosophy there is a huge literature[8] about this concept. Probably a political scientist would use the word 'obligation' rather than 'loyalty'[9] in order to describe the position of national judges in this context, but since in constitutional studies we frequently talk about 'constitutional loyalty',[10] I decided to keep it. Generally speaking, 'dual loyalty' refers to a loyalty to two separate interests that potentially conflict with each other.

This is exactly what we can observe in the role played by national judges, and my intuition is that such dual loyalty can generate antinomies (belonging to one of those two groups identified earlier) and even constitutional conflicts in the multi-level legal system. As a matter of fact, if national judges are well aware of the need to acknowledge the precedence of EU law when it is in conflict with national law, it is more complicated to understand what they should do in the case of collision between EU law provisions and some national constitutional provisions.

A good example of these kinds of antinomies is given by the *Federfarma* case[11] of the Italian State Council (*Consiglio di Stato*).[12] The case concerned an Italian law (Law no. 362/1991) permitting pharmaceutical companies to own municipal pharmacies in Milan. The legislation was partly declared unconstitutional by the Italian Constitutional Court because of the violation of Article 32 of the domestic Constitution (the right to health) 'in that section which did not envisage that a shareholding in companies managing municipal pharmacies is incompatible with all other operations in the sector including the production, distribution, intermediation and scientific information of medicines'.[13] Declaring the unconstitutionality of the provision, the Constitutional Court interpreted the remaining part of

8 On dual loyalty see: I. Zvi Baron, 'The Problem of Dual Loyalty', *Canadian Journal of Political Science*, 2009, pp. 1025 et seq.

9 'By obligation I mean rule-governed conduct, and political obligation specifically refers to laws and law like demand, made by public agencies', J. Shklar, 'Obligation, Loyalty, Exile', *Political Theory*, 1993, pp. 181 et seq., p. 183.

10 'Constitutional loyalty is an intrinsic value principle of all constitutions without which a constitution cannot work properly. Constitutional loyalty particularly requests respect from all state authorities; as manifest in the oaths of loyalty that are sworn by supreme organs of the state; by the duties imposed on civil servants and similar categories of public employees; or in the preconditions of founding a political party. Another arena where constitutional loyalty plays an important, though somewhat neglected, role is the compound state. Where a state consists of at least two tiers, the constitution will have to take care that all tiers are bound to loyalty – loyalty to the constitution itself, but also to each other', A. Gamper, 'On Loyalty and the (Federal) Constitution', *Vienna Journal on International Constitutional Law*, 2010, pp. 157 et seq., p. 157.

11 Cons. St., sez. V, n. 4207 del 2005. On this see: A. Ruggeri, 'Le pronunzie della Corte costituzionale come 'controlimiti' alle cessioni di sovranità a favore dell'ordinamento comunitario? (A margine di Cons. St., sez. V, n. 4207 del 2005)', 2006, www.forumcostituzionale.it/wordpress/wp-content/uploads/pre_2006/350.pdf; O. Pollicino, 'Il difficile riconoscimento delle implicazioni della supremazia del diritto europeo: una discutibile pronuncia del Consiglio di Stato', 2006, www.forumcostituzionale.it/wordpress/wp-content/uploads/pre_2006/531.pdf

12 Cons. St., sez. V, sent. n. 4207/ 2005.

13 Translation by G. Itzcovich, 'Fundamental Rights, Legal Disorder and Legitimacy: The *Federfarma* Case', *Jean Monnet Working Paper*, No. 12/08, 2008, https://jeanmonnetprogram.org/paper/fundamental-rights-legal-disorder-and-legitimacy-the-federfarma-case-2/, p. 16.

the law by offering a judgement that replaced the unconstitutional section with a new norm (a clear example of an additive judgement/*sentenza additiva*). The response of the European Commission was the following: 'The Constitutional Court's interpretation not only discourages but makes it impossible for enterprises operating or linked to enterprises operating in the pharmaceutical distribution to purchase majority or minority holdings in companies managing pharmacies'.[14] On this ground, in a subsequent case, the Italian State Council was asked to disapply the Italian provision as interpreted by the Constitutional Court because of its contrast with EU law. The State Council refused to do so.

In *Federfarma*, the State Council identified another exception to the *Cilfit* doctrine,[15] following a very eccentric reasoning: since a contested Italian norm had been interpreted by the Constitutional Court in a certain way, it had to be conceived as constitutional in nature since the interpretative judgement of the Italian Constitutional Court 'had been issued by the Constitutional Court to safeguard the right to health, which amounts to a "counter-limit" to European law insofar as it is situated in an area, that of fundamental rights'.[16] As a result of this characterisation, 'it, therefore, made no sense to refer to the ECJ for a preliminary ruling "which cannot be taken into account",[17] i.e., which was immaterial to the case':[18] 'If we cannot use the ECJ's decision, why refer to the ECJ?' This rhetoric seems to be the essence of the State Council's decision. The *Federfarma* case, however, is just one of many judgements based on an evident misunderstanding of the basic elements of EU law by the Italian national judges: in *Federfarma*, the State Council confused the Charter of Fundamental Rights of the EU with the Nice Treaty.[19]

Another interesting case is represented by *Cordero Alonso*,[20] where the Spanish judge referring the question to the ECJ asked about the necessity of disapplying a national statute (Article 33 of the Workers' Statute) that had already been acknowledged as inconsistent with the EU principle of non-discrimination by the ECJ in

14 European Commission, letter of 16 March 2005, C (2005) 762/1, infringement proceeding 2004/4928 against Italy, as cited by Itzcovich, 'Fundamental', p. 15.

15 The well-known *Cilfit* case excluded the duty of the national judge of last instance to raise the question, also when: 'previous decisions to the Court have already dealt with the point of law in question, irrespective of the nature of the proceedings which led to those decisions, even though the questions at issue are not strictly identical'. The State Council interpreted this case as a test of the utility/necessity of the decision of the Court. ECJ, C-283/81, *SRL Cilfit e Lanificio di Gavardo SPA v. Ministero della Sanità* [1982] ECR 3415. On the latest development of the *Cilfit* doctrine see ECJ, C-561/19, *Consorzio Italian Management e Catania Multiservizi* and Catania Multiservizi, ECLI:EU:C:2021:799.

16 Itzcovich, 'Fundamental', p. 17.

17 Cons. St., sez. V, sent. n. 4207/ 2005.

18 Itzcovich, 'Fundamental', p. 17.

19 See O. Pollicino, 'Il difficile riconoscimento delle implicazioni della supremazia del diritto europeo: una discutibile pronuncia del Consiglio di Stato (A margine di Cons. St., sez. V, sent. n. 4207/ 2005)', 2006, www.forumcostituzionale.it

20 ECJ, C-81/05, *Cordero Alonso* [2006] ECR I-7569.

a previous judgement.[21] However, the same national provision, after the first ECJ judgement on this matter, had also been interpreted in a way consistent with the constitutional principle of non-discrimination by the Spanish Constitutional Court.[22]

Since the general principle of equality and non-discrimination is a principle of Community law, Member States are bound by the ECJ's interpretation of that principle. That 'applies even when the national rules at issue are, according to the constitutional case-law of the Member State concerned, consistent with an equivalent fundamental right recognised by the national legal system'.[23]

In this case, the national judge was not able to decide which court he should follow (either the ECJ or the domestic constitutional judge) and, in order to avoid a decision that would have been seen as challenging the case law of the Spanish Constitutional Court, decided to refer an interpretive question to the ECJ about the meaning and the scope of the non-discrimination principle in EU law. The ECJ confirmed its previous interpretation, recalling how the *Simmenthal* doctrine and the principle of autonomy of EU law required the disapplication of national law contrasting with European legislation. In this way, the ECJ offered an interpretation of the same principle (principle of non-discrimination) very different from that provided by the Spanish Constitutional Court: although a provision is consistent with the national Constitution it has to be dis-applied if it contrasts with the EU law as interpreted by the ECJ.

These kinds of conflicts, caused by the dual loyalty of national judges to the ECJ and their own Constitutional Courts, have been galvanised over the years by the progressive constitutionalisation of the EU.

5.3 The idea of constitutional conflicts as a direct consequence of the constitutional complexity of the EU

As we saw, the European Union is a complex legal order, since it stems from the interlacing existing between national and supranational legal systems. This implies the existence of shared legal sources and many principles of EU law find their 'roots' in the national legal traditions.

Against this background, the EU is indebted to national constitutional orders since they gave the Union new blood by favouring the circulation of principles and practices that have shaped and reshaped the substance of the Treaties, what I described as the essence of a constitutional exchange (a '*do ut des*', a synallagma) among levels. Such a situation is the outcome of a convergence between the starting positions held by the ECJ (monism) and the national Constitutional Courts (dualism) in the first years of European integration.

21 ECJ, C-442/00 *Rodríguez Caballero* [2002] ECR I-11915.

22 Tribunal Constitucional, judgment No. 306/1993 of 25 October 1993, available at www.tribunalconstitucional.es

23 *Cordero Alonso*, par. 41.

Over the years, this purity was overcome and the Constitutional Courts began to talk about two 'autonomous and separated, although coordinated' systems (the Italian Constitutional Court, for example, in case no. 170/1984). At the same time, the ECJ has demonstrated its appreciation of the efforts of these national actors by assuming – sometimes – a benign and tolerant attitude: some scholars have defined such a situation of partial convergence by using the concept of '(limited) flexibilisation of supremacies'.[24]

Conflicts have had a crucial role in favouring this convergence; take the example of the *Solange* case, for instance. What was the essence of the German Constitutional *diktat* in *Solange I*?[25]

As we know, in 1970 in *Internationale Handelsgesellschaft* the ECJ held that:

> The validity of a Community measure or its effect within a member State cannot be affected by allegations that it runs counter to either fundamental rights as formulated by the constitution of that State or the principles of its constitutional structure.

Notoriously, in *Solange* I – delivered a few years after the ambivalent judgement in *Internationale Handelsgesellschaft* – the German Constitutional Court held that

> as long as [Solange] the integration process has not progressed so far that Community law receives a catalogue of fundamental rights decided on by a parliament and of settled validity, which is adequate in comparison with the catalogue of fundamental rights contained in the Basic Law, a reference by a court in the Federal Republic of Germany to the *Bundesverfassungsgericht* in judicial review proceedings . . . is admissible and necessary.[26]

In other words, the German Court asked for a Bill of Rights and a strong Parliament in a context of separation of powers, the two main ingredients of the most famous definition of Constitution present in the history of European constitutionalism: that of Article 16 of the Declaration of the Rights of Man and of the Citizen (1789).[27] Such chemistry was conceived as the right mix to overcome the democratic deficit characterising the European Communities.

24 V. Ferreres Comella, 'La Constitución española ante la clausola de primacia del Derecho de la Unión europea. Un comentario a la Declaración 1/2004 del Tribunal Constitucional 1/2004', in A. Lopez Castillo, A. Saiz Arnaiz and V. Ferreres Comella, *Constitución española y constitución europea*, Madrid: Centro de Estudios Políticos y Constitucionales, 2005, pp. 77 et seq., pp. 80 et seq.

25 BVerfGE 37, 271 2 BvL 52/71 Solange I-Beschluß.

26 BVerfGE 37, 271 2 BvL 52/71 Solange I-Beschluß.

27 Declaration of the Rights of Man and of the Citizen (1789), Article 16: 'A society in which the guarantee of the rights is not secured, or the separation of powers not determined, has no constitution at all'.

The *Solange* decision and the Italian counter-limits doctrine (*Frontini*[28]) paved the way for a long-lasting confrontation between the ECJ and the national Constitutional Courts.

This reveals how even *prima facie* anti-systemic actions taken by an actor at the national level results, in the end, as characterised by a systemic impact, since they contributed to the development and change of the primacy principle.

As has been noticed, the concept of primacy in *Internationale Handelsgesellschaft*[29] differs from that in *Omega*,[30] since in the latter judgement the ECJ shows an evident openness to the constitutional identity of the Member States.

In *Omega*, the Court said that 'it should be recalled in that context that, according to settled case-law, fundamental rights form an integral part of the general principles of law the observance of which the Court ensures'. In this judgement, the ECJ also acknowledged the necessity, for the EU law primacy, to stop in front of values codified in a national constitution.[31]

This judgement should be regarded as the culmination of a long process, starting with *Solange* I and paving the way for *Dynamic Medien*[32] or *Sayn-Wittgenstein*,[33] which seemed to show greater deference towards those principles embodying the national constitutional identity of the Member States. The *Omega* judgement intended to demonstrate the maturity of the EU legal system and, in general, the outcome of the constitutional dialogue with national interlocutors.

This process of convergence between the languages of the (national and supranational) courts has contributed to the creation of a common axiological field between the different (constitutional) legal orders. This common axiological field

28 Corte costituzionale, sentenza 183/1973.

29 ECJ, 11/70, *Internationale Handelsgesellschaft* [1970] ECR 1125.

30 ECJ, C-36/02 *Omega* [2004] ECR I-9609, par. 41.

31 'There can therefore be no doubt that the objective of protecting human dignity is compatible with Community law, it being immaterial in that respect that, in Germany, the principle of respect for human dignity has a particular status as an independent fundamental right. Since both the Community and its Member States are required to respect fundamental rights, the protection of those rights is a legitimate interest which, in principle, justifies a restriction of the obligations imposed by Community law, even under a fundamental freedom guaranteed by the Treaty such as the freedom to provide services (see, in relation to the free movement of goods, Schmidberger, paragraph 74). However, measures which restrict the freedom to provide services may be justified on public policy grounds only if they are necessary for the protection of the interests which they are intended to guarantee and only in so far as those objectives cannot be attained by less restrictive measures (see, in relation to the free movement of capital, Église de Scientologie, paragraph 18). It is not indispensable in that respect for the restrictive measure issued by the authorities of a Member State to correspond to a conception shared by all Member States as regards the precise way in which the fundamental right or legitimate interest in question is to be protected. Although, in paragraph 60 of Schindler, the Court referred to moral, religious or cultural considerations which lead all Member States to make the organisation of lotteries and other games with money subject to restrictions, it was not its intention, by mentioning that common conception, to formulate a general criterion for assessing the proportionality of any national measure which restricts the exercise of an economic activity', ECJ, C-36/02 *Omega* [2004] ECR I-9609, par. 34–47.

32 ECJ, C-244/06, *Dynamic Medien* [2008] ECR I-505.

33 ECJ, C-208/09, '*Sayn-Wittgenstein*' [2010] ECR I-13693.

can be described as the most evident product of that constitutional exchange defined above as the efficient secret of the European Constitution.

If, as we saw in Chapter 2, multilevel constitutionalism seems not to pay attention to the issue of constitutional conflicts, and if constitutional pluralism attempts to neutralise or to adjust constitutional conflicts, one could say that complexity acknowledges to some/them a positive function in the development of the structure of the legal order. Indeed, constitutional conflicts contribute to 'breaking' the boundaries of the legal spaces and favour the exchange of legal materials (the constitutional synallagma) that, in this book, I have attempted to present as the efficient secret of the European Constitution.

This reveals another important difference: while scholars interested in European constitutional law frequently refer to Habermas[34] in their works and to concepts like coherence or rationality, complexity instead (partly) departs from this tradition.

Rather than to Habermas, the alternative reading suggested by constitutional complexity looks to the idea of conflicts employed, for instance, by Chantal Mouffe[35] and her agonistic pluralism.[36]

Her considerations start from the nexus existing between democracy and conflicts in the attempt to describe an 'agonistic' public sphere conceived as the 'sine qua non for an effective exercise of democracy'.[37]

Another feature of her thought is the scepticism towards those reconstructions based on ideas of universal consensus that claim to 'establish the privileged rational nature of liberal democracy and consequently its universal validity'[38] and that perceive conflicts as mere irrationalities.[39]

34 For instance: J. Habermas, *Moral Consciousness and Communicative Action*, Cambridge MA: MIT Press, 2001; J. Habermas, *The Inclusion of the Other: Studies in Political Theory*, Cambridge MA: MIT Press, 1998.

35 Amongst Mouffe's work, see, in particular, C. Mouffe, *The Return of the Political*, London: Verso, 1993; C. Mouffe, *The Democratic Paradox*, London: Verso, 2000; C. Mouffe, *On the Political*, Abingdon: Routledge, 2005.

36 'I use the concept of agonistic pluralism to present a new way to think about democracy which is different from the traditional liberal conception of democracy as a negotiation among interests and is also different from the model which is currently being developed by people like Jürgen Habermas and John Rawls. While they have many differences, Rawls and Habermas have in common the idea that the aim of the democratic society is the creation of a consensus, and that consensus is possible if people are only able to leave aside their particular interests and think as rational beings. However, while we desire an end to conflict, if we want people to be free we must always allow for the possibility that conflict may appear and to provide an arena where differences can be confronted. The democratic process should supply that arena', C. Mouffe, in 'Hearts, Minds and Radical Democracy', 1998, www.redpepper.org.uk/hearts-minds-and-radical-democracy/

37 Mouffe, *On the Political*, p. 3.

38 Mouffe, *On the Political*, p. 84.

39 'Because for me that is what politics is about. If there is politics in society it is because there is conflict. . . . I started to look at Freud. He does not really develop this idea from the perspective of the collective subject; he develops it more in terms of the individual. I consider the idea of the division of the subject – Eros and Thanatos and the way the concept of the drive is linked to conflict,

Conflict is crucial in the democratic life, and denying it, as Mouffe says, has dangerous consequences since it can lead to authoritarian results as it may be inspired by the belief in a universal and right order.

Mouffe's criticism towards what she defines the 'optimistic anthropology' is strong and induces her to a confrontation with the principal contemporary thinkers Habermas, Rawls, Giddens, Held and Beck.

The legacy of Carl Schmitt is fundamental in this respect: his thought has been 'domesticated' by Mouffe, who tried to extract from his conception of the political (his contraposition friend/enemy) a version of this thought that might be compatible with the democratic premises.[40]

Mouffe is clear in shutting the door of her pluralism to all those positions that deny the democratic premises: 'A democratic society cannot treat those who put basic institutions into question as legitimate adversaries'.[41]

According to Mouffe, democracy is above all the creation of those 'conditions for the conflict to find its expression in agonistic terms'[42] rather than the creation of a 'reconciled society'.

A central point in Mouffe's work is the transformation of the Schmittian dialectic friend/enemy into that between adversary/adversary, following an agonistic concept of conflict (rather than an antagonistic one[43]), since the adversary does

very important for politics. I have also been interested in the work of Elias Canetti, in "Masse und Macht", when he insists that there is a tension between the individuality and the drive to be part of the mass. Again, the idea that we are divided is predominant', C. Mouffe, N. Carpentier and B. Cammaerts, 'Hegemony, Democracy, Agonism and Journalism: An Interview With Chantal Mouffe', *Journalism Studies*, 2006, pp. 964 et seq.; also http://eprints.lse.ac.uk/3020/

40 J. Noonan, *Democratic Society and Human Needs*, Montreal: McGill-Queen's University Press, 2006, p. 193.

41 Mouffe, *On the Political,* p. 120.

42 'How can we then deal with democratic politics? Not by trying to create a reconciled society, or by putting together all different views that are present in society. That would in fact imply a society without politics. Democratic politics should create the conditions for the conflict to find its expression in agonistic terms, avoiding that it becomes antagonistic', Mouffe, in Carpentier and Cammaerts, 'Hegemony'.

In another interview she said: 'This dimension of conflict cannot be eradicated; what you need to know is how to manage it. The traditional view would be to find ways to create a consensus. This is the view that I criticise: the idea that democracy is about trying to reach a consensus. What I say is that, the main task in a democracy is not to reach consensus but to manage dissensus; to manage dissensus so that it does not lead to civil war or so that it is not going to be repressed in authoritarian ways; to find forms which make co-existence possible and in fact will be conducive to some form of freedom and recognition of differences – this is what I understand by tolerance', 'Chantal Mouffe – From Antagonistic Politics to an Agonistic Public Space', 2010, www.academia.edu/30214803/From_antagonistic_politics_to_an_agonistic_public_space_Interview_with_Chantal_Mouffe

43 'There is a crucial difference between antagonism and agonism: a relation is antagonistic when A and B "have no common symbolic space", while it is agonistic when A and B "share a common symbolic space" but wish to organize it in different ways. Thus, by adhering to these principles participants turn to an adversarial mode of interaction and the hostile antagonistic conflict transforms to an exchange of views where the disputants respect one another's beliefs, and so on. Through agonistic contestations participants can reach agreement and common political decisions',

not aim at destroying/eliminating the other but, rather, respects the right to speech and the dissent of the other.[44] Conflict, in Mouffe's view, is not a violent clash but dissent respectful to the other and to democratic institutions. Against this background, conflict is not necessarily subversive but loyal to a context that shares some values without being necessarily homogeneous (in fact, Mouffe prefers to employ 'commonality' instead of 'homogeneity'[45]), but that composes a common symbolic framework.[46] In order to manage conflicts and dissent, a democratic context must give voice to interpretative disagreements by establishing the premises of a 'conflictual consensus'.[47] In this way, Mouffe solves the tension between *pacification* and *conflict*, by arguing that 'pacification, as I see it, is not repressing conflict but it is giving conflict the possibility to take shape in a legitimate way, without destroying the association with the political'.[48]

Mouffe's theory has been hugely studied in political theory and philosophy and focused on the result of this work of adaptation and domestication of Schmitt's categories. It has sometimes been argued that she basically betrayed her Schmittian premises.[49]

Many of these points stress some ambiguities in her thoughts; nevertheless, for the purpose of this study, I cannot go into detail in this while I am limiting myself

E. Erman, 'What Is Wrong With Agonistic Pluralism? Reflections on Conflict in Democratic Theory', *Philosophy and Social Criticism*, 2009, pp. 1039 et seq., p. 1044.

44 Mouffe sums up her relationship with Schmitt as follows: 'To think both with and against Schmitt- this is the thrust of our common endeavour', C. Mouffe (ed.), *The Challenge of Carl Schmitt*, London: Verso, 1999, p. 6.

45 Mouffe, *The Democratic Paradox*, p. 55.

46 'What I understand by the domestication of conflict is not the elimination of conflict but a way to give it a symbolic form and, for this, institutions are absolutely central. I certainly don't believe that the intrinsic logic of agonistic pluralism is to evade formal structure. In fact, what makes the prospect of an agonistic politics impossible is the absence of the necessary institutions', 'Chantal Mouffe – From Antagonistic Politics'.

47 'It needs what I call a "conflictual consensus". We need to accept a common symbolic framework, but within this symbolic framework, of course, there is room for disagreement', C. Mouffe, 'Which Public Space for Critical Artistic Practices?' 2012, https://readingpublicimage.files.wordpress.com/2012/04/chantal_mouffe_cork_caucus.pdf

48 'Of course we need some kind of pacification, if we understand by pacification that conflict is impeded from taking on an antagonistic form .... Obviously, in a democratic society, you cannot have people treating each other as enemies. That is in fact the problem with Schmitt; he is against pluralism because he believes that once it is allowed, it can only express itself in an antagonistic form. My counter-argument would be that not allowing conflict ultimately leads to an authoritarian order. You also have the "good" democrats who say that, if we give way to the idea of conflict and the ineradicability of conflict, then we have to abandon the very idea that we can have democracy. In contrast, I would argue that conflict is ineradicable, but there are different ways in which conflict can express itself. Democracy then becomes the legitimisation of conflict. Its aim is to enable forms of expressing conflict that are not going to destroy the political association. You do not need to negate conflict in order to imagine a democratic society', Mouffe, in Carpentier and Cammaerts, 'Hegemony'.

49 O. Ulas Ince, 'The Return of the Schmittian: Radical Democratic Theory at its Limits', 2009, http://papers.ssrn.com/sol3/papers.cfm?abstract_id=1675583

to adopting her conceptual framework in order to read the relation between actors in a complex legal order.

According to this scheme, actors in a complex legal system share a common framework that, nevertheless, admits the emergence of interpretive disagreements, as I will try to show in this chapter.

According to this construction, the *Solange* saga – as written – could be understood as an example of conflict in these terms, produced by one of these interpretative disagreements described by Mouffe.

In fact, after the first collisions with national Constitutional Courts, progressively the ECJ seemed to get the point by incorporating the concept of the fundamental rights as a premise of the primacy of EU law, and new important provisions have been introduced in the Treaties. Despite this convergence, tension between the ECJ and the Constitutional Courts has not been lacking because of the progressive expansion of the ECJ activity in national fields. Moreover, the product of this convergence gave birth to new kinds of conflicts among interpreters, conflicts due to the existence of legal sources (the principles concerning the protection of fundamental rights) that are now shared by the ECJ and the national Constitutional Courts. As we will see, such a scenario has produced dynamics of interpretive competition.

This is consistent with Mouffe's theory: although the actors of this complex legal system now share the necessity to respect those constitutional goods conceived as fundamental rights according to the multilevel case law, it is always possible to have interpretative disagreements.

5.4 Back to case law: a possible typology of constitutional conflicts

Having recalled the theoretical framework I am going to employ in this chapter, I will move back to the cases.

Applying the scheme of Chantal Mouffe to our ambit, one can identify some examples of 'disagreement over interpretations':

1 Conflicts over the interpretation *stricto sensu* understood and concerning the interpretation of the same and shared principle (*Rodriguez Caballero*, *Cordero Alonso*).
2 Conflicts due to the dual role played by national common judges (*Winner Wetten*, *Filipiak* and *Križan*).
3 Conflicts over the interpretative monopoly caused by an 'octroyée' interpretation of the national constitutional materials (*Mangold* and *Kücükdeveci*).
4 Constitutional conflicts concerning the contrast between EU law – as interpreted by the ECJ – and provisions included in the national constitutions (*Kreil*, *Michaniki*, and *Melki*).

I am not going to deal with all the possible conflicts present in EU law; rather, I shall focus on those conflicts that I call conflicts due to the (partial) convergence occurred among levels (conflicts by convergence). Secondly, I shall focus on constitutional conflicts, i.e. conflicts between the primacy of EU law and the supremacy of national constitutions.[50]

5.4.1 Conflicts over the interpretation **stricto sensu** *understood and concerning the interpretation of the same and shared principle* **(Rodriguez Caballero, Cordero Alonso)**

We have already dealt with the *Cordero Alonso* case in the previous pages, and we also saw how in that case the disagreement caused different interpretations given to a shared principle by two different interpreters.

This confirms that the mere sharing of principles that are common, from a formal point of view, does not mean that the interpreters will agree on the interpretation to give to it.

The referring judge in the *Cordero Alonso* case was just a collateral victim of the interpretive competition between Constitutional Courts and the ECJ, an interpretive competition that paradoxically increased with the progressive constitutionalisation of the EU: the ECJ progressively started acknowledging an important role to the national constitutional materials in its decisions; this 'partial' appropriation of the fundamental rights discourse by the ECJ emerges in a long series of judgements and is most evident in cases such as *Omega*[51] and *Dynamic Medien*.[52] As some authors have pointed out, having a look at those cases, one can perceive a certain concern over the '*octroyée* methodology of construing common constitutional traditions'.[53] However the *Cordero Alonso* case is just one examples of cases where the ECJ has challenged judgements given by national Constitutional Courts, and in the next pages I shall move to other examples of constitutional conflicts.

On 26 February 2013, the ECJ decided *Melloni*,[54] a very important case triggered by a preliminary question raised by the Spanish Constitutional Court.

50 Using the distinction employed by the Spanish Constitutional Court: Tribunal Constitucional, *declaración* 1/2004, www.tribunalconstitucional.es

51 ECJ, C-36/02, *Omega* [2004] ECR I-9609.

52 ECJ, C-244/06, *Dynamic Medien* [2008] ECR I-505.

53 M. Dani, 'Tracking Judicial Dialogue – The Scope for Preliminary Rulings From the Italian Constitutional Court', *Jean Monnet Working Paper*, No. 10/2008, 2008, https://jeanmonnetprogram.org/paper/tracking-judicial-dialogue-the-scope-for-preliminary-rulings-from-the-italian-constitutional-court-2/. See also the reactions to the *Mangold* case (ECJ, C-144/04, *Mangold* [2005] ECR I-9981): R. Herzog and L. Gerken, '[Comment] Stop the European Court of Justice', http://euobserver.com/9/26714. This piece is the translation of an article originally published in German: 'Stoppt den Europäischen Gerichtshof', *Frankfurter Allgemeine Zeitung*, 8 September 2008.

54 ECJ, C-399/11, *Stefano Melloni v. Ministerio Fiscal*, ECLI:EU:C:2013:107. Mr. Melloni, an Italian citizen living in Spain, was convicted in absentia for bankruptcy fraud by a sentence delivered by the Tribunale of Ferrara. On the basis of the Council Framework Decision on the European Arrest Warrant (2002/584/JHA as amended by the Framework Decision 2009/299/JHA), the Italian authorities asked for the activation of the mechanism. Mr. Melloni opposed surrender to the

This preliminary question had gathered the attention of scholars for at least two reasons: first of all, it was raised by the Spanish Constitutional Court, which for the first time had decided to use Article 267 TFEU.

In this sense, *Melloni* represented a link in a longer chain of preliminary questions raised by national Constitutional Courts. The second reason was because the ECJ was expected to say something important about Article 53 of the Charter of Fundamental Rights of the EU, concerning the burning issue of the relationship between the standard of protection ensured to the same right at different levels.

In that case, the ECJ refused a minimalist interpretation of Article 53 by saying that the

> Charter would undermine the principle of the primacy of EU law inasmuch as it would allow a Member State to disapply EU legal rules which are fully in compliance with the Charter where they infringe the fundamental rights guaranteed by that State's constitution.
>
> (par. 58)

The ECJ then added at par. 60:

> It is true that Article 53 of the Charter confirms that, where an EU legal act calls for national implementing measures, national authorities and courts remain free to apply national standards of protection of fundamental rights, provided that the level of protection provided for by the Charter, as interpreted by the Court, and the primacy, unity and effectiveness of EU law are not thereby compromised.

This was seen as a return to an absolute conception of primacy,[55] and in general it sounded very tough. On 13 February 2014, in its follow-up to the *Melloni* decision of the Luxembourg Court, the Spanish Constitutional Court reversed its case law and abided by the indications of the ECJ.[56] The Spanish follow-up to the *Melloni* case was a bit ambiguous because: 'while the outcome does fulfil the mandates of EU law, the reasoning proves quite unsettling'.[57]

Italian authorities, by arguing the violation of the right to defence. The Audiencia Nacional (a special Spanish high court) decided to surrender Mr. Melloni to Italy since it considered the right to defence was respected (Mr. Melloni, in fact, was aware of the trial, opted for the absentia and appointed two lawyers to defend himself). Against the order of the Audiencia Nacional, Mr. Melloni opposed a *recurso de amparo* (a direct action for the protection of constitutional rights guaranteed by the Constitution) before the Spanish Constitutional Court.

55 To quote the formula used, by some scholars: A. Bogdandy and S. Schill, 'Overcoming Absolute Primacy: Respect for National Identity Under the Lisbon Treaty', *Common Market Law Review*, 2011, pp. 1417 et seq.

56 Available at: http://s01.s3c.es/imag/doc/2014-02-20/sentenciaTCextradicion.pdf

57 A. Torres Pérez, 'Melloni in Three Acts: From Dialogue to Monologue', *European Constitutional Law Review*, 2014, pp. 308 et seq.

More generally, this case gives an idea of the very difficult role played by national Constitutional Courts and of the part relativisation, for certain aspects, of their mandate. This decision is in line with other rulings of the ECJ whereby the Luxembourg Court did not show great deference towards national Constitutional Courts. I am referring to the *Filipiak*[58] and the *Winner Wetten*[59] cases, for instance.

5.4.2 Conflicts due to the dual role played by national common judges (Winner Wetten, Filipiak *and* Križan)

Some of these conflicts are strongly related to those multiple loyalties described, and in this respect, other examples of constitutional conflicts are represented by the *Filipiak*[60] and the *Winner Wetten*[61] cases. The *Winner Wetten* case originated from a preliminary reference raised by a German court. In 2006, the German Constitutional Court acknowledged that the legislation on the public monopoly on gambling on sporting competitions existing in two Länder violated Paragraph 12.1 of the Basic Law. At the same time, it decided not to declare the legislation in question unconstitutional and to maintain it in effect until 31 December 2007, sending a sort of 'message' to the legislature to push it to intervene by that date through the use of its discretionary power in order to amend the legislation to save it from being in breach of the Basic Law. Despite this judgement, the ECJ decided to push the referring judge to disapply the legal provision 'saved', for a transitional period, by the German Constitutional Court and concluded that:

> By reason of the primacy of directly-applicable Union law, national legislation concerning a public monopoly on bets on sporting competitions which, according to the findings of a national court, comprises restrictions that are incompatible with the freedom of establishment and the freedom to provide services, because those restrictions do not contribute to limiting betting activities in a consistent and systematic manner, cannot continue to apply during a transitional period.[62]

Filipiak is a very similar case originating from a preliminary question raised by a Polish judge with regard to proceedings on tax issues between Mr Filipiak, a Polish national engaging in economic activity in the Netherlands (where he regularly paid the social security and health insurance contributions required by Dutch legislation) and the Director of the Poznań Tax Chamber. What is interesting to us is that before the judgement in the appeal against the refusal, the Polish

58 ECJ, C-314/08, *Filipiak* [2009] ECR I-11049.
59 ECJ, C-409/06, *Winner Wetten*, [2010] ECR I-08015.
60 ECJ, C-314/08, *Filipiak* [2009] ECR I-11049.
61 ECJ, C-409/06, *Winner Wetten*, [2010] ECR I-08015.
62 ECJ, C-409/06, *Winner Wetten*, [2010] ECR I-08015.

Constitutional Tribunal ruled that the income tax law in question infringed the principles of equality and social justice codified in the Polish Constitution. At the same time, by exploiting its powers *ad hoc*, the Polish Constitutional Tribunal decided to postpone the loss of validity of the legislation until 30 November 2008. By responding to the referring judge, the ECJ concluded that

> the primacy of Community law obliges the national court to apply Community law and to refuse to apply conflicting provisions of national law, irrespective of the judgment of the national Constitutional Court which has deferred the date on which those provisions, held to be unconstitutional, are to lose their binding force.[63]

Another interesting case is *Križan*,[64] which originated from a preliminary reference sent by the *Najvyšší súd Slovenskej republiky* (Supreme Court of Slovakia).

Among other things, the referring judge asked whether Article 267 TFEU requires or enables the supreme court of a Member State to use the preliminary ruling mechanism:

> Even at a stage of proceedings where the constitutional court has annulled a judgment of the supreme court based in particular on the application of the EU framework on environmental protection and imposed the obligation to abide by the constitutional court's legal opinions based on breaches of the procedural and substantive constitutional rights of a person involved in judicial proceedings, irrespective of the EU law dimension of the case concerned that is, where in those proceedings the constitutional court, as the court of last instance, has not concluded that there is a need to refer a question to the [Court of Justice] for a preliminary ruling and has provisionally excluded the application of the right to an acceptable environment and the protection thereof in the case concerned?

The answer delivered further proof of the strong conception of EU law employed by the ECJ in its relationship with national (constitutional) judges, stressing the autonomy to be left to the referring judge to refer to the ECJ:

> The national rule which obliges the Najvyšší súd Slovenskej republiky to follow the legal position of the Ústavný súd Slovenskej republiky cannot therefore prevent the referring court from submitting a request for a preliminary ruling to the Court of Justice at any point in the proceedings which it judges appropriate, and to set aside, if necessary, the assessments made by

63 ECJ, C-314/08, *Filipiak* [2009] ECR I-11049.

64 ECJ, C-416/10, *Krizan & Others atesv. Slovenska Inspekcia Zivotneho Prostredia*, ECLI:EU:C:2013:8.

> the Ústavný súd Slovenskej republiky which might prove to be contrary to European Union law.[65]

The necessity of preserving the direct relationship between the ECJ and national judges was also at the heart of a different decision, the *Melki* case,[66] as we will see.

5.4.3 Conflicts over the interpretative monopoly caused by an 'octroyée' interpretation of the national constitutional materials (Mangold *and* Kücükdeveci)

Another group of cases concerns those conflicts triggered by decisions, so to speak, detrimental for the interpretative sovereignty of Constitutional Courts.

The *Mangold*[67] case represented the realisation of this situation: in order to react to the impulse for flexible labour markets by following a framework agreement reached by the social partners, the German legislation authorised fixed-term

65 'Finally, as a supreme court, the Najvyšší súd Slovenskej republiky is even required to submit a request for a preliminary ruling to the Court of Justice when it finds that the substance of the dispute concerns a question to be resolved which comes within the scope of the first paragraph of Article 267 TFEU. The possibility of bringing, before the constitutional court of the Member State concerned, an action against the decisions of a national court, limited to an examination of a potential infringement of the rights and freedoms guaranteed by the national constitution or by an international agreement, cannot allow the view to be taken that that national court cannot be classified as a court against whose decisions there is no judicial remedy under national law within the meaning of the third paragraph of Article 267 TFEU.

In the light of the foregoing, the answer to the first question is that Article 267 TFEU must be interpreted as meaning that a national court, such as the referring court, is obliged to make, of its own motion, a request for a preliminary ruling to the Court of Justice even though it is ruling on a referral back to it after its first decision was set aside by the constitutional court of the Member State concerned and even though a national rule obliges it to resolve the dispute by following the legal opinion of that latter court'.

66 'The Court has concluded therefrom that the existence of a rule of national law whereby courts or tribunals against whose decisions there is a judicial remedy are bound on points of law by the rulings of a court superior to them cannot, on the basis of that fact alone, deprive the lower courts of the right provided for in Article 267 TFEU to refer questions on the interpretation of EU law to the Court of Justice (see, to that effect, Rheinmühlen-Düsseldorf, paragraphs 4 and 5, and Cartesio, paragraph 94). The lower court must be free, in particular if it considers that a higher court's legal ruling could lead it to give a judgment contrary to EU law, to refer to the Court questions which concern it (Case C-378/08 *ERG and Others* 2010 E.C.R. I-0000, paragraph 32)', par. 42, ECJ, Joined Cases C-188/10 and C-189/10, Melki, [2008] ECR I-09999. On Melki see: A. Dyevre, 'The Melki Way: The Melki Case and Everything You Always Wanted to Know About French Judicial Politics (But Were Afraid to Ask)', in M. Claes, M. De Visser, P. Popelier and C. Van De Heyning (eds.), *Constitutional Conversations in Europe: Actors, Topics and Procedures*, Antwerp: Intersentia, pp. 309 et seq.

67 ECJ, C-144/04, *Mangold* [2005] ECR I-9981. See R. Calvano, 'Il caso "Mangold": la Corte di giustizia afferma (senza dirlo) l'efficacia orizzontale di una direttiva comunitaria non scaduta?', 2006, www.associazionedeicostituzionalisti.it

employment contracts for a maximum of two years. The German legislature also added that within that maximum limit of two years, a fixed-term contract could be renewed up to three times.

The fixed-term employment contracts were accepted without the above condition, if the worker had reached the age limit of 60 – subsequently lowered to 52 years – at the commencement of his employment term. In that case, the ECJ was asked to verify the compatibility of German law with EU directive n. 2000/78, and in particular with the principle of non-discrimination on grounds of age drawn from it.

The Court of Justice recalled that Community law (specifically Article 6, n. 1 of directive 2000/78) had to be construed as precluding

> a provision of domestic law such as that at issue in the main proceedings which authorizes, without restriction, unless there is a close connection with an earlier contract of employment of indefinite duration concluded with the same employer, the conclusion of fixed-term contracts of employment once the worker has reached the age of 52.
>
> (par. 78)

The term for the implementation of the directive was not yet expired, and in fact the *Mangold* case is interesting for the way in which the ECJ resolved the conflict between EU and national laws. The ECJ, in fact, recalled that: 'during the period prescribed for transposition of a directive, the Member States must refrain from taking any measures liable seriously to compromise the attainment of the result prescribed by that directive' (par. 67).

Later, however, the ECJ seemed to 'change' its parameter, shifting its focus from the directive to the general principles of Community law. This intuition is confirmed by the words of the Court, in which it is evident that the conflict at stake is that between national legislation and the principle of non-discrimination on the basis of age, a principle that would find its source 'in various international instruments and in the constitutional traditions common to the Member States' (par. 74).

The ECJ concluded, recalling the duty to disapply of the national judge, that

> it is the responsibility of the national court, hearing a dispute involving the principle of non-discrimination in respect of age, to provide, in a case within its jurisdiction, the legal protection which individuals derive from the rules of Community law and to ensure that those rules are fully effective, setting aside any provision of national law which may conflict with that law . . . . It is the responsibility of the national court to guarantee the full effectiveness of the general principle of non-discrimination in respect of age, setting aside any provision of national law which may conflict with Community law, even where the period prescribed for transposition of that directive has not yet expired.
>
> (par. 77–78)

Hatzopoulos, one of the first commentators of the judgement, read it together with other cases like *Carpenter*[68] and *Karner*:[69] all of these cases are characterised by the material reference to the legal materials of the ECHR and to the general principles. The conclusion reached by Hatzopoulos is that the mix between hard and soft law sources results in influencing the legal reasoning of the ECJ by affecting its linearity. In these cases, the ECJ, in fact, cannot solve its case by appealing to a clear legal parameter and refers to the general principles. This choice sometimes reflects the lack of a strong legal reasoning:

> Since EC hard legislation will be rare in fields in which some EU coordination takes place, the Court will be obliged to control national measures by reference to general principles and fundamental rights, in order to effectively protect the latter. This, however, is not a commendable development, at least by currently applicable legal standards, and all the judgments above have been strongly criticised.[70]

What is interesting to us is the way in which the ECJ took inspiration from the national constitutional materials in order to construct this general principle.

Some German scholars harshly reacted to *Mangold* by questioning the possibility of inferring such a principle from the constitutional traditions common to the Member States.

In an article published in English on *Euobserver*, Herzog and Gerken wrote:

> However, this 'general principle of community law' was a fabrication. In only two of the then 25 member states namely Finland and Portugal is there any reference to a ban on age discrimination, and in not one international treaty is there any mention at all of there being such a ban, contrary to the terse allegation of the ECJ. Consequently, it is not difficult to see why the ECJ dispensed with any degree of specification or any proof of its allegation. To put it bluntly, with this construction which the ECJ more or less pulled out of a hat, they were acting not as part of the judicial power but as the legislature.[71]

Mangold is thus emblematic of that 'octroyée methodology of construing common constitutional traditions'[72] according to which the ECJ has been jeopardising the interpreting sovereignty of national Constitutional Courts.

The ECJ recalled *Mangold* in *Kücükdeveci*,[73] confirming the existence of a general principle of non-discrimination based on age and conceiving this general

68 ECJ, C-60/00, *Carpenter*, [2002] ECR, I-6279.

69 ECJ, C-71/02, *Karner*, [2004] ECR, I-3025.

70 V. Hatzopoulos, 'Why the Open Method of Coordination Is Bad for You: A Letter to the EU', *European Law Journal*, 2007, pp. 309 et seq., p. 337.

71 Herzog and Gerken, '[Comment] Stop the European Court of Justice'.

72 Dani, 'Tracking Judicial Dialogue'.

73 ECJ, C-555/07, *Kücükdeveci*, [2010] ECR I-365.

principle as its parameter. The ECJ acted in this way although the term for implementing the directive had already expired at that time. The Luxembourg Court recalled the EU Charter of Fundamental Rights only to 'prove' the later codification of this general principle, even though the EU Charter was already in force at that time.

As Arnull pointed out, 'the Court of Justice itself was initially rather coy about mentioning Mangold or the general principle of equality'.[74]

However, later on, the ECJ recalled *Mangold* in *Kücükdeveci*,[75] confirming the existence of a general principle of non-discrimination based on age and conceiving this general principle as its parameter, although the term for implementing the directive had already expired at that time, and recalling the EU Charter of Fundamental Rights only to 'prove' the later codification of this general principle despite the fact that the EU Charter was already in force at that time.

More recently, the ECJ recalled *Mangold* also in his *Dansk Industri* case,[76] where the Court reiterated the duty of disapplication in case of violation of the general principle of non-discrimination on grounds of age:

> In order to answer that question, it is appropriate first of all to note that the source of the general principle prohibiting discrimination on grounds of age, as given concrete expression by Directive 2000/78, is to be found, as is clear from recitals 1 and 4 of the directive, in various international instruments and in the constitutional traditions common to the Member States (see judgments in Mangold, C-144/04, EU:C:2005:709, paragraph 74, and Kücükdeveci, C-555/07, EU:C:2010:21, paragraphs 20 and 21). It is also apparent from the Court's case law that that principle, now enshrined in Article 21 of the Charter of Fundamental Rights of the European Union, must be regarded as a general principle of EU law. (see judgements in Mangold, C-144/04, EU:C:2005:709, paragraph 75, and Kücükdeveci, C-555/07, EU:C:2010:21, paragraph 21)[77]

74 A. Arnull, 'What Is a General Principle of EU Law?' in S. Vogenauer (ed.), *Prohibition of Abuse of Law a New General Principle of EU Law?* Oxford: Hart, 2017, pp. 7 et seq., p. 15. Arnull refers to Chacon Navas (ECJ, C-13/05, *Sonia Chacón Navas v. Eurest Colectividades SA* [2006] ECR I-06467) and Palacios de la Villa (ECJ, C-411/05, *Palacios de la Villa* [2007] ECR I-08531), Lindorfer v. Council (ECJ, C-227/04 P, *Maria-Luise Lindorfer v. Council of the European Union* [2007] ECR I-06767) and Bartsch (ECJ, C-427/06, *Bartsch* [2008] ECR I-07245). See also the Opinion AG Mazák, ECJ, C-411/05, *Félix Palacios de la Villa* [2007] ECR I-08531, par. 88–94; Opinion AG Trstenjak, C-282/10, *Maribel Dominguez v. Centre informatique du Centre Ouest Atlantique and Préfet de la région Centre*, ECLI:EU:C:2011:559, par. 140–141.

75 ECJ, C-555/07, *Kücükdeveci* [2010] ECR I-365.

76 ECJ, C-441/14, *Dansk Industri (DI)* ECLI:EU:C:2016:278. See also the distinguishing made by the ECJ in Bartsch, C-427/06, *Bartsch* [2008] I-07245, par. 24

77 ECJ, C-441/14, *Dansk Industri (DI)* ECLI:EU:C:2016:278 par. 22.

Mangold still creates mixed feelings. Looking at the national level, it is no coincidence that after *Mangold*, the German Constitutional Court has indirectly responded to the ECJ with the famous Lisbon decision[78] and then directly with the Honeywell[79] decision before raising its first preliminary question under Article 267 TFEU in the famous *Gauweiler* case.[80] The tip of the iceberg was reached in the already mentioned decision on the Public Sector Purchase Programme (PSPP).[81]

Moreover, the Danish Supreme Court in *Ajos*[82] also took the chance to delimit the competences of the EU. On that occasion, the Danish Supreme Court also rejected the Mangold doctrine by using the *ultra vires* doctrine, arguing that the Danish law on accession to the EU does not cover the general principles of EU law, which cannot have a horizontal direct effect on the domestic legal system.[83] Although the lack of transparency in its legal reasoning does not represent the only ground for criticism of this decision, *Mangold* and its legacy are also an example of the harsh reactions that have been caused by a decision characterised by a questionable use of the comparative method. The fact that the ECJ has not followed the 'mathematical logic of the lowest common denominator' in the reconstruction of a general principle does not represent per se an issue, but the lack of transparency in revealing the domestic sources considered for that purpose triggered tensions and conflicts with national courts. Decisions like *Mangold*[84] have been perceived as a bad move from national Constitutional Courts and commentators,[85] and if the ECJ wants to remedy that it must make sure to involve those Constitutional Courts that are eager to have a proper and loyal dialogue.[86] Indeed, even traditionally cooperative Constitutional Courts – such as the Austrian one – have been sending warnings lately, and this tension later caused important cases like *A. v. B.*[87]

78 BVerfGE 123, 267 www.bundesverfassungsgericht.de/SharedDocs/Entscheidungen/EN/2009/06/es20090630_2bve000208en.html

79 2 BvR 2661/06, www.bundesverfassungsgericht.de/entscheidungen/rs20100706_2bvr266106.html

80 2 BvR 2728/13, par. 29. See also: Case Gauweiler, C-62/14, ECLI:EU:C:2015:400.

81 2 BvR 859/15, www.bundesverfassungsgericht.de/SharedDocs/Entscheidungen/EN/2020/05/rs20200505_2bvr085915en.html;jsessionid=F892FE5330900A9A29FDCBEF992814FE.2_cid392

82 Højesteret, decision no. 15/2014 Dansk Industri (DI) acting for Ajos A/S vs. The estate left by A.

83 N. Lazzerini, *La Carta dei diritti fondamentali dell'Unione europea: I limiti di applicazione*, Milan: Franco Angeli, 2018, p. 131. Zaccaroni argued that on that occasion the Danish Supreme Court basically asked 'the Court of Justice to withdraw from its Kücükdeveci and Mangold case law and to go back to its Dominguez decision', G. Zaccaroni, 'Is the Horizontal Application of General Principles Ultra Vires? Dialogue and Conflict between Supreme European Courts in Dansk Industri', 2018, www.federalismi.it

84 ECJ, C-144/04, *Mangold* [2005] ECR, I-9981.

85 Herzog and Gerken, "[Comment] Stop the European" cit.

86 According to the examples offered by A. Torres Pérez, *Conflicts of Rights in the European Union: A Theory of Supranational Adjudication*, Oxford: Oxford University Press, 2009, p. 118.

87 ECJ, C-112/13, *A v. B and others*, ECLI:EU:C:2014:2195. See also Corte costituzionale, sentenza 269/2017, on that. D. Sarmiento, *Adults in the (Deliberation) Room: A Comment on M.A.S., Quaderni costituzionali*, 2018, pp. 228 et seq.

5.4.4 Constitutional conflicts concerning the contrast between EU law – as interpreted by the ECJ – and provisions included in the national constitutions (Kreil, Michaniki, *and* Melki)

The last group of constitutional conflicts refers to cases of judgements where the ECJ found an incompatibility between a constitutional national provision and EU law. It is not a conflict of 'interpretation' in a narrow sense, but rather a case of real contradiction between EU law and national level.

Kreil[88] is perhaps the most famous case. In *Kreil*, the ECJ de facto affirmed the prevalence of EU law over a national constitutional provision when it held that a general exclusion of women from military posts involving the use of arms (as provided for in Article 12a.4 of the *Grundgesetz*) was in conflict with the content of the Equal Treatment Directive (76/207). Subsequently, the *Grundgesetz* was amended.[89]

This decision concerned the case of Tanja Kreil, who in 1996 applied to join the weapons electronic maintenance service of the German Federal army. Since her application was rejected on the basis of Article 12a.4 of the *Grundgesetz*, she went before the Hannover Administrative Court, claiming that the rejection on the basis of her sex only was contrary to Equal Treatment Directive (76/207), and the local court raised a preliminary question to the ECJ in order to verify the consistency of national provisions with such a directive.

Another interesting case is *Michaniki.*[90] The *Michaniki* case originated from a constitutional reform of 2001, whereby Article 14 of the Greek Constitution was amended. After this reform, Article 14, paragraph 9[91] provided a sort of irre-

88 ECJ, C-285/98, *Kreil* [2000] ECR I-69.

89 Article 12a 4: 'If, during a state of defence, the need for civilian services in the civilian health system or in stationary military hospitals cannot be met on a voluntary basis, women between the age of eighteen and fifty-five may be called upon to render such services by or pursuant to a law. Under no circumstances may they be required to render service involving the use of arms'.

90 ECJ, C-213/07, *Michaniki AE v. Ethniko Simvoulio Radiotileorasis and Ipourgos Epikratias* [2008] ECR I-9999.

91 Article 14, p. 9: 'The ownership, financial standing and means of financing of the media must be disclosed, as stipulated by law.

The measures and restrictions necessary to ensure full media transparency and pluralism shall be specified by law.

It is prohibited to concentrate control of several media of the same or different form.

In particular, it is prohibited to concentrate control of more than one electronic medium of the same form, as specified by law.

The status of owner, partner, main shareholder or management executive of a media undertaking shall be incompatible with the status of owner, partner, main shareholder or management executive of an undertaking which undertakes with the State or a legal person in the public sector in the broad sense to perform works or provide supplies or services.

The prohibition in the previous subparagraph shall also extend to any form of intermediary, such as spouses, relatives or financially dependent persons or companies.

A law shall set out the specific regulations, the sanctions (which may go as far as revocation of a radio or television station's licence and an order prohibiting the signature of, or cancelling, the

buttable presumption of general incompatibility between the sector of the media and that of public contracts in order to promote transparency in the public works sector. On the basis of this provision, a company, Michaniki AE, failed to win the contract at the end of the tendering procedure and brought an action before the Greek Council of State, which referred a preliminary question to the ECJ concerning the interpretation of directive 93/37/EC on public works contracts. The ECJ first recalled that the assessment of the compatibility between EU law and national law goes beyond its jurisdiction in preliminary ruling proceedings. Then it also said that the directive does not forbid per se a Member State from providing other exclusionary measures in order to ensure transparency and equal treatment of the tenderers if these measures are consistent with the principle of proportionality.

However, the Luxembourg Court also stated that:

> Community law must be interpreted as precluding a national provision which, whilst pursuing the legitimate objectives of equal treatment of tenderers and of transparency in procedures for the award of public contracts, establishes an irrebuttable presumption that the status of owner, partner, main shareholder or management executive of an undertaking active in the media sector is incompatible with that of owner, partner, main shareholder or management executive of an undertaking which contracts with the State or a legal person in the public sector in the broad sense to perform a works, supply or services contract.

Finally, it should be noted that, in his Opinion, Advocate General Maduro used the old Article 6.3 TEU, to remember that it was one of the EU's obligations to respect the constitutional identity of the Member States, and this in my view confirms the continuity existing between Article 6.3 TEU (pre-Lisbon version) and Article 4.2 after the coming into force of the Reform Treaty.

Partially different is the *Melki* case.[92]

Before analysing this case, it is necessary to recall that EU law is just one of the factors inducing multiple loyalties in ordinary judges. Similarly, these national judges have a crucial role in the application of the ECHR, and recently scholars have defined them as the natural judges of international law.[93] Against this background, what renders EU law in particular is the preliminary ruling mechanism that makes the relationship between national judges and the ECJ even stronger. The preliminary ruling mechanism has indeed had a fundamental role in the

contract in question), the system of supervision and the guarantees to prevent circumvention of the foregoing subparagraphs'.

92 ECJ, Joined Cases C-188/10 and C-189/10, *Melki*, [2008] ECR I-09999, par. 42.

93 A. Tzanakopoulos, 'Domestic Courts as the "Natural Judge" of International Law: A Change in Physiognomy', in J. Crawford and S. Nouwen (eds.), *Select Proceedings of the European Society of International Law*, Vol. 3, Oxford: Hart, 2011, pp. 155 et seq.

evolution of EU law thanks to the lucky alliance between national judges and the Luxembourg Court.[94] That is why over the years the ECJ has always perceived its relationship with domestic judges as a direct one that cannot be jeopardised by the judicial hierarchies existing at domestic level.[95]

The consequence of this assumption is that the preliminary question may be revoked only by the referring judge, who should be understood as the master of the preliminary reference.[96] This point has been clearly emphasised by the ECJ in a number of cases, including the famous *Melki* case.[97]

This makes it clear why the ECJ is very jealous of its alliance with the national common judges and why it has always reacted in a resolute way to any attempt that might jeopardise such a privileged relationship that has been built over the years.

However, if we change our perspective, we can see that something similar also happens with regard to the relationship between Constitutional Courts and common judges, especially in those legal orders that present an *incidenter* (or indirect) form of control of constitutionality. This *incidenter* control of constitutionality consists of a claim filed by a common judge (known as the judge *a quo*, a Latin expression meaning 'from which', since the question stems 'from'

94 See the reports in A. Slaughter, A. Stone Sweet, and J.H.H. Weiler (eds.), *The European Court and National Courts – Doctrine and Jurisprudence: Legal Change in Its Social Context*, Oxford: Hart, 1997.

95 'National courts have the widest discretion in referring matters to the court of justice if they consider that a case pending before them raises questions involving interpretation, or consideration of the validity, of provisions of community law, necessitating a decision on their part.

It follows from these factors that a rule of national law whereby a court is bound on points of law by the rulings of a superior court cannot deprive the inferior courts of their power to refer to the court questions of interpretation of community law involving such rulings.

It would be otherwise if the questions put by the inferior court were substantially the same as questions already put by the superior court.

On the other hand the inferior court must be free, if it considers that the ruling on law made by the superior court could lead it to give a judgment contrary to community law, to refer to the court questions which concern it.

If inferior courts were bound without being able to refer matters to the court, the jurisdiction of the latter to give preliminary rulings and the application of community law at all levels of the judicial systems of the member states would be compromised', ECJ, 166/73, *Rheinmühlen-Düsseldorf I*, [1974] ECR 33. See also Cartesio: ECJ, C-210/06, *Cartesio*, [2008] ECR I-9641.

96 'A rule of national law whereby a court is bound on points of law by the rulings of a superior court cannot on this ground alone deprive the inferior courts of their power, provided for under article 177, to refer questions to the court for a preliminary ruling. However, in the case of a court against whose decisions there is a judicial remedy under national law, article 177 does not preclude a decision of such a court referring a question to this court for a preliminary ruling from remaining subject to the remedies normally available under national law. Nevertheless, in the interests of clarity and legal certainty, the court must abide by the decision to refer, which must have its full effect so long as it has not been revoked', ECJ, 146/73, *Rheinmühlen-Düsseldorf II*, ECR, 1974, 139.

97 ECJ, Joined Cases C-188/10 and C-189/10, *Melki*, [2008] ECR I-09999, par. 42.

the judge) and is carried out while the underlying proceedings are pending (they are suspended). It is an indirect review of legislation that has a concrete effect – the outcome of the constitutionality review is decisive for the determination of the dispute before the referring judge. In these kinds of proceedings (whose structure resembles that of the preliminary ruling mechanism), national common judges work as doorkeepers,[98] entrusted with the initiation of the proceedings, and their cooperation is essential to the work of the Constitutional Courts.

Starting from the key role played by national judges in the activity of both of these higher Courts (i.e. the ECJ and their Constitutional Courts), one can see how dual preliminarity (*doppia pregiudizialità*[99]) may potentially cause friction or at least competition between them for control over national judges.

Let me clarify first what I mean by dual preliminarity: it refers to those cases where national judges simultaneously raise both a preliminary question to the Court of Justice of the European Union (concerning the validity or interpretation of an EU act) and a question of constitutionality (regarding the validity of a national norm) to their own Constitutional Court.

Undoubtedly these two proceedings differ in scope, object and effects: while the question of constitutionality insists on the domestic provision and usually presents a sort of *erga omnes* effect,[100] the question concerning the EU act has different features (for instance, the issue of the *erga omnes* effect is disputed[101]). Nevertheless, from the perspective of national (common) judges ('*giudici comuni*', i.e. ordinary and administrative judges), both these two preliminary questions can be used in order to obtain the same (sought after) effect: obtaining an argument from a higher court in order to exclude the application (setting it aside or acknowledging its unconstitutionality) of a norm in a case pending before themselves.

While to the common judges dual preliminarity is a technique to enlarge their interpretative and applicative opportunities with regard to the economy of their

98 To quote P. Calamandrei, 'Lettera dedicatoria al prof Enrico Redenti', in P. Calamandrei (ed.), *La illegittimità costituzionale delle leggi nel processo civile*, Padua: Cedam, 1950, XII.

99 M. Cartabia, 'Il processo costituzionale: l'iniziativa. Considerazioni sulla posizione del giudice comune di fronte a casi di "doppia pregiudizialità", comunitaria e costituzionale', *Il Foro italiano*, 1997, 222. For a very similar point of view about the dual preliminarity in English, see M. Cartabia, 'Taking Dialogue Seriously', *Jean Monnet Working Paper*, No. 12/2007, 2007, https://jeanmonnetprogram.org/paper/taking-dialogue-seriously-the-renewed-need-for-a-judicial-dialogue-at-the-time-of-constitutional-activism-in-the-european-union/

100 See A. Pizzorusso, 'Italian and American Models of the Judiciary and of Judicial Review of Legislation: A Comparison of Recent Tendencies', *American Journal of Comparative Law*, 1990, pp. 373 et seq.

101 On this issue, see: A. Trabucchi, 'L'effect «erga omnes» des décisions préjudicielles rendues par la Cour de justice des Communautés européennes', *Revue trimestrielle de droit européen*, 1974, pp. 56 et seq.

pending case (consistently with a logic of inter-court competition[102]), to the Constitutional Courts dual preliminarity can be used as a technique of hidden dialogue[103] with the ECJ (see the *Berlusconi* case[104]). The ECJ instead may perceive dual preliminarity as a menace to the effectiveness of EU law (see the *Melki* case[105]).

This is especially so in a context characterised by different (although sometimes compatible)[106] levels of protection of fundamental rights that are simultaneously disciplined at national (national constitution and legislation), supranational (EU) and international (ECHR) level.

With this scenario in mind, we can now move to the analysis of the *Melki* case.[107]

This case originated from the reform introduced in France by Article 61–1 of the French Constitution by which the *incidenter* control of constitutionality was introduced.[108] This provision was implemented by Institutional Act No. 2009–1523, which amended *Ordonnance* No. 58–1067 of 7 November 1958. After this reform, Article 23–5 of the *Ordonnance*, second paragraph, provided for the priority of the question of constitutionality over the review concerning conformity with EU law:

> In all events the Conseil d'Etat or Cour de Cassation must, when asked to rule on arguments claiming firstly that a provision infringes the rights and freedoms guaranteed by the Constitution, and secondly that it runs counter to the international commitments entered into by France, rule in priority on the transmitting to the Constitutional Council of the application for a priority preliminary ruling on the issue of constitutionality.

102 K. Alter, 'Explaining National Court Acceptance of European Court Jurisprudence: A Critical Evaluation of Theories of Legal Integration', in A. Slaughter, A. Stone Sweet and J.H.H. Weiler (eds.), *The European Court and National Courts – Doctrine and Jurisprudence. Legal Change in Its Social Context*, Oxford: Hart, 1998, pp. 227 et seq.

103 G. Martinico, 'Judging in the Multilevel Legal Order: Exploring the Techniques of "Hidden Dialogue"', *King's Law Journal*, 2010, pp. 257 et seq.

104 ECJ, C-387/02 *Berlusconi* [2005] ECR I-3565.

105 ECJ, Joined Cases C-188/10 and C-189/10, Melki, [2008] ECR I-09999.

106 On this issue see the very famous judgments in *Solange I* (*BVerfGE* 37, S. 271, in https://www.servat.unibe.ch/dfr/bv037271.html) and *II* (BVerfGE 73, 339 (1986)) and *Bosphorus* (ECHR, *Bosphorus Hava v. Ireland*, judgment of 30 June 2005).

107 ECJ, Joined Cases C-188/10 and C-189/10, *Melki*, [2008] ECR I-09999.

108 Article 61–1: 'If, during proceedings in progress before a court of law, it is claimed that a statutory provision infringes the rights and freedoms guaranteed by the Constitution, the matter may be referred by the *Conseil d'État* or by the *Cour de Cassation* to the Constitutional Council, within a determined period. An Institutional Act shall determine the conditions for the application of the present article'. On this, see F. Fabbrini, 'Kelsen in Paris: France's Constitutional Reform and the Introduction of *a posteriori* Constitutional Review of Legislation', *German Law Journal*, 2008, pp. 1297 et seq.

Doubting the compatibility of this provision with the ECJ's case law,[109] the French *Cour de Cassation*[110] referred a preliminary question to the ECJ, asking whether Article 267 TFEU precludes legislation such as that resulting from the French reform

> in so far as those provisions require courts to rule as a matter of priority on the submission to the *Conseil Constitutionnel* of the question on constitutionality referred to them, inasmuch as that question relates to whether domestic legislation, because it is contrary to European Union law, is in breach of the Constitution?[111]

109 'any provision of a national legal system and any legislative, administrative or judicial practice which might impair the effectiveness of Community law by withholding from the national court having jurisdiction to apply such law the power to do everything necessary at the moment of its application to set aside national legislative provisions which might prevent community rules from having full force and effect are incompatible with those requirements which are the very essence of community law. This would be the case in the event of a conflict between a provision of Community law and a subsequent national law if the solution of the conflict were to be reserved for an authority with a discretion of its own, other than the court called upon to apply community law, even if such an impediment to the full effectiveness of community law were only temporary . . . . a national court which is called upon, within the limits of its jurisdiction, to apply provisions of Community law is under a duty to give full effect to those provisions, if necessarily refusing of its own motion to apply any conflicting provision of national legislation, even if adopted subsequently, and it is not necessary for the court to request or await the prior setting aside of such provision by legislative or other constitutional means', ECJ, C-106/77, *Italian Finance Administration v. Simmenthal*, [1978] ECR 629. See also: 'The effectiveness of Community law would be in jeopardy if the existence of an obligation to refer a matter to a constitutional court could prevent a national court hearing a case governed by Community law from exercising the right conferred on it by Article 177 of the EEC Treaty to refer to the Court of Justice questions concerning the interpretation or validity of Community law in order to enable it to decide whether or not a provision of domestic law was compatible with Community law. It must therefore be stated . . . that a national court which in a case concerning Community law declares a provision of national law unconstitutional does not lose the right or escape the obligation under Article 177 of the EEC Treaty to refer questions to the Court of Justice on the interpretation or validity of Community law by reason of the fact that such a declaration is subject to a mandatory reference to the constitutional court', ECJ, C-348/89, *Mecanarte-Metalúrgica da Lagoa v. Alfandega do Porto* [1991] ECR I-3277.

110 The saga is indeed multilevel: Mr. Melki and Mr. Abdeli, were arrested and put into detention after a police control carried out in an area close to the Belgian border, on the basis of Article 78–2, p. 4, of the French Code of Criminal Procedure. The judge deciding on provisional detention decided to refer to the Court of Cassation (as we know the French Constitutional Reform gave the *Court de Cassation* and the *Conseil d'État* a role of filter of the questions raised by the lower courts) the question concerning the consistency with the French Constitution of the possibility to check the identity of persons in a border area. The referring judge had in mind Article 88–1 of the Constitution, which reads 'the Republic shall participate in the European Union constituted by States which have freely chosen to exercise some of their powers in common pursuant to the [Treaties]', insofar as Union law ensures the absence of internal border controls for persons. The Court de Cassation deciding on the possibility to pass the question to the French *Conseil Constitutionnel*, aware of the consequence on European Union law of a decision like that and doubting the mechanism of the priority of the constitutional question devised by the French Reform, raised a preliminary reference to the ECJ.

111 http://curia.europa.eu

Before the ECJ pronounced on this, the French Conseil Constitutionnel (on 12 May 2010)[112] interpreted this provision in a manner consistent with the Simmenthal[113] and Cartesio[114] doctrines. In June 2010, the ECJ decided to take into account the decision of the Conseil Constitutionnel (C-188/10),[115] which had in the meantime attempted to give an interpretation of the legislation consistent with EU law and with the ECJ's case law.

The decision of the ECJ (June 2010) in this respect was just one episode in a multilevel saga that involved all the judicial levels in the EU. In this decision, the ECJ concluded that:

> Article 267 TFEU precludes Member State legislation which establishes an interlocutory procedure for the review of the constitutionality of national laws, in so far as the priority nature of that procedure prevents – both before the submission of a question on constitutionality to the national court responsible for reviewing the constitutionality of laws and, as the case may be, after the decision of that court on that question – all the other national courts or tribunals from exercising their right or fulfilling their obligation to refer questions to the Court of Justice for a preliminary ruling. On the other hand, Article 267 TFEU does not preclude such national legislation, in so far as the other national courts or tribunals remain free:
>
> – to refer to the Court of Justice for a preliminary ruling, at whatever stage of the proceedings they consider appropriate, even at the end of the interlocutory procedure for the review of constitutionality, any question which they consider necessary,
> – to adopt any measure necessary to ensure provisional judicial protection of the rights conferred under the European Union legal order, and
> – to disapply, at the end of such an interlocutory procedure, the national legislative provision at issue if they consider it to be contrary to European Union law.[116]

112 Conseil Constitutionnel, Décision n° 2010–605 DC, www.conseil-constitutionnel.fr/conseil-constitutionnel/francais/les-decisions/acces-par-date/decisions-depuis-1959/2010/2010-605-dc/decision-n-2010-605-dc-du-12-mai-2010.48186.html

113 ECJ, 106/77 *Simmenthal* [1977] ECR I-62.

114 ECJ, C-210/06, *Cartesio*, [2008] ECR I-9641.

115 F. Donnat, 'La Cour de Justice et la QPC: chronique d'un arrêt imprévisible et imprévu', *Recueil Dalloz*, 2010, pp. 1640 et seq.; F. Fabbrini, 'La Corte di Giustizia si pronuncia sulla "legittimità comunitaria" del nuovo modello di giustizia costituzionale francese', *Quaderni Costituzionali*, 2010, pp. 4 et seq.; D. Sarmiento, 'L'affaire Melki: esquisse d'un dialogue des juges constitutionnels et européens sur toile de fond française', *Revue trimestrielle de droit européen*, 2010, pp. 588 et seq.

116 ECJ, Joined Cases C-188/10 and C-189/10, Melki, [2008] ECR I-09999.

Having recalled this, the ECJ concluded that it was up to the referring judge to verify whether the national legislation could be interpreted in accordance with the provisions of European Union law. In doing so, as anticipated, the ECJ exploited the interpretation given by the French *Conseil Constitutionnel* a few weeks before its pronouncement. The *Cour de Cassation*, lastly, drew its own conclusions from the *Melki* judgement and decided not to refer the question of constitutionality to the French *Conseil Constitutionnel*. More generally, in France the *Cour de Cassation* was strongly criticised[117] and accused of having exploited the question to challenge the reform of the constitutionality system.

At the same time, still in *Melki*, the ECJ pointed out the necessity to respect the 'essential characteristics of the system of cooperation between the Court of Justice and the national courts'.[118] It specified that in no case is it possible to infer from the judgement of a Constitutional Court declaring the unconstitutionality of the national legislation the invalidity of the supranational directive, since this would result in a violation of the *Foto Frost* doctrine.[119] Concluding on this typology, it is possible to recall other cases that could be traced back to this group, for instance *Chartry*[120] and, more recently, *A v. B.*[121]

Indeed, the ECJ dealt with a similar case raised by a Belgian court. In March 2011, it declared the case inadmissible because there was no link with EU law.[122] In Belgium, the special law of 12 July 2009 amended Article 26 of the special law of 6 January 1989 regulating the *Court d'Arbitrage* (now the *Court Constitutionelle*). Basically, the Belgian legislation provided that, in case of a conflict between one of the acts listed by Article 134 of the Belgian Constitution and a fundamental right guaranteed by Title II of the Constitution or by an EU law or international provision, the national judges shall first of all refer to the Belgian Constitutional Court the question concerning the conflict between the domestic act and Title II of the Constitution. In this way, this provision seems to imply a priority granted to the question of constitutionality.[123]

117 On this debate, see F.X. Millet, 'La "question prioritaire de constitutionnalité" e il dialogo a singhiozzo tra giudici in Europa', *Giornale di diritto amministrativo*, 2011, pp. 139 et seq.

118 ECJ, Joined Cases C-188/10 and C-189/10, *Melki*, [2008] ECR I-09999.

119 314/85 *Foto-Frost* [1987] ECR 4199: 'It should also be observed that the priority nature of an interlocutory procedure for the review of the constitutionality of a national law, the content of which merely transposes the mandatory provisions of a European Union directive, cannot undermine the jurisdiction of the Court of Justice alone to declare an act of the European Union invalid, and in particular a directive, the purpose of that jurisdiction being to guarantee legal certainty by ensuring that EU law is applied uniformly'.

120 ECJ, C- 457/09, Chartry. [2011] I-00819.

121 ECJ, C-112/13, *A. v. B and Others*, ECLI:EU:C:2014:2195. On the differences between Melki and A v. B see: A. Guazzarotti, *Rinazionalizzare i diritti fondamentali? Spunti a partire da Corte di Giustizia UE, A. c. B. e altri, sent. 11 settembre 2014, C-112/13*, 2014: www.diritticomparati.it

122 ECJ, C- 457/09, Chartry. [2011] I-00819.

123 On the impact of *Melki* on the Belgian case see: P. Popelier, 'Belgium. The Supremacy Dilemma: The Belgian Constitutional Court Caught between the European Court of Human Rights and the European Court of Justice', in P. Popelier, C. Van de Heyning and P. Van Nuffel (eds.), *Human Rights Protection in the European Legal Order: The Interaction Between the European and the*

As said, in *Chartry* the ECJ declared the case inadmissible because there was no link with EU law. In order to understand what the ECJ meant it is necessary to look at the preliminary question as formulated by the referring judge:

> Do Article 6 [EU] and Article 234 [EC] preclude national legislation, such as the Law of 12 July 2009 amending Article 26 of the Law [on the Constitutional Court], from requiring the national court to make a reference to the Constitutional Court for a preliminary ruling, if it finds that a citizen taxpayer has been deprived of the effective judicial protection guaranteed by Article 6 of the European Convention for the Protection of Human Rights and Fundamental Freedoms, as incorporated into Community law, by another national law, [namely] Article 49 of the Law . . . of 9 July 2004, without that national court being able to ensure immediately the direct [effect] of Community law [in the] proceedings before it and without being able also to carry out a review of its compliance with the Convention where the Constitutional Court has recognised the compatibility of the national legislation with the fundamental rights guaranteed by Title II of the [Belgian] Constitution?[124]

Keeping in mind that the judge was referring to the pre-Lisbon wording of Article 6 of the European Union Treaty (TEU),[125] already at first glance one can see how badly this preliminary question was formulated, since it implied the incorporation into EU law of the ECHR, while this is still far from being accomplished. Even after the coming into force of the Lisbon Treaty which, by the wording of Article 6 TEU (Lisbon version),[126] requires the accession of the EU to the ECHR. As we saw, accession has not yet taken place, mainly because of *Opinion 2/13* of the Court of Justice of the EU.[127]

National Courts, Antwerp: Intersentia, 2011, pp. 149 et seq., p. 164. 'It can be argued that the Belgian legislation can be interpreted in conformity with the conditions identified in the Melki case. Indeed the obligation to refer a preliminary question to the Constitutional Court does not prevent the court from lodging another preliminary question before the ECJ. Also the law allows the referring court to adopt provisional measures to ensure judicial protection of the rights conferred under the European Union legal order. Lastly the priority given to the Constitutional Court does not prevent the courts and tribunals to review an Act of Parliament against international or EU law of their own accord, even if in doing so they might contradict the Constitutional Court'.

124 ECJ, C-457/09: Reference for a preliminary ruling from the Tribunal de première instance de Liège (Belgium) lodged on 23 November 2009 – Claude Chartry v. État belge Official Journal C 037, 13/02/2010 p. 0003.

125 Article 6.2 TEU (pre-Lisbon Treaty): 'The Union shall respect fundamental rights, as guaranteed by the European Convention for the Protection of Human Rights and Fundamental Freedoms signed in Rome on 4 November 1950 and as they result from the constitutional traditions common to the Member States, as general principles of Community law'.

126 Article 6.2 TEU: 'The Union shall accede to the European Convention for the Protection of Human Rights and Fundamental Freedoms. Such accession shall not affect the Union's competences as defined in the Treaties'.

127 ECJ, Opinion 2/13, ECLI:EU:C:2014:2454. Moreover, even after accession has been concluded, it will be up to the ECJ to decide whether the ECHR will be incorporated into EU law or not. Looking

It was thus very easy for the ECJ to avoid the 'trap' of a judicial clash with the Belgian Constitutional Court. Since the question raised by the national judge in this case did not regard the EU law provisions *stricto sensu* conceived, the Luxembourg Court concluded that it was not competent to deal with the preliminary question. In doing so, the ECJ recalled Article 51 of the Charter of Fundamental Rights of the EU, stressing how that Charter is 'addressed to the institutions and bodies of the Union with due regard for the principle of subsidiarity and to the Member States only when they are implementing Union law'.[128]

After this overview, it is time to recap. Complex conflicts like those analysed in this chapter are the outcome of a process of partial convergence started after the first conflicts occurred between national and supranational interpreters.

The risk of collision when handling these 'shared' sources (indeed, general principles could be defined as 'multi-sourced equivalent norms')[129] is evident as per judgements like *Cordero Alonso*,[130] in which the ECJ dealt with the question of how to manage this overlapping zone represented by these principles.

The fact that the EU and the national legal systems share some legal materials perhaps explains one of the most ambivalent judgements in the history of EU law, namely *Internationale Handelsgesellschaft*.[131] In that decision, the ECJ first stated its understanding of absolute primacy (primacy even over national constitutional norms) and later added that some of these constitutional norms might inspire the general principles of EU law. However, it also acknowledged that: 'recourse to the

at the ECJ case law devoted to international treaties concluded by the European Communities, one can see how the ECJ has sometimes limited the perfect assimilation between 'Community law proper' and 'Community Agreements' Bourgeois, 'The Effects of International Agreements in European Community Law: Are the Dice Cast?', *Michigan Law Review*, 1984, pp. 1250 et seq., p. 1260. Moreover, more recently, the ECJ has extended the 'WTO exception' (lack of direct effect for WTO law) to the provisions of some other international law treaties. On this see M. Bronckers, 'From "Direct Effect" to "Muted Dialogue": Recent Developments in the European Courts' Case Law on the WTO and Beyond', *Journal of International Economic Law*, 2004, pp. 885 et seq.

128 A similar interpretation of Article 51 had been used by the same Court in the *McB* case, where the ECJ interpreted Article 51 of the Charter in a very restrictive way by showing great deference towards the Member States' legislation and competences. C-400/10 PPU, *McB.* [2010] ECR I-08965: 'First, according to Article 51(1) of the Charter, its provisions are addressed to the Member States only when they are implementing European Union law. Under Article 51(2), the Charter does not extend the field of application of European Union law beyond the powers of the Union, and it does not "establish any new power or task for the Union, or modify powers and tasks as defined in the Treaties". Accordingly, the Court is called upon to interpret, in the light of the Charter, the law of the European Union within the limits of the powers conferred on it.

It follows that, in the context of this case, the Charter should be taken into consideration solely for the purposes of interpreting Regulation No. 2201/2003, and there should be no assessment of national law as such. More specifically, the question is whether the provisions of the Charter preclude the interpretation of that regulation set out in paragraph 44 of this judgment, taking into account, in particular, the reference to national law which that interpretation involves', par. 51–52.

129 For this concept in international law see: T. Broude and Y. Shany (eds.), *Multi-Sourced Equivalent Norms in International Law*, Oxford: Hart, 2011.

130 ECJ, C-81/05, *Cordero Alonso* [2006] ECR I-7569, par. 41.

131 ECJ, 11/70, *Internationale Handelsgesellschaft mbH contro Einfuhr- und Vorratsstelle für Getreide und Futtermittel.* [1970] ECR 01125.

legal rules or concepts of national law in order to judge the validity of measures adopted by the institutions of the Community would have an adverse effect on the uniformity and efficacy of Community law'.[132]

Conflicts like those characterising the 1970s and happening in the *Solange* and in the *controlimiti* saga were conflicts due to the absence (at supranational level) of provisions comparable to those aimed at protecting 'fundamental rights' at the national level, i.e. *conflicts by divergence* or *by absence* of a comparable discipline in EU law. The new conflicts characterising the current phase seem to be, on the contrary, conflicts due to the existence of an area of overlap between the national and supranational level, i.e. conflicts *by convergence* or *by presence* (of an EU law discipline).

As I argue in this book, the current constitutional conflicts are the unexpected consequences of the constitutionalisation of the EU, understood as the progressive attention paid to fundamental rights by EU norms. However, the convergence occurred on the need to protect fundamental rights have not exhausted conflicts and this is due to the ambiguity of constitutionalisation as described in the previous chapters. Indeed, as we saw recalling *Opinion 2/13*, fundamental rights have been seen as a threat to EU law primacy, being one of the pillars of the first notion of constitutionalisation described in this book, referring to the progressive federalisation of the EU.

Not by coincidence, the risk of conflict between national systems and EU law and the need to reserve the autonomy of EU law are also recalled by AG Maduro in Opinion in *Arcelor*:

> In that connection, the Conseil d'État is correct in assuming that the fundamental values of its constitution and those of the Community legal order are identical. It must be pointed out, however, that that structural congruence can be guaranteed only organically and only at the Community level, through the mechanisms provided for by the Treaty. It is that organic identity which is referred to in Article 6 TEU and which ensures that national constitutions are not undermined, even though they can no longer be used as points of reference for the purpose of reviewing the lawfulness of Community acts. If they could, in so far as the content of the national constitutions and the instruments for protecting them vary considerably, the application of Community acts could the subject of derogations in one Member State but not in another. Such an outcome would be contrary to the principles set out in Article 6 TEU and, in particular, to the understanding of the Community as a community based on the rule of law. In other words, the effect of being able to rely on national constitutions to require the selective and discriminatory application of Community provisions in the territory of the Union would, paradoxically, be to distort the conformity of the Community legal order with the constitutional traditions common to the Member States.[133]

132 ECJ, 11/70, *Internationale Handelsgesellschaft mbH contro Einfuhr- und Vorratsstelle für Getreide und Futtermittel* [1970] ECR 01125, par. 3–4.

133 Opinion AG Poiares Maduro, C-127/07, *Société Arcelor Atlantique et Lorraine Société Sollac Méditerrannée Société Arcelor Packaging International Société Ugine & Alz FranceSociété*

I will explore this tension by looking at some examples of the impact of the Charter of Fundamental Rights on the activity of Constitutional Courts. I shall pick two cases: the case of a court like the Italian *Corte costituzionale*, which has been traditionally seen as a competitor of the ECJ, and that of a very cooperative judge such as the Austrian Constitutional Court.

5.5 Conflicts by convergence as one of the unexpected consequences of the constitutionalisation of the EU

A confirmation of the constitutional nature of the Charter of Fundamental Rights can be found in the statements of one of the traditionally most critical courts in the case law of the Court of Justice, the Italian Constitutional Court. I am referring to judgement 269/2017,[134] also commented on in English by scholars,[135] and seen as a harbinger of post-*Simmenthal* rules of engagement in the relationship between national judges and the Court of Justice.

Nevertheless, in that judgement, the Constitutional Court acknowledged – *expressis verbis* – the constitutional relevance of the Charter of Fundamental Rights of the EU:

> Granted the principles of the primacy and direct effect of European Union law as consolidated in both European and constitutional case law, it bears considering that the aforementioned Charter of Rights is a part of Union law that is endowed with particular characteristics **due to the typically constitutional stamp of its contents.**
>
> (emphasis added)

However, as seen, such a constitutionalisation has not killed conflicts. They are still there in order to feed the need for renewal of the EU legal order, and confirmation of this can even be found elsewhere. In search of a traditionally euro-friendly Constitutional Court, it is interesting to look at the Austrian scenario. *A v. B* had its origins in a preliminary reference made by the Austrian Supreme Court. The Austrian case (especially case n. U 466/11–18, U 1836/11–13) is perhaps more relevant than *Melki* to the reasoning of the Italian Constitutional Court judgement 269/2017.[136] The latter did indeed refer to a decision of the Austrian Constitutional

Industeel Loire Société Creusot Métal Société Imphy Alloys Arcelor SA V Premier ministre Ministre de l'Écologie et du Développement durable Ministre de l'Économie, des Finances et de l'Industrie [2008] ECR I-09895, par. 16.

134 Corte costituzionale, sentenza 269/2017.

135 D. Gallo, 'Challenging EU Constitutional Law: The Italian Constitutional Court's New Stance on Direct Effect and the Preliminary Reference Procedure', *European Law Journal*, 2019, pp. 434 et seq.; R. Di Marco, 'The "Path Towards European Integration" of the Italian Constitutional Court: The Primacy of EU Law in the Light of the Judgment No. 269/17', *European Papers*, 2018, pp. 883 et seq.

136 Corte costituzionale, sentenza 269/2017, official translation of the Italian Constitutional Court.

Court to justify the centralisation of decisions concerning conflict with the Charter, arguing that 'other national constitutional courts with longstanding traditions have followed an analogous line of reasoning (see, for example, the decision of the Austrian Constitutional Court, Judgment U 466/11–18; U 1836/11–13 of 14 March 2012)'.[137] That decision of the Austrian Constitutional Court is interesting for a variety of reasons. Firstly, because the Austrian Constitutional Court centralised constitutional review by establishing a unitary yardstick that reflected not only the national constitutional norms and the ECHR (which has the rank of a constitutional source in Austria[138]) but also the equivalent norms of the Charter. Secondly, this decision is relevant because it shows that even traditionally compliant Constitutional Courts – such as the Austrian one – have been issuing warnings lately concerning the potential misuse of the Charter at national level. Thirdly, because the Austrian Constitutional Court also referred to the risks connected to the existence of the overlapping zone represented by those shared norms, as recalled by Article 6 TEU and the Charter:

> In light of the fact that Article 47(2) CFR recognizes a fundamental right which is derived not only from the ECHR but also from constitutional traditions common to the Member States, it must be heeded also when interpreting the constitutionally guaranteed right to effective legal protection (as an emanation of the duty of interpreting national law in line with Union law and of avoiding situations that discriminate nationals). Conversely, the interpretation of Article 47(2) CFR must heed the constitutional traditions of the Member States and therefore the distinct characteristics of the rule of law in the Member States. This avoids discrepancies in the interpretation of constitutionally guaranteed rights and of the corresponding Charter rights.[139]

Precisely because of the centralisation of the judicial review carried out in decision 466/11–18 of the Austrian Constitutional Court, in *A v. B* the Austrian Supreme Court raised a preliminary question in order to clarify the compatibility of this judicial shift with the established case law of the ECJ:

> According to the Oberster Gerichtshof, the effect of that judgment is that Austrian courts may not, of their own motion, refrain from applying a statute that is contrary to the Charter; rather, 'without prejudice to the possibility of making a reference to the Court of Justice for a preliminary ruling', they must lodge an application with the Verfassungsgerichtshof for that law to be struck down. Furthermore, the Verfassungsgerichtshof has ruled that, if a

137 Corte costituzionale, sentenza 269/2017, official translation of the Italian Constitutional Court.

138 P. Cede, 'Report on Austria and Germany', in G. Martinico and O. Pollicino (eds.), *The National Judicial Treatment of the ECHR and EU Laws: A Comparative Constitutional Perspective*, Groningen: Europa Law Publishing, 2010, 55 et seq., p. 63.

139 Austrian Constitutional Court, U 466/11–18, U 1836/11–13, par. 59, official translation of the Austrian Constitutional Court.

> right guaranteed by the Austrian Constitution has the same scope as a right guaranteed by the Charter, it is not necessary to make a request to the Court for a preliminary ruling under Article 267 TFEU. In such circumstances, the interpretation of the Charter would not be relevant for the purposes of ruling on an application for a statute to be struck down, that being a decision which may be given on the basis of rights guaranteed by the Austrian Constitution. The referring court is uncertain whether the principle of equivalence requires the remedy of an interlocutory procedure for the review of constitutionality also to be available in respect of rights guaranteed by the Charter, given that it would prolong the proceedings and increase costs. The objective of securing a general correction of the law through the striking down of a statute that is contrary to the Charter could also be achieved after the proceedings have come to a close. Furthermore, the fact that a right under the Austrian Constitution has the same scope as a right under the Charter does not trigger a waiver of the obligation to make a reference for a preliminary ruling. The possibility cannot be ruled out that the Verfassungsgerichtshof might construe that fundamental right differently from the Court and that, as a consequence, its decision might encroach on the obligations flowing from Regulation No 44/2001.[140]

The issue of the problematic implementation of the Charter is still debated in Austria. According to Klamert, 'the primary law status of the Charter under EU law has created frictions in the established division of competences between the highest courts in Austria'.[141] More recently, the Austrian Supreme Court again referred to the Court of Justice regarding the issue of the concept of equivalence of protection.[142]

In the already mentioned decision 269/2017 of the Italian Constitutional Court quoted both *Melki*[143] and *A v. B*,[144] two decisions that, although they did not originate from preliminary references made by Constitutional Courts, have in a way contributed to redefining the scope enjoyed by national constitutional interpreters. These references can be read in either way. It is possible to argue that, precisely because of these references, the purpose of that *obiter dictum* was not to affect the Simmenthal mandate, as the Italian Constitutional Court was very aware of the relevant supranational case law in this ambit. Others instead see in these references a contradiction in the legal reasoning of the Italian Constitutional Court.[145]

Judgement 269/2017 of the Italian Constitutional Court was seen as a challenge to the principles of European constitutional law.[146] This is a reading given in the

140 ECJ, C-112/13, *A. v. B and Others*, ECLI:EU:C:2014:2195, par. 25–26.

141 M. Klammert, 'The Implementation and Application of the Charter of Fundamental Rights of the EU in Austria', *Acta Universitatis Carolinae Iuridica*, 2018, pp. 88 et seq., p. 88.

142 ECJ, C-234/17, *XC and Others*, ECLI:EU:C:2018:853.

143 ECJ, C-188/10, C- C-189/10, *Aziz Melki, Selim Abdeli*, ECLI:EU:C:2010:363.

144 ECJ, C-112/13, *A. v. B and Others*, ECLI:EU:C:2014:2195.

145 Gallo, 'Challenging', p. 442.

146 Gallo, 'Challenging'.

light of the framework in which this pronouncement was inserted: the post-*Taricco* scenario.[147] *Taricco* is a judgement delivered by the ECJ 'concerning alleged VAT fraud against the national budget' and, in particular, on the question of limitation periods for criminal offences. After the delivery of this decision, the Italian Constitutional Court raised a preliminary question invoking Article 4.2 TEU in relation to the respect of national identity and tried to induce the Luxembourg Court to rethink *Taricco*. Indeed, in *MAS*, the ECJ partly changed its mind, recognising that

> Article 325(1) and (2) TFEU must be interpreted as requiring the national court, in criminal proceedings for infringements relating to value added tax, to disapply national provisions on limitation, forming part of national substantive law, which prevent the application of effective and deterrent criminal penalties in a significant number of cases of serious fraud affecting the financial interests of the European Union, or which lay down shorter limitation periods for cases of serious fraud affecting those interests than for those affecting the financial interests of the Member State concerned, unless that disapplication entails a breach of the principle that offences and penalties must be defined by law because of the lack of precision of the applicable law or because of the retroactive application of legislation imposing conditions of criminal liability stricter than those in force at the time the infringement was committed.[148]

The reflections raised by the doctrine following the *Taricco* saga (and the 'continuation' represented by the 115/2018 decision[149] and, even earlier, in the *obiter dictum* of the 269/2017 judgement of the Constitutional Court) confirm the centrality of constitutional conflicts in the current phase of European law. As we saw, in judgement 269/2017, the Italian Court focused on the possibility of a double violation of the same right, guaranteed at the same time by the Italian Constitution and by the EU Charter of Fundamental Rights:

> The principles and rights laid out in the Charter largely intersect with the principles and rights guaranteed by the Italian Constitution (and by other Member States' constitutions). It may therefore occur that the violation of an individual right infringes, at once, upon the guarantees enshrined in the Italian Constitution and those codified by the European Charter, as recently occurred in reference to the principle of the legality of crimes and punishments. (European Court of Justice, Grand Chamber, Judgement of 5 December 2017, case C 42/17, M.A.S., M.B.)

147 ECJ, C-105/14, *Ivo Taricco et al.*, ECLI:EU:C:2015:555, Corte costituzionale, ordinanza 24/2017, ECJ, C-42/17, *M.A.S., M.B.*, ECLI:EU:C:2017:936, Corte costituzionale, sentenza n. 115/2018.

148 ECJ, C-42/17, *M.A.S., M.B.*, ECLI:EU:C:2017:936, Italian Constitutional Court, sentenza 115/2018.

149 Corte costituzionale, sentenza 115/2018.

In the light of this, the Constitutional Court made an interesting reflection on what we called complex norms in European constitutional law by saying that

> the emergence of the guarantees found in the EUCFR and those provided by the Italian Constitution can generate competing legal remedies. In light of this, for cases of "double prejudice" [doppia pregiudizialità] – i.e. disputes that may give rise to questions of constitutionality and, simultaneously, questions of compliance with Union law.[150]

In these cases:

> This Court holds that, where a law is the object of doubts concerning the rights enshrined in the Italian Constitution or those guaranteed by the Charter of Fundamental Rights of the European Union in those contexts where EU law applies, the question of constitutionality must be raised, leaving in place the possibility of making a referral for a preliminary ruling for matters of interpretation or of invalidity of Union law, under Article 267 TFEU.[151]

What does this mean? In order to understand what provoked the Italian Constitutional Court to deliver decision 269/2017, it is necessary to recall several factors both judicial and extra-judicial in nature that epitomise the background of recent judicial developments in Italy. Judicial politics and inter-court competition[152] have always been crucial to the development of EU law; to a certain extent, the Italian scenario is no different. In particular, Prof. Augusto Barbera,[153] currently a member of the Italian Constitutional Court, delivered an important speech that offers interesting clues in this respect. On that occasion, Justice Barbera mainly recalled the problematic implications stemming from the constitutional chemistry between the ECHR, the Charter and the Italian Constitution, i.e. the still ambiguous scope of application of the Charter, the tension brought about by the *Taricco* saga and the distinction between rules and principles in the Charter. He shared his concerns about the risk of an 'overflowing Charter' ('una Carta traboccante'[154]), reminding us of the wording of Article 51 of the Charter and the lack of a general competence of the EU in the area of fundamental rights' protection. Justice Barbera also criticised several domestic cases in which common courts had directly applied the Charter[155] in

150 Corte costituzionale, sentenza 269/2017, official translation of the Italian Constitutional Court.

151 Corte costituzionale, sentenza 269/2017, official translation of the Italian Constitutional Court.

152 Alter, 'Explaining', pp. 227 et seq.

153 A. Barbera, 'La Carta dei diritti: per un dialogo fra la Corte italiana e la Corte di Giustizia', paper delivered on the occasion of a quadrilateral summit between the French, Italian, Portuguese and Spanish constitutional judges held in Sevilla on 26–28 October 2017, www.cortecostituzionale.it/documenti/convegni_seminari/SIVIGLIA_BARBERA.pdf

154 Barbera, 'La Carta', p. 2.

155 Barbera, 'La Carta', p. 4.

situations that were beyond its scope of application. Finally, Justice Barbera also recalled the third element of the fundamental rights' triangle, i.e. the ECtHR, and devoted several pages to the post-2007 case law of the Italian Constitutional Court concerning the potential for using the Convention as part of the yardstick employed by the *Corte costituzionale*. It is worth noting that the post-2007 case law was provoked by judicial dynamics somewhat similar to those at play now with the Charter, as later confirmed by Justice Viganò in an extra-judicial contribution.[156]

In order to avoid a dangerous (in the eyes of the *Corte costituzionale*) trend that could have *de facto* led to a progressive diffusion of the (constitutional) judicial review of legislation, the Italian Constitutional Court decided to centralise the resolution of conflicts occurring between national norms and the ECHR by using the ECHR as an external and occasional aspect of the yardstick employed to review the constitutionality of certain pieces of legislation. Even after judgements 348 and 349/2007,[157] there were several episodes of resistance by lower courts and even attempts to involve the Court of Justice, as in the *Kamberaj* case.[158]

Can we say that decision 269/2017 is an act of rebellion against the ECJ or an attempt at questioning Simmenthal?

I do not think so. In that judgement, as we saw the *Corte costituzionale* referred to the principle of sincere cooperation and mentioned two ECJ cases, *Melki* and *A. v. B.*

156 F. Viganò, 'La tutela dei diritti fondamentali della persona tra corti europee e giudici nazionali', *Quaderni Costituzionali*, 2019, 39, p. 481 et seq., p. 484.

157 Corte costituzionale, sentenza 348/2007 and sentenza 349/2007. Without going into detail, the main contents of these two decisions can be summarised as follows:

1 The ECHR has a super-primary value (i.e. its normative ranking is halfway between statutes and constitutional norms).
2 In some cases, the ECHR can stand as an 'interposed parameter' for reviewing the constitutionality of primary laws, since the conflict between them and the ECHR can result in an indirect violation of the Constitution.
3 This (no. 2) does not imply that the ECHR has constitutional value; on the contrary, the ECHR has to respect the Constitution.
4 The ECHR cannot be treated domestically in the same way as EU law, as we will see below.
5 The constitutional status accorded to the ECHR implies the necessity to interpret national law in light of ECHR provisions. On this see: F. Biondi Dal Monte and F. Fontanelli, 'The Decisions No. 348 and 349/2007 of the Italian Constitutional Court: The Efficacy of the European Convention in the Italian Legal System', *German Law Journal*, 2008, pp. 889 et seq.; O. Pollicino, 'The Italian Constitutional Court at the Crossroads Between Constitutional Parochialism and Co-operative Constitutionalism. Judgments No. 348 and 349 of 22 and 24 October 2007', *European Constitutional Law Review*, 2008, pp. 363 et seq.; D. Tega, *I diritti in crisi*, Milan: Giuffrè 2012.

158 ECJ, C-571/10, *Kamberaj*, ECLI:EU:C:2012:233.

In fact, this subversive reading of the *Simmenthal* doctrine was rejected by the same Constitutional Court in judgements n. 20/2019[159] and 63/2019.[160] It is now clear that in no case is the effectiveness of supranational judicial remedies called into question. Instead, what happens is that the Constitutional Court, in light of the progressive emergence of EU fundamental rights, wants to be involved in those cases that may represent at the same time a violation of European and domestic law. Why? Because its judgements, unlike those of the ECJ within the preliminary ruling procedure, have *erga omnes* effects. At the same time, in line with the Austrian Constitutional Court, the *Corte costituzionale* sends a message to the ECJ, in the sense that the Court will check that Article 6 is interpreted in a way that is in conformity with the common constitutional traditions:

> Therefore, violations of individual rights posit the need for an erga omnes intervention by this Court, including under the principle that places a centralized system of the constitutional review of laws at the foundation of the constitutional structure (Article 134 of the Constitution). The Court will make a judgment in light of internal parameters and, potentially, European ones as well (per Articles 11 and 117 of the Constitution), in the order that is appropriate to the specific case, including for the purpose of ensuring that the rights guaranteed by the aforementioned Charter of fundamental rights are interpreted in a way consistent with constitutional traditions, which are mentioned in Article 6 of the Treaty on European Union and by Article 52(4) of the EUCFR as relevant sources in this area. Other national constitutional courts with longstanding traditions have followed an analogous line of reasoning (see, for example, the decision of the Austrian Constitutional Court, Judgment U 466/11–18; U 1836/11–13 of 14 March 2012)-[161]

Both the Austrian and the Italian Constitutional Courts – among others – have been sending signals that represent the price the ECJ is paying after problematic decisions like *Mangold* and could jeopardise the inter-judicial cooperation in the long run. Unfortunately, the decision on the PSPP[162] of the German Constitutional Court seems to confirm this risk. Should we despair? I do not think so, since even after these decisions, I would not say that sincere cooperation has failed. On the contrary, the Italian Constitutional Court has raised new preliminary questions

159 Corte costituzionale, sentenza 20/2019. O. Pollicino and G. Repetto, 'Not to Be Pushed Aside: The Italian Constitutional Court and the European Court of Justice', 2019, https://verfassungsblog.de/not-to-be-pushed-aside-the-italian-constitutional-court-and-the-european-court-of-justice/

160 Corte costituzionale, sentenza 63/2019, www.cortecostituzionale.it

161 Corte costituzionale, sentenza 269/2017.

162 2 BvR 859/15, www.bundesverfassungsgericht.de/SharedDocs/Entscheidungen/EN/2020/05/rs20200505_2bvr085915en.html;jsessionid=F892FE5330900A9A29FDCBEF992814FE.2_cid392. A. Baraggia and G. Martinico 'Who Is the Master of the Treaties? The Compact Theory in Karlsruhe', 2020, www.diritticomparati.it/who-is-the-master-of-the-treaties-the-compact-theory-in-karlsruhe/

to the Court of Justice; the *Consob* decision of the Luxembourg Court and the Italian follow-up[163] are recent examples of the fruits of this cooperation. Another example is given by the *O.D. and Others v. Istituto nazionale della previdenza sociale (INPS)* judgement on third country nationals and childbirth and maternity allowances.[164]

This leads me to a related point. When one thinks about 'dialogue' in EU law, preliminary ruling mechanism comes to mind, but despite its importance for the purpose of the evolution of EU law, the preliminary ruling mechanism[165] does not exhaust all the forms of dialogue that can be used by courts in the multilevel legal system.

Instead of recalling the very well-known dynamics of the preliminary ruling mechanism, in this section I am going to introduce the particular nature of judicial interactions involving the Constitutional Courts – normally considered (and that consider themselves) as something different from the 'common' judges and often described as 'negative legislators'[166] – and the ECJ. I shall attempt to explain why they have to be considered as different when compared with interactions between the ECJ and the common national judges, since they are characterised by a more evident competitive nature.

A terminological caveat should be made at this point. The metaphor of dialogue has been widely used by the literature, and this concept is variously understood by different meanings: a vehicle for transplants, an informal means of communication between judicial and political bodies or a new paradigm of judicial relations between actors not belonging to the same legal order.[167]

163 ECJ, C-481/19, *Consob*, ECLI:EU:C:2021:84. This case was triggered by the *Corte costituzionale* by the Italian Constitutional Court by its order 117/2019. See also the follow up of the Italian Constitutional Court to the Consob judgment in sentenza 84/2021.

164 ECJ, O.D. and Others v. Istituto nazionale della previdenza sociale (INPS), ECLI:EU:C:2021:659. On this decision see. D. Gallo, 'Op-Ed: "Migrants' Social Rights in the Dialogue between the CJEU and the Italian Constitutional Court: Long Live Article 267 TFEU!' 2021, https://eulawlive.com/op-ed-migrants-social-rights-in-the-dialogue-between-the-cjeu-and-the-italian-constitutional-court-long-live-article-267-tfeu-by-daniele-gallo/

165 On Article 267 TFEU and dialogue see: R. van Gestel and J. de Poorter, *In the Court We Trust. Cooperation, Coordination and Collaboration Between the ECJ and Supreme Administrative Courts*, Cambridge: Cambridge University Press, 2019.

166 H. Kelsen, 'Il custode della costituzione', in H. Kelsen (ed.), *La giustizia costituzionale*, Milan: Giuffrè, 1981, pp. 231 et seq., p. 256 (H. Kelsen, 'Wer soll der Hüter der Verfassung sein? Abhandlungen zur Theorie der Verfassungsgerichtsbarkeit in der pluralistischen, parlamentarischen Demokratie', *Die Justiz*, 1931, pp. 576 et seq.

167 See the different contributions collected in the volume: F. Fontanelli, G. Martinico, and P. Carrozza (eds.), *Shaping Rule of Law Through Dialogue: International and Supranational Experiences*, Groningen: Europa Law Publishing, 2009. On dialogue as a vehicle for legal transplants, see: D. Barak-Erez, 'An International Community of Legislatures?' in R.W. Bauman and T. Kahana (eds.), *The Least Examined Branch: The Role of Legislatures in the Constitutional State*, Cambridge: Cambridge University Press, 2006, pp. 532 at seq. The literature on judicial dialogue is huge: S. Cassese, 'La funzione costituzionale dei giudici non statali. Dallo spazio giuridico globale all'ordine giuridico globale', *Rivista trimestrale di diritto pubblico*, 2007, pp. 609 et seq.; Y. Shany, *The Competing Jurisdictions of International Courts and Tribunals*, Oxford:

Some authors[168] have attempted to define the essence of the idea of 'dialogue' better by identifying some key elements that should be present when talking about a proper dialogue. However, this notion is still considered by many authors to be misleading and foggy.[169] For all these reasons, in this chapter I am going to adopt more neutral language, writing of 'judicial interactions',[170] i.e. episodes of contact (intentional or casual) between courts that may differ in their degree of intensity, results and typology. Against this background, 'dialogue' can be conceived as a species of the genus 'judicial interaction', characterised by the presence of some specific features, namely the existence of differing viewpoints, symmetry between the interlocutors (i.e. lack of complete authority over the other), mutual recognition and respect, equal opportunity to participate and continuity over time.[171]

Within the notion of 'dialogue', Luc Tremblay proposed an interesting distinction between dialogue as a conversation and dialogue as a deliberation. The former implies a conversation that does not aim at reaching a specific purpose in mind; this is the case of a casual meeting between friends talking about trivialities, while the latter is aimed at a specific purpose and attempts to achieve a common agreement, at solving problems collectively.[172] In this context, even 'conflicts' (and constitutional conflicts[173] in particular) can be traced back to the idea of judicial interactions.[174] Within this macro-group, I am going to distinguish between

Oxford University Press, 2003; Y. Shany, *Regulating Jurisdictional Relations Between National and International Courts*, Oxford: Oxford University Press, 2007; C. L'Heureux-Dube, 'The International Judicial Dialogue: When Domestic Constitutional Courts Join the Conversation', *Harvard Law Review*, 2001, pp. 2049 et seq.; A.M. Slaughter, 'A Global Community of Courts', *Harvard International Law Journal*, 2003, pp. 191 et seq.; S. Choudry, 'Globalization in Search of Justification: Towards a Theory of Comparative Constitutional Interpretation', *Indiana Law Journal*, 1999, pp. 819 et seq., p. 821; A. McCrudden, 'A Common Law of Human Rights? Transnational Judicial Conversations on Constitutional Rights', *Oxford Journal of Legal Studies*, 2000, pp. 499 et seq.; A. Stone Sweet, *On Law, Politics and Judicialization*, Oxford: Oxford University Press, 2002; A. Stone Sweet, *Governing With Judges: Constitutional Politics in Europe*, Oxford: Oxford University Press, 1992; A.M. Slaughter, 'Judicial Globalization', *Virginia Journal of International Law*, 2000, pp. 1104 et seq.; R. Hirschl, *Towards Juristocracy, the Limits and the Consequence of the New Constitutionalism*, Cambridge MA: Harvard University Press, 2004; G.N. Tate and T. Vallinder (eds.), *The Global Expansion of the Judicial Power*, New York: New York University Press, 1995; M.R. Ferrarese, 'When National Actors Become Transnational: Transjudicial Dialogue between Democracy and Constitutionalism', *Global Jurist*, 2009, pp. 1 et seq.

168 Torres Perez, *Conflicts*, pp. 118 et seq.

169 For instance, see: G. de Vergottini, *Oltre il dialogo fra le Corti*, Bologna, Il Mulino, 2010; E. D'Alterio, *La funzione di regolazione delle corti nello spazio amministrativo globale*, Milan: Giuffrè, 2010, pp. 194 et seq.

170 de Vergottini, *Oltre il dialogo*, pp. 194 et seq.

171 For this conception of judicial dialogue, see Torres Perez, *Conflicts of Rights*, pp. 118 et seq.

172 L.B. Tremblay, 'The Legitimacy of Judicial Review: The Limits of Dialogue between Courts and Legislatures', *International Journal of Constitutional Law*, 2005, pp. 617 et seq.

173 On constitutional conflicts, M. Kumm, 'The Jurisprudence of Constitutional Conflict: Constitutional Supremacy in Europe Before and After the Constitutional Treaty', *European Law Journal*, 2005, pp. 262 et seq.

174 On the importance of conflicts in pluralistic systems, see: D. Halberstam, 'Constitutional Heterarchy: The Centrality of Conflict in the European Union and the United States', in J. Dunoff

cooperative and competitive judicial interactions, by specifying the particular features of the second typology.

Constitutional Courts have not given up their counter-power mission in spite of the partial convergence occurring between the language of their constitutions and that of the EU Treaties.

This confirms that conflicts are still in the everyday agenda and why some of the most evident developments in the complex legal order have found their engine in those conflicts (which have been a factor of innovation), especially in the field of fundamental rights protection, which has experienced different tensions and frictions among judges.

Even going beyond the relationship between the EU and Member States, it is possible to see how conflicts have played a systemic function by favouring confrontation and change in the complex legal order.

In this sense, it has been argued that it is possible to compare judgements such as *Bosphorus*[175] to the famous *Solange* case. As we know, the *Solange* method[176] implies the recognition of a 'reserve jurisdiction' for domestic courts and the acknowledgement to EC law of a sort of limited primacy: such primacy is guaranteed as long as it does not affect the national constitutional fundamental principles.[177]

In the *Bosphorus*[178] case, the ECtHR refused to review an EC regulation implementing a UN Security Council resolution, although the content of such an EC act was restrictive of the property right. The conclusion reached by the Strasbourg Court was persuaded by the comparability between the system of safeguarding fundamental rights guaranteed at the EU level and that provided by the ECHR. In *Bosphorus*, thus, the ECtHR used the same formula ('as long as') adopted by the German Constitutional Court in *Solange* to introduce a sort of presumption of comparability, preventing a clash between jurisdictions.[179]

---

and J. Trachtman (eds.), *In Ruling the World? Constitutionalism, International Law and Global Governance*, Cambridge: Cambridge University Press, 2009, pp. 326 et seq.

175 EtCHR, *Bosphorus Hava v. Ireland.* Application no. 45036/98), www.eui.eu/Documents/DepartmentsCentres/AcademyofEuropeanLaw/CourseMaterialsHR/HR2009/DeWet/DeWetBackgroundReadingCase3.pdf

176 On the *Solange* method see N. Lavranos, 'Towards a Solange-Method Between International Courts and Tribunals?', in Y. Shany and T. Broude (eds.), *The Shifting Allocation of Authority in International Law: Considering Sovereignty, Supremacy and Subsidiarity*, Oxford: Hart, 2008, pp. 217 et seq.

177 Lavranos, 'Towards a Solange-Method', p. 232. See N. Lavranos, 'Regulating Competing Jurisdictions Among International Courts and Tribunals', *Heidelberg Journal of International Law*, 2008, pp. 575 et seq.

178 EtCHR, *Bosphorus Hava v. Ireland.* Application no. 45036/98), www.eui.eu/Documents/DepartmentsCentres/AcademyofEuropeanLaw/CourseMaterialsHR/HR2009/DeWet/DeWetBackgroundReadingCase3.pdf

179 'Paradoxically, the safeguard of core rights, far from being the reason for the application of the counter-limit doctrine, was used as a harmonizing platform, and both tribunals sacrificed their own particular conception to pledge allegiance to the Court of Justice, or to support it', G. Martinico and F. Fontanelli, 'The Hidden Dialogue: When Judicial Competitors Collaborate', *Global Jurist*, 2008, pp. 1 et seq.

In the aforementioned cases, courts, despite the *prima facie* impression of judicial clash, preferred to depart from their original positions by achieving a compromise that has been defined as a process of 'integration through rights'.[180]

Again, this confirms the importance of judicial interactions in these dynamics and the existence of a circulation of models (interpretative techniques, approaches, styles) among judges.

The consequence of the emergence of constitutional conflicts cannot be a priori perceived, and in this sense the literature on conflicts shares the principle of non-apriorism that characterises the theory of complexity.

5.6 The importance of a consistent interpretation as a technique for recognising fully fledged 'conflicts'

Although conflicts are inevitable, they are also very costly and not always able to have a systemic impact or, according to another terminology, a positive impact (in this sense, what has been argued by scholars in other disciplines is still valid[181]).

Judges and scholars have tried to minimise them although, as said, it must be clear that conflict belongs to the usual life of constitutional politics.

Constitutional conflicts, as defined by Kumm (conflicts between supremacies or, in other words, primacy and supremacy),[182] are peculiar in the way they are produced by particular antinomies, real antinomies. It is in the interest of the actors to avoid them according to a rationalistic view, which is, however, questioned by the approach employed by Mouffe and, more generally, by the literature on conflicts;[183] as scholars have pointed out, judges when performing their role do not ignore political pressures or motivations.[184] As said, complexity recognises the physiology

180 L. Scheeck, 'The Relationship Between the European Courts and Integration Through Human Rights', *Zeitschrift für ausländisches öffentliches Recht und Völkerrecht*, 2005, pp. 837 et seq.

181 For instance: G. Simmel, *Der Konflikt der modernen Kultur*, Rome: Bulzoni, 1918, Italian translation G. Simmel, *I conflitti della cultura moderna*, Rome: Bulzoni, 1976, pp. 87–89 and p. 100.

182 Kumm, 'The Jurisprudence of'.

183 J. Knight, *Institutions and Social Conflict*, Cambridge: Cambridge University Press, 1992; A. Pizzorno, *Le classi sociali*, Bologna: Il Mulino, 1959; A. Pizzorno, *Le radici della politica assoluta*, Milan: Feltrinelli, 1993; C. Crouch and A. Pizzorno, *Conflitti in Europa*, Milan: Etas libri, 1977; R. Dahrendorf, 'Toward a Theory of Social Conflict', *Journal of Conflict Resolution*, 1958, pp. 170 et seq.; R. Dahrendorf, *Essays in the Theory of Society*, Stanford: Redwood City: Stanford University Press, 1968; G. Azzariti, *Critica della democrazia identitaria*, Rome-Bari; Laterza, 2005; F. Cazzola, 'Sui conflitti: primi appunti', 2008, www.cirpac.it/pace/sui-conflitti-primi-appunti-e-citazioni/; G. Azzariti, *Diritto e conflitti. Lezioni di diritto costituzionale*, Rome-Bari: Laterza, 2010.

With regard to EU law and conflicts see: Halberstam, 'Constitutional Heterarchy'; M. Dani, 'Economic and Social Conflicts, Integration and Constitutionalism in Contemporary Europe', *LSE 'Europe in Question' Discussion Paper Series*, 13/2009, 2009, http://papers.ssrn.com/sol3/papers.cfm?abstract_id=1518629; see also: A. Somek, 'The Social Question in a Transnational Context', *LSE 'Europe in Question' Discussion Paper Series*, 39/2011, 2011, http://papers.ssrn.com/sol3/papers.cfm?abstract_id=1865720

184 On this debate from a sceptical perspective see: A. Grimmel, 'Integration and the Context of Law: Why the European Court of Justice Is Not a Political Actor', 2011, https://ideas.repec.org/p/erp/scpoxx/p0048.html

of conflicts and their potential significance for the change and development of the complex system.

It does not aim at cancelling or minimising them because that would go against the logic of complexity.

Complexity and theory of conflicts share their non-apriorism, and complexity is fed by conflicts that protect and preserve diversity and pluralism that are essential in a true, complex legal order.

One might wonder if the employment of the idea of 'agonistic pluralism' contradicts the evolutionary model of constitutionalism described in Chapter 3.

I would say no, at least not necessarily. We saw that evolutionism does not deny the role of agents and have already defined what Hayek meant by action in this respect.

Conflicts are based on actions but not on deliberate planning, in the sense that, although they are produced by agents, agents do not trigger them with the intention of producing constitutional changes.

As noted in Chapter 3, Hayek distinguished between 'action' and human 'design'[185] and, regaining this distinction, one could argue that only the latter is deeply present in the very idea of constructivism.

In this scheme, in fact, the action and the role of the agent would not be excluded from the constitutional dynamics, but these actions are not performed with the intent of producing a legal change. Constitutional conflicts are usually inspired by contingent reasons and do not necessarily imply the intention to contribute to the change of that set of values and principles characterising the relationship with the other relevant actors in the multilevel arena.

However, although complexity does not give a magic formula for eliminating conflicts,[186] it is possible to infer some considerations that might be helpful to guide the interpreter in a complex legal system.

Complexity offers, in fact, another good reason for endorsing an 'open' reading of national constitutions.

When is there a real antinomy between the Constitution, on the one hand, and EU law, on the other, when both are applicable simultaneously?

185 'Spontaneous orders are the result of human action but are not the result of deliberate design (Hayek 1973: 37). Stated another way, a spontaneous order is an unintended consequence of the nonetheless purposeful action of multiple individuals. This is what distinguishes spontaneous orders from what Hayek characterizes as made orders. Made orders, which may also be described as artificial orders, organizations or taxis are deliberately constructed by an individual or group of individuals. Think a corporation or a marching band. Grown orders or spontaneous orders are different. If an order is like a sentence, then a spontaneous order is like a sentence with no author. It is as if the words, aware of the rules of grammar, arranged themselves into a meaningful structure that conveyed a sentiment that no individual word in the sentence intended to convey. A spontaneous order is a side effect not the goal of individual human action', N.P. Martin and V. Henry Storr, 'On Perverse Emergent', *Studies in Emergent Order*, 2008, pp. 73 et seq., p. 76.

186 It cannot do that for theoretical and practical reasons since it would go against its premises and against its survival course, as diversity is at the basis of complexity.

Legal theorists[187] usually distinguish between virtual and real antinomies: the former can be resolved through interpretation, while the latter represents a real example of irreconcilable normative conflicts.

I am going to link this distinction to the idea of constitutional openness.

Today, national constitutions do not provide an exhaustive list of fundamental rights, as a consequence of that constitutional openness described by Saiz Arnaiz,[188] making these constitutions reference international and supranational law to ensure the protection of some constitutional goods. For instance, with regard to the Italian case, it was said that the general clause of protection of fundamental rights contained in Article 2, the Constitution is to be considered an 'open' norm.[189] This reading of Article 2 has allowed the Constitutional Court to recognise and guarantee the so-called new rights (for instance, data protection, environmental rights) and to keep the Constitution up to date with respect to the need to protect the 'person' (*principio personalista*).

As for Portugal, the fundamental provision is Article 16 of the Constitution,[190] which recognises that international human rights treaties have a complementary role to the Constitution.[191] A similar provision is Article 20, paragraph 1 of the Romanian Constitution: 'Constitutional provisions concerning the citizens' rights and liberties shall be interpreted and enforced in conformity with the Universal Declaration of Human Rights, with the covenants and other treaties Romania is a party to'.

Finally, the most important confirmation of human rights treaties' special ranking in Spain is Article 10.2,[192] acknowledging that they provide interpretive guidance in the application of human rights-related constitutional clauses (even if the Spanish Constitutional Court specified that this does not implicate that human rights treaties have a constitutional status[193]).

187 On the antinomies see for example N. Bobbio, *Teoria generale del diritto*, Turin: Giappichelli, 1993, pp. 213 et seq., p. 218; R. Guastini, *Le fonti del diritto e l'interpretazione*, Milan: Giuffrè, 1993, pp. 409 et seq.

188 Saiz A. Arnaiz, *La apertura constitucional al derecho internacional y europeo de los derechos humanos. El articulo 10.2 de la Constitucion española*, Madrid: Centro de Estudios Políticos y Constitucionales, 1999.

189 Article 2 Constitution of the Italian Constitution: 'The Republic recognizes and guarantees the inviolable rights of the person, both as an individual and in the social groups where human personality is expressed'.

190 Article 16 of the Portuguese Constitution: '1. The fundamental rights enshrined in this Constitution shall not exclude such other rights as may be laid down by law and in the applicable rules of international law. 2. The provisions of this Constitution and of laws concerning fundamental rights shall be interpreted and construed in accordance with the Universal Declaration of Human Rights'.

191 Portuguese Constitutional Court, decision 345/99, available at www.tribunalconstitucional.pt. The episode is mentioned by F. Pereira Coutinho, 'Report on Portugal', in G. Martinico and O. Pollicino (eds.), *The National Judicial Treatment of the ECHR and EU Laws: A Comparative Constitutional Perspective*, Groningen: Europa Law Publishing, 2010, pp. 351 et seq., p. 360.

192 Article 10 of the Spanish Constitution: (2) 'The norms relative to basic rights and liberties which are recognized by the Constitution shall be interpreted in conformity with the Universal Declaration of Human Rights and the international treaties and agreements on those matters ratified by Spain'.

193 Tribunal Constitucional, sentencia 30/1991, available at www.tribunalconstitucional.es

Looking at the question from this perspective, it seems that no problem of real inconsistency could ever exist for those supranational principles that might be interpreted in light of constitutional law or for those national legislations that might be interpreted in light of EU law. On the contrary, more problems exist for those supranational principles or national legislations that do not do so.

If the interpreter was not able to find a way of solving the antinomy, conflict will be inevitable.

According to this scheme, consistent interpretation, a very well-known doctrine in EU law (see *Von Colson*[194] and *Marleasing*[195]), might serve as a filter for identifying real conflicts. More generally, consistent interpretation is a typical doctrine of multilevel systems,[196] since it guarantees some flexibility in the relationship between laws of different orders and entrusts judges with the role of gatekeepers (see *Hermés*[197] and *Dior*[198] on the relationship between EU and WTO laws). The literature described the obligation of consistent interpretation as recognition of EU law's 'indirect effect' and primacy, which is particularly convenient when the conflict between norms cannot be solved with the *Simmenthal* doctrine, because EU provisions lack direct effect.

As stressed by Rodin,[199] consistent interpretation has been acquiring increasing importance in EU law: the *Simmenthal* doctrine rigidly dictates a unilateral conclusion of constitutional conflicts (i.e. conflicts between constitutional supremacy and the primacy of EU law), while the consistent interpretation makes it possible to 'filter' constitutional conflicts, to the extent possible.

Of course, in this case, if we limit our perspective to the mere hierarchical relationship between national and supranational laws, supremacy exists and it belongs to either the national Constitution or to EU law, but here further disagreement will emerge between the interpreters, since it is not possible to find a supreme norm understood in a univocal manner.

This approach responds to an open conception of consistent interpretation and to an open conception of the Constitution, although normally scholars distinguish between different forms of consistent interpretation, depending on the document to be taken as reference by the interpreter (interpretation consistent to the Constitution; interpretation consistent to public international law; interpretation consistent to EU law).[200]

194 ECJ, 14/83, *Von Colson* [1985] ECR 1891.

195 ECJ, C-106/89, *Marleasing* [1990] ECR I 4345.

196 Even in the US: Charming Betsy 'canon', 6 U.S. (2 Cranch) 64 (1804).

197 ECJ, C-53/96, *Hermès International (a partnership limited by shares) v. FHT Marketing Choice BV* [1998] ECR I-3603.

198 ECJ, C-300/98 and C-302/98, *Dior and others* [2000] ECR 11307.

199 S. Rodin, 'Back to Square One: The Past, the Present and the Future of the Simmenthal Mandate', Paper Presented at the 8th ECLN, Madrid, 6–8 October 2010 (on file with author).

200 M. Luciani, 'Le funzioni sistemiche della Corte costituzionale, oggi, e l'interpretazione "conforme a"', 2007, www.federalismi.it

This analysis tends to emphasise the axiological superiority of the Constitution over public international and EU laws and conceives the national Constitution as the apex and the moment of closure of the domestic legal system.

According to another construction, constitutions should not be understood as a moment of closure but, rather, as documents (or a set of principles) open to those external influences that can enrich the protection of the goods estimated as fundamental.[201]

Going beyond a formalistic logic, constitutions can be influenced by the international and supranational documents and doctrines if this can improve, for instance, the protection of fundamental rights.

According to this scheme, there is no clear border between domestic and supranational/international law, the latter being the engine of a sort of steady process of constitutional update and improvement.

As a consequence, there is no need to break down consistent interpretation into the three forms seen earlier; in fact, consistent interpretation is arguably an open instrument.[202]

This seems to me to be a construction that better responds to the complex (i.e. interlaced) nature of the multilevel system, where a sharp distinction between levels is not always possible.

At the same time, this does not prevent Constitutional Courts from defending their fundamental charters or conflicts from emerging. To this end, they can make use of those techniques already recalled, such as, the counter-limits or *Solange* doctrines, triggering new conflicts that will feed the polemical spirit of EU law, i.e. that physiological interaction and confrontation between constitutional levels/poles.[203]

201 A. Ruggeri, 'Interpretazione conforme e tutela dei diritti fondamentali, tra internazionalizzazione (ed "europeizzazione") della Costituzione e costituzionalizzazione del diritto internazionale e del diritto eurounitario', 2010, https://www.rivistaaic.it/it/rivista/ultimi-contributi-pubblicati/antonio-ruggeri/interpretazione-conforme-e-tutela-dei-diritti-fondamentali-tra-internazionalizzazione-ed-europeizzazione-della-costituzione-e-costituzionalizzazione-del-diritto-internazionale-e-del-diritto-eurounitario

202 Ruggeri, 'Interpretazione conforme'.

203 G. Martinico, *Lo spirito polemico del diritto europeo. Studio sulle ambizioni costituzionali dell'Unione*, Rome: Aracne, 2011.

6 On the future of constitutional conflicts

6.1 On European monstrosity

In 2005, Nico Krisch opened his essay 'Europe's Constitutional Monstrosity'[1] by recalling that in 1667 Pufendorf had described the Holy Roman Empire as *monstro simile*.

Starting from this anecdote, Krisch lingered on the mismatch between the classical constitutionalism and the European one, given the irregularities and inconsistencies that the supranational integration process has when compared to the nation-state model.

In those pages the citation of Pufendorf slipped away too quickly without reflecting on the meaning to be attributed to the Latin word *monstrum*.

Today 'monster' refers to one whose features are considered 'unnatural', this word having a mainly negative meaning.

However, in Latin *monstrum* stood for both 'monster' and 'miracle', so much so that *monstra* were the signs of God. Something similar happened with the Greek *téras*, which originally meant the first sign from God, a sign capable of inducing terror.

With Homer, *téras* referred to all the divine signs, not so much seen as acts 'against nature' but rather 'beyond nature'.[2]

A partial change of meaning occurred with the Latin word *monstrum*, which derived from the Latin *monēre* (warning); that is the origin of the verb *monstrare*, which also meant those signals that broke the rules of the divine nature (in this respect, for example, cataclysms and natural disasters were read as a sign of anger of the gods).

Trying to regain the etymology of the word, one could say that this book wanted to be an essay on the 'monstrosity' of the EU, its prodigiousness (which is expressed in its 'non-regularity' – i.e. not in perfect correspondence with the national model of constitutionalism).

It is probably because of its 'monstrosity' that European law produces consternation among constitutionalists accustomed to traditional patterns of power.

1 N. Krisch, 'Europe's Constitutional Monstrosity', *Oxford Journal of Legal Studies*, 2005, pp. 321 et seq.

2 S. Sebenico, *I Mostri dell'Occidente medievale: Fonti e diffusione di razze umane mostruose, ibridi ed animali fantastici*, Trieste, 2005, www.sslmit.units.it/crevatin/Anthropology.htm

DOI: 10.4324/9781003056522-6

The aim of this book was to present one of the possible constitutional interpretations of the EU integration process by introducing the idea of constitutional complexity and investigating some of the problematic consequences of the EU structural features.

At the end of the journey proposed, we can now provide our research question with an answer.

I described the EU as a complex legal order produced by the interaction among constitutional levels/poles, which is characterised by some precise features: non-reducibility, non-predictability, non-determinism and non-reversibility.

Starting from this, I defined the order as the product of the interaction among the levels and the steady exchange (what I termed the *constitutional synallagma* in the first part of the volume) between the constitutional materials of the levels/poles as the efficient secret of the European Constitution.

Secondly, I linked the idea of complexity to an evolutionary understanding of order and, borrowing Hayek's distinction between constructivism and evolutionism, read the last 30 years of constitutional politics at EU level in light of this dichotomy. I also tried to emphasise how the years between 1992 and 2010 were dominated by the constructivist attempt to reduce complexity by giving the EU a constituent process resembling the revolutionary and continental idea of constituent process.

As we have seen, these events have not (always, at least) produced the desired effects, and the issue of constitutional conflicts has not gone away. On the contrary, conflicts are still crucial in the constitutional life of the EU and sometimes they can play a systemic function by favouring the transformation of the basic principles of the EU.

I described the *Solange* saga as an example of this, but other recent cases might be found, including the *Kadi* and *Taricco* sagas recalled in Chapters 1 and 5.

The bridge between complexity and literature on conflicts is offered by non-reductionism and non-apriorism, and consistent with this, there is no a priori criterion for identifying in advance conflicts provided with systemic influence.

More recently, as we saw, constitutional pluralists (à la Bobić[3]) also seem to regain the importance that conflicts may have in the long run for the sustainability and innovation of the system. This seems to me a major change that somehow reduces the differences, which, however, still persist. Think for instance of the difference in approach towards federalism, sometimes perceived by constitutional pluralists as a threat to the speciality of the EU.[4]

This is not a detail and has deep methodological and substantial consequences. From a methodological point of view, the approach endorsed by constitutional pluralism ends up neglecting the contribution that comparative law may have in European studies. In other words, it exalts the EU special nature understood as non-comparability. From a substantial point of view, it ends up losing a part of the mosaic

3 A. Bobić, 'Constructive Versus Destructive Conflict: Taking Stock of the Recent Constitutional Jurisprudence in the EU', *Cambridge Yearbook of European Legal Studies*, 2020, pp. 60 et seq.

4 Bobić, 'Constructive Versus Destructive', pp. 64.

and betraying the very premises of constitutional pluralism, and here we return to the considerations made on the presumed monism of many constitutional pluralists.

6.2 Pushing the incoming tide back? Some notes on Brexit

In *Bulmer (HP) Ltd v. J Bollinger SA*, a famous British case, Lord Denning, one of the most influential lawyers in the history of the United Kingdom, described the impact of Community law over the British legal system by using the image of the 'incoming tide' that 'flows into the estuaries and up the rivers. It cannot be held back'.[5]

Brexit was all about repelling the tide in order to come back to the original conformation of British sovereignty. It was inspired by this goal: a titanic challenge against history that aims to achieve what Lord Denning could not even conceive in the 1970s. In this sense, Brexit can be defined as an effort to push the tide of EU law back to recover the original meaning of British sovereignty, understood as parliamentary supremacy[6] in a context characterised by a partly written constitution.

Brexit was also a landmark event in the characterisation of the relationship between the EU and its Member States. The 'incoming tide' described by Lord Denning showed all its force in the moment of maximum friction, that is, the withdrawal of EU membership. However, even after Brexit, the inextricable knot that the membership created will not vanish magically in one blow. Brexit set a milestone for EU law, and the ECJ has been one of its main interpreters. From this standpoint, the legacy of Brexit is destined to last beyond the individual case of the UK and to affect the future of the EU legal order.

As written at the beginning of this work, for many aspects, Brexit paradoxically confirms the complex nature of the EU legal system. Brexit has not produced a return to the status quo for the British Constitution. Indeed, EU law has changed the nature of the British legal system thanks to the power given to national judges in light of the *Simmenthal* doctrine.[7]

As Bogdanor recently pointed out, the *Simmenthal* doctrine transformed the political constitution into something different.[8] Indeed, in his view, the European Union Withdrawal Act 2018 sought 'to do something quite unprecedented in the constitutional history of the modern world by withdrawing Britain from a protected constitution into an unprotected one'.[9] This explains why soon after Brexit the populist government of Boris Johnson has targeted judicial power and the UK Supreme Court in particular.[10] The EU integration, moreover, has created ties that bind even after the exit, and all the added value in terms of protection of

5 HP Bulmer Ltd & Anor v. J. Bollinger SA & Ors [1974] EWCA Civ 14.

6 A.V. Dicey, *Introduction to the Study of the Law of the Constitution*, Oxford: Oxford All Souls College, 1885.

7 ECJ, 106/77 *Simmenthal* [1977] ECR I-62.

8 V. Bogdanor, *Beyond Brexit: Towards a British Constitution*, London: I.B. Tauris, 2019, p. 274.

9 V. Bogdanor, 'Brexit and Our Unprotected Constitution', 2018, https://consoc.org.uk/wp-content/uploads/2018/02/Brexit-and-our-unprotected-constitution-web.pdf

10 J. Croft and J. Blitz, 'Lawyers Fear Tories Are Planning "Revenge" Against Supreme Court', 2019, www.ft.com/content/60f97382-1b4e-11ea-97df-cc63de1d73f4

fundamental rights created by years of European integration has been converted in domestic laws. This confirms, again, that the 'incoming tide' has changed the geology of the British legal system. Another confirmation of that is the persisting role of the Court of Justice according to the text of the Withdrawal Agreement, which maintained its jurisdiction during and even beyond the transition period.

Apart from the ECJ's jurisdiction over cases or proceedings pending at the end of the transition period, or events occurring before that date, the ECJ will also have some jurisdiction over entirely new cases arising after that date. In this sense, as Peers clarified, there are four different categories of 'continued jurisdiction',[11] each of which relates to specific norms of the Withdrawal Agreement. They have to do with citizens' rights,[12] financial settlement,[13] the Protocol on Ireland and Northern Ireland and that on Cypriot bases.

All of this, in my view, confirms the complex nature of the EU legal system, with non-reversibility one of the pillars of complex systems.

In light of this, my reader could wonder why I have not devoted an entire chapter to Brexit while analysing the current challenges posed to EU integration. My answer would be the following: while Brexit has for sure had a huge impact of the activity of the EU institutions after the 2016 referendum, it has not really represented a crisis for the EU as such. Brexit could have represented the source of major internal fractures among the EU Member States, but this was not the case. On the contrary, the EU has acted as a whole in a firm and almost coherent manner, and because of that, it was also accused of acting in a too tough manner vis-à-vis the UK.[14]

Sure, issues have been raised even after the exit of the UK, in particular with regard to the situation in Northern Ireland; perhaps in the long run, the EU will pay the price of such a political divorce, but Brexit also showed how difficult and problematic leaving the EU is. In this respect, with all its flaws, Article 50 TEU managed to tame in a political manner an issue that in other contexts would have led to a violent conflict.

That is why I decided to devote some space to Brexit in the last chapter, as I think it could be a potential source of new conflicts in the long run.

In this respect, Article 50 TEU can be compared to secession clauses, although scholars have distinguished between withdrawal and secession.[15] Secession clauses are traditionally ambiguous and rarely aim at facilitating the exit.[16] On the

11 S. Peers, 'The End – or a New Beginning? The EU/UK Withdrawal Agreement', *Yearbook of European Law*, 2020, pp. 122 et seq., p. 185.

12 Art. 158 of the Withdrawal Agreement.

13 Art. 160 of the Withdrawal Agreement.

14 J.H.H. Weiler, 'Brexit, the Irish Protocol and the "Versailles Effect"', 2021, www.ejiltalk.org/brexit-the-irish-protocol-and-the-versailles-effect/

15 C. Closa, 'Interpreting Article 50: Exit, Voice and . . . What About Loyalty?' in C. Closa (ed.), *Secession From a Member State and Withdrawal From the European Union: Troubled Membership*, Cambridge: Cambridge University Press, 2017, pp. 187 et seq.

16 S. Mancini, 'Secession and Self-Determination', in M. Rosenfeld and A. Sajó (eds.), *The Oxford Handbook of Comparative Constitutional Law*, Oxford: Oxford University Press, 2012, pp. 495 et seq.

contrary, they are frequently drafted to make secession difficult and conditional upon the respect of some procedures and values – thus preserving axiological continuity and respect of the rule of law.[17] Article 50 TEU represents such ambiguity in both the lack of an explicit mention of the possibility of revoking the notification and in clarifying how many times the extension can be requested.

However, for the EU the main legacy of Brexit will probably be the outcome of the *Wightman* case,[18] where the ECJ interpreted Article 50 TEU. This was the first time that the ECJ engaged with the interpretation of this provision and aimed to clarify the functioning of the withdrawal process. *Wightman* disclosed the tensions between national sovereignty and EU membership and opened some potential issues in the exercise of national right to revocation of the withdrawal decision.

Wightman was the first occasion for the Luxembourg Court to offer an interpretation of Article 50 TEU, and, as in other 'historical' decisions, it tried to give continuity to its case law by reading Article 50 TEU in combination with other provisions. There, the Luxembourg Court openly used the constitutional jargon inaugurated with the *Les Verts* case.[19] Not by chance, *Les Verts*, together with the *Kadi* judgement[20] and *Opinion 2/13*,[21] is mentioned in paragraph 44 in order to recall the constitutional and *sui generis* nature of the European Treaties.[22]

17 As Norman recalled 'the perceived advantages of handling secessionist politics and secessionist contests within the rule of law rather than as "political" issues that lie outside of, or are presumed (by the secessionists) to supersede, the law', W. Norman, *Negotiating Nationalism: Nation-Building, Federalism, and Secession in the Multinational State*, Oxford: Oxford University Press, 2006, pp. 178. See also G. Martinico, '"A Message of Hope": A Legal Perspective on the Reference', in G. Delledonne and G. Martinico (eds.), *The Canadian Contribution to a Comparative Law of Secession: Legacies of the Quebec Secession Reference*, London: Palgrave, 2019, pp. 249 et seq.; T. Ginsburg and M. Versteeg, 'From Catalonia to California: Secession in Constitutional Law', *Alabama Law Review*, 2019, pp. 923 et seq.

18 ECJ, C-621/18 *Wightman e a.* ECLI:EU:C:2018:999. On this decision see: G. Martinico and M. Simoncini, 'Wightman and the Perils of Britain's Withdrawal', *German Law Journal*, 2020, pp. 799 et seq.; M. Simoncini and G. Martinico, 'A Knot Not to Be Cut? The Legacy of Brexit over the CJEU', *Politics and Governance*, 2021, pp. 77 et seq.

19 ECJ, C-294/83, *Les Verts v. Parliament*, ECLI:EU:C:1986:166.

20 ECJ, C-402/05 P, *Kadi and Al Barakaat International Foundation/Council and Commission*, ECLI:EU:C:2008:461; see also Opinion of Advocate General Poiares Maduro in C-402 & 415/05 P, *Kadi and Al Barakaat International Foundation/Council and Commission*, ECLI:EU:C:2008:30, Opinion of Jan. 23, 2008. On the *Kadi* saga see Matej Avbelj, Filippo Fontanelli, and Giuseppe Martinico (eds.), *Kadi on Trial: A Multifaceted Analysis of the Kadi Judgment*, Abingdon: Routledge, 2014; M. Simoncini, 'Risk Regulation Approach to EU Policy Against Terrorism in the Light of the ECJ/CFI Jurisprudence', *German Law Journal*, 2009, pp. 1526 et seq.

21 ECJ, Opinion 2/13, *On the Draft Agreement Providing for the Accession of the European Union to the Convention for the Protection of Human Rights and Fundamental Freedoms*, ECLI:EU:C:2014:2454.

22 ECJ, C-621/18 *Wightman e a.* ECLI:EU:C:2018:999, par. 44: 'In that respect, it must be borne in mind that the founding Treaties, which constitute the basic constitutional charter of the European Union (judgment of 23 April 1986, Les Verts v. Parliament, 294/83, EU:C:1986:166, paragraph 23), established, unlike ordinary international treaties, a new legal order, possessing its own institutions, for the benefit of which the Member States thereof have limited their sovereign rights, in ever wider fields, and the subjects of which comprise not only those States but also their

The Court offered a reading of Article 50 TEU in context by attempting, in other words, to interpret this provision in light of the values that characterise the integration process. For example, the reference to the impact of the possible exit of the United Kingdom on EU citizenship[23] is confirmation of the systematic reading given by the Court.[24]

It is interesting to note that, in *Wightman*, on the specific issue of the revocability of the notification, the ECJ opted for a construction other than that endorsed by the High Court of England and Wales[25] and by the Supreme Court of the United Kingdom in the *Miller* I saga.

On those occasions, both British courts denied the Government's ability to exercise the power of notification of the intention to leave the Union under Article 50 TEU to the European Council without parliamentary involvement. The non-revocability of the notification had been one of the fundamental pillars of the judges' reasoning and served as an external – referring to a non-national norm – premise of that judgement. Indeed, Article 50 TEU offered margins for either option, as scholars had already pointed out:

> The point is arguable either way. It could be argued that since a notification to withdraw is subject to a Member State's constitutional requirements, the Treaty therefore leaves to each Member State the possibility of rescinding that notification in accordance with those requirements. On the other hand, it could also be argued that Article 50 only provides for two possibilities to delay the withdrawal of a Member State from the EU once notification has been given (an extension of the time limit, or a different date in the withdrawal agreement). There's no suggestion that this is a non-exhaustive list. Therefore, the notification of withdrawal can't be rescinded.[26]

nationals (Opinion 2/13 (Accession of the European Union to the ECHR) of 18 December 2014, EU:C:2014:2454, paragraph 157 and the case-law cited)'.

23 D. Sarmiento, 'Brexit and EU Citizenship After Wightman', 2018, https://despiteourdifferencesblog.wordpress.com/2018/12/12/brexit-and-eu-citizenship-after-wightman/

24 ECJ, C-621/18 *Wightman e a.* ECLI:EU:C:2018:999, par. 64: 'It must also be noted that, since citizenship of the Union is intended to be the fundamental status of nationals of the Member States (see, to that effect, judgments of 20 September 2001, Grzelczyk, C-184/99, EU:C:2001:458, paragraph 31; of 19 October 2004, Zhu and Chen, C-200/02, EU:C:2004:639, paragraph 25; and of 2 March 2010, Rottmann, C-135/08, EU:C:2010:104, paragraph 43), any withdrawal of a Member State from the European Union is liable to have a considerable impact on the rights of all Union citizens, including, inter alia, their right to free movement, as regards both nationals of the Member State concerned and nationals of other Member States'.

25 *R (Miller) v. Secretary of State for Exiting the European Union*, [2016] EWHC 2768.

26 S. Peers, 'Article 50 TEU: 'The Uses and Abuses of the Process of Withdrawing From the EU', 2014, http://eulawanalysis.blogspot.com/2014/12/article-50-teu-uses-and-abuses-of.html; see also J. Rylatt, 'The Irrevocability of an Article 50 Notification: Lex Specialis and the Irrelevance of the Purported Customary Right to Unilaterally Revoke', 2016, https://ukconstitutionallaw.org/; C. Streeten, 'Putting the Toothpaste Back in the Tube: Can an Article 50 Notification Be Revoked?' 2016, https://ukconstitutionallaw.org/2016/07/13/charles-streeten-putting-the-toothpaste-back-in-the-tube-can-an-article-50-notification-be-revoked/

I think that, on those occasions, the reference to Article 50 TEU was appropriate. Over the years, UK membership in the Union has created complex rules in the etymological sense of the term: a set of norms that are the result of a tangled knot between domestic law and European law. This made the reference to the law of the EU Treaties inevitable for the correct reading of the question posed to the British courts in the case of the *Miller* I saga. The wording itself of Article 50 TEU, moreover, refers to domestic law when it reads that 'any Member State may decide to withdraw from the Union in accordance with its own constitutional requirements'. This confirms the legal interlacement created by the European integration process. However, precisely because of the impact that the question of revocability of the notification had on the margin of manoeuvre of the UK Parliament, commentators stressed the excessive brusqueness of some of the relevant passages in the *Miller* I saga. They also criticised the choice not to raise a preliminary question to the ECJ.[27] Returning to *Wightman* of the ECJ, one can see how the Luxembourg Court started from a premise similar to that employed by the British courts – the inextricability of national and supranational legal systems. This was then reaffirmed by the ECJ itself in paragraph 45 of the *Wightman* judgement, which also included a reference to the *Achmea*[28] case.[29]

Indeed, *Wightman* is interesting as it offers a confirmation of the difficult distinguishability between national and supranational legal systems and the complex nature of European law. Another example of the complex context triggered by the Europeanisation of the national system are the *Miller* I decisions of the High Court and the UK Supreme Court, especially in the passages devoted to the importance of EU integration for the genesis of a new category of rights.[30]

Nevertheless, if in the *Miller* I saga[31] the British courts opted for the non-revocability of the notification to justify the involvement of Parliament, the ECJ

27 S. Peers, 'Brexit: Can the ECJ Get Involved?' 2016, http://eulawanalysis.blogspot.com/2016/11/brexit-can-ecj-get-involved.html

28 ECJ, C-284/16, *Slowakische Republik (Slovak Republic) v. Achmea*, ECLI:EU:C:2018:158.

29 ECJ, C-621/18 *Wightman e a.* ECLI:EU:C:2018:999, par. 45: 'According to settled case-law of the Court, that autonomy of EU law with respect both to the law of the Member States and to international law is justified by the essential characteristics of the European Union and its law, relating in particular to the constitutional structure of the European Union and the very nature of that law. EU law is characterized by the fact that it stems from an independent source of law, namely the Treaties, by its primacy over the laws of the Member States, and by the direct effect of a whole series of provisions which are applicable to their nationals and to the Member States themselves. Those characteristics have given rise to a structured network of principles, rules and mutually interdependent legal relations binding the European Union and its Member States reciprocally as well as binding its Member States to each other (judgment of 6 March 2018, Achmea, C-284/16, EU:C:2018:158, paragraph 33 and the case-law cited)'.

30 See, e.g., UKSC, *Miller I*; *R (HS2 Action Alliance Ltd) v. Secretary of State for Transport* [2014], par. 69.

31 *R (Miller) v. Secretary of State for Exiting the European Union* [2016] EWHC 2768, at par. 11 and 17; UKSC, *Miller I*; *R (HS2 Action Alliance Ltd) v. Secretary of State for Transport* [2014] UKSC,

instead came to a different conclusion in *Wightman*. Indeed, in *Miller* I litigation, the non-revocability of the Article 50 notification was the agreed assumption on which the courts had proceeded. The ECJ followed a different path and did so by relying on the systematic reading of Article 50 TEU[32] and recalling the aims of the integration process.

In so doing, it also paid particular attention to the values of liberty and democracy, especially in the part of the judgement recalling the *Kadi* case.[33] Moreover, after discarding the parallel with the decision to request an extension of the negotiations pursuant to Article 50.3 TEU, the ECJ focused on Article 49 TEU in order to reiterate that the decision to join the EU is based on a free and voluntary commitment.[34] Finally, by illustrating the parallels between Article 49 TEU and Article 50 TEU, the ECJ concluded, regarding the revocability of the notification, that

> in those circumstances, given that a State cannot be forced to accede to the EU against its will, neither can it be forced to withdraw from the EU against its will. However, if the notification of the intention to withdraw were to lead inevitably to the withdrawal of the Member State concerned from the EU at the end of the period laid down in Article 50(3) TEU, that Member State could be forced to leave the EU despite its wish – as expressed through its

par. 26: 'In these proceedings, it is common ground that notice under [A]rticle 50(2) (which we shall call "Notice") cannot be given in qualified or conditional terms and that, once given, it cannot be withdrawn. Especially as it is the Secretary of State's case that, even if this common ground is mistaken, it would make no difference to the outcome of these proceedings, we are content to proceed on the basis that that is correct, without expressing any view of our own on either point. It follows from this that once the United Kingdom gives Notice, it will inevitably cease at a later date to be a member of the European Union and a party to the EU Treaties'.

32 ECJ, C-621/18 *Wightman e a.* ECLI:EU:C:2018:999, par. 61–67.

33 ECJ, C-621/18 *Wightman e a.* ECLI:EU:C:2018:999, par. 61–62: 'As regards the context of Article 50 TEU, reference must be made to the 13th recital in the preamble to the TEU, the first recital in the preamble to the TFEU and Article 1 TEU, which indicate that those treaties have as their purpose the creation of an ever closer union among the peoples of Europe, and to the second recital in the preamble to the TFEU, from which it follows that the European Union aims to eliminate the barriers which divide Europe.

It is also appropriate to underline the importance of the values of liberty and democracy, referred to in the second and fourth recitals of the preamble to the TEU, which are among the common values referred to in Article 2 of that Treaty and in the preamble to the Charter of Fundamental Rights of the European Union, and which thus form part of the very foundations of the European Union legal order (see, to that effect, judgment of 3 September 2008, Kadi and Al Barakaat International Foundation v. Council and Commission, C-402/05 P and C-415/05 P, EU:C:2008:461, paragraphs 303 and 304)'.

34 ECJ, C-621/18 *Wightman e a.* ECLI:EU:C:2018:999, par. 63: 'As is apparent from Article 49 TEU, which provides the possibility for any European State to apply to become a member of the European Union and to which Article 50 TEU, on the right of withdrawal, is the counterpart, the European Union is composed of States which have freely and voluntarily committed themselves to those values, and EU law is thus based on the fundamental premise that each Member State shares with all the other Member States, and recognizes that those Member States share with it, those same values (see, to that effect, judgment of 25 July 2018, Minister for Justice and Equality (Deficiencies in the system of justice), C-216/18 PPU, EU:C:2018:586, paragraph 35)'.

> democratic process in accordance with its constitutional requirements – to reverse its decision to withdraw and, accordingly, to remain a Member of the EU. Such a result would be inconsistent with the aims and values referred to in paragraphs 61 and 62 of the present judgment. In particular, it would be inconsistent with the Treaties' purpose of creating an ever closer union among the peoples of Europe to force the withdrawal of a Member State which, having notified its intention to withdraw from the EU in accordance with its constitutional requirements and following a democratic process, decides to revoke the notification of that intention through a democratic process.[35]

Another interesting passage in the judgement is that – and this is a rare thing in the case law of the Court – the ECJ looked at the preparatory works of the second Convention (concerning the Treaty establishing a Constitution for Europe[36]) in order to support its decision. In particular, it recalled that all amendments proposed about the possibility of expelling a Member State in order to avoid the risk of abuse during the withdrawal procedure had been rejected.[37] This is a curious 'exhumation' of the preparatory works of a text that never came into force, which is the Treaty establishing a Constitution for Europe. At the same time, the ECJ, aware of the risk of an excessively unilateral reading of this provision, tried to limit the timeframe in which such a decision could be taken, when it says (repeatedly, as if to reassure itself) that:

> As the Advocate General stated in points 94 and 95 of his Opinion, the sovereign nature of the right of withdrawal enshrined in Article 50(1) TEU supports the conclusion that the Member State concerned has a right to revoke the notification of its intention to withdraw from the EU, for as long as a

35 ECJ, C-621/18 *Wightman e a.* ECLI:EU:C:2018:999, par. 65–67.

36 C. Margiotta, 'Vizi e virtù della secessione. A proposito dell'articolo 59 del progetto di Costituzione europea', *Ragion Pratica*, 2004, pp. 257 et seq.

37 ECJ, C-621/18 *Wightman e a.* ECLI:EU:C:2018:999, par. 68–70: 'The origins of Article 50 TEU also support an interpretation of that provision as meaning that a Member State is entitled to revoke unilaterally the notification of its intention to withdraw from the European Union. That article largely adopts the wording of a withdrawal clause first set out in the draft Treaty establishing a Constitution for Europe. Although, during the drafting of that clause, amendments had been proposed to allow the expulsion of a Member State, to avoid the risk of abuse during the withdrawal procedure or to make the withdrawal decision more difficult, those amendments were all rejected on the ground, expressly set out in the comments on the draft, that the voluntary and unilateral nature of the withdrawal decision should be ensured. It follows from the foregoing that the notification by a Member State of its intention to withdraw does not lead inevitably to the withdrawal of that Member State from the European Union. On the contrary, a Member State that has reversed its decision to withdraw from the European Union is entitled to revoke that notification for as long as a withdrawal agreement concluded between that Member State and the European Union has not entered into force or, if no such agreement has been concluded, for as long as the two-year period laid down in Article 50(3) TEU, possibly extended in accordance with that provision, has not expired. That conclusion is corroborated by the provisions of the Vienna Convention on the Law of Treaties, which was taken into account in the preparatory work for the Treaty establishing a Constitution for Europe'.

> Withdrawal Agreement concluded between the EU and that Member State has not entered into force or, if no such agreement has been concluded, for as long as the two-year period laid down in Article 50(3) TEU, possibly extended in accordance with that provision, has not expired.[38]

In so doing, the Court seemed to limit the risks associated with the unilateral nature of the revocability of the intention to leave in the two-year period – except for what is established by Article 50.3 TEU. However, even during this period, a situation of evident uncertainty could be generated, increasing the confusion surrounding the activity of the EU institutions and the instability of the markets. These considerations of the Court were followed by a procedural clarification when it added that:

> In the absence of an express provision governing revocation of the notification of the intention to withdraw, that revocation is subject to the rules laid down in Art[icle] 50(1) TEU for the withdrawal itself, with the result that it may be decided upon unilaterally, in accordance with the constitutional requirements of the Member State concerned.[39]

The lack of reference to the concept of national identity has been one of the fundamental differences between the Opinion of the Advocate General and the ruling of the ECJ. There is another difference, however, that should be emphasised. While the Advocate General tried to find, in the principle of good faith and sincere cooperation – Article 4 TEU – a limit to this sovereign choice of the Member State concerned, this reference disappeared in the judgement of the ECJ. These are probably the most critical issues of the *Wightman* case, and they could pave the way for a dangerous domino effect in the long run.

6.3 Past and future of constitutional conflicts

Before closing this volume, it is worth recalling why the 'constitutional conflicts' will continue to play a central role in the life of the EU, and to do so in the final chapter of the first edition of this book, I focused on four factors: the EU's future accession to the ECHR, the financial crisis, the consequences (one might say, the aftermath) of the roar of the mega-constitutional politics of the season of the Conventions and the enlargement to the East.[40]

38 ECJ, C-621/18 *Wightman e a.* ECLI:EU:C:2018:999, par. 57.

39 ECJ, C-621/18 *Wightman e a.* ECLI:EU:C:2018:999, par. 58.

40 On this see O. Pollicino, *L'allargamento ad est dell'Europa e rapporti tra Corti costituzionali e Corti europee. Verso una teoria generale dell'impatto interordinamentale del diritto sovranazionale?* Milano: Giuffrè, 2010, pp. 443 et seq.

In Chapters 1 and 4, we saw that the first two factors have played a role in the multiple crises that have been affecting the EU over recent years, but what about the other two?

The post-enlargement developments have been among the potential factors of crisis and constitutional conflicts in light of both the constitutional heterogeneity 'introduced', in terms of constitutional traditions[41] in the European context', and the strong pro-sovereignty clauses present in some Eastern European countries.[42]

As is well known, Poland and Hungary have taken the lead in jeopardising the EU values enshrined in Article 2 TEU. These countries have been characterised by the approval of measures that attack the independence of the judiciary, that centralise the power of the executives in office, that restrict the freedom of the press and that close universities.[43]

In addition, Article 7 TEU provides for the possibility of sanctions, to be decided following a complicated procedure, in the event of a serious and persistent breach by a Member State of the Union's values as enshrined in Article 2 TEU.

If it is true that Article 7 TEU has been useless so far, it is also true that the ECJ has remedied that by adapting the infringement procedure to comply with cases of violation of values.[44] Thanks to this, the ECJ has recognised the breach of EU values committed by Poland, Hungary and other countries[45] in many cases. In other cases, originating from a preliminary ruling mechanism, the ECJ recognised the conflict between EU law and national measures as jeopardising the

41 H. Rasmussen, 'Present and Future Judicial Problems After Enlargements and the Post-2004 Ideological Revolt', *Common Market Law Review*, 2007, pp. 1661 et seq.; G. de Vergottini, 'Tradizioni costituzionali comuni e Costituzione europea', 2005, https://www.forumcostituzionale.it/wordpress/wp-content/uploads/pre_2006/135.pdf

42 On this see A. Albi, '"Europe" Articles in the Constitutions of the Central and Eastern European Countries', *Common Market Law Review*, 2005, pp. 399 et seq.; A. Albi, *EU Enlargement and the Constitutions of Central and Eastern Europe*, Cambridge: Cambridge University Press, 2005; O. Pollicino, *Allargamento dell'Europa a Est e rapporto tra corti costituzionali e corti europee: verso una teoria generale dell'impatto interordinamentale del diritto sovranazionale?*, 2010, Milan: Giuffrè, pp. 262 et seq.

43 W. Sadurski, *Poland's Constitutional Breakdown*, Oxford: Oxford University Press, 2019; T. Drinóczi and A. Bień-Kacała, *Rule of Law, Common Values, and Illiberal Constitutionalism: Poland and Hungary within the European Union*, Abingdon: Routledge, 2020.

44 K.L. Scheppele, D. Kochenov, and B. Grabowska-Moroz, 'EU Values Are Law, After All: Enforcing EU Values Through Systemic Infringement Actions by the European Commission and the Member States of the European Union', *Yearbook of European Law*, 2020, pp. 3 et seq.; A. Jakab and D. Kochenov (eds.), *The Enforcement of EU Law and Values. Ensuring Member States' Compliance*, Oxford: Oxford University Press, 2017.

45 Among others, see ECJ, C-78/18 – Commission v. Hungary (Transparence associative), ECLI:EU:C:2020:476; ECJ, C-715/17 – Commission v. Poland (Mécanisme temporaire de relocalisation de demandeurs de protection internationale), ECLI:EU:C:2020:257. For an overview see: R. Mańko, *Protecting the Rule of Law in the EU Existing Mechanisms and Possible Improvements*, European Parliamentary Research Service, 2019, www.europarl.europa.eu/RegData/etudes/BRIE/2019/642280/EPRS_BRI(2019)642280_EN.pdf

independence of the judiciary by confirming the important role of EU law in the preservation of constitutional values and safeguards.[46]

By attempting to challenge the authoritarian drift in Poland and Hungary, the EU – in particular the ECJ – has in fact sought, first and foremost, to avoid the emptying of procedural guarantees and to substantiate the rule of law,[47] relying on Article 19 TEU and Article 4.3 TEU.[48] The national Constitutional Courts in this context – after having proposed opposing them – have been controlled by governments and more recently have responded in a long-distance duel with the Court of Justice. I will focus on two examples that seem to me emblematic of how, in these contexts, EU law has been evoked in bad faith.

The first example has to do with the ambiguity of Article 4.2 TEU, which has been exploited to question supranational loyalty by populists; the EU has been an easy target for sovereigntists.

Recently, Constitutional Courts have come under siege, with scholars criticising them for their abuse of the national (or, according to another terminology, constitutional[49]) identity argument. As we saw in the Preface, Halmai[50] has criticised the German *Bundesverfassungsgericht* for providing other Constitutional Courts with a problematic series of techniques – namely the *ultra vires* and the identity reviews – by triggering a dangerous escalation of constitutional conflicts. Similar criticism has been directed to the supporters of constitutional pluralism, since they would be responsible for offering arguments to autocrats, sovereigntists and populists in order to justify violations of the values enshrined in Article 2.[51]

As written previously in this book, I think that constitutional pluralism has nothing to do with that. In this sense, it is interesting to see how the Hungarian Constitutional Court manipulated the concept of national identity stemming from Article 4 TEU by interpreting it as an isolated concept, and how it read it in light of its own concept of constitutional identity. This case is a perfect example of how national actors can sometimes cite a norm of the EU Treaties to justify a claim

46 For instance, ECJ, C-216/18 PPU, *Minister for Justice and Equality v. LM*, ECLI:EU:C:2018:586.

47 ECJ, C-619/18, *Commission v. Poland (Independence of the Supreme Court)*, ECLI:EU:C:2019:531, para 72. On this reading see X. Groussot and G. Martinico, 'Mutual Trust, the Rule of Law and the Charter: A New Age of Judicial Activism', 2020, https://eulawlive.com/long-read-mutual-trust-the-rule-of-law-and-the-charter-a-new-age-for-judicial-activism-by-xavier-grousot-and-giuseppe-martinico/. More recently L. Mancano, 'You'll Never Work Alone: A Systemic Assessment of the European Arrest Warrant and Judicial Independence', *Common Market Law Review*, 2021, pp. 683 et seq.

48 ECJ, C-64/16, *Associação Sindical dos Juízes Portugueses*, EU:C:2018:117, paras. 31–41.

49 On the difference see: E. Cloots, *National Identity in EU Law*, Oxford: Hart, 2015, p. 163 and G. Di Federico, *L'identità nazionale degli stati membri nel diritto dell'Unione europea. Natura e portata dell'art. 4, par. 2, TUE*, Naples: Editoriale Scientifica 2017, p. 15.

50 Halmai, 'Abuse', pp. 23 et seq.

51 Kelemen and Pech, 'Why Autocrats'; F. Fabbrini and A. Sajó, 'The Dangers of Constitutional Identity', *European Law Journal*, 2019, pp. 457 et seq.

that is against the very essence of the Treaties. In its 2016 decision, the Hungarian Constitutional Court argued that

> according to Article 4 (2) TEU, 'the Union shall respect the equality of Member States before the Treaties as well as their national identities, inherent in their fundamental structures, political and constitutional, inclusive of regional and local self-government.' . . . The Constitutional Court of Hungary interprets the concept of constitutional identity as Hungary's self-identity and it unfolds the content of this concept from case to case, on the basis of the whole Fundamental Law and certain provisions thereof, in accordance with the National Avowal and the achievements of our historical constitution – as required by Article R) (3) of the Fundamental Law. The Constitutional Court establishes that the constitutional self-identity of Hungary is a fundamental value not created by the Fundamental Law – it is merely acknowledged by the Fundamental Law. Consequently, constitutional identity cannot be waived by way of an international treaty – Hungary can only be deprived of its constitutional identity through the final termination of its sovereignty, its independent statehood. **Therefore the protection of constitutional identity shall remain the duty of the Constitutional Court as long as Hungary is a sovereign State. Accordingly, sovereignty and constitutional identity have several common points, thus their control should be performed with due regard to each other in specific cases.**[52]
>
> (emphasis added)

Here, the Hungarian Constitutional Court first started from Article 4.2 TEU (which employs the concept of national identity). Secondly, it used the concept of 'constitutional identity', coupling it with the preservation of sovereignty (a term that is not used in Article 4.2. TEU). Thirdly, it read the concept of constitutional identity in light of Article R.3, offering in this way an alternative reading of the same concept.

In so doing, it completely disregarded the fact that in Article 4 TEU, national identity must be read in system with the concept of sincere cooperation stemming from its paragraph 3. In other words, the alternative reading of constitutional identity offered by the Hungarian Constitutional Court is in evident conflict with the meaning of the provision of the Treaty recalled by the Hungarian judges. Moreover, in a case in which the application of EU law was at stake, the Hungarian Court did not use Article 267 TFEU to consult the ECJ on how to interpret the national identity clause.

After the judgement, the notion of constitutional identity was codified in the Hungarian Constitution in 2018 with the approval of the seventh amendment.

52 Hungarian Constitutional Court, Decision 22/2016, http://www.europeanrights.eu/public/sentenze/Ungheria_30novembre2016.pdf, par. 62–66.

Now Article R.4 reads: 'The protection of the constitutional identity and Christian culture of Hungary shall be an obligation of every organ of the State'.[53]

Elsewhere, I tried to stress the risk of a unilateral reading of Article 4.2 TEU and the need for a systematic approach.[54] Against this background, I have two main recommendations when dealing with case law involving Article 4.2 TEU. My first recommendation regards the need for a systematic interpretation of the clause. In other words, this clause should not be read in splendid isolation, but in context, since it is instead a star in a broader constellation of values guaranteed by the EU Treaties. My second point directly stems from the first: Article 4.2 should not be detached from the reference to the moment of commonality (common principles and values) recalled in Articles 2 and 6 TEU. This was clear in the wording of Article 6 pre-Lisbon formula, where both national identity and common constitutional traditions were disciplined in the same provision. It is likely that the decoupling that occurred in Lisbon was a mistake galvanising the temptations of a unilateral and decontextualised reading of the identity clause. In other words, national courts are not allowed to use national identity as a weapon to violate the fundamental goods protected by Article 2 TEU, Article 4.3 TEU and Article 6 TEU. A reading like that advanced by the Hungarian Constitutional Court does not make any sense from a legal point of view.

Thus, as said, a systematic interpretation is needed, but one could wonder what the 'system' is in a multilevel context like that characterising European constitutional law. Although the ECJ is the interpreter of Article 4.2 TEU, we should refrain from the temptation of making national identity a purely European concept. In this respect, I think that national Constitutional Courts have the right to advance a proper interpretation of what national identity is in their legal system within the preliminary ruling mechanism, triggering in this way an exchange of arguments with the ECJ. The Luxembourg Court would not be bound by the interpretation given by the national Constitutional Courts but should respectfully take it into account by giving reasons in case of an outcome that does not take their view on board. This is the only way of avoiding a *contra litteram* interpretation of Article 4.2 TEU, in my view.

Against this background, the use of the preliminary ruling mechanism is key to distinguishing loyal (under Article 4.3 TEU) and bad courts. In this sense, again, what the Hungarian Constitutional Court did in 2016 does not have anything to do with a proper use of Article 4.2 TEU as the Hungarian judges did not activate Article 267 TFEU on that occasion.

53 Art. Q.4 of the Hungarian Constitution.

54 G. Martinico, 'Taming National Identity: A Systematic Understanding of Article 4.2 TEU', *European Public Law*, 2021, pp. 447 et seq.; G. Martinico and O. Pollicino, 'G. Martinico, O. Pollicino, Use and Abuse of a Promising Concept: What Has Happened to National Constitutional Identity?', *Yearbook of European Law*, 2020, pp. 228 et seq.

This does not exclude using national identity as part of the toolkit of the ECJ. However, inevitably the wording of this clause has created expectations in domestic Constitutional Courts that have, perhaps not by coincidence, raised preliminary references to the Luxembourg Court, trying to contribute to the interpretation of what national identity is. Giving the impression of considering national identity a purely European concept would risk losing the Constitutional Courts that could feel excluded from a dialogue with the ECJ. Make no mistake: the fact that in *Weiss* and *M.A.S.*[55] the ECJ did not use national identity in its legal reasoning should not lead to considering it as a marginal card from a strategic point of view. Indeed, in my view, the Italian Constitutional Court was very clever in its reference by showing how the threat of a conflict may indeed trigger dialogue by obliging the interlocutor to pay attention to a rigorous reconstruction of the national legal and factual background. It was again clever when it recalled paragraph 53 of *Taricco*, when the ECJ had opened a margin by stating that 'if the national court decides to disapply the national provisions at issue, it must also ensure that the fundamental rights of the persons concerned are respected'.[56] Finally, it also offered an alternative option to its interlocutor (eventually endorsed by the ECJ) by recalling the argument based on the constitutional traditions common to the Member States in order to question the *Taricco* rule.

The second example I would like to recall has to do with Poland. Indeed, more recently the Polish Constitutional Court overcame Hungarian colleagues by acting as the most disloyal[57] Constitutional Court of the EU with its decision K/3/21.[58] This ruling states that Articles 1, 2 and 19 of the Treaty on European Union are in conflict with the Constitution.[59] This move is an evident reaction to the case law of the ECJ, which had relied on the procedural rule of law to impose the protection of

55 For instance, case ECJ, C-493/17, *Weiss and Others*, ECLI:EU:C:2018:1000; ECJ, C-42/17, M.A.S. e M.B, par. 53, ECLI:EU:C:2017:936.

56 ECJ, C-105/14, *Taricco*, ECLI:EU:C:2015:555.

57 On loyalty and disloyalty in EU law see: T. Flynn, 'Constitutional Pluralism and Loyal Opposition', *International Journal of Constitutional Law*, 2021, pp. 241 et seq.

58 Polish Constitutional Court, decision 3/21, https://trybunal.gov.pl/en/hearings/judgments/art/11662-ocena-zgodnosci-z-konstytucja-rp-wybranych-przepisow-traktatu-o-unii-europejskiej

59 From an official translation of a part of the decision one can grasp the essence of the ruling:

'1. Article 1, first and second paragraphs, in conjunction with Article 4(3) of the Treaty on European Union (Journal of Laws – Dz. U. of 2004 No. 90, item 864/30, as amended) – insofar as the European Union, established by equal and sovereign states, creates "an ever closer union among the peoples of Europe", the integration of whom – happening on the basis of EU law and through the interpretation of EU law by the Court of Justice of the European Union – enters "a new stage" in which:

a) the European Union authorities act outside the scope of the competences conferred upon them by the Republic of Poland in the Treaties;
b) the Constitution is not the supreme law of the Republic of Poland, which takes precedence as regards its binding force and application;
c) the Republic of Poland may not function as a sovereign and democratic state

the independence of national judges. Here again one can notice the manipulative approach followed by the Polish Constitutional Court.

This decision follows another decision of the same court in which it had declared that interim measures imposed on it by the Luxembourg Court are unconstitutional and accused the ECJ of imposing 'ultra vires obligations'.[60]

In all these cases – and here we come back again to the difference between good and bad conflicts – the Polish Constitutional Court did not raise a preliminary question before rendering its ruling. Once again, it acted in a disloyal manner by manipulating the text of the Treaties and of its own Constitution, since

> in reality, there is no conflict between the TEU and the Polish Constitution. According to Article 45 of the Polish Constitution, all courts shall be independent and impartial and, as discussed above, the Constitutional Tribunal is currently neither independent nor impartial.[61]

– is inconsistent with Article 2, Article 8 and Article 90(1) of the Constitution of the Republic of Poland.

2. Article 19(1), second subparagraph, of the Treaty on European Union – insofar as, for the purpose of ensuring effective legal protection in the areas covered by EU law – it grants domestic courts (common courts, administrative courts, military courts, and the Supreme Court) the competence to:

   a) bypass the provisions of the Constitution in the course of adjudication – is inconsistent with Article 2, Article 7, Article 8(1), Article 90(1) and Article 178(1) of the Constitution;
   b) adjudicate on the basis of provisions which are not binding, having been revoked by the Sejm and/or ruled by the Constitutional Tribunal to be inconsistent with the Constitution

   – is inconsistent with Article 2, Article 7, Article 8(1), Article 90(1) and Article 178(1), and Article 190(1) of the Constitution.

3. Article 19(1), second subparagraph, and Article 2 of the Treaty on European Union – insofar as, for the purpose of ensuring effective legal protection in the areas covered by EU law and ensuring the independence of judges – they grant domestic courts (common courts, administrative courts, military courts, and the Supreme Court) the competence to:

   a) review the legality of the procedure for appointing a judge, including the review of the legality of the act in which the President of the Republic appoints a judge – are inconsistent with Article 2, Article 8(1), Article 90(1) and Article 179 in conjunction with Article 144(3)(17) of the Constitution;
   b) review the legality of the National Council of the Judiciary's resolution to refer a request to the President of the Republic to appoint a judge – are inconsistent with Article 2, Article 8(1), Article 90(1) and Article 186(1) of the Constitution;
   c) determine the defectiveness of the process of appointing a judge and, as a result, to refuse to regard a person appointed to a judicial office in accordance with Article 179 of the Constitution as a judge – are inconsistent with Article 2, Article 8(1), Article 90(1) and Article 179 in conjunction with Article 144(3)(17) of the Constitution'.

60 Polish Constitutional Court, decision P 7/20, https://trybunal.gov.pl/postepowanie-i-orzeczenia/wyroki/art/11589-obowiazek-panstwa-czlonkowskiego-ue-polegajacy-na-wykonywaniu-srodkow-tymczasowych-odnoszacych-sie-do-ksztaltu-ustroju-i-funkcjonowania-konstytucyjnych-organow-wladzy-sadowniczej-tego-panstwa

61 M. Lasek-Markey, 'Poland's Constitutional Tribunal on the Status of EU Law: The Polish Government Got All the Answers It Needed From a Court It Controls', 2021, https://europeanlawblog.

Moreover, constitutional pluralism has been recalled in an instrumental manner by the Polish government in its White Paper on judicial independence:

> The legal system of the European Union is based on **constitutional pluralism** of the member states. It means that there are multiple constitutional systems – on one side there are national systems of the Member States, on another, the European framework, having its "constitutional charter" in the Treaties: Treaty of the European Union and Treaty on the Functioning of the European Union (see: ECJ opinion No 1/91, ECR 1991/10, s. I-6102). Each country has specific constitutional solutions that are rooted in its history and legal traditions and these differences are protected by the treaty law of the European Union. Article 4 of the Treaty on European Union quoted above shows that the Union respects national identity which is inherent in the fundamental political and constitutional structures of the member states. **Constitutional identity, a core value of each national community, determines not only the most fundamental values and resulting tasks for state authorities, but also sets the limit for regulatory intervention of the European Union.**[62]
>
> (emphasis added)

In Chapter 2, we already saw how powerfully Avbelj challenged this argument by stressing that accepting this kind of instrumental use of constitutional pluralism by autocrats means neglecting the normative core of constitutional pluralism.[63] Instead of blaming constitutional theorists for having favoured autocrats, we should battle to avoid such an instrumental use of noble concepts. Otherwise, autocrats will become monopolists of categories belonging to the toolbox of constitutional law scholars.

While the EU is not comparable to the level of democracy achieved at the domestic level thus far, it should be taken into account that it does not intend to replace the State, understood as the primary guarantor of fundamental rights. Thus, when considering the democratic nature or lack thereof of the EU, we should consider its complementarity to the State level. The EU has also improved, especially after the Lisbon Treaty, which marked its tenth anniversary in 2019 and which made the Charter of Fundamental Rights of the EU binding. At the same time, the EU also offers new paths to improve national democracy. European integration is now not only about purely economic matters, and, above all, this cooperation does not accept the loss of guarantees that protect fundamental rights. As we saw in Chapters 1 and 2, constitutionalism, understood as a philosophical-political phenomenon, cannot be reduced to its state epiphany but is rather enriched by the

eu/2021/10/21/polands-constitutional-tribunal-on-the-status-of-eu-law-the-polish-government-got-all-the-answers-it-needed-from-a-court-it-controls/

62 The Chancellery of the Prime Minister, 'White Paper on the Reform of the Polish Judiciary', 2018, www.statewatch.org/media/documents/news/2018/mar/pl-judiciary-reform-chanceller-white-paper-3-18.pdf

63 M. Avbelj, 'Constitutional Pluralism and Authoritarianism', *German Law Journal*, 2020, pp. 1023 et seq., pp. 1026–1028.

contribution made by EU law, which provides further arguments to limit and channel the claims of political power into procedural paths. In this scenario, on the one hand, European constitutionalism is not based on the denial of the state or national constitutionalism; on the contrary, as Milward has also pointed out,[64] the state is and remains a fundamental actor of government. However, European constitutionalism adds value to the achievements of the state experience over time, offering extra protection for the system of fundamental rights, especially when it is the state that contradicts the values of democracy and neglects the teaching of post-WWII constitutionalism from which our constitutions and the Union are derived.

All this confirms that today the EU is the main antidote to the new wave of populism (either authoritarian or otherwise) that has developed in some of its Member States.

My last point at the end of the first edition of this book was regarding the legacy of the failure of the Constitutional Treaty. Indeed, in recent years we have been experiencing a substantial decline of the constructivist approach, and I explained this in light of different reasons analysed in Chapter 4. One of the reasons for this decline is that we are still paying the price for the mega-constitutional politics of the Convention. According to Bin, the Constitutional Treaty has discovered a nerve – that of constitutional symbolism – using 'words' that have come to recall dangerous and misleading domestic analogies (law, constitution, minister), causing real worry about the existence of a plan to transform the EU into a state. In his view, this has changed the context by detonating 'dramatically latent conflicts, which are concealed by the silences and evasions of the constitutions themselves'.[65]

The point developed by Bin relied on that scholarship[66] that views in a positive way the silence present in constitutions (referring to 'elements of dormant suspension'[67]), since silence would serve as a way to avoid the emergence of conflicts.

In other words, the seasons of the Conventions would have broken a sort of silent pact between the EU and its Member States, recalling dangerous (for the states' sovereignty) analogies and paving the way for new conflicts.

This reconstruction captures only a part of the phenomenon: conflicts have always been part of the EU constitutionalisation process even when some 'F-words' had not been pronounced, but of course, the fear of the domestic analogy is at the

64 A. Milward, *The European Rescue of the Nation-State*, Berkeley and Los Angeles: University of California Press, 1992.

65 R. Bin, 'Gli effetti del diritto dell'Unione nell'ordinamento italiano e il principio di entropia', in *AA.VV., Scritti in onore di Franco Modugno*, Naples: Jovene, 2011, pp. 363 et seq., 372–373. My own translation.

66 M. Foley, *The Silence of Constitutions: Gaps, 'Abeyances', and Political Temperament in the Maintenance of Government*, New York: Routledge, 1989, p. 198.

67 Foley, *The Silence of Constitutions: Gaps*, p. 3.

heart of the case law of the German Constitutional Court,[68] especially after the *Lissabon Urteil*.[69]

However, again, as I tried to present in Chapter 5, conflicts belong to the life of constitutional polities. This has been argued by huge scholarship in sociology and political science (mainly with regard to social conflicts[70]), but more generally conflicts belong to the essence of constitutionalism as such, which has a 'polemical' (and not irenical) nature, being founded on a never-ending friction between liberty and power, as Luciani wrote.[71]

All this shows that the mega-constitutional politics of the season of the Conventions has not only failed to magically solve (and indeed it could not) all the democratic problems of the EU but has also opened another 'fracture'. This fracture could have serious effects on the future of the EU – as occurred in the Canadian constitutional odyssey – confirming, therefore, the 'polemical' spirit of European constitutional law,[72] which is fed by the conflicts stemming from the complexity of the EU.

In this sense, reflecting on European complexity is particularly relevant today. The EU is in need of reform, and the discontent expressed by the German Constitutional Court's case law[73] (right or wrong) confirms this. This is a political issue that needs to be developed in fora other than the courts, which often also suffer from the excessive passivity of political actors. Often this passivity is instrumental, because national political actors sometimes like to use the shortcomings of the EU as an excuse for domestic purposes. For the first time in many years, the subject of reforms to the European architecture could really be taken up again. Indeed, as mentioned in Chapter 4, a partial exception to this trend of decline of

68 BVerfG, 2 BvC 4/10 and BVerfG, 2 BvE 8/11 del 28.2.2012. 'It is in this sense that integration cannot be well understood as an autonomously "constitutional" phenomenon in its own right, as some of integration's most fervent advocates like to maintain. Rather, despite the EU's extensive normative power, the process of integration lacks the autonomous capacity to legitimize itself in democratic and constitutional terms. For that, the integration process still very much needs the nation-state and national constitutional oversight, whether legislative, executive, or judicial. The most recent decision of the German Federal Constitutional Court regarding national-parliamentary oversight is simply a concrete expression of this continuing dependence', P. Lindseth, 'National Parliaments in European Integration: Europeanization, Renationalization, or Reconciliation?' 2012, https://eutopialaw.wordpress.com/

69 BVerfGE 123, 267.

70 J. Knight, *Institutions and Social Conflict*, Cambridge: Cambridge University Press, 1992; A. Pizzorno, *Le classi sociali*, Bologna: il Mulino 1959; A. Pizzorno, *Le radici della politica assoluta*, Milano: Feltrinelli, 1993; C. Crouch and A. Pizzorno, *Conflitti in Europa*, Milano: Etas libri, 1977; R. Dahrendorf, 'Toward a Theory of Social Conflict', *The Journal of Conflict Resolution*, 1958, pp. 170 et seq.; R. Dahrendorf, *Essays in the Theory of Society*, Stanford: Stanford University Press, 1968.

71 Luciani, 'Costituzionalismo irenico'.

72 G. Martinico, *Lo spirito polemico del diritto europeo. Studio sulle ambizioni costituzionali dell'Unione*, Rome: Aracne 2011.

73 More recently see: German Constitutional Court, 5 May 2020, – 2 BvR 859/15–2 BvR 1651/15–2 BvR 2006/15–2 BvR 980/16.

constructivism and a possible boost for future reforms is represented by the Conference on the Future of Europe.

Once activated, the Conference was immediately attacked, and the start of the work was surrounded by irony and scepticism, with few people connected to the streaming events. This was for many reasons, partly because at the beginning it was seen as a product of Macron. Also, the platform is not appealing,[74] but one has to understand that the improvement of supranational democracy is not a disconnected issue from the future of national democracy. On the contrary, the EU has played an important role as a remedy to populism and sovereignism, which means that the future of state democracy also depends on the improvement of the EU. These are not two separate choices, but a single battle in respect of the complex structure that I have described in the book.

74 https://futureu.europa.eu/?locale=en

Index

Note: Numbers followed by 'n' represents notes

absolute primacy 105n119, 178
accession to the ECHR 3n10, 27n147, 33, 115, 204
agonistic pluralism 150, 156, 158n47, 191
Art. 2 TEU 32, 121, 205, 208
Art. 4.2 TEU 77, 92, 105–112, 126, 183, 206, 207–208
Art. 6 TEU 3, 7n34, 36, 40, 106, 110, 112, 114, 177, 179, 181, 208
austerity 120, 123, 129, 139, 141
Avbelj, M. viii, 44n28, 55, 75, 91, 211

Bagehot, Walter 1, 16, 86n46
Barber Protocol 92, 96, 97
Besselink, Leonard 41, 78, 79
Bin, R. 212
Bobić, A. 74n170, 196
Bogdandy, A. 105–109, 111
Bosphorus 189
Brexit 60, 61, 121, 197–199
Bundesverfassungsgericht see German Constitutional Court

Canada xiv, 57, 85, 102–105
Cartesio 175
Charter of fundamental Rights of the European Union *see* EUCFR
Charter of Nice *see* EUCFR
Chartry 176, 177
Cilfit 152
Claes, M. 6, 7, 109
common constitutional traditions 8, 64, 106, 108, 110, 148, 150, 160, 166, 186, 208
common judges 159, 162, 171–172, 187
comparative constitutional law xiv, 75, 198
complex antinomies xviii, 56, 148–149
complexity: in action 148–153, 190–191; to constitutional synallagma examples 63–65; as *efficient secret* of European Constitution 56–75; idea of a complex order 65–75; non-determinability (non-determinism) 57n92, 58, 63, 148; non-reducibility 3, 57n92, 58, 60–62, 73, 148; non-reversibility 3, 57n92, 58–60, 196, 198; unpredictability 62–63; *see also* constitutional conflicts
Conseil Constitutionnel 174–176
consistent interpretation 99, 190, 193, 194
constituent power 81–85
constitutional ambition 5, 76, 91, 100, 120–121, 141
constitutional conflicts viii, xviii, 35, 45–48, 70–71; consistent interpretation 190–194; contrast between EU law 169–180; as direct consequence of constitutional complexity of EU 153–159; interpretative monopoly 164–168; issue of 17, 42–43, 53, 149; national common judges dual role 162–164; neutralising 77; over the interpretation 160–162; possible typology of 159; unexpected consequences of constitutionalisation of EU 180–190
constitutional constructivism 2, 38, 77, 90
Constitutional Courts vii, ix, 50, 63, 108, 111, 118, 132, 154, 159–160, 168, 173, 189, 194, 206, 208–209; *see also* German Constitutional Court
constitutional evolutionism 2, 38, 77
constitutional failure 102
constitutional historical contextualism 11, 13
constitutional identity 37, 54, 106, 112, 155, 170, 206, 207, 208, 211

constitutionalisation xvi–xvii, 3–10, 15, 37, 39, 77, 89–90, 99, 131, 179, 180–190, 213
Constitutional Odyssey 85, 101, 102, 105, 213
constitutional openness 192
constitutional pluralism 9, 16, 43–55, 74, 79, 148, 156, 196–197, 206, 211
constitutional politics xiv, xvii, 76–78, 91, 100–104, 111, 120, 132, 196
constitutional processualism 11–13
constitutional scepticism 11, 12, 84, 85
constitutional serialism 11–13
constitutional supremacy 52, 193
constitutional synallagma 2, 6, 59, 63, 69n145, 75, 92, 148, 156, 196
constitutional theory 15, 16, 17n97, 44, 48, 81n28
constitutional tolerance 10, 11, 15, 62, 63
Constitutional Treaty 5, 12–13, 17, 63, 76–79, 100, 104–105, 131, 212
constructivism xiii, xvii, 2, 38, 95, 132, 191; *versus* constitutional evolutionism 77–90; European constitutionalism 90–92
Controlimiti see Counter-limits
Cordero Alonso 159, 160
Corte costituzionale see Italian Constitutional Court
cosmopolitan communitarism 10–11
Costa/Enel 8n40, 18, 19, 60
counter-limits 35, 50, 64, 108, 111n147, 151n12, 155, 179
Court d'Arbitrage 176
cultural sources of law 6, 91, 93
Curtin, D. 91, 93, 95, 96, 97
Czech Constitutional Court 112n149, 134, 137n97

Danish Second Home protocol 96
De Búrca, G. 13, 18
Delmas Marty, M. 65, 66, 67n133, 68, 69
democratic deficit xiv, 15, 53, 104, 119, 131, 154
De Witte, B. 13, 93, 95, 123, 125n24, 128–130
direct effect 15, 30, 60, 61, 95, 98–99, 114, 168, 180, 193, 201n29
discontents of European constitutionalism 5, 90–92
disorder 17, 39, 63n113, 69, 70, 71, 80
Doppia pregiudizialità see dual preliminarity
dualism 48, 79, 153
dual preliminarity 172, 173, 184
Dynamic Medien 160

ECHR 28–31, 37, 59, 116, 166, 170, 181, 185, 189, 204; Article 53, 27; EU accession to 3n10, 27n147, 33, 115, 204
ECJ 15, 17, 19, 22, 25, 29–30, 33, 51n64, 59, 88n55, 95, 100, 114, 117, 133, 161–162, 167, 170–171, 183, 187, 199, 201, 208–209, 210
economic crisis 120, 121, 139, 141
ECtHR 3, 23n127, 28–30, 115–116, 117n174, 176n124, 185, 189
efficient secret 1–2, 10–17, 56–63
EFSF 122, 124
EFSM 122
Eleftheriadis, P. 46, 47n42, 48n47, 49, 51, 52
enlargement 106n120, 144, 204, 205
EU Accession to the ECHR 3n10, 27n147, 33, 115, 204
EUCFR 92, 95, 100, 105, 112, 113, 115–119, 167, 184, 186, 202
EU constitutionalism 5, 8, 9, 16, 92, 131
EU law 117n173, 126, 164, 174–176, 178n129, 180
euro 122
euro-crisis 125, 128–129
European Central Bank, ECB 54, 65, 122, 132n71
European Constitution xvii, 1–38, 42, 53, 56–63, 76, 80, 89, 137, 156, 196
European constitutional law viii, xv, 2, 4, 6–8, 16–17, 41, 79, 141, 149, 156, 182–184, 208, 213; *Kadi saga* 18–26; relationship between autonomy and fundamental rights 26–34
European Convention of Human Rights *see* ECHR
European Conventions 82, 89n61
European Court of Human rights *see* ECtHR
European Court of Justice *see* ECJ
European economic governance 123, 124, 127, 130, 135, 136
European Financial Stabilisation Mechanism *see* EFSM
European Financial Stability Facility *see* EFSF
European Stability Mechanism (ESM) 122, 123n19, 124, 129n46, 131, 132, 139, 140
Euro Plus Pact 122, 123, 125
Eurozone 54n76, 124n23, 125, 126n32, 127n35, 136n97

evolutionary constitutionalism 69, 80–81, 83, 85–88, 90
evolutionism 2, 38, 70, 73, 76, 77, 80, 120, 191, 196

federalism 74, 75n172, 142, 196
Federfarma 151, 152
Filipiak 118, 159, 162
Fiscal Compact 121, 123n19, 125, 125n24
Fossum, J.E. 17n97, 87n54, 88, 90
Friedrich, D. 75
fundamental rights 92, 95, 100, 105, 112, 113, 115–119, 167, 184, 186, 202

Gauweiler 132, 168
General principles of Community Law 20, 90n63, 106n120, 165, 177n126
German Constitutional Court 9, 53–54, 65, 110–112, 118, 133–136, 154, 162, 168, 206
Grimm, D. 12, 14
Grogan Protocol 96

Habermas, J. 156–157
Haegeman 30
Halberstam, D. 190n182
Halmai, G. vii, 206
Haltern, U. 13, 15
Hayek, F.A. xiii, 70, 72–73, 79, 87–88, 142, 191n184, 196
hidden dialogue 173
Hijack of *acquis communautaire* 92–93, 95
Honeywell 117, 168
Hungary 137, 138, 205, 206, 207, 208

Incidenter 171, 173
interaction xvii, 6–8, 17, 40, 49, 61, 68, 118, 150, 196
intergovernmentalism xiv, 6, 90, 93–94, 100, 123, 130, 137
Internationale Hadesgeselschaft 41
interpretative competition 111, 159, 160
Italian Constitutional Court 50, 62, 151–152, 154, 180, 182, 184–186, 187n162, 209

judicial activism 63, 94, 98
judicial dialogue 50, 61, 108
judicial interaction 50, 61, 80, 149, 150n6, 187–189, 190

Kadi 17–26, 33–35, 196, 199, 202
Kelemen, R.D. vii, 54–55, 150, 206
Komárek, J. ix, 51
κόσμος (spontaneous/natural order) 70, 79, 93
Kreil 159, 169
Krisch, N. 9, 44, 48, 66, 91, 195
Kücükdeveci 159, 164, 167, 168n84
Kumm, M. viii, 43, 48–49, 52–53, 190

Laval 143, 144
Les Verts 19, 199
Lisbon Treaty ix, 59, 76, 92, 100, 105, 112, 115, 118, 143, 177, 212
Lissabon Urteil (Lisbon judgment) 111, 118
Luciani, M. 43, 213
Luxembourg Court 17, 22, 25, 29–30, 33, 59, 95, 114, 117, 133, 161–162, 167, 170–171, 183, 187, 199, 201, 208–209, 210

Maastricht Treaty 83, 92, 94, 95, 98, 105n119, 118, 121, 136
Maduro, M. Poiares 5, 8, 16, 20, 43–44, 48–52, 92, 121, 140, 170, 179
Mangold 118, 164–168, 186
MAS 183
Mayer, F. 42
mega constitutional politics xiv, 93, 101–104, 120, 132, 204, 212–213
Melki 30, 164, 170–171, 173, 176–177, 180
Melloni 17, 30, 116, 161
Menéndez, A.J. 17n97, 87n54, 88, 90
Michaniki 159, 169, 170
monism 46–48, 151, 153, 197
Morin, E. 56, 58, 71n151
Mouffe, Chantal ix, 149–150, 156–159, 190
Mox Plant 31
multilevel constitutionalism 14–16, 39–42, 50, 53, 105, 156
multiple loyalties 149, 150, 151, 162, 170

natural sciences 56, 71
non-determinability 57n92, 58, 63, 148
non-exclusivity of state constitutionalism 39
non-reducibility 3, 57n92, 58, 60–62, 73, 148
non-reversibility 3, 57n92, 58–60, 196, 198

Omega 106n120, 108n133, 155, 160
opinion 2/13 3, 17–18, 26–34, 37, 177, 179, 199
ordering pluralism 67
ordo-liberalism 136, 141–147

Pandemic Crisis Support 132n74, 133n75, 140
Pech, L. vii, 54–55, 206
Pernice, I. 14, 15, 40, 41, 50, 92
pluralism under International law 47, 48n47, 48n48
"pluralisme de fusion" (pluralism of fusion) 67, 68
"pluralisme de separation" (pluralism of separation) 67, 68
pluralisme ordonné 65–68
political constitutionalism 5
political sources of law 80, 91, 95
populism 121, 212, 214
preliminary ruling 28n153, 33, 59, 96–97, 108, 114, 118, 135, 152, 163–164, 170–173, 175, 177, 181–182, 187, 205, 208
primacy of EU law 86n50, 105n119, 108, 130, 159, 160, 161, 193
Pringle 132
proportionality 5, 25, 40, 64, 65, 133, 134, 135n90, 144, 155n32, 170
PSPP 54, 65, 133, 134, 135n89, 136, 168, 186
Pupino 98–99

radical pluralism 43n27, 46n42, 47
Reform Treaty 3n10, 76, 77, 99, 100, 108, 170; *see also* Lisbon Treaty
Revolutionary Constitutionalism 78, 81, 87, 89
Rodriguez Caballero 159, 160
Ruggeri, A. 108
rule of law 18, 35, 53, 79n16, 91, 120, 137–139, 179, 181, 199, 206, 209
Russell, P. 101, 102, 103, 104

Sayn-Wittgenstein 155
Schill, S. 105–109, 111
Schmitt, Carl 157, 158
semi-permanent treaty revision process 13, 78, 93
social pillar 145
Solange saga 159, 196
solidarity 88n55, 113, 120, 133, 141, 144, 145
sovereignism 214
Spanish Constitutional Court 153, 160, 161
Strasbourg court *see* ECtHR
supranationalism 90, 93, 123, 137
Switzerland 7n37, 85
systemic pluralism 44, 48

Taricco 183, 184, 196, 209
τάξις (constructed/artificial order) xiii, 70, 79–80, 88n56, 93–95
terrorism xiii
TEU 124; Article 2 32, 121, 205, 208; Article 4.2 77, 92, 105–112, 126, 183, 206, 207–208; Article 6 3, 7n34, 36, 40, 106, 110, 112, 114, 177, 179, 181, 208
TFEU 31n167, 59n96, 65, 114, 124–125, 211; Article 136 122; Article 218.11 26; Article 258 136; Article 260 126; Article 267 28n153, 33, 59, 161, 164, 174–175, 182, 208; Article 273 126; Article 344 28, 31
Treaty on the European Union *see* TEU
Treaty on the Functioning of the European Union *see* TFEU
Tribunal constitucional see Spanish Constitutional Court

unpredictability 3, 57n92, 58, 62, 63, 73, 148

values 5, 11, 21, 36, 199; common 32, 68, 70n147; violations in Article 2 vii, 55, 205–206
Van Gend en Loos 18, 19, 21, 30, 60, 83
Viking 143, 144

Walker, N. 11–12, 14–15, 43, 48–49, 55, 70, 84–85
Weiler, J.H.H. 4, 11
Weiss 54, 65, 132, 133, 134, 209
Wiener, Antje 11
Winner Wetten 118, 159, 162

www.ingramcontent.com/pod-product-compliance
Lightning Source LLC
LaVergne TN
LVHW010549300926
849162LV00002B/275
* 9 7 8 0 3 6 7 4 6 7 0 3 6 *